W9-BXC-680

500 ESSENTIAL CULT BOOKS
The Ultimate Guide

500 **ESSENTIAL** CULT BOOKS

The Ultimate Guide • Gina McKinnon

with Steve Holland

STERLING

New York / London
www.sterlingpublishing.com

500 Essential Cult Books: The Ultimate Guide

Copyright © 2010 by The Ilex Press Limited

All images copyright © their respective copyright holders

10 9 8 7 6 5 4 3 2 1

Published by Sterling Publishing Co., Inc.
387 Park Avenue South, New York, NY 10016
Distributed in Canada by Sterling Publishing
c/o Canadian Manda Group, 165 Dufferin Street
Toronto, Ontario, Canada M6K 3H6

ISBN: 978-1-4027-7485-0

For information about custom editions, special sales, premium and
corporate purchases, please contact Sterling Special Sales
Department at 800-805-5489 or specialsales@sterlingpub.com.

This book was conceived, designed, and produced by
ILEX
210 High Street
Lewes
East Sussex BN7 2NS
UK
www.ilex-press.com

For Ilex:
Publisher: Alastair Campbell
Creative Director: Peter Bridgewater
Managing Editor: Nick Jones
Editor: Ellie Wilson
Commissioning Editor: Tim Pilcher
Art Director: Julie Weir
Senior Designer: Emily Harbison
Designers: Chris & Jane Lanaway

Printed in China

Color Origination by Ivy Press Reprographics

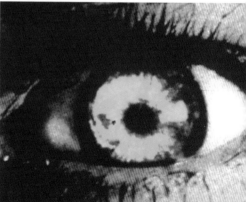

CONTENTS

INTRODUCTION

GINA MCKINNON

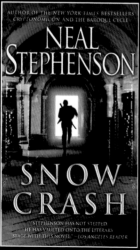

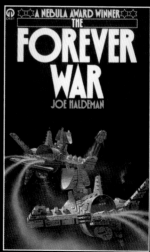

What is it that makes a book cult? Why do certain words on a page attain cult status, while others simply become popular or successful? And how is it that books that are neither popular, successful—or even any good—manage cult kudos? These are questions we had to answer not once but 500 times in making the selections for this volume.

The fact that some cult authors distance themselves from the label didn't help. Barry Gifford, author of *Wild at Heart* (a cult book later made into a cult movie by David Lynch), told us he didn't mind his most famous novel being selected here, but that to him, cult "just means it is a title of particular interest that has not sold as many copies as *Gone with the Wind*."

The phenomenon clearly needs further definition before we explain how we whittled the endless possibilities of cult literature down to an essential 500.

WHAT MAKES A BOOK CULT?

After much thought, and chatting with literary types, we'd cautiously assert that what characterizes all the books included here is a peculiar ability to speak to the reader, a kind of authorial empathy, which allows the cult book to transcend being merely liked, or even loved, and inspire a fierce, unquestioning devotion. Recommend-ability and covetousness are also key symptoms. Here we have the kind of book that, the minute the last page is turned, it is pressed into the hands of your best book buddy as you mutter, "You've just got to read this." Here are the books that you buy in each and every new edition (and you might well find yourself doing this a lot—cult books are seldom returned by borrowers). Another symptom is youth appeal: these are the texts that caught your imagination as a teenager or young adult, and which stay forever embedded in your brain, a kind of emotional literary baggage that you won't ever lose and wouldn't want to.

WHAT WE PUT IN . . . AND WHAT WE LEFT OUT

For me, *The Catcher in the Rye*, *Hangover Square*, and *Ask the Dust* tick all these boxes. Your top three cult classics will certainly be different. Indeed, you might loathe mine. But this divisiveness is what makes the cult genre so exciting.

And yes, the general consensus is now that cult is a genre in its own right. A genre that nonetheless promiscuously embraces other genres: fiction (classics, westerns, adventure novels, erotica), as well as memoir, popular science, and political works may all be considered cult and are all featured here. Such diversity suggests that you might well be wary of some of the titles included; heck, you might even prefer to use them as a doorstop. But, the aim is for you to be tempted into a new voyage of literary discovery, for you to discover the shared power of all these books to excite, thrill, provoke, and amaze, no matter what shelf the librarian or bookseller chooses to stack them on.

That we have chosen the books from all manner of bookshelves goes some way to explaining the inevitable omissions from our final selection. Doubtless some of the other omissions are a generational thing; often the cult book is so tied up with the counterculture or zeitgeist of a certain epoch that some texts may be forgotten or be considered too parochial to appeal to the modern reader. That said, peering through the keyhole into bygone cultures is a quintessentially cult preoccupation: Kerouac and Hunter S. Thompson, Goethe and Voltaire are all authors who achieved poster-child status for their generations, and their most famous books are the stuff of cult legend.

CAN A CULT BOOK BE A MAINSTREAM BOOK?

Short answer: yes. Both *Jane Eyre* and *Pride and Prejudice* made our final selection. This is not because they are studied at schools and universities

Nicholson Baker

SALMAN RUSHDIE

Mezzanine

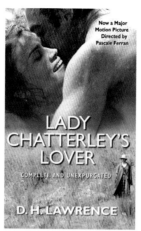

Now a Major
Motion Picture
Directed by
Pascale Ferran

LADY
CHATTERLEY'S
LOVER

COMPLETE AND UNEXPURGATED

D. H. LAWRENCE

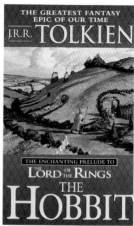

THE GREATEST FANTASY
EPIC OF OUR TIME

J.R.R. TOLKIEN

THE ENCHANTING PRELUDE TO
THE LORD OF THE RINGS

THE
HOBBIT

THE
GINGER
MAN

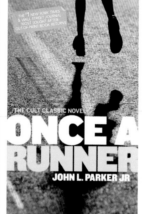

THE #1 NEW YORK TIMES
& WALL STREET JOURNAL
MOST SOUGHT AFTER
OUT-OF-PRINT BOOK RETURNS

THE CULT CLASSIC NOVEL

ONCE A
RUNNER

JOHN L. PARKER JR

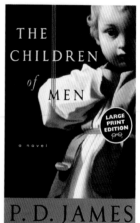

THE
CHILDREN
of MEN

LARGE
PRINT
EDITION

a novel

P. D. JAMES

JANE
EYRE

CHARLOTTE
BRONTË

Complete and Unabridged

with an introduction by MARY M. THREAPLETON

RAYMOND CARVER

This third man, an old friend of my wife's, he was on his way to spend the night. His wife had died

cathedral

THE INTERNATIONAL BEST-SELLER
NORTHERN LIGHTS
Now a major movie starring Nicole Kidman and Daniel Craig

FILMED AS

THE
GOLDEN
COMPASS

PHILIP PULLMAN

worldwide. Rather, it's because of their legions of devoted fans—fans so devoted in fact, they dress in the attire of these books' heroes and heroines, read a flood of fan fiction, and subscribe to contemporary magazines devoted to their authors. Nor does cult preclude commercial success. That's why we've included modern bestsellers like the *Da Vinci Code*; love it or loathe it, you can't deny the fervor of the fans who will go to extraordinary lengths to crack the secret of the code, visiting key locations in the book, and generally showing their devotion to Dan Brown's implausible potboilers.

And of course there is a darker side to the devotion that comes with the territory of cult. You'll find amid these pages a review for *Mein Kampf*, for instance. Are we honestly endorsing the terrifyingly blatant anti-Semitism of history's most reviled villain? Of course not. But include it we had to, for the sake of the millions whose fate was sealed by this infamous volume's cult following.

Still, you can rest assured that Hitler's inane diatribe against the world is just one rotten egg in a nest of otherwise Fabergé-like recommended reads. It's a selection that we hope you find diverting and surprising, but at the same time as comforting as a pair of old slippers.

And so, on to the books.

HOW TO USE THIS BOOK

The main aim of this book is for you to discover new books, or rediscover old ones—in short, to get you reading more. As such the book is organized to help you get the most from it.

Divided into ten categories, characterized by genre or theme, each section has an introduction, followed by a "top ten" selection of the best titles in that category, and then the "best of the rest" in that section.

Each entry has a brief plot summary (for fiction) or synopsis (non-fiction) followed by a review. To help you select from the 500 entries, each book has been given a star rating out of five. There are very few one-star entries here—we've tried to include must-read books, after all. If a review receives only one or two stars the accompanying review will explain why. At the opposite end of the scale the five-star entries are the crème de la crème of cult books: brilliant writing, plots, or ideas, and even sometimes all three.

Since sex, drugs, and rock 'n' roll feature profusely, we felt it best to have a recommended readership age range. A is for all ages, 12+ won't be suitable for youngsters, and 15+ may have some adult themes and swearing. As for 18+, well, let's just say these aren't books you'd care to give your grandmother for Christmas.

After each review we suggest "further reading," that is; the best of what's available by the same author. The "see also" recommendations include not only comparable titles included in this book, but also many which aren't: we do want you to sow your cult book oats as far and wide as possible.

Some of the books are reasonably obscure, but we've made sure all of them are in print or at least available online. And don't forget your local library will stock most of them too, so there's no excuse not to dive in, select your pick of these 500 titles, and lose yourself in a unique, inspiring, and incredible cult book.

ANTHONY
BURGESS

A CLOCKWORK
ORANGE

Catch-22

One of the Great Novels of the Century

Joseph Heller

With a new preface by the author

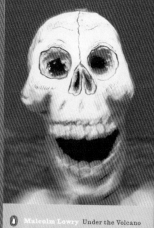

Malcolm Lowry   Under the Volcano

GEN

Funny, colourful and

Geoff Ryman

253

THE JOURNEY OF 253 LIFETIMES

'A TRIUMPH' New Statesman

BARRY

GIFFORD

WILD at

"Gifford's spun another taut, electric tale
where the writing not only comes in
strobelight bursts but is as charged and
potent." —DETAILS

HEART

THE NUMBER ONE BESTSELLER

THE

LOVELY
BONES

Compulsive enough to read in a single sitting,
brilliantly intelligent, elegantly constructed
and ultimately intriguing'
The Times

ALICE SEBOLD

WHITE
NOISE
DON DELILLO

'ONE OF THE MOST
IRONIC, INTELLIGENT,
GRIMLY FUNNY VOICES
TO COMMENT ON LIFE IN
PRESENT-DAY AMERICA'
JAYNE ANNE PHILLIPS

THOMAS
PYNCHON
THE CRYING OF
LOT 49

ANGELA CARTER

NIGHTS AT THE CIRCUS

JEAN-

na

PAUL

SARTKE

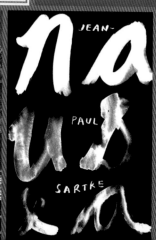

Paul
Auster

ADAPTATION BY
Paul Karasik and
David Mazzucchelli
NEW INTRODUCTION BY
Art Spiegelman

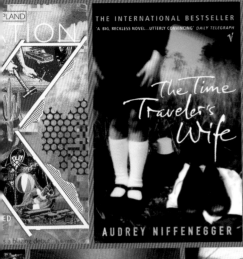

THE INTERNATIONAL BESTSELLER

'A BIG, RECKLESS NOVEL...UTTERLY CONVINCING' *DAILY TELEGRAPH*

The Time Traveler's Wife

AUDREY NIFFENEGGER

Jorge Luis Borges Labyrinths

"Astonishing...breathtaking. You are seduced completely."
— *The Washington Post Book World*

MEMOIRS OF A
GEISHA

ARTHUR GOLDEN

NOW A MAJOR MOTION PICTURE

'Seductive metaphysical thrillers, as stylish, urgent and unnerving as the best detective fiction.'
Literary Review

The
New York
Trilogy

a fictional memoir
a fan's notes
frederick exley

CHAPTER 1

CULT CLASSICS

MODERN HITS,
ALL-TIME FAVORITES,
AND EVERYTHING IN-BETWEEN

The juxtaposition of the words "classic" and "cult" might have some of you scratching your heads. "But I thought those words could never go together," you might say, "like chick and literature." We beg to differ.

This chapter contains books that are so much a part of the collective literary psyche, such required rites-of-passage reading, that they could not be labeled anything but "classic." They are, though, books that have something of that magical, if arbitrary, series of ingredients that also make them perfect examples of the cult book canon.

There's a wide range of titles and genres, so have a flick through and we're sure there will be something that appeals to your inner cult bookworm.

★
★
★
★
★

Writer: Bret Easton Ellis
Publisher: Viking, 1991

ISBN US: 978-0679735779
ISBN UK: 978-0330448017

18+ # AMERICAN PSYCHO

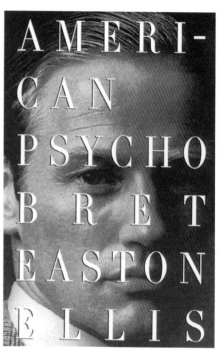

Plot: Easton Ellis spends the first third of *American Psycho* painting the respectable (if we can call it that) face of Patrick Bateman, only hinting at the gory psychosis to come. Bateman's is a blank, bland world of investment banking by day, expensive restaurants and cocaine-snorting by night. A world where "you can always be in better shape," where grown men cry if they can't get a dinner reservation, and where wearing white socks with gray trousers is the ultimate faux pas.

As the book progresses the other face of Bateman is presented, and it's not a pretty sight: graphic scenes of killing, rape, and torture are depicted with the same sangfroid as earlier depictions of dinner dates, trips to the drycleaners, and workouts in the gym. Among the horror and the mutilation, Bateman finds time to deliver critical appreciations on the work of iconic 1980s pop acts from Genesis to Whitney Houston—unlikely yet ironic commentaries on the vacuity of pop culture.

Review: A stunningly accomplished critique of twentieth-century American society, or a misogynistic gore-fest: critics were divided on publication. With hindsight, it's hard to see how the novel could be considered anything *but* a savage indictment of the New York elite, 1980s pop culture, and the burgeoning machismo of the time; the bitterly dark humor and bland personalities could hardly point to anything else.

Besides, few could challenge the originality and brilliance of the Bateman character, and the nebulous atmosphere that Easton Ellis builds around his increasingly unreliable narration. The book might be dripping with blood, but it is also packed with satire and, as satires go, they don't come much more controversial, successful, or cult than this.

FURTHER READING: *The Rules of Attraction; Glamorama; Less Than Zero*
SEE ALSO: *Fight Club* (Chuck Palahniuk); *Story of My Life* (Jay McInerney)

★
★
★
★
★

Writer: Anthony Burgess
Publisher: Heinemann, 1962

ISBN US: 978-0393312836
ISBN UK: 978-0141182605

18+

A CLOCKWORK ORANGE

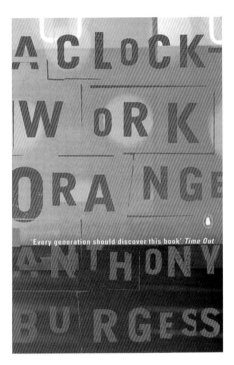

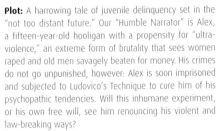

Plot: A harrowing tale of juvenile delinquency set in the "not too distant future." Our "Humble Narrator" is Alex, a fifteen-year-old hooligan with a propensity for "ultra-violence," an extreme form of brutality that sees women raped and old men savagely beaten for money. His crimes do not go unpunished, however: Alex is soon imprisoned and subjected to Ludovico's Technique to cure him of his psychopathic tendencies. Will this inhumane experiment, or his own free will, see him renouncing his violent and law-breaking ways?

Review: Small in stature, vast in ideas, Burgess creates a chillingly realistic portrayal of the darker side of adolescence. The clothes, the love of music, the parental conflict, and the slang (Alex uses "Nadsat," an evocative fictional argot devised by Burgess) create a perfect picture of Alex and his gang of "droogs." Indeed, a more timeless evocation of the selfishness and arrogance of adolescence has probably never been written.

Not that Alex's behavior is the stuff of your usual teenage rebellions: his moral compass is indubitably awry. This allows Burgess to bring innumerable ideas into the novel, not least a principal concern of the author that, "Duality is the Ultimate Reality," i.e. that opposite forces in life are inevitable, meaning that evil is necessary and natural—despite all the horrors that come with it.

Kubrick's 1971 movie version of *A Clockwork Orange*, banned in the United Kingdom by its own director, has helped make Burgess' dystopian tale the stuff of cult legend. The story is all the more successful given that, we, the reader, whom Alex addresses as "my brothers," are all along coerced into empathizing with a character who is not in the least bit sympathetic.

FURTHER READING: *The Enderby Quartet*
SEE ALSO: *Fahrenheit 451* (Ray Bradbury)

★ **Writer:** Luke Rhinehart
★ **Publisher:** William Morrow, 1971
★

ISBN US: 978-0879518646
ISBN UK: 978-0006513902

18+ THE DICE MAN

the dice man

'Novelist of the century'
Loaded

LUKE RHINEHART

Plot: Luke Rhinehart, a psychiatrist, bored of the constraints of middle-class living, decides to determine his next life move with a roll of the dice—whether it be what to eat, whether to leave his wife, even whether to rape. Mentioning this latter transgression is not a plot spoiler. In fact, this, perhaps the most famous episode in the book, happens fairly early on in the story. What follows is a litany of misdeeds, each one more distasteful than the next.

Review: We can look at Rhinehart's cult bestseller two ways: either the author cuts a subversive swathe through the repressive psychology of the 1970s, or he is, as one character notes, enjoying the "sick rebellion of an elephantine child." What's really disappointing is that this rebellion, that is Rhinehart's deep-seated fury at the usual social, moral, and political conventions of the epoch, finds no better outlet than various violent sexual acts of aggression. Okay, so he founds a program based on his psychiatric research, which might be considered a level up from his other misdeeds, but the "Fuck without Fear for Fun and Profit Program" doesn't exactly elevate the novel from the level of crassness.

Still, you can't argue with the success of *The Dice Man.* Not only was it a bestseller but it soon developed a cult following, with people enacting the book's mantra, "not my will, oh Die, but Thy will be done!" It seems only fitting then, that you roll the die to decide whether to read it. Albeit with insider information from someone who has already done so: the sex and violence is so over-the-top, the repeated claims of unconventionality so overplayed, the nihilism so extreme, the book actually gets quite boring.

FURTHER READING: *The Search for the Dice Man, The Book of the Die*
SEE ALSO: *Fight Club* (Chuck Palahniuk)

★
★
★
★

Writer: Douglas Coupland
Publisher: St. Martin's Press, 1991

ISBN US: 978-0312054366
ISBN UK: 978-0349108391

15+

GENERATION X

'Funny, colourful and accessible, this is a blazing debut' THE TIMES

Plot: Here we have Andy, Dag, and Claire, friends and neighbors, who have cut themselves adrift from their middle-class backgrounds to do menial jobs in Palm Springs, California. It's the early 1990s, in the aftermath of the Reagan years: recession, yuppies, and eighties pop culture are all fresh in our trio's minds. To make sense of their disaffected lives they tell one another "bedtime stories," some of which are grounded in reality, while they locate others in Texlahoma, a mythic world that is stuck in 1974.

All three of the central characters have a "terminal wanderlust," suffer from "successophobia," and "homeowner envy." Just in case these terms don't mean anything to us, Coupland offers handy definitions in the margins of the book, adding an extra, and welcome, dimension to the narrative.

Review: Possibly one of the most misunderstood books of the twentieth century, *Generation X* is assumed to have been an apologia for the slacker generation, the children of the baby boomers who have turned their backs on careers and prospects for a life of moping, groping, and doping. Some critics hated it for that very reason, while others with a keener eye saw through the disaffection of Andy, Dag, and Claire as a lament for the cultural wasteland of the time.

There's no doubting the book's merits—the stories are often funny, and there is much to be admired in Coupland's style. But the trio's sense of entitlement seems so grasping, their apathy so unnecessary when you think of the cultural void and bleak job market we're enduring at the start of the twenty-first century. We might, therefore, call *Generation X* a late-twentieth-century period piece. But, hey, sometimes looking at old stuff can be fun.

FURTHER READING: *Shampoo Planet;*
Girlfriend in a Coma; Generation A
SEE ALSO: *Bright Lights, Big City* (Jay McInerney);
Less than Zero (Bret Easton Elllis)

★
★
★
★

Writer: Jean Paul-Sartre
Publisher: Gallimard, 1938

ISBN US: 978-0811201889
ISBN UK: 978-0141185491

15+ LA NAUSÉE (NAUSEA)

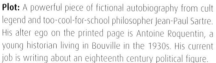

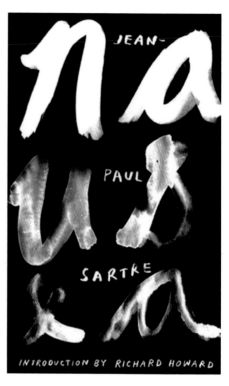

Plot: A powerful piece of fictional autobiography from cult legend and too-cool-for-school philosopher Jean-Paul Sartre. His alter ego on the printed page is Antoine Roquentin, a young historian living in Bouville in the 1930s. His current job is writing about an eighteenth century political figure.

Written in the form of a fictional diary, *Nausea* confronts us with Roquentin's innermost thoughts on the nature of his being as he begins to suffer an increasing sense of alienation from his everyday bourgeois life. He has also developed an increasing awareness in the objects that surround him. "I exist," he says, "that is all, and I find it nauseating."

Review: Through Roquentin, Sartre explores the key existentialist concept of whether a person is a free agent and able to determine their own course in life via free will. So far, so comprehensible. It's when Roquentin starts to lose

his grip on reality that Sartre might also be said to lose his grip on the reader—Roquentin's hyper-awareness of the world around him, and his wondering at the existence of objects, are complex concepts to grasp. He questions, for instance, why inanimate objects should have names. A seat might well be called a "dead donkey," he says, which would do nothing to change the essence of its being.

The best solution, if these tougher aesthetic and intellectual concepts trouble you, is to let them wash over you like a beautiful Mediterranean wave: think too much about them, though, and you might get seasick.

FURTHER READING: *The Age of Reason*
SEE ALSO: *The Outsider* (Albert Camus);
She Came to Stay (Simone de Beauvoir)

★
★
★
★
★

Writer: Milan Kundera
Publisher: Gallimard, 1984

ISBN US: 978-0061148521
ISBN UK: 978-0571135394

15+

L'INSOUTENABLE LÉGÈRETÉ DE L'ÊTRE
(THE UNBEARABLE LIGHTNESS OF BEING)

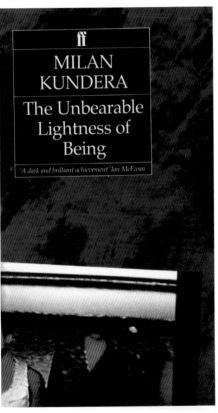

Plot: Tomas, a self-confessed womanizer, has "designed his life in a way that no woman could move in with a suitcase." He then meets Tereza who becomes his second wife, but this second marriage does not see Tomas renouncing his adulterous ways. The backdrop is Prague, 1968, where, before long, the Russian tanks have rolled in, taking away political freedoms as well as personal ones, and seeing Tomas and Tereza exiled to Geneva.

In the midst of all this sex and politics, Kundera undertakes a philosophical inquiry as to whether we should live a life of "lightness," that is, living for the moment; or "heaviness," following Nietzsche's philosophy of eternal return. It is reasonable to surmise, considering the fate of the central protagonists by the novel's climax, that the conclusion to this authorial inquiry is one that is left open-ended.

Review: This prize-winning novel was both a critical and commercial smash, but there are flaws: the characters are not fully drawn; feminists loathe Tomas' philandering (actually, so vile are his justifications for his "erotic friendships" that the misogynists might ally themselves with the feminists for once); and finally—and perhaps most difficult—is Kundera's depiction of loving human relationships as "weighty" or "kitsch"—the only "selfless love" in the book being that which Tomas and Tereza have for their dog Karenin.

If all this sounds like rather an unusual recommendation for a novel, here come the positives. Humor, tragedy, diverting digressions, and philosophy echo through the book with acuity: "Our life is a sketch for nothing, an outline with no picture," Kundera says, and it's this kind of sentiment that keeps you reading, laughing, crying and, for the most part, enjoying through to the bitter end.

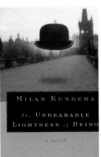

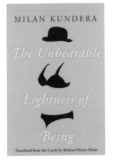

FURTHER READING:
The Book of Laughter and Forgetting
SEE ALSO: *The Sheltering Sky* (Paul Bowles);
Love in the Time of Cholera (Gabriel Garcia Marquez)

★
★
★

Writer: Giuseppe Tomasi di Lampedusa
Publisher: Feltrinelli, 1958

ISBN US: 978-0679731214
ISBN UK: 978-0099512158

15+ IL GATTOPARDO (THE LEOPARD)

Plot: *The Leopard* not only plots the history of Italian unification (the *Risorgimento*), but is also a character study of Prince Fabrizio, the head of an aristocratic Sicilian family, the Salinas, in the 1860s. In Fabrizio, Lampedusa depicts a proud man, a bully who cannot grasp the inevitability of change and the fall of the nobility.

Hosting this melancholy family saga is the arid landscape of Sicily, a place where, for its people, political change is just another event "outside our control." This resigned, fatalist view, is, Lampedusa suggests, down not just to the landscape and climate, but to a succession of rulers who "landed by main force" and who taxed Sicily but "did nothing for her."

Review: Unpublishable, divisive, stylistically challenging, rich with metaphor, Italy's bestselling novel ever, a masterwork of the imagination. Lampedusa's only novel, *The Leopard*, is all these things.

The author, who died before the book was published, did not live to learn of the polarized views of this work: on the one hand he came in for a lot of flack, due to his aristocratic background (he was the last in a line of Italian princes), and the church weren't overly impressed by the anticlerical nature of the book either. On the other hand, *The Leopard* has become one of Italy's most cherished and important works of literature. You get the feeling the author himself would be saddened by the public's reaction, sadness and pessimism being a mood that reverberates through his famous novel.

FURTHER READING: This was his only novel; Lampedusa's other work does not bear comparison
SEE ALSO: *The Garden of the Finzi Continis* (Giorgio Bassini)

★
★
★
★
★

Writer: Mikhail Bulgakov
Publisher: Moskva Journal, 1966

ISBN US: 978-0679760801
ISBN UK: 978-0140455465

15+

MASTER I MARGARITA
(THE MASTER AND MARGARITA)

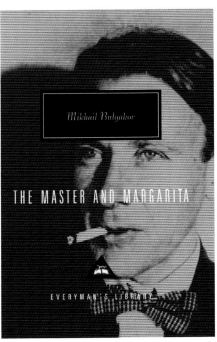

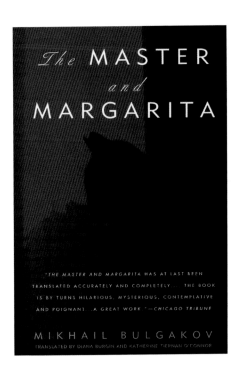

Plot: Two narratives coexist in Bulgakov's maverick satire. In Moscow a satanic magician named Woland carries out a demented terror campaign. His magic is of the black variety: he makes a bureaucrat disappear; he predicts the decapitation of a famous editor (Woland subsequently commandeers his apartment); and, as a *pièce de résistance*, he holds a ball for Moscow's wickedest residents. Simultaneously, an unpublished novel about Pontius Pilate is woven into the story. Its author, "The Master," whose love is the adulterous Margarita, is in a psychiatric hospital, demented by rejection and criticism of his book. Further dramatis personae range from a talking cat to a lunatic named Ivan Homeless. All in all, there is much for the gray cells to work on here.

Review: Mikhail Bulgakov died before he saw his satirical tour de force published in book form. Nor did he live to see the influence his novel had on future writers (Pelevin, Rushdie, Pynchon); as protest literature goes, this one continues to

knock people's socks off. And there was much to protest about when Bulgakov began writing *The Master and Margarita* in 1928: living in Russia during the worst excesses of Soviet totalitarianism, he also saw all of his plays banned in 1929 (despite earlier having been Stalin's favorite playwright).

So there's no doubting that *The Master and Margarita* is at once challenging, important, and hugely influential—but is it worth reading? Well, if you like a linear plotline with identifiable characters, stay away. If you like shadowy allegory and dark humor, dust off your library card and make a request for one of the screwiest adventures in twentieth-century literature. Heck, you might even buy a copy—it's a book that lends itself well to multiple readings.

FURTHER READING: *The Heart of a Dog*
SEE ALSO: *Midnight's Children* (Salman Rushdie); *The Clay Machine-Gun* (Viktor Pelevin)

★
★ **Writer:** Jack Kerouac   **ISBN US:** 978-0140283297
★ **Publisher:** The Viking Press, 1957   **ISBN UK:** 978-0141182674
★

12+ ON THE ROAD

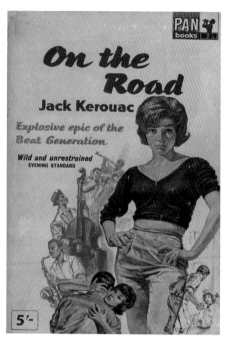

Plot: Inspired by his friend "the strange Dean Moriarty," Sal Paradise decides to make a journey by road across America in "one great red line," east to west. The two young men's subsequent life on the road—the excitement, the strangeness, and the freedom—make up the plot of the novel, combining to represent a life of nonconformity, and, with it, a search for freedom.

Review: A lyrical travelog by the King of the Beats, or the "new Buddha of American prose" as Ginsberg called him. This praise of his peers aside, it was not all plain sailing for Kerouac and his most famous work: it took six years for him to find a publisher for *On the Road*, by which time the author himself was disenchanted with the counterculture he had espoused. Also problematic was the fact that the immediate postwar austerity the novel describes had given way to the biggest economic boom-time America had ever seen.

For the modern reader the book can be equally problematic, as Kerouac's "spontaneous prose" may appear rambling and dated; that women are ornaments in Sal's life, and on the periphery of the story, also dates the book; and a third issue is the naive depiction of African Americans. And yet . . .

And yet this monumental cult classic still inspires travelers the world over and continues to delight with its feast of rhythmic language and a swinging poetic vibrancy. The dual nature of the novel—the exuberant style and iffy politics—is epitomized in perhaps its best-known passage, where Paradise wishes he were "a Negro, feeling that the best the white world had offered me was not enough ecstasy for me, not enough life, joy, kicks, darkness, music, not enough night."

A must-read.

FURTHER READING: *The Dharma Bums; Big Sur*
SEE ALSO: *Naked Lunch* (William Burroughs)

★
★
★
★
★

Writer: Jacqueline Susann
Publisher: Bernard Geis,1966

ISBN US: 978-0802135193
ISBN UK: 978-1860498879

15+

VALLEY OF THE DOLLS

Plot: A hugely entertaining romp through the ups and downs of three women negotiating the snakes and ladders game that was the entertainment industry in the 1960s. Anne, Jennifer, and Neely all crave glittering careers and success: Anne from Lawrencevillle, Massachusetts comes to New York to work in television; Jennifer is a blonde bombshell of little talent who, thanks to her exquisite physique, becomes a French "art house" movie star; Neely is the talented one—even winning an Oscar—but her addiction to uppers and downers sees her spiraling into a vortex of depression.

Through the three women those shining beacons of fame and fortune, Hollywood, Broadway, and Vegas, come in for a pasting. Our three heroines don't fare much better, as an unfortunate triumvirate of disappointments in love, sex, and career sees their beloved dolls (prescription drugs) become ever more appealing. It doesn't end well for anyone: abortion, divorce, insanity, addiction, and stomach pumps, all being part of the bumpy ride down.

Review: *Valley of the Dolls* is said to be an inspiration for the "sex and shopping" oeuvre of Jackie Collins in the 1980s. It might also be answerable for the "chick lit" genre. But let's not hold that against Susann. Her roman à clef (it is based on her own life experience) showing that the glitter of fame and fortune is nothing more than fool's gold, is entertaining, enduring, and, for the times, subversive. In short, *Valley of the Dolls* is that rare thing: a cult classic which is truly deserving of that label.

FURTHER READING: *The Love Machine; Once is Not Enough*
SEE ALSO: *What Makes Sammy Run* (Budd Schulberg); *Peyton Place* (Grace Metalious)

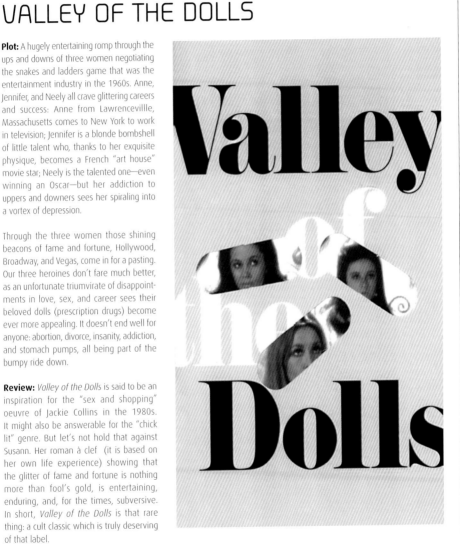

ESSENTIAL CULT BOOKS

500

23

CULT CLASSICS
Top 10 Classics

★
★ **Writer:** Geoff Ryman **ISBN US:** 978-0312182953
★ **Publisher:** Flamingo, 1998 **ISBN UK:** 978-0006550785

15+ # 253 THE PRINT REMIX

Geoff Ryman

253

THE JOURNEY OF 253 LIFETIMES

'A TRIUMPH' New Statesman

Plot: A tube train on the Bakerloo line of the London Underground is seven and a half minutes away from crashing. There are 252 seats on the train, all occupied, plus the driver, which makes 253. The book is made up of 253 brief character studies of each passenger, telling of their looks, personalities, and innermost thoughts—each in 253 words.

Review: *253* began life as a hypertext on the web, where readers could link to connections between each character in terms of mutual friends and work places, as well their likes and dislikes. Its reincarnation to the printed page, with footnotes instead of weblinks, could have made it all seem a bit tricksy or contrived, but, actually, it works.

FURTHER READING: *The Unconquered Country; The Warrior Who Carried Life* (both of the fantasy/sci-fi ilk)
SEE ALSO: *House of Leaves* (Mark Danielewski); *Exercises in Style* (Raymond Queneau)

★
★ **Writer:** Colin MacInnes **ISBN US:** 978-0749005405
★ **Publisher:** MacGibbon & Kee, 1959 **ISBN UK:** 978-0140021424

12+ # ABSOLUTE BEGINNERS

Absolute Beginners

Colin MacInnes

Plot: A snapshot of the birth of youth culture in 1950s London, as seen through the eyes of an unnamed photographer in the last of his teenage years. He—and the hep cats and squares of his acquaintance—are "absolute beginners," dealing with a changing world where young people have disposable incomes for the first time and the freedom to do what they want with it.

Review: Capturing the excitement of a period when the "teenager" was born is this book's best feature. Its perfunctory treatment of London's race riots is possibly its worst. On balance, it's an exuberant literary joy ride with a plethora of memorable characters (Ed the Ted, Crepe Suzette, and Mr. Cool to name but three).

FURTHER READING: *City of Spades; Mr. Love and Justice*
SEE ALSO: *The Lonely Londoners* (Samuel Selvon)

Writer: John O'Hara
Publisher: Harcourt Brace, 1934

ISBN US: 978-0375719202
ISBN UK: 978-0099518327

ISBN US: 978-0375719202
ISBN UK: 978-0099518327

15+

APPOINTMENT IN SAMARRA

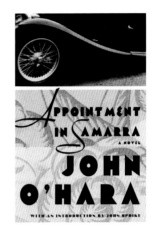

Plot: The title (from Maugham, used as an epigraph) implies the inevitability that death will find the protagonist Julian English. English runs a struggling car dealership in Gibbsville, Pennsylvania, based on O'Hara's home town of Pottsville and split along lines of religion and class. He throws a drink in the face of a bartender, makes drunken passes at women, and commits other faux pas. Fearing that his social status, financial position, and relationship with his wife are ruined, he commits suicide.

Review: English's inescapable decline is due to his inadequacy and insecurity. O'Hara litters the novel with brand names (badges of status), hints at matters sexual (uncommon at the time), and faultlessly pitched dialog. His first novel, O'Hara was already mastering many of his writing strengths, which would blossom in *Butterfield 8*, *Pal Joey*, and elsewhere.

FURTHER READING: *Ten North Frederick*
SEE ALSO: *Now in November* (Josephine W. Johnson);
The Grapes of Wrath (John Steinbeck)

Writer: Ayn Rand
Publisher: Random House, 1957

ISBN US: 978-0451191144
ISBN UK: 978-0141188935

ISBN US: 978-0451191144
ISBN UK: 978-0141188935

12+

ATLAS SHRUGGED

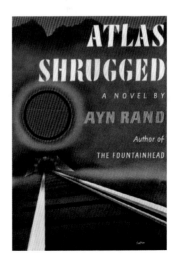

Plot: Dagny Taggart is trying to keep her railroad company afloat in difficult times when the economy is moving toward collectivisim, and the government is pressuring and manipulating businesses in order to control commerce. She teams up with Hank Rearden, a self-made steel magnate, to discover why some of the finest minds in business are disappearing. They find that, under the guidance of the mysterious John Galt, they have gone on strike, withdrawing their creativity and allowing the economy to collapse.

Review: In parts science fiction, mystery, romance, and philosophical discourse, *Atlas Shrugged* was the culmination of Rand's fiction writing, through which she explored the notion of Objectivism—the idea of selfish egoism. The book was met with mostly hostile reviews but was a bestseller and influential in libertarian circles.

FURTHER READING: *We the Living; Anthem; The Fountainhead*
SEE ALSO: *Letters of Ayn Rand* (ed. Michael S. Berliner);
Journals of Ayn Rand (ed. David Harriman)

★
★
★
★

Writer: Barack Obama
Publisher: Crown, 2006

ISBN US: 978-0307455871
ISBN UK: 978-1847670830

THE AUDACITY OF HOPE

12+

Synopsis: Taking its title from a 2004 keynote speech at the Democratic Convention, *The Audacity of Hope* is part manifesto, part biography that sets out (then Senator) Barack Obama's beliefs, both political and personal, and examines how he came to hold them. Chapters focus on issues of family, foreign policy, the Constitution, faith, and race, and the difference between the two political parties.

Review: Subtitled "Thoughts on reclaiming the American Dream," Obama introduced a number of ideas (such as health care reform) in the book that split critics on a political level, but his insight and ability to present his ideas was almost universally applauded. Four months after publication, Obama announced his (ultimately successful) candidacy for president, the move sometimes attributed to the reaction and endorsements he received while promoting the book.

FURTHER READING: *Dreams from My Father; Change We Can Believe In*
SEE ALSO: *The American Journey of Barack Obama* (*Life* magazine); *Barack Obama in His Own Words* (Lisa Rogak)

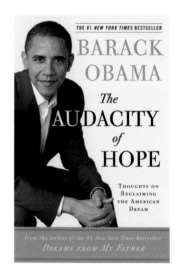

★
★

Writer: Kevin Sampson
Publisher: Jonathan Cape, 1998

ISBN US: 978-0224050555
ISBN UK: 978-0099267973

AWAYDAYS

18+

Plot: *Awaydays* explores the world of football (soccer) hooliganism in England in the late 1970s. Paul Clarty is our central protagonist, a clever lad from a nice home—but not clever or nice enough to avoid falling in with The Pack, a mob of violent Tranmere Rovers fans.

Review: The world of the football hooligan is an ugly one, and if you don't like ugliness, such as head-butting, bare-knuckle fights, box cutters, and the like, best give this novel a miss. On the other hand, it's an authentic take on late-seventies England, when gangs of "casuals" dressed in Fila tracksuits and Adidas trainers roamed the streets, and bands like Joy Division and Echo and the Bunnymen were in fashion. Not the best of books about malcontented youth in Margaret Thatcher's Britain, but worth a look.

FURTHER READING: *Powder; Clubland*
SEE ALSO: *The Damned United* (David Peace); *The Football Factory* (John King); *Marabou Stork Nightmares* (Irvine Welsh)

★
★
★
★

Writer: Jim Carroll
Publisher: Tombouctou Books, 1978

ISBN US: 978-0140249996
ISBN UK: 978-0140249996

15+

THE BASKETBALL DIARIES

Plot: A novelization of the diaries of the young Carroll, as he does his growing up on the streets of New York from 1963–1966.

Review: Those looking for a straightforward chronicle about a young man excelling at the game of basketball, forget it. Like so many youngsters Carroll allows his childish hopes and dreams to vanish in the headier allure of sex and drugs.

At once very funny and depressing, only those suffering from the acutest memory loss will not recognize something of their teenaged years in the young Jim's story. By this I don't mean the glue-sniffing, purse-snatching, shooting-up, or hustling of gay men, I mean the trials and tribulations of coming of age, both sexually and intellectually—no matter when or where you did it.

FURTHER READING: *Forced Entries* (poetry)
SEE ALSO: *Wonderland Avenue: Tales of Glamour and Excess*
(Danny Sugerman)

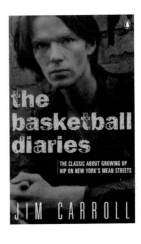

the
**basketball
diaries**

THE CLASSIC ABOUT GROWING UP
HIP ON NEW YORK'S MEAN STREETS

JIM CARROLL

★
★
★
★

Writer: Richard Farina
Publisher: Random House, 1966

ISBN US: 978-0140189308
ISBN UK: 978-0140189308

15+

BEEN DOWN SO LONG IT LOOKS LIKE UP TO ME

Plot: "Turn on, tune in, drop out," Timothy Leary said in 1966. Farina's Gnossos Pappadopoulis, a fictional creation from that year, is the very epitome of the phrase: jobless, and with no direction, Pappadopoulis heads back to his old college town to indulge in all manner of hippie behavior: psychedelics, women, and a search for the meaning of life.

Review: *Been Down So Long It Looks Like Up to Me* had the makings of a cult classic from the moment it burst forth into the world: the author died in a motorcycle accident two days after its publication, contemporary reviewers loathed it, and it has an inventive narrative that recalls "the Beats." Far out, and forever "in," this is required countercultural reading.

FURTHER READING: His untimely death meant no more books, but if you like folk music, give his *Celebrations for a Grey Day* a listen
SEE ALSO: *Gravity's Rainbow* (Thomas Pynchon), dedicated to Farina

NEL

BEEN DOWN
SO LONG IT LOOKS
LIKE UP TO ME

COMPLETE AND UNEXPURGATED

BY RICHARD FARINA
THE WILDEST, SEXIEST, MOST TURNED-ON
UNDERGROUND NOVEL SINCE *CATCHER IN THE RYE*

Writer: Roger Kahn
Publisher: Harper and Row, 1972

ISBN US: 978-0060883966
ISBN UK: 978-0060883966

THE BOYS OF SUMMER

Synopsis: A bitter-sweet memoir charting the history of the Brooklyn Dodgers baseball team. The book tells of the author's own childhood through to his life as a cub reporter on *The New York Herald Tribune*, and, finally, presents his time covering the team for two league seasons.

Review: Like the very best sports books, the personal—and the human—are neatly bound into the journalistic narrative here. Kahn's own coming of age is linked with the ups and downs of the National League baseball team, particularly during the twilight years of its success. Separate chapters devoted to the lives of the team's players in middle-age are a particularly nice touch to a book that is resplendent with nice touches.

FURTHER READING: *Memories of Summer*
SEE ALSO: *Fever Pitch* (Nick Hornby)

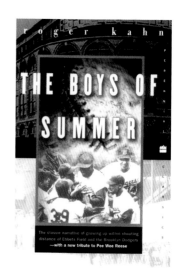

Writer: Jay McInerney
Publisher: Vintage, 1984

ISBN US: 978-0394726410
ISBN UK: 978-0747589204

BRIGHT LIGHTS, BIG CITY

Plot: A young New York socialite is falling apart: his famous model wife has left him and his job at *Prestigious Magazine* is not going to plan. Can parties and cocaine abuse provide the relief he needs?

Review: McInerney's distinctive use of the second person has us absorbing the decadent world of 1980s New York as if by osmosis. At first the repeated "you" jars, but soon we get into its beat and that of the protagonist's beloved Bolivian Marching Powder (cocaine). That he works in a verification department is no coincidence: verification of life itself is what this young man strives for. It's this existential edge to the novel, and its surprisingly touching take on loss, that makes it a more fulfilling read than other "brat pack" novels of the era.

FURTHER READING: *Story of My Life;*
Model Behavior; Brightness Falls
SEE ALSO: *The Year of Magical Thinking* (Didion)

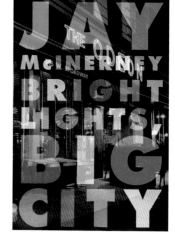

★
★
★
★

Writer: Hanif Kureishi
Publisher: Faber, 1990

ISBN US: 978-0140131680
ISBN UK: 978-0571142743

15+

THE BUDDHA OF SUBURBIA

Plot: "I'm an Englishman born and bred, almost." The famous opening lines of Kureishi's 1990 instant hit set the tone for what's to come—race and racism is a central theme. But the principle obsession of Karim, our seventeen-year-old narrator, is how he can escape the South London suburbs. A dream that is realized when his Indian father becomes a guru to his white neighbors—in other words, the Buddha of Suburbia.

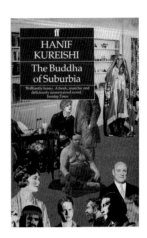

Review: After writing film scripts (*My Beautiful Launderette* being the most successful), Kureishi broke into novel writing with this bildungsroman set in the late 1970s. Although readers from outside the UK might be bored by the obsession with social class, the emotional and sexual adventures of Karim as he fumbles through adolescence should have universal appeal.

FURTHER READING: *The Black Album; Intimacy and Other Stories*
SEE ALSO: *A Suitable Boy* (Vikram Seth); *Anita and Me* (Meera Syal)

★
★
★

Writer: Ethan Canin
Publisher: Random House New York, 2001

ISBN US: 978-0375759932
ISBN UK: 978-0747557906

15+

CARRY ME ACROSS THE WATER

Plot: An accomplished patchwork history of a war veteran, August Kleinman, in the middle of the twentieth century. The book begins with a letter from Japan, then drifts to and fro through Kleinman's life: escaping Nazi Germany, fighting in World War Two, starting his own beer business in Pittsburgh, and falling in and out of love.

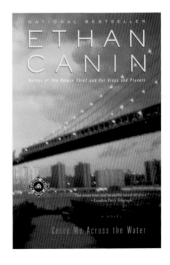

Review: If an old man's life history sounds more mundane than mesmerizing, more conventional than fashionably cult, then rest assured that the novel's form, with its episodic peepholes into Kleinman's complex life, is satisfyingly diverting. He's a man who "takes the advice of no one" (following his mother's advice, ironically enough), which sees him lead a bold and successful life, but not one without its mistakes.

FURTHER READING: *Blue River; America, America*
SEE ALSO: *2666* (Roberto Bolano)

★
★
★
★

Writer: Joseph Heller
Publisher: Simon and Schuster, 1961

ISBN US: 978-0684833392
ISBN UK: 978-0099470465

15+ # CATCH-22

Plot: War in all its bloody and nonsensical horror is satirized in Heller's seminal work. Our central character is John Yossarian, a bombardier in the 256th squadron stationed in Pianosa, Italy, during World War II. His conflict lies in whether to question his Colonel and authority or die a hero.

Review: This 500-plus paged paean to pacifism split opinion on publication in 1961. Perhaps the main criticism was that Yossarian takes the universal tragedy of war personally. What can't be denied, though, is that the horrors, sounds, and personal tragedies of war (including the hostility that exists between men in the same uniforms) fill these pages with eye-opening might. Depressing, difficult, and funny in equal measure.

FURTHER READING: *Something Happened; Closing Time*
SEE ALSO: *Birdsong* (Sebastian Faulks)

★
★
★
★
★

Writer: Raymond Carver
Publisher: Knopf, 1983

ISBN US: 978-0679723691
ISBN UK: 978-0099449850

18+ # CATHEDRAL

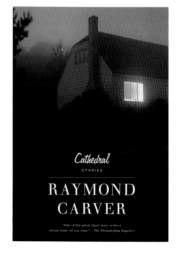

Synopsis: The lovers and losers in Carver's fourth short story collection are fighting a losing battle against the human existence. Among the favorites are: "Cathedral," in which a seeing man and a blind man gain a mutual understanding when they draw a picture together; "Chef's House," in which a recovering alcoholic spends a summer by the sea; and "Vitamins," in which a husband and wife are divided by alcohol, betrayal, and dietary supplements.

Review: Bespectacled wannabe writers have attended many a creative writing course in an attempt to recreate Carver's much lauded minimalist style. But that's the thing with genius. It is inimitable. This collection is Carver at his best, fused with alcohol, cathartic moments, wry observation, and choppy prose. Outstanding.

FURTHER READING: *What We Talk About When We Talk About Love;*
Will You Please be Quiet, Please?
SEE ALSO: *Don't Tell Me the Truth About Love* (Dan Rhodes);
Short Stories (Guy de Maupassant); *Complete Stories*
(Flannery O'Connor)

★
★
★
★

Writer: Ian McEwan
Publisher: Jonathan Cape, 1978

ISBN US: 978-0099755111
ISBN UK: 978-0099755111

18+

THE CEMENT GARDEN

Plot: Our narrator is Jack, brother to Julie, Sue, and Tom. When their father dies, closely followed by their mother, the elder siblings pour cement over their mother's body in the cellar to avoid adult interference. The consequences are disastrous: Jack has incestuous longings for Julie, Tom dresses in girl's clothes and, in the brooding hot summer, a smell emanates from the cellar, arousing the suspicions of Julie's new "bloke," Derek.

Review: Dark and disturbing, impeccably written, it could be argued that this, McEwan's first novel, is his best; certainly it is the one that has attracted the most devoted cult following. The stand-out scene is saved for last, leaving the reader ogling in fascinated revulsion at the inevitable conclusion.

FURTHER READING: *First Love, Last Rites; Enduring Love; Saturday*
SEE ALSO: *Les Enfants Terribles* (Jean Cocteau)

★
★
★
★

Writer: Kai Hermann and Horst Rieck
Publisher: Stern, 1979

ISBN US: 978-0553208979
ISBN UK: 978-0553261370

18+

CHRISTIANE F. WIR KINDER VOM BAHNHOF ZOO

Synopsis: *Wir Kinder Vom Bahnhof Zoo* is the product of two months of interviews with the teenaged drug addict Christiane Felscherinow, who frequented the Bahnhof Zoo area of Berlin, a notorious hang-out for heroin addicts in the 1970s. Christiane and her friends' comings and goings are described candidly, and at times harrowingly, in this account of her life from the ages of twelve to fifteen.

Review: "Just say no to drugs" is a message you might have heard before but if you want your children to heed it, you could do worse than pressing this grubby little exposé into their hands: it shocked Germany in the 1970s and is no less eye-opening now. Honest and disturbing, Christiane's descent into the nightmare of heroin addiction makes for sobering reading.

FURTHER READING: This was a solo-effort from Christiane F.'s journalist alter-egos
SEE ALSO: *The Basketball Diaries* (Jim Carroll)

ESSENTIAL CULT BOOKS

500 ESSENTIAL CULT BOOKS

31

CULT CLASSICS
Best of the Rest

★
★ **Writer:** Paul Auster. Adpated by Paul
★ Karasik and David Mazzucchelli
★ **Publisher:** Avon Books, 1994

ISBN US: 978-0140097313
ISBN UK: 0-571-22633-7

15+ CITY OF GLASS

Plot: A wrong number (or is it?) provides the catalyst for Quinn, a writer, to become involved in a strange adventure, which sees him impersonating a detective, named Paul Auster, and taking on a case to protect a man from his possibly psychotic father.

Review: Originally published as part of his famous *New York Trilogy*, Paul Auster was persuaded to have the work adapted in comic form in the early 1990s. The story does not suffer in the transition. Mazzucchelli's black and white illustrations, maps, and graphics lend an existential edge that perfectly complements the dream-like atmosphere of the original and enhances the absorption of its detective story element. Very unsettling, but very good.

FURTHER READING: A unique collaboration,
but see Auster's other fiction
SEE ALSO: *The New York Trilogy* **(Paul Auster)**

★
★ **Writer:** Victor Pelevin
★ **Publisher:** Vagrius, 1996

ISBN US: 978-0571201266
ISBN UK: 978-0571201266

15+ THE CLAY MACHINE GUN

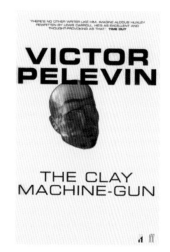

Plot: Petr Voyd is one of four patients undergoing treatment at a Moscow psychiatric clinic in the early 1990s. In a separate plotline, he is also Petka, a captain in the Red Army during the Russian civil war, aide to Chapaev, a Bolshevik hero. Instructed by Chapaev, Petr/Petka explores the meaning of reality in an attempt to fill a void at the center of his existence.

Review: It might seem like the profusion of influences, themes, and plotlines here come from different planets, but somehow they all hang together in one beautiful universe of madness by the novel's end. Hated by the Russian literary establishment, feted by his legions of (mainly young) fans, Pelevin might well split opinion but is far too important to be missed.

FURTHER READING: *Omon Ra; The Sacred Book of the Werewolf*
SEE ALSO: *The Master and Margarita* **(Mikhail Bulgakov)**

★
★
★
★

Writer: Bohumil Hrabal
Publisher: Ceskoslovensky, 1965

ISBN US: 978-0810112780
ISBN UK: 978-0349101255

15+

CLOSELY OBSERVED TRAINS

Plot: A comic coming-of-age story about Milos Hrma, a young railroad apprentice in Bohemia in 1945. Hrma is preoccupied by two questions: will he ever succeed in losing his innocence to a woman, and how much longer can he bear to observe the trains carrying German soldiers, goods, and munitions to the Eastern front?

Review: Impotence is the keyword of this masterly novella, reflecting both the failure of Hrma to rise to the occasion with his girlfriend Masha, and the powerlessness of the Czech people under Nazi occupation. Hrabal addresses both these issues with two acts—one sexual, one heroic—that see his main protagonist lose his innocence. Celebrations of humanity don't come any more tragicomic than this.

Hrabal's comedy, comic and poignant in equal measure.

FURTHER READING: *Too Loud a Solitude;*
The Little Town Where Time Stood Still
SEE ALSO: *The Good Soldier Svejk* (Jaroslva Hasek)

★
★
★
★
★

Writer: Flannery O'Connor
Publisher: Farrar, Straus, Giroux, 1971

ISBN US: 978-0374515362
ISBN UK: 978-0571245789

12+

THE COMPLETE STORIES

Synopsis: Flannery O'Connor's entire short story output in one complete collection. O'Connor was the master of the genre and her stories are notable for their tragicomic tone, freakish characters, and religious and social themes.

Review: The word most often associated with O'Connor's work is "grotesque," of which she said, "Anything that comes out of the South is going to be called grotesque by the northern reader, unless it is grotesque, in which case it is going to be called realistic." Her window on the world of the South includes a granddaughter being beaten on the head with a rock, a morally superior woman being throttled in a doctor's waiting room, and death by bull. Whether these tales are "grotesque" or "realistic" is immaterial when you have short-story telling this good.

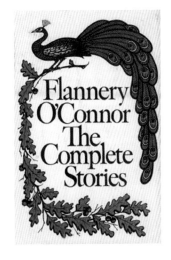

FURTHER READING: *Wise Blood*
SEE ALSO: *And the Ass Saw the Angel* (Nick Cave);
A Feast of Snakes (Harry Crews)

★
★
★

Writer: Jonathan Franzen
Publisher: Farrar, Straus and Giroux 2001

ISBN US: 978-0312421274
ISBN UK: 978-0007232444

15+ THE CORRECTIONS

Plot: The Lambert Family—notably parents Enid and Alfred—must face up to the secrets and lies, that is, "make corrections" to the mistakes of their past. More than a family saga, though, *The Corrections* also looks at America's political world identity—interesting considering it was published only days before the 9/11 attacks.

Review: Without doubt Franzen's main achievement in *The Corrections* was to put family at the heart of the Great American novel once again. However its strengths are also its limitations: in representing the spirit of life in the U.S. at the turn of the millennium from an educated middle class, learned perspective, he neglects the stories of the poor and the needy. Not a universal novel then, but a funny and challenging one, nevertheless.

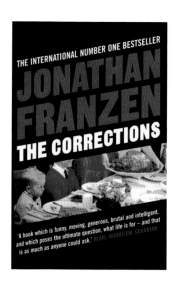

FURTHER READING: *Strong Motion*
SEE ALSO: *White Noise* (Don DeLillo)

★
★
★

Writer: Edna O'Brien
Publisher: Hutchinson, 1960

ISBN US: 978-0452263949
ISBN UK: 978-0752881164

15+ THE COUNTRY GIRLS

Plot: *The Country Girls* chronicles the adolescent years of Caithleen, a romantic young girl, and Baba, her friend. Afraid of their parents, priests, and the nuns in their convent school, they escape rural east Clare to Dublin, where they enjoy the hedonism and harsh lessons the city has to offer.

Review: Wise, tender, and true, *The Country Girls* is a coming-of-age novel that bears comparison with the very best of the genre. It's such an important novel in Irish literature, in part because of the outrage it caused on publication: O'Brien's parish priest ordered copies to be burned, the Irish censor called it "a smear on Irish womanhood," and the author's own mother inked out the naughty bits. It's more than a frank account of sexual awakening though—the narrative is clever and absorbing and has rightly been compared to Joyce.

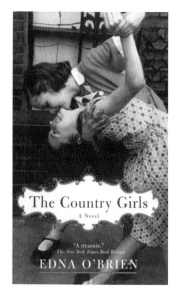

FURTHER READING: *Girl with Green Eyes; Girls in Their Married Bliss*
SEE ALSO: *The Gathering* (Anne Enright); *The Heather Blazing* (Colm Toibin)

★
★
★
★

Writer: Thomas Pynchon
Publisher: Lippincott, 1966

ISBN US: 978-0060913076
ISBN UK: 978-0099532613

15+

THE CRYING OF LOT 49

THOMAS
PYNCHON
THE CRYING OF
LOT 49

Plot: Returning from a Tupperware party, Mrs. Oedipa Maas discovers she has been named as executrix in an ex-lover's will. Uncovering the truth behind his assets sees her journeying across America and opening a Pandora's Box of strange characters and possible conspiracies.

Review: *The Crying of Lot 49* is characterized by clever and darkly humorous prose, a caustic wit, and unerring cynicism. It's often said this is the easiest of Pynchon's work, and a slender volume it is too. So, if you have a penchant for a one-stop Pynchon shop, dive in. If you have fear and loathing of the willfully erudite, skip to the next cult book.

FURTHER READING: *Gravity's Rainbow*
SEE ALSO: *The New York Trilogy* (Paul Auster); *White Noise* (Don DeLillo)

★
★
★

Writer: Donald Goines
Publisher: Holloway House, 1974

ISBN US: 978-2070498048
ISBN UK: 978-0870678974

18+ # DADDY COOL

Plot: Larry Jackson is Daddy Cool, a black contract killer whose fortunes take a nosedive when he discovers his beloved daughter is being pimped out by her boyfriend.

Review: The daily grind of a hired killer is mundanely presented, which seems to normalize the brutality and violence of the gangster lifestyle. Goines was no stranger to the harsh urban landscape of the 1970s depicted here—despite a homely upbringing, he became a heroin addict in the army, turning to pimping, gambling, and other criminal activity to feed his habit when he got out. An inevitable stint in jail saw him penning his first book, and he wrote an impressive sixteen novels before his untimely death in 1974. *Daddy Cool* is considered his best work.

FURTHER READING: *Black Gangster; Dopefiend*
SEE ALSO: *Trick Baby* (Iceberg Slim)

★
★
★

Writer: Arthur Koestler
Publisher: Jonathan Cape, 1940

ISBN US: 978-0553265958
ISBN UK: 978 0099 424 918

15+

DARKNESS AT NOON

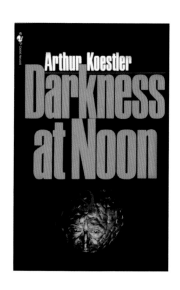

Plot: An old-guard Communist, Rubashov, is unsurprised when he is arrested by two officials one day. They imprison him and he soon goes on trial. The plot of *Darkness at Noon* tells of his incarceration, and the three hearings that lead to a depressing ending.

Review: The verisimilitude of Koestler's powerful account of Rubashov's troubles is not unaffected by his not naming the government that holds Rubashov captive—all revolutionary dictatorships are being held to account here, though Stalin's regime is uppermost in our minds. In his preface Koestler dedicates the work to the "men who were victims of the so-called Moscow Trials." His central character Rubashov is, he tells us, a "synthesis" of their lives, but his story is nevertheless a moving tribute to the tyranny of victims everywhere.

FURTHER READING: *The Gladiators; Arrival and Departure*
SEE ALSO: *Appointment in Samarra* (John O'Hara)

★
★
★
★

Writer: Nathanael West
Publisher: Random House, 1939

ISBN US: 978-0811218221
ISBN UK: 978-0141023656

15+

THE DAY OF THE LOCUST

Plot: Art graduate Tod Hackett works in the film industry as a set designer while awaiting inspiration for his paintings. He meets a series of fading stars, aspiring starlets, and ineffective hangers-on whose emptiness and loathing turns to violence at a Hollywood premiere.

Review: During the Depression, Nathanael West was immersed in the lives of the semi-successful. The author of a handful of novels, he ran hotels offering free accommodation to writers; the sale of one took him to Hollywood where he struggled to make any impact as a screenwriter. His novel reflects these people on the fringes of success whose dreams have failed to come true—West's own story. Just as he seemed to be on the cusp of success, he died in a car crash.

FURTHER READING: *The Dream Life of Balso Snell; Miss Lonelyhearts; A Cool Million*
SEE ALSO: *The Beautiful and Damned* (F. Scott Fitzgerald); *Play It As It Lays* (Joan Didion)

★
★
★
★
★

Writer: Nikolai Gogol
Publisher: 1842 in Russia

ISBN US: 978-0486426822
ISBN UK: 978-0140448078

12+ DEAD SOULS

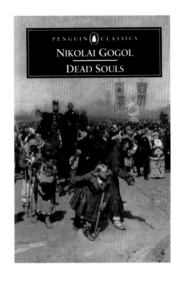

Plot: Light on plot, heavy on character assassination, this is the story of Pavel Ivanovich Chichikov's attempt to swindle a fortune via the acquisition of the rights of dead serfs, the "dead souls" of the title. His plan is to offer local landowners a novel form of tax avoidance. But will it work?

Review: Gogol draws a cynical picture of the characters of Russian provincial life: greedy, suspicious, affected, and complacent. His aim was to change Russia, and he was driven mad by his desire to do so (as well as by the writing of this book), eventually committing suicide. A tragic fate to end the gestation of a comic masterpiece.

FURTHER READING: *The Collected Tales of Nikolai Gogol*
SEE ALSO: *Master and Margarita* (Mikhail Bulgakov);
Notes from the Underground (Fydor Dostoyevsky)

★
★
★
★

Writer: George and Weedon Grossmith
Publisher: J. W. Arrowsmith, 1892

ISBN US: 978-0140437324
ISBN UK: 978-0140621570

12+ THE DIARY OF A NOBODY

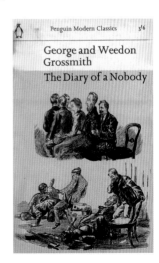

Plot: Charles Pooter is a city worker with a suburban home in London, a respectable wife, and an altogether inflated opinion of his own importance. The "diary" chronicles everything from his status anxieties (many) to his daring innovations in interior design (a painted bathtub) and his anxieties about his son Lupin's courtship of the shocking Daisy Mutlar.

Review: How can a work so solidly rooted in late-Victorian suburbia still be relevant—let alone laugh-out-loud funny—today? The secret of its enduring appeal lies in the authors' (who were brothers) keen, yet not unkind, understanding of human nature, especially as it relates to embarrassment, social climbing, and family ties. The hapless Pooter may be the perennial butt of everyone's jokes, but it is impossible to look at him and not see something of ourselves.

FURTHER READING: The brothers collaborated once only on the diaries
SEE ALSO: *The Inimitable Jeeves* (P. G. Wodehouse);
Vile Bodies (Evelyn Waugh)

★
★ **Writer:** Günter Grass   **ISBN US:** 978-0679725756
★ **Publisher:** Luchterhand, 1959   **ISBN UK:** 978-0099466048

15+   DIE BLECHTTROMMEL (THE TIN DRUM)

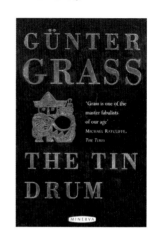

Plot: Through the eyes of a dwarf, Oskar Matzerath, we learn of three decades of life in Danzig (now Gdansk, Poland) during the rise of Hitler, Nazi rule, and, finally, during the defeat and partition of Germany.

Review: This is not a conventional historical novel. It is also a character study of the grotesque Matzerath, who at age four decides he will not grow into an adult and is later institutionalized for a murder he did not commit. With *The Tin Drum*, Grass captured the guilty sentiment of Germany in the postwar era, and painfully told the world of the role the *petit bourgeoisie* played in the German catastrophe. It was a huge success and one neither he, nor any other West German writer, has been able to emulate since.

FURTHER READING: *Cat and Mouse; The Dog Years*
(the other two titles making up the Danziger trilogy of books,
of which *The Tin Drum* is the first)
SEE ALSO: *Midnight's Children* (Salman Rushdie)

★
★ **Writer:** Heinrich Böll   **ISBN US:** 978-0140187281
★ **Publisher:** Kiepenheuer und Witsch, 1974   **ISBN UK:** 978-0749398989

15+   DIE VERLORENE EHRE DER KATHARINA BLUM
(THE LOST HONOR OF KATHARINA BLUM)

Plot: A cautionary tale of what can happen to an ordinary person when they are hounded by the press. After meeting a criminal at a party, Katharina Blum is caught up in a media circus that ultimately leads to murder.

Review: Red tops, gutter press, tabloids, yellow press—call them what you will, but the sensationalist journalists who prey on the innocent, as well as the guilty, are given short shrift here. The book highlights the lengths investigative reporters will go to for a story, and the snowball effect of this invasion of privacy: Katharina's friends and family are also tainted by the news story that circles round her like a vulture. Still fiercely relevant.

FURTHER READING: *Group Portrait with a Lady; The Safety Net*
SEE ALSO: *Vernon God Little* (D .B. C. Pierre)

★
★
★
★

Writer: Peter Biskind
Publisher: Simon and Schuster, 1998

ISBN US: 978-0684857084
ISBN UK: 978-0747544210

15+

EASY RIDERS, RAGING BULLS

Synopsis: The full and frank story of the last Golden Age of Cinema, from the release of *Easy Riders* to the dawn of the blockbuster in the late 1970s.

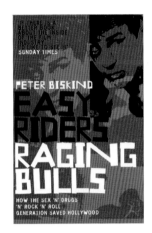

Review: Based on interviews with the key players in Hollywood at the time, the sex, drugs, and rock 'n' roll culture that led to a new dawn of inventiveness on the silver screen is divertingly told. Gossip junkies will love the anecdotes from on and off set, while film buffs will enjoy the story of how some of cinema's greatest ever films (*The Godfather*; *Chinatown*; *Jaws*) were made. It's a cautionary tale of sorts, relating how the personal peccadilloes of cinema's great and good led to the situation, where, to use an old cliché, "they don't make them like that anymore."

FURTHER READING: *Down and Dirty Pictures: Miramax, Sundance, and the Rise of Independent Film*
SEE ALSO: *Hollywood Babylon* (Kenneth Anger); *The Kid Stays in the Picture* (Robert Evans)

CULT CLASSICS
Best of the Rest

★
★
★
★

Writer: José Saramago
Publisher: Editorial Camhino, 1995

ISBN US: 978-0156035583
ISBN UK: 978-1860466854

12+

ENSAIO SOBRE A CEGUEIRA (BLINDNESS)

Plot: A thought-provoking parable in which a doctor in an unidentified city is suddenly struck blind. He is not the only one, and soon finds himself, together with his wife, shunted by the government to a military-style asylum, where they are forced to live side-by-side with others similarly afflicted.

Review: The epidemic and its consequences illustrate what can happen—in any place, at any time—when society breaks down. There is greed, selfishness, horrible acts of violence; at the same time there is humanity and hope, the latter mostly tied to the character of the doctor's wife. Stylistically the novel is a challenge, being bereft of the usual grammatical rules, which only adds to the uneasiness of a book that questions the very nature of humanity.

FURTHER READING: *The History of the Siege of Lisbon*
SEE ALSO: *The Plague* (Albert Camus); *Lord of the Flies* (William Golding)

Writer: Tom Robbins
Publisher: Houghton Mifflin, 1976

ISBN US: 978-0553349498
ISBN UK: 978-1842430248

15+ EVEN COWGIRLS GET THE BLUES

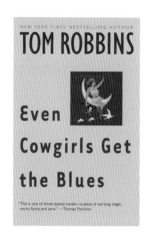

Plot: Sissy Hankshaw, born with extra large thumbs, goes hitchhiking across America where she meets a melting pot of characters, including Bonanza Jelly Bean and the cowgirls of the Rubber Rose Ranch. Gatecrashing the plot are anarchic, yet pleasing, asides on topics such as the rectal temperature of bees and other life forms.

Review: The art of reflecting the mindset of a counterculture via the printed page is a skill few authors have mastered. Tom Robbins is such an author, and *Even Cowgirls Get the Blues* is such a book. Its message of peace, love, and understanding made it a favorite of 1970s hippies, but it hasn't dated, and eccentric free-wheeling types should enjoy it to this day.

FURTHER READING: *Another Roadside Attraction*
SEE ALSO: *Walden* (Henry David Thoreau);
Trout Fishing in America (Richard Brautigan)

Writer: Frederick Exley
Publisher: Harper and Row, 1968

ISBN US: 978-0679720768
ISBN UK: 978-0679720768

12+ A FAN'S NOTES

Synopsis: Ostensibly an account of a fan's love of the former New York Giants' halfback Frank Gifford. Actually about Exley's misfit status, as a man destined to be on the sidelines of life . . . or so he would have himself and the reader think.

Review: The confessional genre—or misery memoir—became hugely successful in the early noughties, but before it was even invented Exley sought catharsis in writing the depressing story of his life. Despite the alcoholism, though, despite the time spent in institutions, despite his unerring—and self-confessed—ability to fail, we are well-disposed toward him and his "nearly heroic drinking." Besides, he can hardly be said to be a failure when his *A Fan's Notes* is such a legendary cult read.

FURTHER READING: *Pages from a Cold Island; Last Notes Home*
SEE ALSO: *A Million Little Pieces* (James Frey)

★
★
★

Writer: Harry Crews
Publisher: Atheneum, 1976

ISBN US: 978-0684842486
ISBN UK: 978-0684842486

15+

A FEAST OF SNAKES

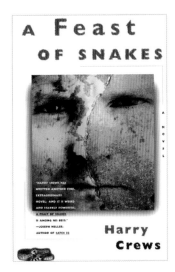

Plot: A sublime mix of post-modernism, Southern hicks, perverse humor . . . and rattlesnakes. The setting is Mystic, Georgia, location of the annual "Rattlesnake Roundup." The protagonist is Joe Lon Mackey, a trailer-park loser whose glory days as the Boss Snake of the Mystic Rattlers football team is long gone. The action is Joe's personal journey into ruin.

Review: Locating Joe's inner turmoil in the midst of the Rattlesnake Roundup is inspired. The Roundup, Joe says, is "Just a bunch of crazy people cranking up to git crazier. But that's all right. Feel on the edge of doing something outstanding myself." That he does, precipitating a bizarre set of events which include castration, suicide, and murder.

FURTHER READING: *The Gospel Singer; The Knock-Out Punch*
SEE ALSO: *Joe* (Larry Brown)

★
★
★

Writer: Nick Hornby
Publisher: Victor Gollancz, 1992

ISBN US: 978-1573226882
ISBN UK: 978-0140293449

12+

FEVER PITCH

Synopsis: The autobiographical memoir of a high school English teacher's tortured relationship with Arsenal, a North London soccer team. The highs and lows of his own life seem to mirror, and be echoed by, the triumphs and travails of his team on the pitch.

Review: Hugely successful, *Fever Pitch* was read by a generation of men who picked up a book about football and discovered, somewhat to their surprise, that it was as much an analysis of hope, depression, despair, and the difficulties of being a man as a celebration of the "beautiful game." They didn't mind; the book launched Hornby's career and was followed by a string of acute and perceptive novels.

FURTHER READING: *High Fidelity; About a Boy; A Long Way Down*
SEE ALSO: *Brilliant Orange* (David Winner); *The Damned United* (David Pearce)

★
★
★
★

Writer: Chuck Palahniuk
Publisher: W.W. Norton & Co, 1996

ISBN US: 0-393-03976-5
ISBN UK: 978-0099765219

18+ FIGHT CLUB

Plot: Intending to show the lack of social cohesion among late twenty-first-century males, Palahniuk presents a self-help group addict who joins a club, a club where men fight bare-knuckled according to a strict set of rules. Its creator, the über-masculine Tyler Durden, sees "fight club" as a catalyst for his '"Project Mayhem" to bring down capitalist society.

Review: *Fight Club*, Palahniuk's first novel, is boundary-breaking, bleak, and zeitgeist-y, and was canonized as a cult classic way before the 1998 movie. Lovers of style over substance may not go in for his conversational tone (in a *Guardian* interview Palahniuk admitted he doesn't go in for "all those abstract, chicken-shit descriptions"), but it matters not. His message comes across loud and clear without such detail, namely: "Your life comes down to nothing and not even nothing, oblivion."

FURTHER READING: *Choke*
SEE ALSO: *Stiffed: The Betrayal of the American Man*
(Susan Faludi); *The Game* (Neil Strauss)

★
★
★
★

Writer: Rohinton Mistry
Publisher: McClelland & Stewart, 1995

ISBN US: 978-1400030651
ISBN UK: 978-0571230587

15+ A FINE BALANCE

Plot: Dina Dalai escapes her abusive brother and, because of failing eyesight, must hire others to help make dresses. Ishvar Darji and his nephew Omprakash are low-caste tailors, survivors of a family massacre, who come to Mumbai to work for her. Maneck Kohlah, a student who had befriended a political activist, is seeking lodgings. Despite their diverse backgrounds, the four become unlikely friends.

Review: Set against the background of civil unrest of the mid-1970s Emergency, the story graphically portrays a time of corruption, exploitation, and intolerance. To most Western readers (and, thanks to Oprah's Book Club, there were many), the background of social deprivation and political injustice will be as distant as a Dickens novel and just as powerful.

FURTHER READING: *Tales from Firozsha Baag;*
Such a Long Journey; Family Matters; The Scream
SEE ALSO: *A Suitable Boy* (Vikram Seth);
Shataram (Gregory David Roberts)

★
★
★
★

Writer: Donald Barthelme
Publisher: G. P. Putnam's Sons, 1987

ISBN US: 978-0140112450
ISBN UK: 978-0141180946

15+

FORTY STORIES

Synopsis: *Forty Stories* is an inappositely pedestrian title for a highly unusual collection. Being saturated with characters, settings, imagination, idiosyncrasies, and experimentation, the stories are hard to define as a collective entity. For instance, the characters include: Goethe, a lion, Sinbad, a sick daughter, Bluebeard, two elderly lesbians, a "bogle" (a kind of spirit), and a dysfunctional married couple.

Review: One reviewer has said of this collection that the stories "follow the emotional logic of a dream." Like a dream, some of the tales are satisfying, others unnerving, while others still, "Bluebeard," for instance, stick with you after reading, leaving you wondering, "what did it all mean?" Barthelme's randomness is both loved and loathed—only by reading him will you find out which applies to you.

FURTHER READING: *Sixty Stories*
SEE ALSO: The short stories of Dave Eggers

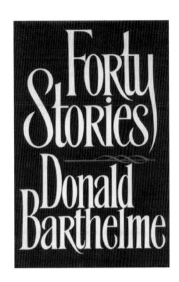

500 ESSENTIAL CULT BOOKS

43

CULT CLASSICS
Best of the Rest

★
★
★

Writer: James Baldwin
Publisher: Dial Press, 1956

ISBN US: 978-0385334587
ISBN UK: 978-0141032948

15+

GIOVANNI'S ROOM

Plot: In 1950s Paris, an American man, David, struggles between his unconventional "tastes" (his homosexuality) and his strong sense of conventional morality, wavering between his relationship with a woman, Hella, and a passionate love affair with Italian bartender Giovanni.

Review: It's a quick read but the atmosphere is no less heavy and brooding for that. Baldwin fans admire the pared-down nature of his writing, which nonetheless deals with a host of ideas about death, sexual preference, and belonging. The dialog can seem a bit preachy at times, but, overall, the book is an emotional slap in the face, and a reminder of just how repressive the postwar era really was.

FURTHER READING: *Go Tell It on the Mountain; Another Country*
SEE ALSO: *Disgrace* (J. M. Coetzee)

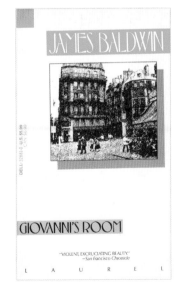

★
★
★
★
★

Writer: F. Scott Fitzgerald
Publisher: C. Scribner's Sons, 1925

ISBN US: 978-0743273565
ISBN UK: 978-0140620184

THE GREAT GATSBY

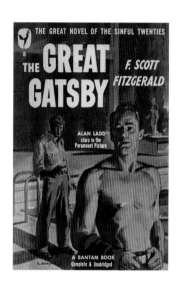

Plot: The enigmatic Jay Gatsby lives at West Egg in a moneyed world of making "plans to do nothing," hosting garden parties, and getting "roaring drunk"; the world, that is, of 1920s high society. Against this background Gatsby pursues his extravagant love for Daisy Buchanan. The action is seen through the eyes of his captivated neighbor, Nick Carraway.

Review: Our first glimpse of Gatsby is a shadowy figure standing in the garden of his mansion; as the book progresses we are no further illuminated as to his character. No matter. That Gatsby remains a puzzle is part of the point of this stunning evocation of the excesses and hypocrisy of the fashionable and the wealthy who "sneer at Gatsby on the courage of his own liquor."

FURTHER READING: *Tender is the Night; The Beautiful and Damned*
SEE ALSO: *A Farewell to Arms* (Ernest Hemingway);
The Grapes of Wrath (John Steinbeck)

★
★
★
★

Writer: Danilo Kis
Publisher: Harcourt Brace Jovanovich, 1978

ISBN US: 978-1564782731
ISBN UK: 978-1564782731

GROBNICA ZA BORISA DAVIDOVICA
(A TOMB FOR BORIS DAVIDOVICH)

Synopsis: A collection of seven short stories, each telling the tale of one individual's life and thematically linked (political hypocrisy, death, and betrayal all feature highly). The tales mostly deal with Eastern Europe in the early part of the twentieth century, though the story "Dogs and Books" takes us back to fourteenth-century France and the forced conversion of a Jewish man to Christianity.

Review: Wide in scope, dense in detail, Kis lends both a universal and microcosmic bent to his stories—no mean feat, and one which will not be to everybody's taste. The stories all end tragically, which is all the more upsetting when we consider that the lives depicted are all meant to have been real.

FURTHER READING: *Garden; Ashes*
SEE ALSO: *Too Loud a Solitude* (Bohumil Hrabal);
The Question of Bruno (Aleksandar Hemon)

★
★
★
★

Writer: Patrick McGrath
Publisher: Penguin Books, 1989

ISBN US: 978-0679776215
ISBN UK: 978-0140126532

15+

THE GROTESQUE

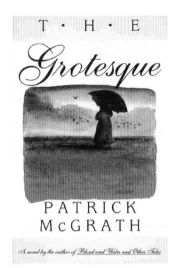

Plot: The unreliable narration of the brain damaged, wheel-chair bound, and sexually frustrated Sir Hugo Coal tells of a missing person, murder, and Coal's fear that what the Butler saw, or indeed plans, is more than he is letting on.

Review: The suffocating traditionalism of the English country manor house cries out for the horror treatment, and McGrath does it to perfection here. The work has been called "modern gothic," but what is masterful is that McGrath is not tempted by the explicit possibilities that modern fiction offers, instead ensuring that hideously shocking details—in short, the "grotesque"— are served up with polite, restrained good manners, for all their grisly subject matter. Murder most foul, indeed.

FURTHER READING: *Asylum; Port Mungo*
SEE ALSO: *The Monk* (Matthew Gregory Lewis):
The Castle of Otranto (Horace Walpole)

★
★
★
★

Writer: Dave Eggers
Publisher: Simon and Schuster, 2000

ISBN US: 978-0375725784
ISBN UK: 978-0330456715

15+

A HEARTBREAKING WORK
OF STAGGERING GENIUS

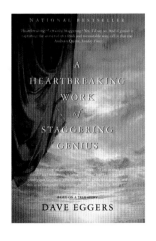

Synopsis: Based on the real experiences of Eggers, his heartbreaking work chronicles the consequences of the death of both his parents from cancer, after which he is left as the sole guardian of his eight-year-old brother Toph.

Review: If you find the title of Eggers' critically acclaimed memoir hyperbolically off-putting, rest assured that the author keenly points out the book's flaws, suggesting in the preface that the first 109 pages, "are all some of you might want to bother with." There is also an anxiety that the book does not appear mawkish, creating a self-conscious aspect to the piece that you'll either love or hate. Misery memoir dressed up as masterly metafiction, or narcissistic ramblings of a wannabe reality TV show star? As the TV show says: you decide.

FURTHER READING: *McSweeny's Quarterly* –
Eggers edits this periodic literary journal
SEE ALSO: *A Million Little Pieces* (James Frey);
Generation X (Douglas Coupland)

★
★
★

Writer: Mark Z. Danielewski
Publisher: Pantheon, 2000

ISBN US: 978-0375703768
ISBN UK: 978-0385603102

15+ HOUSE OF LEAVES

Plot: There are several narratives, or leaves, to this novel, making it hard to reduce to a plot summary. But let's try: firstly we have a manuscript regarding "the Navidson record," a documentary film about a haunted house. Secondly, there are footnotes to this manuscript by a young L.A. tattooist called Johnny Truant. Finally we have footnotes to these footnotes by a collective known as "The Editors."

Review: A 700-page, genre-defying, divisive hunk of a novel that you will either love or hate. Influenced by Nabokov, Escher paintings, and Sam Raimi's movies, Danielewski creates at once a bone-chilling horror tale, a love story, a satire on academia, and a headache for lovers of a linear narrative.

FURTHER READING: *The Whalestoe Letters* – so complex was the House of Leaves that a collection of some of letters within the book was published as a separate edition
SEE ALSO: An honest to goodness stand-alone title which defies comparison

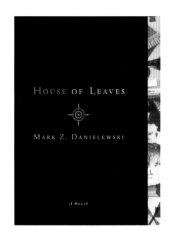

★
★
★

Writer: Dodie Smith
Publisher: Atlantic, Little Brown Books, 1948

ISBN US: 978-0312316167
ISBN UK: 978-0099460879

12+ I CAPTURE THE CASTLE

Plot: The "crumbling ruin" of a Suffolk castle is home to the Mortmain family: our heroine Cassandra, whose story is told through her imaginary journal; her Father, a once published author suffering from writer's block; her elder sister, Rose, a hopeless romantic; and step-mother Topaz, a lover of nature. The crux of the story is Cassandra's lessons in the confusions and disappoint-ments of first love.

Review: What makes this account of an eccentric family's life cult? Certainly it's not stylistically challenging, explicit, or particularly unconventional. There is, however, one central theme that often attracts a cult following: that of the creative writing process. Indeed Cassandra's attempts to "capture" the world around her, for our money, explains both the ongoing popularity and cult status of this book, which is witty and warm in equal measure.

FURTHER READING: *The 101 Dalmatians*
SEE ALSO: *Pride and Prejudice* (Jane Austen); *The Pursuit of Love* (Nancy Mitford)

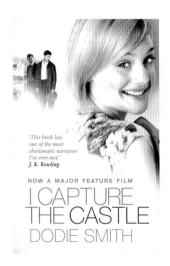

'This book has one of the most charismatic narrators I've ever met.'
J. K. Rowling

NOW A MAJOR FEATURE FILM

I CAPTURE THE CASTLE
DODIE SMITH

★
★
★

Writer: David Foster
Publisher: Fourth Estate, 1999

ISBN US: 978-1841150369
ISBN UK: 978-1841150369

15+

IN THE NEW COUNTRY

Plot: Australia, old and new, clash when a man in a gorilla suit wins the Sydney to Surf race. Detective Harley Christian investigates, while Ad Hock, a local entrepreneur, attempts to organize a school reunion.

Review: David Foster has a strong cult following in his native Australia and has perhaps not received the worldwide recognition he deserves. In her critical study, Susan Leaver points out this might be because he has difficult qualities but these "are, of course, also those that make his books rewarding to read." *In the New Country* Foster uses those qualities to full effect: brilliant satire, literary tricks and experiments, and a unique view of the place of Australia in the modern world. If you like Carl Hiaasen, you'll like David Foster.

FURTHER READING: *The Glade within the Grove; Dog Rock*
SEE ALSO: *Tourist Season* (Carl Hiaasen)

★
★
★
★
★

Writer: Robert Walser
Publisher: Bruno Cassirer, 1909

ISBN US: 978-1852425050
ISBN UK: 978-1852425050

15+

JAKOB VON GUNTEN (INSTITUTE BENJAMENTA)

Plot: More an amalgam of imaginings than a linear narrative, *Institute Benjamenta* is, on the surface at least, Jakob von Gunten's chronicle of his life at a school for servants.

Review: It's all too easy to give up on Walser's picaresque novel: concentration is key to getting anything out of Jakob's perplexing stream of consciousness. Read between his oddball fantasies (of being a Napoleonic soldier, for instance), and the ambiguous daydreams (such as fondling a "wall of worries"), and you will not only find some semblance of a story, but drop your jaw in wonder at Jakob's random soliloquizing ("I'd like to be rich and smash my head in," for instance). Walser spent his last twenty-seven years in a mental asylum; this madcap 1909 creation will not have you wondering why.

FURTHER READING: *The Tanner Family; The Assistant*
SEE ALSO: *The Notebooks of Malte Laurids Brigge* (Rainer Maria Rilke); *The Castle* (Franz Kafka)

★
★
★
★

Writer: Charlotte Brontë
Publisher: Smith, Elder & Co, 1847

ISBN US: 978-0307455192
ISBN UK: 978-0140620115

JANE EYRE

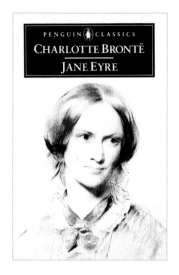

PENGUIN CLASSICS
CHARLOTTE BRONTË
JANE EYRE

Plot: Orphaned into the care of a wealthy aunt, our heroine, Jane Eyre, suffers the cruel regime of Lowood charity school, becomes a governess, and falls in love with a Mr. Edward Rochester; a love that is not without its complications.

Review: *Jane Eyre* is a romance, a rite-of-passage, and a social commentary rolled into one. The writing is excellent, with haunting images of dreams and nightmares, nature and the supernatural, set against the practical Jane, who is presented as a spirited, independent woman navigating the patriarchy of the time. Thus, Charlotte Brontë creates a feminist icon in her heroine, with her rebellious voice and steadfast refusal to conform. For that, reader, we should salute her.

FURTHER READING: *Shirley; Vilette*
SEE ALSO: *Wuthering Heights* **(Emily Brontë);**
Pride and Prejudice **(Jane Austen)** *Agnes Grey* **(Anne Brontë)**

★
★
★
★

Writer: Jorge Luis Borges
Publisher: New Directions Publishing, 1962

ISBN US: 978-0811216999
ISBN UK: 978-0141184845

LABYRINTHS

Synopsis: Short—and very short—fiction, and essays, in the first English-language anthology of Argentine author Jorge Luis Borges' work. Borges' vision is futuristic, mathematical, serpentine: a world where an enormous library of books in every permutation of 410 pages exists, where a man who encounters a stranger discovers the stranger is himself, and where a strange world slowly takes over reality.

Review: Avant-garde, inventive, original, brilliant—just some of the critics' puffery about Borges' work. It's worth pointing out, though, that his arch cleverness won't suit all literary palettes. Still, you've got to admire a writer who—though clearly rampant with ideas—eschews the novel, confining himself to a dazzling range of short prose pieces.

FURTHER READING: *The Book of Imaginary Beings*
SEE ALSO: *Cosmicomics* **(Italo Calvino);** *Collected Stories*
(Gabriel García Márquez); *Life: A User's Manual* **(Georges Perec)**

Jorge Luis Borges **Labyrinths**

★
★
★

Writer: Mario Vargas Llosa
Publisher: Editorial Seix Barral, 1977

ISBN US: 978-0312427245
ISBN UK: 978-0571167777

15+

LA TIA JULIA Y EL ESCRIBIDOR
(AUNT JULIA AND THE SCRIPTWRITER)

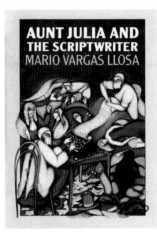

Plot: Set in Lima, Peru, in the 1950s, this comic romp has two narrative threads connected by an aspiring author, Mario. The first narrative sees Mario conducting a passionate affair with his aunt Julia. The second narrative is a series of vignettes about a hugely successful scriptwriter of racy soap operas, Pedro Camacho, whom Mario befriends.

Review: Observing Mario as he learns his craft is a lot of fun, particularly as Mario is the fictionalized version of the young Mario Vargas Llosa. The hodge-podge of stories in the scriptwriter section is even more enjoyable. Oh, and before you ask, she's not a blood aunt, but his "Uncle Lucho's sister-in-law." Doesn't make the family any less hopping mad about their infraction, though.

FURTHER READING: *The Bad Girl; The Feast of the Goat*
SEE ALSO: *What Little Vargas Didn't Say*
(Aunt Julia, aka Julia Urquidi)

★
★
★
★

Writer: Georges Perec
Publisher: Hachette, 1978

ISBN US: 978-0879237516
ISBN UK: 978-0099449256

15+

LA VIE MODE D'EMPLOI
(LIFE: A USER'S MANUAL)

Plot: A fictional Parisian apartment block is split into a grid of rooms, each of which—along with the objects contained therein and its occupants—are examined in minute detail in each of ninety-nine chapters.

Review: If we did not know that Perec belonged to the Oulipo group of writers—whose aim is to put a mathematical kind of structure and form back into fiction—we might call this a rummage sale of a novel, but we know better. The novel, written over the course of nine years, has in fact been planned to within an inch of its life. Inventive, exciting, and with nary a linear plot line in sight, Perec's 1978 Médics Prix-prize winner is an experimental masterwork. As to whether you can use the book as a self-help guide for life: no, course not. If you fancy a nice line in writing experimental fiction, however, it might just become your bible.

FURTHER READING: *A Void*
SEE ALSO: *Exercises in Style* (Raymond Queneau);
If on a Winter's Night, a Traveler (Italo Calvino)

★
★
★
★

Writer: Boris Vian
Publisher: Gallimard, 1947

ISBN US: 978-0966234633
ISBN UK: 978-0966234633

15+

L'ECUME DES JOURS
(FOAM OF THE DAZE)

Plot: *Foam of the Daze* centers around Colin, a man of independent means, who is obsessed with finding love and eventually falls for, and marries, Chloé. When she contracts the delicate condition of "a water-lily on the lung," her cure is Colin's (financial) ruin. Meanwhile, Colin's talking pet mouse offers rays of hope, word-play abounds, and a daydream-like quality wafts over everything like a scent concocted by a particularly crazed scientist.

Review: It's been called science fiction, romance, and a surrealist tour de force. Suffice to say, the plot line above does not do justice to this extraordinary book, which, despite losing in translation some of the signature word play of the original French, is a cult book of major importance.

FURTHER READING: *Blues for a Black Cat and Other Stories*
SEE ALSO: *Zazie in the Metro* (Raymond Queneau)

★
★
★
★

Writer: Alain Fournier
Publisher: Editions Emile-Paul Frères, 1913

ISBN US: 978-0141441894
ISBN UK: 978-0140182828

15+

LE GRAND MEAULNES
(THE WANDERER)

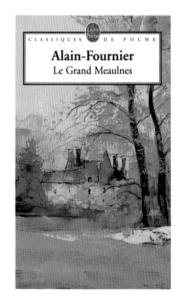

Plot: Hero worship. A mysterious chateau. Love at first sight. A sexual awakening. A masquerade ball. A gypsy in disguise. A betrayal of friendship. A gun shot. These, in part, make up Alain Fournier's story of Augustin Meaulnes and his relentless pursuit of a beautiful young girl, Yvonne de Galais.

Review: Using the first person narration of Meaulnes' school-friend François, Fournier leads us into an almost hypnotic state as we are guided through the hero's adventures with poetic adulation. Add the dreaminess of Meaulnes' first sexual encounters, and his deeply felt pain at the realization that such feelings come at a price, and you have a timeless cult classic of adolescent love.

FURTHER READING: Fournier died before he could build on the success of *Le Grand Meaulnes*
SEE ALSO: *Bonjour Tristesse* (Françoise Sagan);
The Great Gatsby (F. Scott Fitzgerald)

★
★
★
★

Writer: Colette
Publisher: J. Ferenczi, 1932

ISBN US: 978-0940322486
ISBN UK: 978-0140183245

15+

LE PUR ET L'IMPUR
(THE PURE AND THE IMPURE)

Synopsis: An assortment of men and women (named "ghosts" by Colette) talk to the author about their sex lives in this series of dialogs written in the early twentieth century.

Review: Madonna, eat your heart out. Here is a woman who, during her time as a music hall actress, was first to bare her breasts and to simulate sex on the Paris stage. Colette was not afraid to shock, and she also had a fine line in erotic fiction. A survey of sexual desire in *fin-de-siècle* Paris might be the best summary for *Le Pur et L'Impur*, and a well-crafted survey, at that—indeed, Colette herself claimed it as her *chef d'oeuvre*.

FURTHER READING: *The Claudine Quartet; Gigi*
SEE ALSO: *Bonjour Tristesse* (Françoise Sagan);
Delta of Venus (Anaïs Nin)

CULT CLASSICS
Best of the Rest

★
★
★
★
★

Writer: Bret Easton Ellis
Publisher: Penguin, 1985

ISBN US: 978-0679781493
ISBN UK: 978-0330447973

18+

LESS THAN ZERO

Plot: Clay is one of the "in" crowd. When he comes home to L.A. from his New Hampshire college for Christmas vacation he takes up with his old friends: spending their parents' money, bed-hopping, gobbling drugs, and losing themselves in an increasingly warped party scene.

Review: There are echoes of the aristos of De Laclos' *Dangerous Liaisons* here: too much time, and too much wealth, creating an unfulfillment that is relieved only by self-absorption and outrageous sexual shenanigans. Permeating this narcissistic lifestyle are the music and designer clothing brands of the 1980s. The novel holds up a mirror to the pop culture of those times, although the image reflected back is definitely not a flattering one.

FURTHER READING: *The Rules of Attraction;*
Glamorama; American Psycho
SEE ALSO: *The Story of My Life* (Jay McInerney)

★
★ **Writer:** Fay Weldon
★ **Publisher:** Hodder and Stoughton, 1983

ISBN US: 978-0345323750
ISBN UK: 978-0340589359

15+

THE LIFE AND LOVES OF A SHE-DEVIL

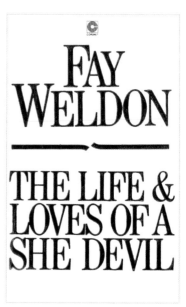

Plot: Seized by a diabolic fury when she discovers her husband is having an affair with a gorgeous romantic novelist, the plain Ruth Pratchett exacts a series of destructive acts of revenge.

Review: Love, hate, envy, and revenge form a violent quadrangle of emotion at the heart of Weldon's 1983 smash hit. Ardently feminist at the time of writing, now less so, Weldon recently said of the 1980s, "Women were so much in the habit of being good it would do nobody any harm if they learned to be a little bad." That feminism now flounders in the doldrums should not detract from this enjoyable tragicomic novel's universal appeal. A must read for scorned lovers.

FURTHER READING: *The Fat Woman's Joke*; *Wicked Women*
SEE ALSO: *The Robber Bride* (Margaret Atwood); *The First Wives' Club* (Olivia Goldsmith)

★
★
★

Writer: Simone de Beauvoir
Publisher: Gallimard, 1943

ISBN US: 978-0393318845
ISBN UK: 978-0007204649

15+

L'INVITEE (SHE CAME TO STAY)

Plot: A fictional account of a turbulent time in the legendary open relationship between de Beauvoir and Jean-Paul Sartre. A couple of naïve young intellectuals, Pierre and Françoise, consumed with love for one another, nevertheless allow a beautiful young woman, Xaviere, into their lives.

Review: Three's a crowd. No book relays the impossibility of the love triangle better than this, de Beauvoir's stunning debut. But let's not reduce her novel to themes of romance and sexuality. Ranked side-by-side with Sartre, de Beauvoir was a high priestess of existentialism, and this book is a key text in that movement, examining as it does our power of choice in life—of which Françoise's, incidentally, is at once shocking and painful by the novel's end.

FURTHER READING: *The Mandarins*;
The Second Sex (the classic feminist text)
SEE ALSO: *Nausea* (Jean-Paul Sartre)

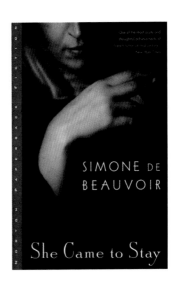

★
★
★
★

Writer: Kazuo Koike and Goseki Kojima
Publisher: Dark Horse, 2000

ISBN US: 978-1569715024
ISBN UK: 978-1569715024

15+

LONE WOLF AND CUB VOLUME 1
THE ASSASSIN'S ROAD

Plot: In which we are introduced to Ogami Itto, a disgraced ronin, who, with his baby son Daigoro, wanders Japan during its mid-Edo period. With his samurai sword at his side, and carrying the banner "son for hire, sword for hire," Ogami is primed for many violent confrontations as he takes on the role of hired assassin.

Review: Split into nine short stories, this is the first in a series of twenty-eight graphic novels about Ogami and his son. The ronin's skills as a prodigious swordsman are matched by Goseki Kojima's fearless black, white, and gray visuals and the fast-paced writing of Kazuo Koike, which together create a thrilling epic of swordplay and adventure. For the softer of heart, the father/son dynamic lends an emotional edge.

FURTHER READING: Volumes 2–28
SEE ALSO: *Ronin* (Frank Miller)

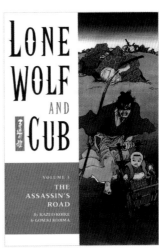

★
★
★
★

Writer: Alice Sebold
Publisher: Little Brown, 2002

ISBN US: 978-0316044936
ISBN UK: 978-0330485388

15+ # THE LOVELY BONES

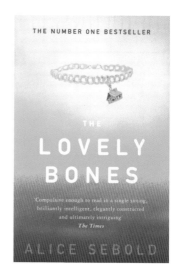

THE NUMBER ONE BESTSELLER

Plot: Raped, stabbed, and dismembered, fourteen-year-old Susie Salmon watches over her family and friends from heaven and relates how they come to terms with her brutal death. At first reluctant to believe she is dead, they eventually concede when part of her body is found. Over the years, they slowly move on with their lives, falling in and out of love, having families. Susie herself is also able to move on.

Review: The novel draws on Sebold's own horrific experience as a rape victim who discovered that her attacker's previous victim had been killed and dismembered. What could have been a mawkish, pity-filled novel is actually surprisingly warm and moving as we learn more about the characters through the eyes of Susie.

FURTHER READING: *Lucky; The Almost Moon*
SEE ALSO: *The Virgin Suicides* (Jeffrey Eugenides);
A Certain Age or Pure (Rebbecca Ray)

THE

**LOVELY
BONES**

Compulsive enough to read in a single sitting,
brilliantly intelligent, elegantly constructed
and ultimately intriguing'
The Times

ALICE SEBOLD

★
★
★

Writer: John Fowles
Publisher: Jonathan Cape, 1966;
revised edition 1977

ISBN US: 978-0440351627
ISBN UK: 978-0099743910

15+ # THE MAGUS

JOHN
FOWLES

Plot: The sober 1950s: an Englishman fearing commitment spurns his girl-friend for a new life teaching in a private school on a Greek island. Here he becomes entangled in the trickeries of a wealthy landowner on a remote corner of the island. What are the reasons behind the psychological games played by Maurice Conchis on the young Nicholas Urfe? And where does the line between the real world and mysticism lie?

Review: If you like a slight book with an obvious meaning, you'd best avoid this whopper of a novel (700-plus pages), with its cascade of literary, philosophical, and psychological pretensions. Sex, death, and violence add spice, but the ending will bamboozle even the most erudite of readers. A good summer beach read—you'll certainly need to put in the hours to fully appreciate it.

FURTHER READING: *The French Lieutenant's Woman; The Collector*
SEE ALSO: *The Alchemist* (Paulo Coelho); *Midnight's Children*
(Salman Rushdie)

THE MAGUS
'AN ASTONISHING ACHIEVEMENT' ANTHONY BURGESS

★
★
★
★
★

Writer: Arthur Golden
Publisher: Knopf, 1997

ISBN US: 978-1400096893
ISBN UK: 978-0099498186

18+

MEMOIRS OF A GEISHA

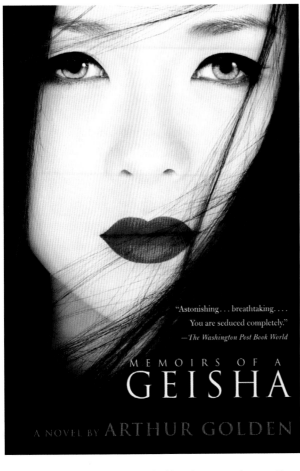

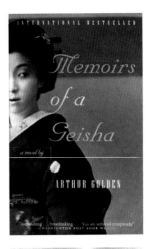

Plot: *Memoirs of a Geisha* chronicles the life and times of Chiyo Sakamoto, from her dark days of poverty in a fishing village via her instruction in the arts of the Geisha, through to adulthood where she becomes Sayuri, Japan's most celebrated Geisha.

Review: The build up to—and tragedy of—World War II lends drama to what is essentially a love story. Told in flashbacks to a fictional translator, Sayuri recounts her life and loves with intrigue and romance, and she is certainly a convincing character. The exotic silks of the geisha attire, the soft blossoms of the Japanese landscape, and the erotic maneuverings of the geisha as they carry out their work make this a sensual, if not seductive, experience.

FURTHER READING: So far Golden hasn't rushed out a sequel to the phenomenally successful *Geisha*
SEE ALSO: *Geisha of Gion: The Memoir of Mineko Iwasaki* (The Geisha interviewed by Golden for research with her own version of her life story)

★
★
★
★
★

Writer: Nicholson Baker
Publisher: Weidenfeld and Nicholson, 1988

ISBN US: 978-0679725763
ISBN UK: 978-0140140026

15+

THE MEZZANINE

Plot: An office worker, Howie, travels up an escalator during his lunch hour.

Review: Nicholson Baker's first novel could be described as a mini-master-piece. Come again? Yes, you might wonder how a story about one man's lunch hour deserves this lofty label, but the masterly nature of this short novella does not lie in its plot. Rather, it is the quality marginalia and trivia of Howie's mind that absorb us: in a series of lengthy footnotes we are treated to his obsessions and innermost thoughts on the efficacy of drinking straws, the inventor of the wing-flap spout on milk cartons, as well as musings on shoelaces and staplers among other inanimate objects. Grand, sweeping epic this is not. Quite the contrary, in fact . . . and so much the better for it.

FURTHER READING: *Vox; The Fermata; A Box of Matches*
SEE ALSO: *A La Récherche du Temps Perdu* (Marcel Proust);
La Nausée (Jean Paul Sartre)

★
★
★
★

Writer: Jeffrey Eugenides
Publisher: Farrar, Strauss, Giroux, 2002

ISBN US: 978-0312427733
ISBN UK: 978-0747561620

15+

MIDDLESEX

Plot: From its now-famous opening lines onward, *Middlesex* grips the reader with a fascinating story of how and why Calliope Stephanides, born with a rare genetic condition, is "born twice": first as Calliope, a girl, and later as Cal, a teenage boy—a story that takes in eighty years of Stephanides' family history.

Review: What's fascinating here is that the book, while ostensibly about Cal, is really, as Eugenides has said, the history of a gene, from 1922 (when Cal's grandparents create it) through his parents' lives, until it finally makes its way into the narrator's body, creating a hermaphrodite. It's an imaginative and extensively researched latter-day Greek epic, which won Eugendies the Pulitzer Prize for fiction in 2003.

FURTHER READING: *The Virgin Suicides*
SEE ALSO: *Myra Breckinridge* (Gore Vidal);
The Wasp Factory (Iain Banks)

★
★
★

Writer: Jean Genet
Publisher: Marc Barbezat, 1946

ISBN US: 978-0802130884
ISBN UK: 978-0140033045

15+

THE MIRACLE OF THE ROSE

Plot: A foundling, taken in by a poor provincial family, becomes a brilliant scholar, later a petty criminal, and finally ends up one of France's literary glitterati. This is not the plot to *The Miracle of the Rose* but rather a snapshot of the life of Jean Genet, one of France's most singular writers. The book itself is an autobiographical account of his time spent at Mettray, a reform school for boys, with additional episodic passages about his time at Fontrevault prison.

Review: Explicitly homosexual, *The Miracle of the Rose* deals with Genet's erotic desires for the rough boys who were his fellow detainees at Mettray, as well as a fantasy element about a murderer Harcamone, idolized by the prisoners at Fontrevault. That Jean-Paul Sartre wrote a huge book about Genet is testament to his talent and enduring appeal.

MIRACLE
OF THE ROSE
BY JEAN GENET

FURTHER READING: *Our Lady of the Flowers*
SEE ALSO: *My Season in Hell* (Arthur Rimbaud)

★
★
★
★

Writer: Martin Amis
Publisher: Jonathan Cape, 1984

ISBN US: 978-0140088915
ISBN UK: 978-0099461883

15+

MONEY A SUICIDE NOTE

Plot: *Money* charts the decline of John Self, an ad-man—drunk, porn-addicted, and habitually masturbating—who is lured to America, where he suffers a series of setbacks while trying to make the movie of his life.

Review: Although his characters are always immaculately named, (Spunk Davis, Lorne Guyland, and Fielding Goodney feature here), Amis is often accused of not drawing them in depth. Not so here, however, where the main protagonist is really not the narrator but money itself, and its pervasive hold over eighties Britain and the States—a situation brilliantly depicted by Amis. Add a complex plot and moments of wild satire, and we have a post-modern masterpiece, whose first person narration is perfectly suited to the egocentricity of its time.

Savage, audacious and
demonically funny –
a story of urban
excess

MARTIN AMIS

FURTHER READING: *The Rachel Papers; London Fields; Dead Babies*
SEE ALSO: *Before She Met Me* (Julian Barnes); *My Idea of Fun*
(Will Self)

★
★
★

Writer: Edward Abbey
Publisher: Lipincott, 1975

ISBN US: 978-0061129766
ISBN UK: 978-0141187624

18+ # THE MONKEY WRENCH GANG

Plot: "The dust clouds darken the desert blue, pale sand and red dust drift across the asphalt trails and tumbleweeds fill the arroyos." These are the colors and textures of the American wilderness that permeate Abbey's 1975 cult hit. The story concerns a hodgepodge of eco-warriors, the gang of the title, on a mission to rescue the wilderness from Big Government and Big Business, which threaten this ancient landscape with industrial development.

Review: Abbey's novel was the hippest of all books to be seen hanging out your back pocket in 1970s America. Which is not to say that his "ecologically sound protest book" suffers from a twenty-first-century analysis. On the contrary: It is a book that pulsates with comic energy, as well as a stringent environmental message to preserve the American wilderness—a message that is anything but dated.

FURTHER READING: *Desert Solitaire*
SEE ALSO: *Trout Fishing in America*
(Richard Brautigan); *Walden* (Henry David Thoreau)

Writer: Richard Russo
Publisher: Knopf, 1986

ISBN US: 978-0375412868
ISBN UK: 978-0394744094

★
★
★

078
500

15+

MOHAWK

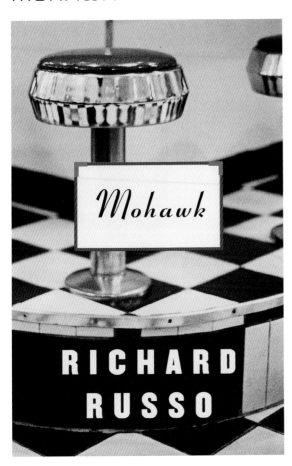

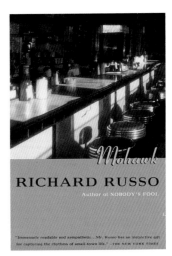

Plot: Mohawk, New York, is a town going nowhere fast, and its residents are on a similarly accelerated journey to the metaphorical back of beyond. Prime example: Dallas Younger. He lives in Mohawk with his wife Anne and their son Randall, who, though bright, won't do his homework; dumbasses are where it's at in Mohawk, it seems.

Review: We're presented with a man and town here whose glory days have passed him/them by. In fact, thinking of the song of that riff by Bruce Springsteen, it's what the man himself might have written if he'd given up music for novels,

and had gotten, like Russo, a Ph.D. Clever and compassionate, this is a heartfelt, but not slushy, look at America in flux.

FURTHER READING: *Empire Falls*;
The Risk Pool; *Nobody's Straight*
SEE ALSO: *Housekeeping* (Marilynne Robinson)

★
★
★
★

Writer: Gore Vidal
Publisher: Little, Brown, & Co, 1968

ISBN US: 978-0141180281
ISBN UK: 978-0349103655

18+

MYRA BRECKINRIDGE

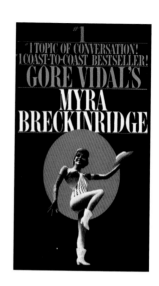

Plot: Sexually timid, un-emancipated, female: Myra Breckinridge, the lead player in Vidal's 1968 satirical triumph, is none of those things. After a sex change operation in Copenhagen, Myron Breckinridge comes to Hollywood as Myra and gets a teaching job at her Uncle Buck Loner's academy for wannabe movie stars. (Think *Fame*—but with pot, orgies, and anal rape.)

Review: Vidal is the foremost cultural satirist in contemporary America, and his chosen targets here are the patriarchy, traditional gender roles, and the tyranny of conventional sexual identity. Contemporary critics seemed particularly keen to use the word "vulgar" to describe the book. We've moved on since then, of course, although Vidal's vision of "Woman Triumphant" retains its power to inspire—be you man, woman, or transsexual.

FURTHER READING: *Live from Golgotha; Myron*
SEE ALSO: *Middlesex* (Jeffrey Eugenides)

★
★
★

Writer: Desmond Morris
Publisher: Jonathan Cape, 1967

ISBN US: 978-0385334303
ISBN UK: 978-0099482017

12+

THE NAKED APE

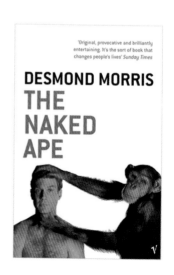

'Original, provocative and brilliantly entertaining. It's the sort of book that changes people's lives' *Sunday Times*

DESMOND MORRIS

THE NAKED APE

Synopsis: Drawing on his experience as a zoologist, Desmond Morris examines the "animal qualities" of human beings and how these affect our behavior in key areas such as sex, parenting, violence, and eating. *The Naked Ape* was the first mainstream book to undertake such a study of humans as an animal species.

Review: Banned in some countries, burned by the church in others—just two of the strong reactions to the publication of Morris' anthropological tour de force in 1967. Even if the contemporary reader might be readier to accept our part in primate evolution, *The Naked Ape* remains essential reading, being packed with golden nuggets of controversy and fascinating tidbits on what makes us unique in the animal kingdom.

FURTHER READING: *The Human Zoo*
SEE ALSO: *The Selfish Gene* (Richard Dawkins);
The Origin of Species (Charles Darwin)

★
★
★
★
★

15+

Writer: Haruki Murakami
Publisher: Shinchosa, 1994

ISBN US: 978-0679775430
ISBN UK: 978-0099448792

NEJIMAKI-DORI KURONIKURU
(THE WIND-UP BIRD CHRONICLE)

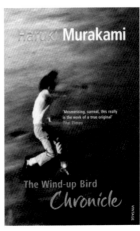

Plot: Life is not going well for Toru Okada. He has lost his job, he is on the receiving end of a series of disturbing dirty phone calls, and his cat goes missing. Then, there is the small matter that his wife does not return home from work. In Okada's quest to find both cat and wife, a parade of bizarre encounters and happenings explode the hitherto quiet conventionality of his suburban existence.

Review: Embedded in the mystery element of Murakami's masterwork is a political leitmotif, associated with massacres committed by Japanese soldiers in China in World War II. Essentially though, this is a compelling story that leaves the reader in a miasma of discombobulated surrealism. Not recommended for those lacking in imagination.

FURTHER READING: *Norwegian Wood; A Wild Sheep Chase*
SEE ALSO: *The New York Trilogy* (Paul Auster)

★
★
★
★

15+

Writer: Paul Auster
Publisher: Faber and Faber, 1987

ISBN US: 978-0140131550
ISBN UK: 978-0571152230

THE NEW YORK TRILOGY

Synopsis: Three stories with a maverick take on the detective genre make up this trilogy: *City of Glass* tells of Quinn, who becomes embroiled in a dysfunctional family's affairs after a wrong number; in *Ghosts* a voyeuristic drama is played by characters named after colors; and lastly, we have a missing person's case in *The Locked Room*.

Review: Name games, identity issues, coincidence—all writer's tricks exploited in this trio of tales, which have been described as "post-modern thrillers." Not giving much by way of explanation, the spooky vagueness of Auster's writing leaves us feeling exposed and unsettled—a feeling exaggerated by the spare quality of the language. More "post-modern" than "thriller" though, really.

FURTHER READING: *Mr. Vertigo; Moon Palace; Timbuctu*
SEE ALSO: *White Noise* (Don DeLillo); *The Crying of Lot 49* (Thomas Pynchon)

★
★
★
★

Writer: Angela Carter
Publisher: Chatto and Windus, 1984

ISBN US: 978-0140077032
ISBN UK: 978-0099388616

15+ # NIGHTS AT THE CIRCUS

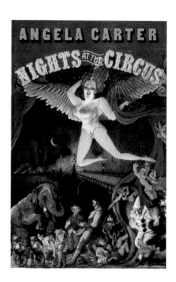

Plot: Part swan, part woman, Sophie Fevvers, "the most famous aerialiste of her day," a member of Colonel Kearney's circus, inspires the slogan, "Is she fact or fiction?" Jack Walser, an American journalist, is keen to find out, and so he joins the circus on a tour through London, St. Petersburg, and Siberia to investigate.

Review: This is a magical, burlesque, rip-roaring adventure from start to finish, with episodes of wild eccentricity thrown in for good measure. At its center is the independent, hugely exuberant Fevvers, who concocts a carnival of language and strangenesses. Yes, the language at times can be overwhelmingly ornate, but Angela Carter doesn't care: "I write overblown, purple, self-indulgent prose—so fucking what?" Quite!

FURTHER READING: *The Bloody Chamber; Wise Children*
SEE ALSO: *The Leto Bundle* (Marina Warner); *Travels with a Circus* (Katie Hickman)

★
★
★

Writer: David Peace
Publisher: Serpent's Tail, 1999

ISBN US: 978-0307455086
ISBN UK: 978-1846687051

18+ # NINETEEN SEVENTY-FOUR

Plot: The first book in Peace's "Red Riding Quartet" sets an ugly tone. It's 1974 in Yorkshire, England, and Ed Dunford, crime correspondent for the *Evening Post*, must deal with police corruption and pedophiles during his investigations into the story of the brutal murder of a ten-year-old girl.

Review: If there was a literary equivalent of a swear box, Peace would be a few dollars short: the profanity count is high. Sensitive folk might also be repelled by the blood and gore approach to crime writing. It's not that you need a strong stomach, or that the brutality is gratuitous, necessarily. It's just that other writers achieve the same gutsy effect without the visceral hyperbole. Spare and staccato prose make up for this overly graphic detail, though.

FURTHER READING: *1977; 1980; 1983; The Damned United*
SEE ALSO: *Wire in the Blood* (Val McDermid); *The Black Dhalia* (James Ellroy)

★
★
★

Writer: Paulo Coelho
Publisher: Editora Rocco, 1988

ISBN US: 978-0061122415
ISBN UK: 978-0722532935

12+

O ALQUIMISTA

(THE ALCHEMIST: A FABLE ABOUT FOLLOWING YOUR DREAM)

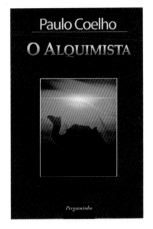

Plot: Santiago, an Andalusian shepherd boy, leaves Spain and after a spot of globetrotting meets the Alchemist who guides him towards fulfillment of his own "Personal Legend."

Review: It's not many books that can claim to have changed the lives of millions. Who'd have thought that Coelho's 1988 novel, written in two weeks by an ex-convict and ditched by its first publisher for poor sales, would go on to do just that? Coelho (a man who believes in angels, no less) may

not suit all tastes—particularly the unspiritual—but it'd be a hard-hearted person who would scoff at the message at its center: don't give up on your childhood dreams, for they may well be realized.

FURTHER READING: *The Devil and Miss Prym; Veronika Decides to Die*
SEE ALSO: *Jonathan Livingston Seagull* (Richard Bach); *The Road Less Travelled* (Scott Peck)

★
★
★
★
★

Writer: John Steinbeck
Publisher: Covici Frede, 1937

ISBN US: 978-0142000670
ISBN UK: 978-0141023571

12+

OF MICE AND MEN

Plot: George and his simple-minded friend Lennie Small, drifters on a miserable quest for ranch work during the Great Depression, dream of some day owning land of their own. Small is in fact a giant of a man, possessing a strength that ultimately sees the two friends' dreams cede to a tragic and bloody nightmare.

Review: Although the book is firmly grounded in the harsh realities of its epoch, there are universal themes to consider here: friendship, the dangers of mob mentality, and the destructive nature of man's condition. The title, borrowed from Robert Burns' philosophical poem "To a Mouse," is a reminder that our best efforts in life may in fact leave us with nothing "but grief and pain for promised joy."

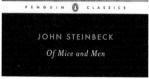

PENGUIN CLASSICS

JOHN STEINBECK
Of Mice and Men

FURTHER READING: *East of Eden; The Grapes of Wrath*
SEE ALSO: *The Heart Is a Lonely Hunter* (Carson McCullers)

★
★

Writer: John L. Parker, Jr.
Publisher: Cedarwinds Publishing, 1978

ISBN US: 978-1416597889
ISBN UK: 978-1416597889

12+

ONCE A RUNNER

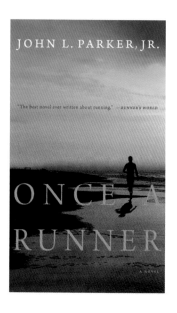

JOHN L. PARKER, JR.

"The best novel ever written about running." —*RUNNER'S WORLD*

ONCE A
RUNNER

A NOVEL

Plot: Quenton Cassidy, a banned college runner, trains under the supervision of Bruce Denton, an Olympic athlete, in order to compete in, and win, a mile race in under four minutes.

Review: *Once a Runner* has been canonized as a cult classic by the running fraternity ever since its first publication in the seventies; *Runner's World* magazine called it "the best novel ever written about running." Non-runners might not be similarly enthused: the shifts in perspective are disorienting, the long build up to the climax an endurance test in itself, and the mentions of Achilles tendons and calluses are rather off-putting. We say this as self-confessed couch-potatoes, incidentally. If you run long-distance, the considered view is you will love this book.

FURTHER READING: *Again to Carthage*
SEE ALSO: *The Loneliness of the Long Distance Runner*
(Alan Sillitoe); *What I Talk About When I Talk About Running*
(Haruki Murakami)

★★★★

Writer: Jeanette Winterson
Publisher: Pandora Press, 1985

ISBN US: 978-0802135162
ISBN UK: 978-0099935704

5+

ORANGES ARE NOT THE ONLY FRUIT

Plot: Here is Jeanette, the adopted daughter of a Bible-bashing Pentecostalist. For fear she will mix with "the Heathens," Jeanette is kept away from school (the "Breeding Ground") and subjected to innumerable quizzes on the Bible. After Jeanette confesses her "unnatural passions" for another girl, her mother undertakes a one-woman mission to save her soul.

Review: Fairy tales and dreams are interspersed with straightforward prose taking us to an allegorical level which is discordant with the otherwise well-crafted storytelling. Nonetheless, a very funny and touching story about a young girl discovering her sexual preference—all the more moving as it is partly based on Winterson's own experience.

FURTHER READING: *Sexing the Cherry; The World and Other Places*
SEE ALSO: *Ruby Fruit Jungle* (Rita Mae Brown);
The Well of Loneliness (Radclyffe Hall)

★★★

Writer: Jaroslav Hasek
Publisher: A Synek Publishers, 1923

ISBN US: 978-0140449914
ISBN UK: 978-0140449914

12+

OSUDY DOBRÉHO VOJÁKA ŠVEJKA ZA SVĚTOVÉ VÁLKY
(GOOD SOLDIER ŠVEJK)

Plot: The genial Svejk, a Czech, is conscripted into the army of the Austro-Hungarian Empire as it fights in World War I. Despite his ostensible willingness to serve—and his obedience to the orders of ludicrous officers, priests, and NCOs—he somehow never quite makes it to the front, instead finding himself spreading (unwitting) havoc and frustration behind the lines.

Review: Don't be put off by the weight of this tome—it's light, likeable stuff and has had a huge influence on Czech literature. Hasek himself was a drifter who lived a life of adventure, and his stories are episodic and full of irony, wit, and broad humor. Underneath, though, lies a sad anger that so many lives be wasted in the futile wars of empire.

FURTHER READING: *The Good Soldier Svejk* was Hasek's
only notable achievement
SEE ALSO: *Closely Observed Trains* (Bohumil Hrabal)

★
★
★

Writer: Patrick Süskind
Publisher: Diogenes Verlag, 1985

ISBN US: 978-0307277763
ISBN UK: 978-0140120837

15+ # PERFUME

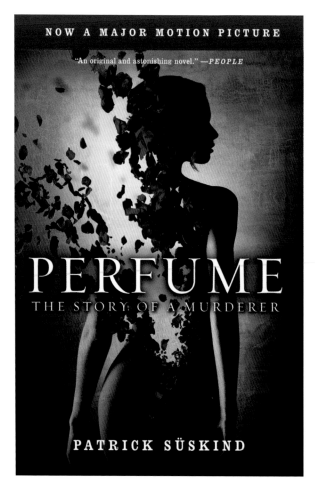

Plot: In the rank-smelling slums of eighteenth-century France, an infant, Jean-Baptiste Grenouille, is born at a fish stall. Although he has no personal body odor, Grenouille soon develops a kind of olfactory super-sense, which sees him turning from perfumer's assistant to serial killer.

Review: In the 1980s you would have been nothing short of painfully unfashionable if you had not read Patrick Süskind's *Perfume*; novels do not come much more cult than this. Nor much stranger. Even if the dramatic arc is fairly conventional—leading to a pungent and grisly denouement—the unique premise and vivid writing combine to form an assault on the senses unlike any other in twentieth-century literature. A must-read . . . and don't hold your noses.

FURTHER READING: *The Pigeon; On Love and Death*
SEE ALSO: *The Odor* (George Herbert); *Flush* (Virginia Woolf)

★
★
★
★

Writer: Oscar Wilde
Publisher: Ward, Lock and Co, 1891
ISBN US: 978-1580493932
ISBN UK: 978-0099511144

THE PICTURE OF DORIAN GRAY

Plot: Cad about town, renowned beauty, and epitome of youthful self-indulgence, Dorian Gray makes a Faustian pact that his portrait should age instead of his physical being. His wish comes true and the excesses of a hedonistic lifestyle do not weather him; instead, his portrait slowly decays, becoming the outward manifestation of a diabolical new direction.

Review: There is something of the fairy tale here, with its allegories and metaphors, recalling Wilde's own fairy tale collection of 1888. As with all fairy tales, caution is in its heart: Wilde may have been playing out a fantasy of his own contained passions, but at the same time he warns of the dangers of such fantasies. A fairy tale ending it is not.

FURTHER READING: *The Complete Fairy Tales of Oscar Wilde;*
The Importance of Being Earnest
SEE ALSO: *Faust* (Johann Wolfgang von Goethe);
Dr. Faustus (Thomas Mann)

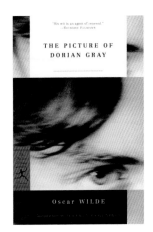

★
★
★
★

Writer: Jane Austen
Publisher: T. Eggerton, 1813
ISBN US: 978-0553213102
ISBN UK: 978-0141439518

PRIDE AND PREJUDICE

Plot: Mrs. Bennet wants to marry off her five daughters. Elizabeth, the most level-headed of the offspring, is courted by the enigmatic Mr. Darcy, whom she snubs until a series of misunderstandings are worked out.

Review: If you wonder how a nineteenth-century book, which is neither explicit, exotic, nor experimental in form, can be considered "cult," you need only consider the rapturous following Austen enjoys to this day: devoted fans make pilgrimages to the Jane Austen center in Bath and can even subscribe to *Jane Austen's Regency World* magazine. Some of them also write sequels to her books. Not bad for someone whose (latterly) most popular book divided the critics on its publication. If you have not read one of the best loved books in the English language, you are in for a treat.

FURTHER READING: *Sense and Sensibility; Emma*
SEE ALSO: *Pride and Prejudice and Zombies*
(Jane Austen and Seth Grahame-Smith), an ultra modern
retelling of Austen's classic, now a cult hit in its own right

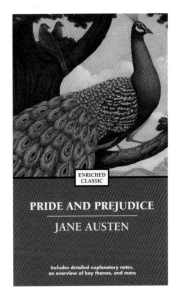

★
★
★
★
★

Writer: Muriel Spark
Publisher: Macmillan, 1961

ISBN US: 978-0060931735
ISBN UK: 978-0140278712

12+

THE PRIME OF MISS JEAN BRODIE

Plot: Six young girls in the junior form of the Marcia Blaine school, Edinburgh, are taught the ways of the world, but not in the ways of the curriculum, by their eccentric tutor Miss Jean Brodie.

Review: Miss Jean Brodie is an unforgettable example of a character that transcends the story for which it was created. She strikes a chord with her maverick teaching style (for instance showing her students slides of Italian fascist conventions). Not that this isn't also a novel of ideas, a central one being, as our eponymous heroine points out, "It is important to recognize the years of one's prime." Oh, and might we add that this is a very funny novel to boot.

FURTHER READING: *The Ballad of Peckham Rye; The Driver's Seat*
SEE ALSO: *Poor Things* (Alasdair Gray)

★
★
★

Writer: Graham Greene
Publisher: William Heinemann, 1955

ISBN US: 978-0143039020
ISBN UK: 978-0099478393

THE QUIET AMERICAN

Plot: As the French Army grapple with the Viet Minh in Indochina in the 1950s, two men in Saigon are involved in a romantic and political struggle. Pyle, a naïve young CIA agent, is the "quiet American" of the title. The second is a British foreign correspondent, Fowler, who brings Pyle down—for which his motives are dubious.

Review: If ever one novel was said to be its author's defining work, *The Quiet American* is Greene's. The messy romantic dalliances, American intervention in world affairs, and religion that feature are favored themes of the author. One criticism is that Phoung, the beautiful local woman at the center of the love triangle, does not get much of a say. Her mute status does, however, highlight the flaws of the two male principals.

FURTHER READING: *A Burnt Out Case;*
The Power and the Glory; Our Man in Havana
SEE ALSO: *A Woman of Bangkok* (Jack Reynolds);
Under the Volcano (Malcolm Lowry)

Writer: John Updike
Publisher: Knopf, 1960

ISBN US: 978-0449911655
ISBN UK: 978-0141187839

★
★
★
★

15+

RABBIT, RUN

PULITZER PRIZE-WINNING AUTHOR

JOHN **VOLUME ONE**
UP**THE**DIKE
RABBIT
NOVELS
RABBIT, RUN
RABBIT REDUX

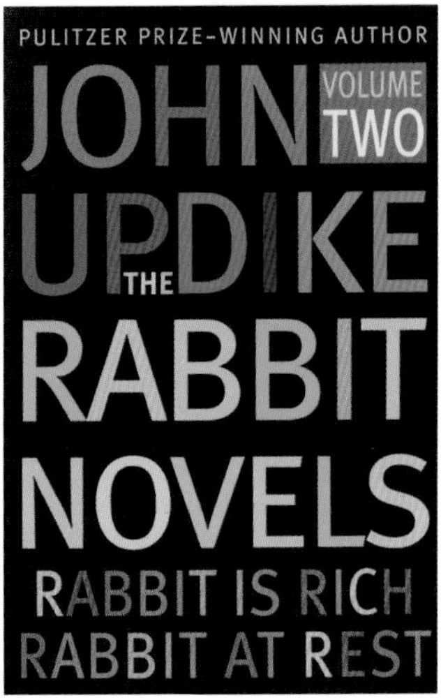

PULITZER PRIZE-WINNING AUTHOR

JOHN **VOLUME TWO**
UP**THE**DIKE
RABBIT
NOVELS
RABBIT IS RICH
RABBIT AT REST

Plot: Dissatisfaction is at the centre of *Rabbit, Run*, which tells of the early years of adulthood of ex-high-school basketball star Harry "Rabbit" Angstrom. It is Harry's dissatisfaction with his town, his job, his wife, and his child—in short, his life—which sees him carrying out a series of self-centered and ultimately self-destructive actions, including adultery and sexual coercion.

the stifling morality of the 1950s. He might not be likeable, but his everyman qualities make Rabbit an enduringly successful cult character.

Review: The personal and financial struggles of Updike's middle class salesman, "Rabbit," resonated with millions of Americans, as did Rabbit's travails in three sequels. In each book Updike perfectly evokes the mood of its epoch—here

FURTHER READING: The rest of the *Rabbit books*; *The Witches of Eastwick*
SEE ALSO: *Revolutionary Road* (Richard Yates); *The Sportswriter* (Richard Ford)

★
★
★

Writer: Julio Cortazar
Publisher: Sudamericana Sociedad Anónima, 1963

ISBN US: 978-0394752846
ISBN UK: 978-0394752846

12+ RAYUELA (HOPSCOTCH)

Plot: *Hopscotch* is the story of Horacio Oliveira, an Argentinean writer living in Paris, who later returns to Buenos Aires. What makes it a stand-out cult title is its non-linear structure, which means the novel can be read in any order—indeed, in a "table of instructions" Cortazar urges his readers to do so.

Review: Conventionality is torn asunder in Cortazar's fragmented "anti-novel." Not only is the format unusual, but his characters scoff at the norm. As one says, "People who make dates are the same kind who need lines on their writing paper, or who always squeeze up from the bottom on a tube of toothpaste."

In summary, *Hopscotch* will probably only appeal if your tastes—literary and otherwise—are unconventional.

FURTHER READING: *Bestiary*
SEE ALSO: *The Savage Detectives* (Robert Bolano)

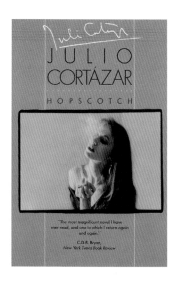

★
★
★

Writer: Donna Tartt
Publisher: Knopf, 1992

ISBN US: 978-0449911518
ISBN UK: 978-0140167771

15+ THE SECRET HISTORY

Plot: In a prologue to the main narrative we witness the murder of a wealthy college student, Bunny Corcoran. As the story begins in earnest we meet Richard Papen, our narrator, whose induction into a clique of classics students at an elite New England college sees him adopt their upper-class way of life, before becoming party to Corcoran's murder, the second in which his new friends have been involved.

Review: It's a story of guilt based on the *Crime and Punishment* model, though in this instance the parties involved are as randy as they are remorseful. On the downside, the references to Ancient Greek (and Latin) literature and philosophy repeat worse than a Gyros from your local kebab shop. Still, its compelling stuff: murder mystery for brainiacs, you might say.

FURTHER READING: *The Little Friend*
SEE ALSO: *The Name of the Rose* (Umberto Eco)

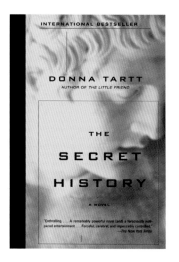

★
★
★
★

Writer: Italo Calvino
Publisher: Giulio Einaudi Editore, 1979
ISBN US: 978-0156439619
ISBN UK: 978-0099430896

12+

SE UNA NOTTE D'INVERNO UN VIAGGIATORE (IF ON A WINTER'S NIGHT A TRAVELER)

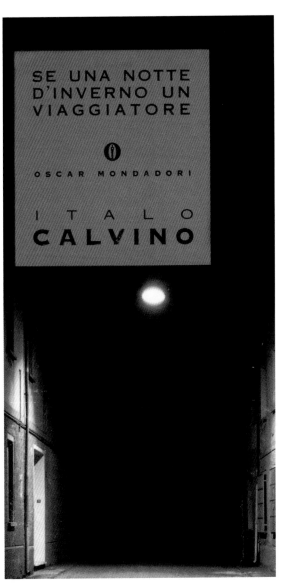

Plot: A reader commences *If on a Winter's Night a Traveler* only to discover the printers have botched the binding: the first section is repeated many times over. When he revisits the bookshop he discovers the book is not by Calvino but a Polish author and meets Ludmilla, who has found her copy to be similarly afflicted.

Review: "You are about to begin reading Italo Calvino's new novel, *If on a Winter's Night a Traveler*. Relax. Let the world around you fade." Such are the famous opening words from Calvino's 1979 novel about books, reading, and writing. Writers will love the literary gamesmanship and delight in images such as the comparison of books left unbought in bookstores to stray dogs in the pound. Readers, meanwhile, should enjoy the ten stories within the narrative, each a parody of a different writing style. If such an experimental and writerly book does not have cult written, and read, all over it, then we don't know what does.

FURTHER READING: *Invisible Cities*
SEE ALSO: *New York Trilogy* (Paul Auster); *Labyrinths* (Jorge Borges)

500 ESSENTIAL CULT BOOKS

71

CULT CLASSICS
Best of the Rest

★
★
Writer: Paul Bowles
Publisher: John Lehmann, 1949

ISBN US: 978-0060834821
ISBN UK: 978-0141023427

15+

THE SHELTERING SKY

Plot: A married couple from New York, Port and Kit Moresby, attempt to put the spark back into their relationship by traveling to the deserts of Africa. Their destination, however, is uncivilized, and the environment vast and cruel: will they, never mind their marriage, survive?

Review: Critics and reviewers have highlighted the state of disaffection which Bowes imbues in his characters, reflecting the general malaise of the postwar period. The problem is that the existential torpor they encounter in the voluminous sandy desert is a bit like the sand you cannot shake from your clothes or body after a day on the beach: it's everywhere—and it's a bit annoying. You can see why the Beats liked Bowles and buddied up with him in Tangiers. But, unlike the Beats, this does not excite, shock, or amaze.

FURTHER READING: *The Spider's House*;
Without Stopping (autobiography)
SEE ALSO: *The Woman in the Dunes* (Kobo Abe) –
another existential novel with an abundance of sand

★
★
★
Writer: Tama Janowitz
Publisher: Crown, 1986

ISBN US: 978-0671745240
ISBN UK: 978-0747574606

15+

SLAVES OF NEW YORK

Plot: A prostitute whose pimp has a double PhD, an artist with delusions of grandeur, and Eleanor, an unsuccessful jewelry designer, come together in a series of interlocking stories about life in the bohemian world of Manhattan around 1985.

Review: So accurately does Janowitz depict those living on the margins of eighties society that *Slaves of New York* has been called dated, or even a period piece. Not fair, say those who enjoy her tales of junkies trying to come off drugs, and, anyway, what's wrong with period accuracy? What's more, Janowitz's vignettes on these disaffected Noo Yorkers are told with satiric brio, and are laugh-out-loud funny from the opening paragraph on. For females, at least . . .

FURTHER READING: *The Male Cross Dresser's Support Group*;
A Cannibal in Manhattan
SEE ALSO: *Bright Lights, Big City* (Jay McInerney); *Story of My Life*
(Bret Easton Ellis); *I Was Gonna Be Like Paris* (Emily Listfield)

★
★
★

Writer: Jodi Picoult
Publisher: Faber & Faber, 1992

ISBN US: 978-0743431019
ISBN UK: 978-0340897300

15+ # SONGS OF THE HUMPBACK WHALE

Plot: Told through the narrations of five protagonists. Jane Jones leaves her emotionally abusive husband, Oliver, taking her daughter Rachel from San Diego to Stow, Massachusetts, where her brother Joley works on a farm owned by Sam, who becomes Jane's lover. Rachel, only fifteen, falls in love with Sam's son, Hadley. Their romance is threatened when Oliver arrives, hoping to take his estranged family home.

Review: Picoult has said that—unlike others who process childhood trauma through writing—her uneventful childhood gave her something to write about: the solid core of family and relationships. Using multiple perspectives offers a multitude of views on the same events and emotional tangles as the various characters test the bonds of love and compassion that exist between them.

FURTHER READING: *Picture Perfect; Nineteen Minutes*
SEE ALSO: *Before I Die* (Jenny Downham);
It's the Little Things (Erica James)

★
★
★
★

Writer: Johann Wolfgang von Goethe
Publisher: Weygandsche Buchhandlung, 1774

ISBN US: 978-0140445039
ISBN UK: 978-0140445039

12+ # THE SORROWS OF YOUNG WERTHER

Plot: When visiting a village, a sensitive young man, Werther, identifies the bucolic beauty of the area with a charming young woman, Lotte. Love soon turns to misery and despair when Werther discovers that Lotte does not reciprocate his feelings, and that she is engaged to Albert, an older man.

Review: *The Sorrows of Young Werther* was a worldwide bestseller before the term was even invented. Success has its problems, though: an avalanche of pirated editions appeared, and the book was condemned for advocating suicide. Nonetheless, this was perhaps the first book to have a true cult following, as swathes of young men identified with the tormented Werther, dressing like him and even allegedly killing themselves. The high-flown "Sturm und Drang" language may deter some, but those who have weathered the storms of unrequited love may "draw consolation" from Werther's sorrows—a hope that Goethe states in his preface.

FURTHER READING: *Prometheus; Goetz von Berlichingen*
SEE ALSO: *The New Sorrows of Young W* (Ulrich Plenzdorf);
Kabale und Liebe (Schiller)

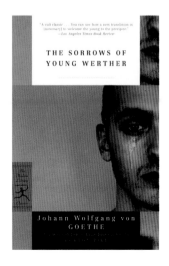

★
★
★
★

Writer: William Faulkner
Publisher: Harrison Smith, 1929

ISBN US: 978-0679732242
ISBN UK: 978-0099475019

15+

THE SOUND AND THE FURY

Plot: *The Sound and the Fury* charts the decline of the Compson family, told via the interior monolog of three brothers, Benjy, Quentin, and Jason. Each section ostensibly relates to one day, but time shifts allow the story to cover thirty years of Compson family history, as well as the South's problems in the post-civil war era.

Review: Sometimes a book's cult status goes hand-in-hand with the fact it's a challenging read for the masses. This is just such a book. Get past the meandering streams of consciousness, staccato narratives, and the sometimes difficult Southern vernacular, and you too can join the ranks of the too-cool-for-school who have ticked this off their cult books check list.

FURTHER READING: *As I Lay Dying*
SEE ALSO: *The Sun Also Rises* (Ernest Hemingway);
Invisible Man (Ralph Ellison)

★
★
★

Writer: Richard Ford
Publisher: Harvill Press, 1986

ISBN US: 978-0679762102
ISBN UK: 978-0747585176

12+

THE SPORTSWRITER

Plot: One Easter week in the life of Frank Bascombe: sports journalist, divorced man, bereaved father. Frank takes us through seven days filled with ordinary places and people: he goes to church, sees a couple of women, speaks to his friends—and comes, quietly, to some tentative conclusions about the meaning of life.

Review: Ford's books are loved by critics on both sides of the Atlantic, and on reading this it's not hard to see why. Not only is the writing precise, light, and open, with memorable dialog and wonderful descriptions of 1980s America, it is not afraid to tackle big questions of life and love. It's not bad on small questions of life, either—in particular about baseball and shopping.

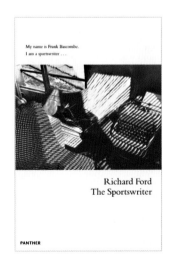

FURTHER READING: *Rock Springs* (short story collection);
Independence Day (sequel to *The Sportswriter*)
SEE ALSO: *Where I'm Calling From* (Raymond Carver);
A Fan's Notes (Frederick Exley)

★
★
★

Writer: Jay McInerney
Publisher: Atlantic Monthly Press, 1988

ISBN US: 978-0679722571
ISBN UK: 978-0747584902

18+

THE STORY OF MY LIFE

Plot: What happens to the girl who has everything? Meltdown, it seems, if we are take Alison Poole's life as a template. The party-girl narrator of McInerney's satire of 1980s high-living, Poole, spends her nights playing Truth or Dare while snorting up mountains of cocaine, and her days taking that much-traveled literary journey on a road to nowhere.

Review: In this, McInerney's third novel, he creates a hollow world where jaded characters are but empty shells of human beings. The success of the book is in the implied bitter consequences of such shallow living, as well as the believable narrative voice of Poole—which is all the more remarkable for having been written by a man.

URTHER READING: *Ransom; Bright Lights, Big City*
SEE ALSO: *Less Than Zero; The Rules of Attraction* (Bret Easton Ellis)

★
★
★

Writer: John Gray
Publisher: Granta Books, 2002

ISBN US: 978-0374270933
ISBN UK: 978-1862075962

15+

STRAW DOGS

Synopsis: *Straw Dogs* is a philosophical work which examines what it is that makes us human. Positing the notion that humans "can be no more masters of their destiny than any other animal," Gray points to an uncertain future for the human race while launching a scathing attack on humanists.

Review: From the pen of British philosopher John Gray, this divisive work had that country's cultural elite at loggerheads. The nihilistic world-view was deplored by some, its critique on the progress (or lack thereof) of humanity lauded by others. If you've a short attention span you might appreciate the bite-size chunks of philosophy, but, bear in mind so pessimistic are these chunks, that you might find them hard to swallow.

FURTHER READING: *False Dawn: The Delusions of Global Capitalism; Black Mass: Apocalyptic Religion and the Death of Utopia*
SEE ALSO: *The Selfish Gene* (Richard Dawkins);
The Naked Ape (Desmond Morris)

ESSENTIAL
CULT BOOKS

500

75

CULT CLASSICS
Best of the Rest

★
★
★
★
★

Writer: Knut Hamsun
Publisher: Philipsen, 1890

ISBN US: 978-0374525286
ISBN UK: 978-1841952062

15+ # SULT (HUNGER)

Plot: Here we have the daily struggles of a writer as he weaves his way, starving and world-weary, through the streets of Christiana (now Oslo) at the turn of the twentieth century, encountering angry landladies, generous newspaper editors, and a mysterious veiled woman along the way.

Review: Paul Auster, and many other writers, have heaped praise on Hamsun, celebrating him as one of the founding fathers of modernist writing. There is much for the lay reader to enjoy also, in this journey inside the mind of a writer going physically and mentally to the dogs. The fact that much is based on Hamsun's own life makes his woes all the more alarming (he begs a butcher for a bone; he pawns his clothes; he eats woodchips). Those with ambitions to write, take heed.

FURTHER READING: *Growth of the Soil*
SEE ALSO: *The Art of Hunger* (Paul Auster);
Notes from the Underground (Fyodor Dostoyevsky)

★
★
★
★

Writer: Kobo Abe
Publisher: First American Edition Knopf, 1964;
first Japanese edition 1962

ISBN US: 978-0679733782
ISBN UK: 978-0141188522

15+ # SUNA NO ONNA (THE WOMAN IN THE DUNES)

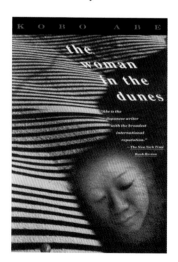

Plot: Niki Jumpei is an amateur entomologist who, while searching for a rare beetle, becomes imprisoned in a sandpit in a peculiar village. Alongside him in the gaping pit is one of the villagers, a young widow. Together they must shovel sand to prevent the approaching dunes from engulfing the entire locale.

Review: An existential novel, and a study in alienation and conformity: as you might expect, this is not an easy read. Feminists might ask why Jumpei treats his fellow victim so cruelly. The narrator's digressions on his frustrated sexuality and the lengthy descriptions of sand might also be an issue for some. Exceptional for those readers, though, who like both the surreal and the unsettling.

FURTHER READING: *The Ruined Map; The Art Sakura*
SEE ALSO: *The Stranger* (Albert Camus); *Nausea* (Jean-Paul Sartre)

Writer: Armistead Maupin
Publisher: Chronicle Publishing Company, 1978

ISBN US: 978-0061358302
ISBN UK: 978-0552998765

TALES OF THE CITY

15+

Plot: The first installment in Maupin's trailblazing *Tales of the City* series. The book centers around the goings-on at 28 Barbary Lane, a boarding house in San Francisco in the 1970s—home to a veritable fruit basket of highly colorful characters.

Review: Okay, so this is not literary fiction, and book snobs may not fall for Maupin's laidback style. But let's not forget that like another social commentator, Dickens, Maupin's work had to meet the needs of newspaper serialization, and it shares something of the former's page-turning pace. More importantly though, like Dickens, Maupin is a social revolutionary, presenting straights and gays coexisting without fanfare or fuss for perhaps the first time in a work of fiction. Add a genuinely surprising ending, and we defy you to resist—guilty pleasure though this may be.

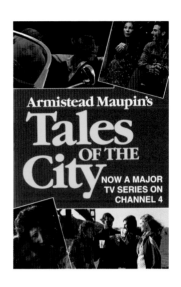

FURTHER READING: *Further Tales of the City;*
More Tales of the City; Babycakes
SEE ALSO: *Martin Chuzzlewit* **(Charles Dickens)**

Writer: Horace McCoy
Publisher: A. Barker, 1935

ISBN US: 978-1852424015
ISBN UK: 978-1852424015

THEY SHOOT HORSES, DON'T THEY?

15+

Plot: Most of the action in this short novel takes place during a "Marathon Dance Craze," inspired by the Depression-era contests in which dance pairs competed to be the last couple standing and win a cash prize. Robert Syverten, we learn as the story opens, is being sentenced for murder in the first degree for killing his dancer partner, Gloria Beatty. As the novel and the dance competition develop, it becomes clear that Gloria—with her pessimistic outlook and suicidal notions—was all too willing a "victim."

Review: Existentialism meets brutal poverty, in this, McCoy's mini-masterpiece—a desperately bleak combination if ever there was one. A slim volume, but one heavy with ideas.

FURTHER READING: *Kiss Tomorrow Goodbye*
SEE ALSO: *The Heart Is a Lonely Hunter* **(Carson McCullers);**
Miss Lonelyhearts **(Nathanael West)**

★
★
★

Writer: Audrey Niffenegger
Publisher: Macadam Cage, 2003

ISBN US: 978-0156029438
ISBN UK: 978-0099464464

15+ THE TIME TRAVELER'S WIFE

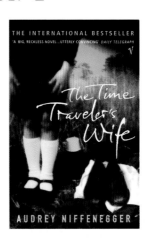

Plot: Henry and Clare DeTamble seem to be your normal, everyday couple, with the usual worries and woes. But there is an additional dimension to their relationship—Henry has been diagnosed with Chrono-Displacement Disorder, which sees him involuntarily displaced into the past or future at the drop of a hat.

Review: Time-travel aside, this is a conventional love story where Henry's "stomach lurches" when he meets Clare for the first time. Thus, irritated critics did not know whether to put the book in the "romance" or "sci-fi" bracket. Who cares? Above all this is a fun story of a loving couple whose predicament should strike a chord or two with those among us who've ever had a long-distance relationship.

FURTHER READING: This was Niffenegger's first novel—
a follow up we await with bated breath
SEE ALSO: *The Adjustment Team* (Philip K. Dick);
Solaris (Stanislaw Lem)

★
★
★
★

Writer: Irvine Welsh
Publisher: Martin, Secker & Warburg, 1993

ISBN US: 978-0393314809
ISBN UK: 978-0749336509

18+ TRAINSPOTTING

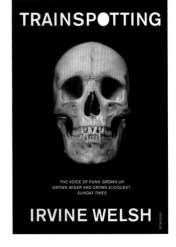

Plot: A series of intense and energetic vignettes tell the story of Mark Renton and his heroin-addicted friends Spud, Sick Boy, and the psychotic Begbie as they raise drug-induced merry hell in Scotland's capital, Edinburgh.

Review: Unflinching account of heroin addiction by an ex-user? Check. Gritty urban realism? Check. Free flowing slang and Scots dialect? Check. It could only be *Trainspotting*: the cult book of the 1990s. The fainthearted may not be able to stomach dead babies, vomit, and needles galore; the lazy may be deterred by the long passages written in the Edinburgh vernacular. Those who persevere are treated to a hilarious—if no-holds barred—account of the results of mass unemployment in the post-Thatcher period in Britain.

FURTHER READING: *The Acid House; Porno; Reheated Cabbage*
SEE ALSO: *Young Adam* (Alexander Trocchi); *How Late It Was, How Late* (James Kelman)

★
★
★
Writer: Iceberg Slim
Publisher: Holloway House Publishing, 1967
ISBN US: 978-0870679339
ISBN UK: 978-0862415945

 # TRICK BABY

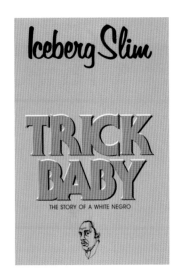

Plot: Trick Baby, aka White Folks, is, as the book's strap-line suggests, "the story of a white negro." He's white and the son of a black mother, so he must, locals assume, have been born as the result of a trick; that is, a white man must have paid his mom for sex. After a horrible sexual assault, she loses the plot, and Trick Baby turns to a life on the con.

Review: There's no denying the authenticity of the material—Slim pimped out his first prostitute at the age of eighteen and pimped his way through life thereafter, until he tried his hand at writing at the age of forty-two. He's a natural, the vibrant slang of his upbringing only adding to the quality of this entertaining tale.

THE STORY OF A WHITE NEGRO

FURTHER READING: *Pimp*
SEE ALSO: *Daddy Cool* (Donald Goines)

★
★
★
Writer: Richard Brautigan
Publisher: Four Seasons Foundation, 1967
ISBN US: 978-0395500767
ISBN UK: 978-0099747710

 # TROUT FISHING IN AMERICA

Synopsis: Richard Brautigan takes us back to basics with forty-seven loosely connected passages ostensibly about finding an unspoiled trout stream for fishing. At the book's heart, though, is a critique of 1960s mainstream society and culture.

Review: Imagine a time when a book of rampant experimentation could be a two million-copy seller. The time was the late 1960s: the post-beat period, the hippie years, a time when Richard Brautigan captured the spirit of a genera-tion. But *Trout Fishing in America* is more than just a hippie tract: there are genuinely funny and surreal moments—an old woman is mistaken for a trout stream, for instance. The book can and should, then, be read quite apart from its status as a counterculture classic. Even though it does assuredly deserve that label.

Richard Brautigan's

Trout Fishing in America,
The Pill versus the Springhill Mine Disaster,
and In Watermelon Sugar

FURTHER READING: *A Confederate General in Big Sur*
SEE ALSO: *Walden* (Henry David Thoreau)

ESSENTIAL CULT BOOKS
500
79
CULT CLASSICS
Best of the Rest

★
★
★
★

Writer: Iris Murdoch
Publisher: Chatto & Windus, 1954

ISBN US: 978-0140014457
ISBN UK: 978-0099429074

12+ UNDER THE NET

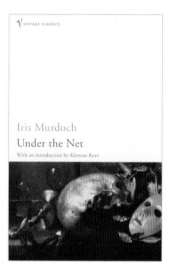

Plot: Returning to London after a stint in Paris, writer and translator Jake Donaghue tries to find someone to sponge off, a place to rest his head, and, last but not least, work. En route he encounters a mixed bunch of acquaintances, from a glamorous film star to a dodgy book maker, and his old pal, the enigmatic philosopher Hugo Belfounder.

Review: Before Murdoch penned this, her debut novel, she wrote the first academic work in English on Jean-Paul Sartre. Indeed, there is a miasma of academia wafting over *Under the Net*, but it's not oppressive: the novel is both engaging and accessible. The gloomy evocation of London in the 1950s, the blossoming artistry of the writer Jake, and his drifting search for personal identity, create the dazzling promise Murdoch would more than live up to in her future twenty-five novels.

FURTHER READING: *The Sea, the Sea; A Severed Head; The Bell*
SEE ALSO: *Nausea* (Jean-Paul Sartre); *The Mandarins* (Simone de Beauvoir)

★
★
★
★

Writer: Malcolm Lowry
Publisher: Jonathan Cape, 1947

ISBN US: 978-0060955229
ISBN UK: 978-0141182254

15+ UNDER THE VOLCANO

Plot: *Under the Volcano* belongs to that unusual category of novels set in just one day—the day in question here being the Mexican Day of the Dead festival in 1938 Quauhnahuac (a fictional Cuernavaca). Against a backdrop of mescal, heat, fascism, a dead dog, a storm, and more mescal, the ex-wife of the British consul, Geoffrey Firmin, attempts a reconciliation. Tragedy, however, ensues.

Review: A tough nut to crack, this. It's one of those books where the words on the page look beautiful, and indeed synchronize together beautifully, but do not immediately compute in the brain. For instance, "Over the town, in the dark tempestuous night, backwards revolved the luminous clock," ends one chapter, ambiguously. Difficult, but poetically pleasing. Enjoyed best at the second, or even third, reading.

FURTHER READING: *Ultramarine; Hear Us O Lord from Heaven*
SEE ALSO: *The Savage Detectives* (Roberto Bolaño);
The Quiet American (Graham Greene)—another ex-pat tale

★
★
★

Writer: Bruce Chatwin
Publisher: Jonathan Cape, 1988

ISBN US: 978-0140115765
ISBN UK: 978-0099770015

15+

UTZ

Plot: Cold War Prague: Kaspar Utz collects Meissen porcelain, a small flourish of individuality in the oppressive Communist state. Even when travel abroad offers him a chance for defection, he returns to his small apartment overlooking the Jewish cemetery and his prized and beloved collection.

Review: The book begins with Kaspar Utz's death, and his funeral—a sorry "valedictory" affair that he himself arranged for twenty people, of which only two show up. The narrator, a young academic interested in Utz, muses on life and death with a sorrowful grace throughout the rest of the novel, although mostly, it has to be said, this is a book about collecting things. Short, but sweet.

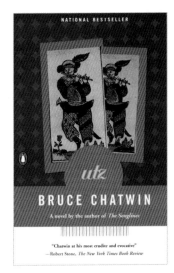

FURTHER READING: *The Songlines; In Patagonia*
SEE ALSO: *The Emigrants* (W. G. Sebald)

★
★
★

Writer: Nicholson Baker
Publisher: Random House, 1992

ISBN US: 978-0679742111
ISBN UK: 978-1862070967

18+

VOX

Plot: Love, or rather lust, on the telephone wire. A man, Jim, and a woman, Abby, separately call an adult party line. They are turned on by one another's voices, and soon begin a one-to-one conversation. *Vox* is the account of their steamy chat.

Review: Hats off to Nicholson Baker, who consistently experiments with form and content when so many contemporary novelists stick to boring old conventionality. Baker's signature method is taking in the minutiae of life, the everyday objects that surround us. Here he looks at the accoutrements of modern sex and in so doing offers us a vision that is no less meaningful than if he had written a stonking 700-page epic. Short, not sweet . . . and gratifyingly uncouth.

FURTHER READING: *Fermata; The Mezzanine; A Box of Matches*
SEE ALSO: *Choke* (Chuck Palahniuk)

ESSENTIAL CULT BOOKS

500

81

CULT CLASSICS
Best of the Rest

★
★
★
★

Writer: Iain Banks
Publisher: Macmillan, 1984

ISBN US: 978-0684853154
ISBN UK: 978-0349101774

15+ THE WASP FACTORY

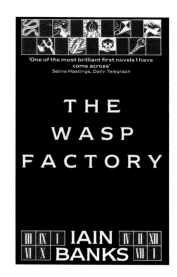

Plot: Here we have sixteen-year-old Frank Cauldhaume, his eccentric father, his lunatic brother, and a factory of wasps that the teenager uses as a crystal ball. With all the ingredients of gothic horror (animal cruelty, child murder, a remote island setting) and a gruesome twist that makes *The Sixth Sense* look like *Scooby-Doo*, this is not one for the squeamish.

'One of the most brilliant first novels I have come across'
Selina Hastings, *Daily Telegraph*

THE WASP FACTORY

Review: Reviewers at the time of publication recoiled at the *Wasp Factory*'s grotesque horrors: "Unparalleled depravity" (*The Irish Times*), "A silly, gloating and sadistic . . . yarn" (*Sunday Express*), "A joke to fool literary London?" (*The Times*). Others marveled at its originality, black humor, and powerful imagination. With hindsight an analysis of this macabre work can be no less bifurcated.

FURTHER READING: *Walking on Glass; The Crow Road*
SEE ALSO: *Morvern Callar* (Alan Warner); *Darkmans* (Nicola Barker); *The Blind Assassin* (Margaret Atwood)

IAIN BANKS

★
★
★
★

Writer: Lionel Shriver
Publisher: Counterpoint, 2003

ISBN US: 978-0061124297
ISBN UK: 978-1852424671

15+ WE NEED TO TALK ABOUT KEVIN

WINNER OF THE ORANGE PRIZE FOR FICTION

Plot: An epistolary novel told in the form of letters from a mother (Eva) to her estranged husband (Franklin) telling their family's story pre- and post a bloody high-school massacre carried out by their son (the eponymous Kevin). Eva examines her own culpability in the matter and asks whether her ambivalent maternal feelings may be to blame.

We Need to Talk About KEVIN.
LIONEL SHRIVER

Review: Critics have questioned how Shriver can write about the unconditional love a mother is supposed to feel when she isn't a mother herself; others claim its depiction of the vulnerability of the new mother will resonate with most women with children. That it so polarized opinion on publication, and that it makes for compelling reading, make it a must-read cult book.

FURTHER READING: *Ordinary Decent Criminals;*
The Post-Birthday World
SEE ALSO: *Vernon God Little* (D. B. C. Pierre);
Stuart: A Life Backwards (Alexander Masters)

'A courageous book which will resonate with everyone who has had a child or thought about having one' *Jenni Murray*

★
★
★
★

Writer: Budd Schulberg
Publisher: Random House, 1941

ISBN US: 978-0679734222
ISBN UK: 978-0679734222

WHAT MAKES SAMMY RUN?

12+

Plot: What was Hollywood like in the 1940s? Did only egocentric, backstabbing scumbags make it to the top? What makes Sammy run? The answers to these questions are all to be found in Schulberg's 1941 story of Sammy Glick, a newspaper copyboy who backstabs his way to becoming a top screenwriter for the movies.

Review: If anyone should know about the black rotten core of the movie industry, it was Schulberg: he had been a screenwriter for four years before he wrote *What Makes Sammy Run?* Later he found huge success in the screenwriting field, a success that is remarkable considering the unflattering picture painted of the studio bosses in this, his first novel. Remarkable, but unsurprisingly so: Schulberg was an awesome talent.

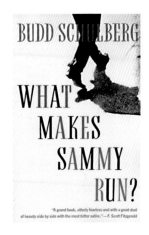

FURTHER READING: *The Disenchanted*
SEE ALSO: *Valley of the Dolls* (Jacqueline Susann)

★
★
★
★

Writer: Raymond Briggs
Publisher: Hamish Hamilton, 1982

ISBN US: 978-0140094190
ISBN UK: 978-0140094190

WHEN THE WIND BLOWS

A

Plot: Trusting in the "Powers That Be," an elderly couple, Hilda and James, prepare for a nuclear attack with the help of pamphlets such as "The House-holder's Guide to Survival." However, their homemade air-raid shelter will not protect them from the radioactive fallout that blows in the wind after an attack from the Soviets.

Review: With hindsight we could label this Cold War paranoia, but that would be to criminally overlook the very real apocalyptic anxieties of the 1980s. In using the Everyman name "Bloggs" for his retirees, and gently depicting them with endearingly realistic cartoons, Brigg imbues his case against the bomb with a universal resonance. A tearjerker, but one nourished by a tender veracity.

FURTHER READING: *Fungus the Bogeyman: Ethel and Earnest*
SEE ALSO: *9/11: The Illustrated 9/11 Commission Report*
(Sid Jacobson and Ernie Colon); *Red Alert* (Peter George)

★
★
★
★

Writer: Don DeLillo
Publisher: Viking, Penguin, 1985

ISBN US: 978-0140283303
ISBN UK: 978-0140283303

15+ # WHITE NOISE

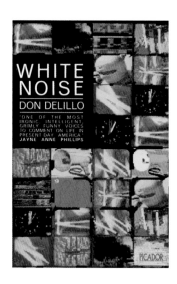

Plot: Meet Jack Gladney: The inventor of Hitler studies at colleges in North America, professor at the aptly named "College-On-The-Hill," and five times married (to four wives). When a chemical spill creates an "airborne toxic event" in his town and surrounding area, Gladney must confront his, his wife Babette's, and America's deepest modern fear: that of their own mortality.

Review: With car crash seminars, a visit to the Most Photographed Barn in America, and a postal chess game between one of Gladney's children and a mass-murderer, DeLillo creates a host of unforgettable fragments of modern life, if not an unforgettable cast of characters in his breakthrough novel. Though written in 1985 its comment on our common obsession with death, TV, shopping, and so on is no less thought-provoking now. Post-modernism at its blackly comic best.

FURTHER READING: *Underworld; Falling Man*
SEE ALSO: *The Corrections* (Jonathan Franzen);
The Crying Lot of 49 (Thomas Pynchon)

★
★
★
★

Writer: Jean Rhys
Publisher: Andre Deutsch, 1966

ISBN US: 978-0140818031
ISBN UK: 978-0141182858

15+ # WIDE SARGASSO SEA

Plot: A prequel/parallel companion to Charlotte Brontë's *Jane Eyre*, told from the viewpoint of Bertha Mason, the madwoman in the attic at Thornfield Hall. Antoinette Cosway here is a white Dominican who marries Mr. Rochester. How she becomes the morbidly troubled Bertha is woven around events related by Brontë.

Review: Jean Rhys' writings drew on bitter memories of lost love, loneliness, and instability (both financial and emotional). Her part-Creole heritage and Dominican upbringing also inform the character of Antoinette. Rejected and abandoned, Antoinette slips toward madness, although the ending—predetermined by Brontë's novel—is given a twist as Antoinette takes control of her life in her last moments. Winner of the W. H. Smith and Heinemann awards.

FURTHER READING: *After Leaving Mr. Mackenzie;*
Quartet; Voyage in the Dark; Good Morning, Midnight
SEE ALSO: *Jane Eyre* (Charlotte Brontë); *Foe* (J. M. Coetzee)

Writer: Barry Gifford
Publisher: Grove Press, 1990

ISBN US: 978-0802134530
ISBN UK: 978-0140445039

18+ WILD AT HEART THE STORY OF SAILOR AND LULA

Plot: To escape the clutches of her disapproving mother, Lula Pace Fortune goes on the run with her boyfriend Sailor Ripley, who is fresh from serving a two-year stint in prison for manslaughter. A road-trip, a love story, a neo-noir, Lula's and Sailor's stories make for exhilarating reading.

Review: Gifford employs the leitmotifs of the noir genre—violence, sweet love turned sour, hard drinking, a hard-boiled private eye—and gives them a welcome modern twist. Even those who have seen David Lynch's 1990 movie will get something from the paper and ink version of the story on which it was based: for one the writing has a sultry, unique quality of its own; for another, the endings are different.

FURTHER READING: *Port Tropique; The Wild Lives of Sailor and Lula*
SEE ALSO: *The Grifters* (Jim Thompson)

Writer: Jung Chang
Publisher: Globalflair, 1991

ISBN US: 978-0743246989
ISBN UK: 978-0007176151

12+ WILD SWANS

Synopsis: Family memoir told as a fictional narrative, following three generations of women in twentieth-century China. Our eyes are opened to China's invasion by Japan, World War II, the Nationalist-Communist Civil War, and the effects of Mao's cultural revolution in the 1960s.

Review: Chang bravely, painfully, shows us the cruel and brutal side of communism, as well as its personal tragedies; she has said the most difficult moment for her to write about was her father's descent into insanity after his denunciation by the Communist party. Not only is this a meticulous record of a period in history, but a personal one of Chang, her mother, and her grandmother, and all the more gripping for that.

FURTHER READING: *Mao: The Unknown Story*
SEE ALSO: *Life and Death in Shangahi* (Nien Cheng)

THE HANDMAID'S TALE

Margaret Atwood

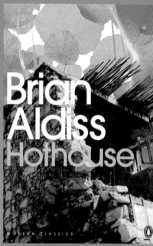

Brian Aldiss
Hothouse

MODERN CLASSICS

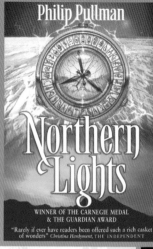

Philip Pullman

Northern Lights

WINNER OF THE CARNEGIE MEDAL
& THE GUARDIAN AWARD

"Rarely if ever have readers been offered such a rich casket
of wonders" *Christina Hardyment*, THE INDEPENDENT

GU
GAL

DOUG

FILM TI
WITH AN
ROB

BONE

1

OUT FROM BONEVILLE

ONE OF *TIME*
MAGAZINE'S 100
BEST NOVELS

XII

WATCHMEN

DC

ALAN MOORE
DAVE GIBBONS

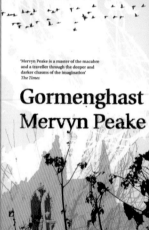

'Mervyn Peake is a master of the macabre
and a traveller through the deeper and
darker chasms of the imagination'
The Times

Gormenghast
Mervyn Peake

NOW A MAJO
Starring Hugh Jackman

THE
PREST
CHRISTOPHE

VINTAGE **SHELLEY**

FRANKENSTEIN

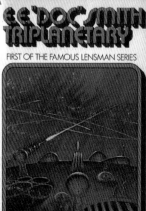

V2890/$1.25

EE'DOC'SMITH
TRIPLANETARY

FIRST OF THE FAMOUS LENSMAN SERIES

8B

95¢

The Last Unicorn
a novel by
Peter S. Beagle

JEFF

Battlefield Earth
i saga of the year 3000

L. Ron Hubbard

BLACK HOLE

CHARLES BURNS

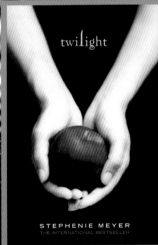

twilight

STEPHENIE MEYER
THE INTERNATIONAL BESTSELLER

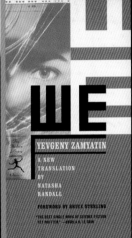

WE

YEVGENY ZAMYATIN

A NEW
TRANSLATION
BY
NATASHA
RANDALL

FOREWORD BY BRUCE STERLING

"THE BEST SINGLE WORK OF SCIENCE FICTION
YET WRITTEN." —URSULA K. LE GUIN

PART ONE OF THE DUNE TRILOGY

FRANK
HERBERT
DUNE

WINNER OF THE HUGO AWARD AND NEBULA AWARD

SLAUGHTER HOUSE 5

Kurt Vonnegut

FUTURE WORLDS, DIFFERENT PLANETS, AND A LITTLE DASH OF HUMOR

The sci-fi and fantasy genres offered us rich pickings for our selection of cult books. Both the ardent enthusiasm of the sci-fi or fantasy fan, and the experimental, "anything goes" qualities of these genres lend themselves fantastically well to the label "cult."

Of course, you might be a sci-fi novice, in which case you've a constellation of variety to look forward to in this chapter: future worlds, past worlds reinvented, and epic space battles all feature in our selection.

And they're not all aimed at techies either. Some of the books are only flushed with a tinge of sci-fi, others are very funny: these might be the ones to start with for those who know little of the genre. An intergalactic voyage of discovery awaits you—if you dare. Meanwhile, sci-fi lovers of old can blast into the past of treasured favorites (time travel is a staple of the genre, after all) and maybe even find something new. So, what are you waiting for?

★
★
★
★
★

Writer: Katsuhiro Otomo
Publisher: Dark Horse, 2000

ISBN US: 978-1935429005
ISBN UK: 978-1840232578

15+ # AKIRA

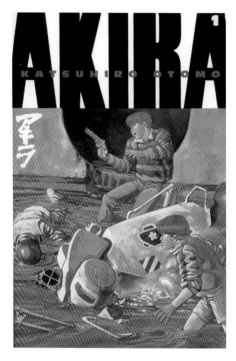

Plot: In a post-apocalyptic Neo Tokyo, there is civil unrest as the government attempts to maintain totalitarian order in the society it has rebuilt, while a terrorist resistance movement opposes the corruption within the system. Motorcycle gangs battle it out to rule the streets, and during one such turf war, teenage delinquents Kaneda and Tetsuo encounter a strange, wizened child who has escaped from a government facility. The boy, who has psychokinetic powers, defends himself from being run over by causing Tetsuo's motorcycle to explode, and both are then spirited away by armed soldiers. This experience causes Tetsuo's own latent psychic abilities to awaken, generating great interest and concern among the government scientists studying him. The early attempts of their predecessors to create super-powered humans had brought about the destruction of Tokyo several decades ago, and as Tetsuo gets drunk on his own power, he becomes obsessed with discovering more about one of those early test subjects: a child known only as Akira.

Review: Katsuhiro Otomo's cyberpunk epic demonstrated to Western audiences that there was more to *manga* than magical girls with huge eyes. Despite the trappings of futuristic technology (the motorbikes in particular are a fanboy's wet dream) and humans with super abilities, *Akira*'s main themes reflect the fears of Japanese society during the eighties: government corruption, rebellious younger generations, and the possible disastrous consequences of rushing to embrace new technologies. Against the beautifully detailed, ruined backdrop of what was once present-day Tokyo, Otomo's vision may seem dystopian and bleak, yet ultimately it offers hope for the future. An animated feature film of *Akira* was released in 1988, and although the plot was condensed, it too proved to be a seminal work.

FURTHER READING: *Domu: A Child's Dream;*
The Legend of Mother Sarah
SEE ALSO: *Akira Club* (Otomo);
Ghost in the Shell (Masamune Shirow)

★
★
★
★

Writer: Philip K. Dick
Publisher: Doubleday, 1968

ISBN US: 978-0194792226
ISBN UK: 978-1857988130

15+

DO ANDROIDS DREAM OF ELECTRIC SHEEP?

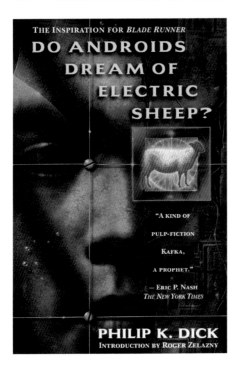

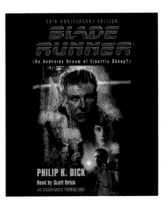

Deckard's success in tracking and killing the androids gives him the means to buy a goat, which Rachel kills. Deckard quits his job and travels to the desert where he finds what he believes to be a real toad. It is, in fact, artificial, but Deckard cares for it anyway.

Review: Where the movie *Blade Runner* revolves around the question of whether Deckard is an android (replicant), the book's protagonist is more concerned with what it really means to be human, which is defined as the ability to feel empathy and tested using Voight-Kampff, which measures emotional responses to the harming of animals.

Dick's constant concern about the nature of reality is evident here in religion, the ability to control moods, and the incongruity of a society that encourages the care and ownership of artificial animals but sends bounty hunters to kill artificial humans. Pervasive throughout the novel is the use of technology to artificially stimulate human lives, whether it is the television's *Barney Friendly* show perpetually playing in the background, the Penfield Mood Organ—with choices ranging from depression to the desire to watch TV—or Mercerism, a religion based on the use of empathy boxes where adherents share a single experience.

FURTHER READING: *Now Wait for Last Year;*
We Can Build You
SEE ALSO: *Solaris* (Stanislaw Lem);
Beyond Apollo (Barry Malzberg)

Plot: In the post-World War III world of depopulated San Francisco, 1992, radiation has forced most of the population off-world and killed most of the animals. Their scarcity makes real animals a status symbol, and those who cannot afford the real thing buy electric duplicates.

Rick Deckard, a bounty hunter working for the San Francisco Police Department, is ordered to execute six "andys"—androids indistinguishable from humans in almost every criterion—who have escaped from slavery on Mars and integrated themselves on Earth. Deckard accepts the job despite the fact that one of the senior bounty hunters has already been killed in the task.

Trapped in a loveless marriage, Deckard finds it easy to fall in love with Rachel, who reveals herself to be an android. Deckard begins to question the morality of his job.

★
★
★
★
★

Writer: Ray Bradbury
Publisher: Ballantine, 1953

ISBN US: 978-0345342966
ISBN UK: 978-0006546061

12+

FAHRENHEIT 451

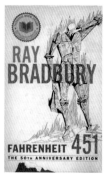

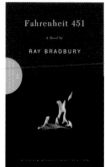

Plot: Inspired by newsreel of Nazi book-burning and named for the temperature at which paper ignites, Bradbury's *Fahrenheit 451* concerns a future in which humanity is protected against anything offensive or confusing. Books—contradictory and full of elusive and ambivalent ideas—are destroyed by firemen. One fireman, Montag, becomes obsessed with books after he takes one home and reads it. When his crime is discovered, Montag kills his supervisor and escapes to a community where each person memorizes a book.

Review: Bradbury had examined the question of censorship and the growing impact of technology on reading habits in short stories and, while this was clearly an attack on the McCarthyism of the early 1950s, it resonates still, thanks to regular headlines decrying—or calling for—the removal of books from library and school shelves. His short story "Bright Phoenix" (1963), in which citizens of a small town foil book burners by memorizing texts, was written in 1947, predating

the appearance of "The Fireman" (1951)—the original novella-length story Bradbury expanded to create *Fahrenheit 451*—although it appeared later.

Bradbury offers few details of the dystopia created by the this book-burning society beyond the notion that people are unhappy (Montag's wife attempts suicide, despite being a poster girl for the passive acceptance of repression). Montag swaps a homogenized society for one where each person could not be more individual, although the community he finds himself in is as passive in its own way as the world he left behind. Rather than leading a revolution, it will flourish only once the rest of the world has come to its senses.

FURTHER READING: *The Martian Chronicles*; *The Illustrated Man*
SEE ALSO: *Brave New World* (Aldous Huxley); *Nineteen Eighty-Four* (George Orwell)

Writer: Isaac Asimov
Publisher: Gnome Press, 1951

ISBN US: 978-0553293357
ISBN UK: 978-0586010808

FOUNDATION

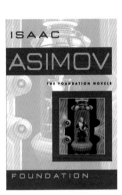

Book two—*Foundation and Empire*—sees even greater threats to the Foundation as it repels attacks from the decaying old Empire, battles internal corruption, and faces the rise of an irresistible mutant leader, the Mule. In the third book, Seldon's secret Second Foundation emerges.

Review: When Asimov wrote "The Encyclopedists," he had penned only three dozen stories and sold around half of them. From a minor writer, his first story published in 1939, Asimov emerged in 1941 as a major talent, writing "Nightfall" (often cited as one of the finest SF stories ever published), formulating the Three Laws of Robotics, and creating the basis for his Foundation series.

Plot: Hari Seldon is a psychohistorian—the science of predicting large scale changes in populations—who convinces the authorities that the Galactic Empire is dying and threatening to plunge 12,000 worlds into an age of barbarism. Too late to prevent the fall, Seldon sets up two foundations: one of scientists and encyclopedists to record all human knowledge in an Encyclopedia Galactica in the hope that this will reduce the period of unenlightenment; the other a secret organization of psychohistorians which emerges only later in the story.

Told in a series of stories set between twenty and seventy-five years apart, *Foundation* reveals what happens in the first 175 years of the Seldon Plan as the Foundation copes with a series of crises from neighboring barbaric planets. Through the use of trade and economic incentives and the religion of Scientism, the Foundation guides and controls newly emerging planets.

Asimov said that the series began with a notion thought up on the way to a meeting with editor John W. Campbell to write the story of a Galactic Empire that crumbled—taking its inspiration from Edward Gibbon's *History of the Decline and Fall of the Roman Empire*, although, while writing, the twenty-four-volume *Historian's History of the World* and Toynbee's *A Study of History* provided ideas. Complexly plotted and without a bug-eyed monster in sight, the Foundation trilogy introduced many readers to a more sophisticated form of science fiction. In 1966, the series was given a special Hugo Award for Best All-time Novel Series.

FURTHER READING: *Foundation's Edge;*
Foundation and Earth; Prelude to Foundation;
Forward the Foundation; Robots and Empire
SEE ALSO: *Foundation's Fear* (Gregory Benford);
Foundation and Chaos (Greg Bear);
Foundation's Triumph (David Brin)

★
★
★
★
★

Writer: Mervyn Peake
Publisher: Eyre & Spottiswoode, 1950
ISBN US: 978-0879516284
ISBN UK: 978-0099288893

15+

GORMENGHAST

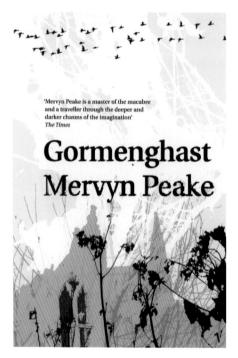

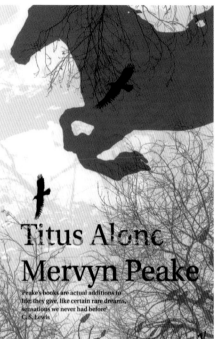

Plot: The titular Gormenghast is a vast and decaying castle that also serves as an entire kingdom, filled with labyrinthine passages and stifled by ancient, meaningless ritual. Titus Groan, the long-awaited male heir, is a young man rebelling against the role set out for him and longing to escape to the world outside. Meanwhile Steerpike, an ambitious former kitchen boy who has managed to swiftly ascend the social ladder, resorts to murder in order to gain control of Gormenghast outright. His treachery is eventually uncovered and the now-insane Steerpike seeks refuge within the remotest areas of Gormenghast, killing at random. As the lower levels of the castle are flooded by torrential rain, Titus must eventually face the killer and defend his unwanted birthright.

Review: The first book of Peake's surreal Gothic fantasy trilogy, *Titus Groan*, sets the scene for this, the second book of the series, with the birth of Titus and the introduction of Gormenghast's eccentric, often grotesque inhabitants. Unlike Tolkien's magical Middle-Earth, which spanned continents,

Gormenghast is a claustrophobic, stifling world in microcosm, shut away from the outside to the extent that most believe that nothing else exists. As Titus' mother tells him, "All roads lead to Gormenghast." The reader can empathize with Titus' teenage rebellion as he struggles to discover and be his own person; eventually he achieves it, though the cost is the loss of innocence and all he has known. Sadly, Peake's early death from Parkinson's disease prevented the completion of all the *Titus* books he had planned; the third book, *Titus Alone*, was published posthumously in 1959 and suffered due to heavy-handed editing. A revision by Langdon Jones in 1970 was better received, though Peake's writing still appears to have suffered somewhat during his illness.

FURTHER READING: *Titus Groan*; *Titus Alone*
SEE ALSO: *Vast Alchemies* (G. Peter Winnington); *Mervyn Peake: Two Lives and Mervyn Peake: The Man and His Art* (Sebastian Peake)

★
★
★
★

Writer: Margaret Atwood
Publisher: McClelland & Stuart, 1985

ISBN US: 978-0307264602
ISBN UK: 978-0099740919

12+

THE HANDMAID'S TALE

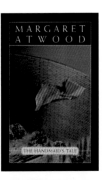

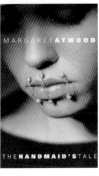

Plot: In a near future, we have the Republic of Gilead—a repressive state where women are assigned the role of breeder, wife, or housekeeper. This is a place of traditional values, where questions are not asked and dissent is unadvisable at the risk of punishment by public hanging or radiation poisoning.

Our central protagonist is Offred who, being one of the few women left in Gilead with functioning sex organs, is given the role of "Handmaid" or breeder. Not that Offred may choose her partner in this assignation. Rather, she is obliged to have sex with the Commander (named Fred, hence Offred), her designated mating partner, in order to produce offspring for him and his wife.

But Offred remembers past freedoms and past sensualities, she remembers her husband and daughter. It comes as no surprise, then, that she is tempted when a group of dissidents try to claim her as one of their own.

Review: Sci-fi in the vein of Orwell in that Atwood's dystopia has a terrifying resonance and, through simple, well-structured language, is utterly believable. We care hugely for Offred and will her "tiny peepholes of possibility" for the future to become gaping giant chasms of change. This makes the novel's obscure ending rather frustrating.

Thematically the book is very powerful. Hailed as a seminal feminist text, the book's cogency about the politicization of women's bodies elicits a good think from the reader. But whether, like the author, you identify yourself with feminism or not (Atwood now says she's not sure), you must still read *The Handmaid's Tale*. It's a cracking story, brilliantly written, and if it gets you thinking about gender politics as well, then so much the better.

FURTHER READING: *The Blind Assassin; Alias Grace*
SEE ALSO: *1984* **(George Orwell);** *Brave New World* **(Aldous Huxley)**

★
★
★
★
★

Writer: Douglas Adams
Publisher: Pan Books, 1979

ISBN US: 978-0345453747
ISBN UK: 978-0330437981

12+

THE HITCHHIKER'S GUIDE TO THE GALAXY

DOUGLAS ADAMS

FILM TIE-IN EDITION
WITH AN AFTERWORD BY
ROBBIE STAMP

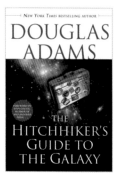

Plot: Arthur Dent begins a bewildering journey through the universe in the company of his friend, Ford Prefect, who has revealed himself to be an alien collecting data on Earth for a hitchhiker's guide. Escaping Earth shortly before the planet is demolished to make way for an intergalactic bypass, and after being forced to listen to some particularly bad Vogon poetry, Arthur and Ford are picked up by Zaphod Beeblebrox, the two-headed President of the Universe, on the run in a stolen spaceship.

Arthur is of particular interest to the mice (actually multidimensional aliens) who believe that in him may lay the ultimate question to life, the universe, and everything, the answer to which—already calculated by the universe's second greatest computer, Deep Thought—is 42. As Deep Thought says, "That quite definitely is the answer. I think the problem . . . is that you've never actually known what the question was."

The mice build a computer powerful enough to discover the ultimate question and call it Earth. Its ten-million-year program is five minutes from completion when Earth is destroyed. The mice believe that Arthur, a last-minute byproduct of the program, will have the Question imprinted on his brain. All they need to do is dissect it.

Review: *Hitchhiker's Guide to the Galaxy* began life as a radio show broadcast in 1978 and, by word of mouth, became a cult classic, repeated numerous times. It was rerecorded as LPs, novelized, and turned into a hit TV show and movie.

In crafting this hilarious SF comedy, Adams proved that the two genres were not mutually exclusive and lovingly sends up everything from bureaucracy to bad poetry as Everyman Dent discovers the absurdity of the universe. The early novels diverge from other forms of the story, so there are always happy surprises to be had.

FURTHER READING: *The Restaurant at the End of the Universe; Life, the Universe, and Everything; So Long, and Thanks for All the Fish; Mostly Harmless*
SEE ALSO: The *Discworld* novels (Terry Pratchett)

Writer: Yevgeny Zamyatin
Publisher: E. P Dutton, 1924

ISBN US: 978-0812974621
ISBN UK: 978-0140185850

12+

MY (WE)

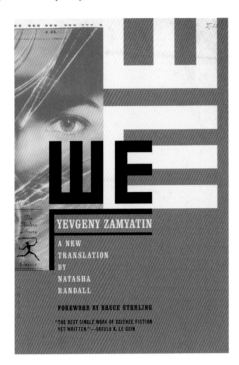

Plot: Set 1000 years in the future, Zamyatin's *We* tells of the One State, a technology-based society where human emotion and sensuality have ceded to logic and reason—all of society's problems are solved by mathematical equations, for instance. Subordination, subjugation, and submission are the One State's watchwords; freedom, sex, cigarettes, alcohol—and even real food—are pleasures that were enjoyed by "the ancients," while the One State's ruler, The Benefactor, is re-elected each year in a series of rigged votes. In this future dystopia, people are known by a letter and a number, not a name. D-503, a law abiding digit in this strange glass city, plays by the rules, until his lust for female dissident I-330 sees him embroiled in a plan to overthrow The Benefactor. This we learn from intimate access to D-503's journal entries, which form the basis of the narrative of the book.

Review: Much has been made of the "borrowings" of *1984* and *Brave New World* from *We*. It's a fascinating literary love triangle: in a 1946 review of *We*, Orwell stated he preferred it to Huxley's novel, as it had a "political point that the other lacked." Orwell was, though, influenced by both. This political point Orwell liked is what gives *We* its enduring appeal: in presenting his vision of a state where individual freedoms are vanished (let's not forget he wrote the book in the early days of the Soviet Union), Zamyatin's work has a universality that's an unwelcome flash of recognition to the modern reader. The actual writing—which can be fussy at times—stands up less well to the test of time. But it would be churlish of this lowly reviewer to suggest that *We* is anything short of a sci-fi masterpiece, and one that still holds a power to enthrall today.

FURTHER READING: *We* is the sole work of fiction by Zamyatin in English translation but you can try his essays if you're feeling brainy, *A Soviet Heretic: Essays,* for instance
SEE ALSO: *1984* (George Orwell); *Brave New World* (Aldous Huxley)

★
★
★
★
★

Writer: William Gibson
Publisher: Ace Books, 1984

ISBN US: 978-0441012039
ISBN UK: 978-0006480419

15+

NEUROMANCER

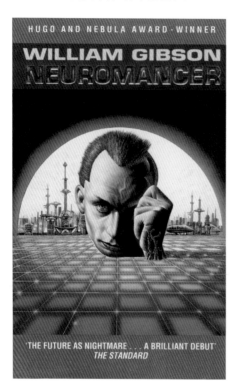

Review: Not the first but certainly the defining novel of the cyberpunk movement—"cyber" for its computers, gadgets, and virtual worlds, "punk" for the street-smart protagonists and low-lifes who inhabit these urban landscapes lit with neon and reflective chrome. "The sky above the port was the color of television, tuned to a dead channel"—the book's opening line meshes technology with the downbeat of crime noir. Multinational corporations have outgrown governments and the underclasses living in the urban sprawl of expanding, overcrowded cities live out pointless, chemically dulled or stimulated existences.

Packed with jargon and slang derived from computer and drug culture, Gibson's voice is the deadpan of hardboiled private eyes relocated to post-industrial mean streets. If Raymond Chandler is alive and well and writing science fiction, he may well be using the name William Gibson.

Neuromancer, Gibson's debut novel, won the Hugo, Nebula, and Philip K. Dick awards and was named by *Time* magazine as one of the top 100 novels since 1923. He has since escaped into the mainstream, as has some of the terminology he has used in his novels. The development of the world wide web and online gaming in particular are steps towards Gibson's vision of cyberspace.

Plot: Case, a master computer hacker, stole data from his employer and paid the price: mycotoxins have shredded his nerve endings making it impossible for him to jack into the matrix of cyberspace. In Chiba City, hustling for money to pay for repairs to his system, Case becomes embroiled with the cybernetically enhanced Molly and a plot to steal the saved conscience of a legendary hacker known as The Dixie Flatline on behalf of ex-military officer Armitage. It's a race against time: Armitage may have paid for his cure at a black clinic, but he has also inserted a medical time-bomb in Case—slowly dissolving sacs of mycotoxin bonded to his blood vessels.

Investigating Armitage, Case discovers that he is acting for an artificial intelligence known as Wintermute, one half of an AI—the other half known as Neuromancer—which, when united, will become a single super-AI.

FURTHER READING: *Count Zero;*
Mona Lisa Overdrive; Burning Chrome
SEE ALSO: *Software, Wetware, Freeware,*
and *Realwhere* **(Rudy Rucker);** *Eclipse, Eclipse*
Penumbra, and *Eclipse Corona* **(John Shirley);**
Mirrorshades: The Cyberpunk Anthology
(ed. Bruce Sterling)

★
★
★
★
★

Writer: Alan Moore and Dave Gibbons
Publisher: DC Comics, 1986

ISBN US: 978-1401219260
ISBN UK: 978-1848560062

15+

WATCHMEN

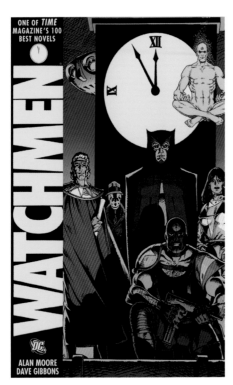

someone is gunning for masked heroes seems vindicated. Accusations that his irradiated, atomically altered body has caused cancer in those closest to him drive Doctor Manhattan into exile on Mars. These events are somehow connected with the disappearance of a group of writers, artists, and musicians but, before he can solve the mystery, Rorschach is imprisoned. With the nuclear clock poised close to midnight, it becomes a race against time to free Rorschach and unravel the conspiracy.

Review: In précis, *Watchmen* sounds little more than a rip-roaring, albeit intricately plotted, superhero comic. The reality is a complexly layered, richly detailed graphic novel where prose and images mesh perfectly. The series (originally published in twelve installments) discarded the clutter of comics—descriptive captions and sound effects—and told its story using a rigid panel structure, clean-line art, and a vivid color palette, creating a tale that had a wholly different look and feel to the average comic.

Plot: The emergence of masked vigilantes in the late 1930s and the accidental creation of a man with genuine superpowers, Doctor Manhattan, have altered the future as we know it. Their influence won the U.S. the Vietnam conflict, and Richard Nixon is still in power, although the Cold War is escalating despite the strategic advantage America has.

The Keene Act outlawed vigilantism in 1977 and most of the costumed crimefighters retire, bar those sanctioned by the government (Doctor Manhattan, now involved in subatomic research, and The Comedian) and the mentally unstable Rorschach. When The Comedian is killed, Rorschach's investigation involves other former comrades, Nite Owl (Daniel Dreiberg), Silk Spectre (Laurie Juspeczyk)—whose relationship with Doctor Manhattan is falling apart—and Ozymandias (Adrian Veidt). When the latter narrowly escapes being killed, Rorschach's paranoid belief that

Emphasizing character and motivation (often lacking in monthly comic books) opened *Watchmen* up to an audience that would not normally find satisfaction in graphic storytelling. Critically acclaimed, *Watchmen* was one of *Time* magazine's 100 greatest novels of all time, and *Entertainment Weekly* named it the thirteenth most important novel of the previous twenty-five years.

FURTHER READING: *The League of Extraordinary Gentlemen* (Moore and Kevin O'Neill); *Martha Washington* (Gibbons and Frank Miller)
SEE ALSO: *The Adventures of Luther Arkwright* (Bryan Talbot); *Sandman* (Neil Gaiman and various artists)

★
★
★
★
★

Writer: George Orwell
Publisher: Secker & Warburg, 1949

ISBN US: 978-0452284234
ISBN UK: 978-0141187761

12+ # 1984

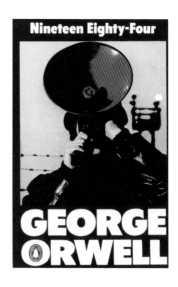

Plot: War is peace. Freedom is slavery. Ignorance is strength. These are the slogans of "the Party," the totalitarian government of Orwell's dystopia, Oceania. Winston Smith is a worker in the Party's Ministry of Truth. His rebellions of starting a relationship with fellow party worker, Julia, and showing interest in the anti-government community, the Brotherhood, ultimately sees Smith facing his worst fears in the nightmarish Room 101.

Review: *1984* is written in a deceptively simple style for a novel so buzzing with intellectual ideas. Far from being dated, concepts such as "thought crimes," historical revisionism, and the all-seeing eye of Big Brother may even render this political novel more relevant and thought-provoking today than it was on its publication.

FURTHER READING: *Animal Farm* (the most akin to 1984 in its politics); *Keep the Aspidistra Flying* (for the writing)
SEE ALSO: *We* (Zamyatin);
The Handmaid's Tale (Margaret Atwood)

★

Writer: L. Ron Hubbard
Publisher: St. Martin's Press, 1982

ISBN US: 978-1592120536
ISBN UK: 978-1592120079

12+ # BATTLEFIELD EARTH

Plot: Subtitled "A saga of the year 3000," by which time mankind has been enslaved for a thousand years by the Psychlos. Humans live in scattered, isolated tribes. Illiterate hunter Jonnie Goodboy Tyler is captured by Terl, the Psychlo's chief of security, who has been sent to Earth as punishment. Terl is desperate to buy his way off the planet, which he plans to do by using human slaves to dig uranium ore. Jonnie leads the rebel forces and frees the planet.

Review: Inactive as a fiction writer since the 1950s—he was the creator of Dianetics and founder of the controversial Church of Scientology—Hubbard returned to his pulp writing roots with a sprawling alien invasion yarn. As bad as the plot is, the writing, characterless and inept, is worse. And just when you think it's all over, it isn't.

FURTHER READING: *Final Blackout; Fear; Typewriter in the Sky*
SEE ALSO: *Childhood's End* (Arthur C. Clarke); *The Genocides* (Thomas M. Disch); *Footfall* (Larry Niven and Jerry Pournelle)

★
★
★
★

Writer: Charles Burns
Publisher: Pantheon Books, 2005
ISBN US: 978-0375714726
ISBN UK: 978-0224077781

18+

BLACK HOLE

Plot: "It took a while, but they finally figured out it was some kind of new disease that only affected teenagers. They called it the 'teen plague' or 'the bug' and there were all kinds of unpredictable symptoms . . . For some it wasn't too bad—a few bumps, maybe an ugly rash . . . Others turned into monsters or grew new body parts . . ." Against this background, the graphic novel's story switches between the lives of four characters: Chris, who catches the disease from her boyfriend Rob, and Keith, infected by a tail-bearing woman called Eliza.

Review: A powerfully evocative tale of teenage life, claustrophobic and tragic. The plague is a metaphor for burgeoning adulthood as adolescents awaken sexually and make the transition from children to adults. The artwork is bold monochrome, heavy on the black, and sometimes deeply disturbing.

FURTHER READING: *Skin Deep; Blood Club; Big Baby*
SEE ALSO: *Ghost World* (Daniel Clowes); *Summer Blonde* (Adrian Tomine)

★
★
★

Writer: Cormac McCarthy
Publisher: Random House, 1985
ISBN US: 978-0679728757
ISBN UK: 978-0330312561

15+

BLOOD MERIDIAN

Plot: The Wild West in the 1850s. A one-time innocent teenager, the Kid, joins forces with an Indian scalp-hunting cadre, who, though initially on an official mission, turn instead to murder and chaos. The Kid's story ends ambiguously, decades later, after a strange reunion with the book's main antagonist, Judge Holden.

Review: *Blood Meridian* has all the trademarks of McCarthy's work: the spare, yet spell-binding language, the desolate landscapes, the unerring violence. What sets this book apart is that the story was based on fact, on the exploits of the notorious Glanton gang. The mythology of the west has never been so accurately, nor compellingly, depicted.

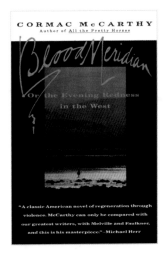

FURTHER READING: *The Road; No Country for Old Men*
SEE ALSO: *Little Big Man* (Thomas Berger)

500 ESSENTIAL CULT BOOKS

101

INCREDIBLE WORLDS
Best of the Rest

★
★
★
★

Writer: Jeff Smith
Publisher: Cartoon Books, 1991

ISBN US: 978-1888963144
ISBN UK: 978-1888963144

 A

BONE

OUT FROM BONEVILLE

Plot: Chased from Boneville and separated from his cousins, Fone Bone stumbles across a forested valley, populated by talking animals and terrifying creatures. He is befriended by Thorn, a young girl whose forgotten past leads them both into a quest to prevent the nightmarish Lord of Locusts from enslaving the land.

Review: Despite an initially lukewarm response, Jeff Smith's comic book series soon became a major and critical success, combining physical and verbal humor with epic, dramatic storytelling. Smith's strong, clean linework is also a perfect marriage of contrasts, from the cartoonish-looking Bones to the detailed world of the Valley, creating a series that is accessible to adult and younger readers alike.

FURTHER READING: *Rose* (with Charles Vess);
Stupid, Stupid Rat Tails
SEE ALSO: *Carl Barks Library*;
The Complete Pogo (Walt Kelly)

★
★
★
★

Writer: Aldous Huxley
Publisher: Chatto & Windus Ltd, 1932

ISBN US: 978-0060929879
ISBN UK: 978-0099518471

12+

BRAVE NEW WORLD

Plot: Six hundred years in the future, human beings are born in test tubes and conditioned into different behaviors as part of a hierarchical caste system. John, from "The Savage Reservation," used as a counterpoint to the "world state," comes to this dystopian brave new world and, repelled by its dehumanizing of birth, life, and death, attempts to teach its people about manhood and freedom.

Review: Bertrand Russell cautioned that *Brave New World* "Is all too likely to come true." Let's hope not. Babies are electrocuted to suppress their love of nature and books, promiscuity is encouraged, and society is valued over the individual. Dark and disturbing, full of ideas and ambiguity, this is sci-fi at its most inventive . . . and most portentously powerful.

FURTHER READING: *The Doors of Perception*
SEE ALSO: *We* (Zamyatin); *1984* (George Orwell);
The Handmaid's Tale (Margaret Atwood)

★
★
★
★
★

15+

Writer: Walter M. Miller, Jr.
Publisher: Lippincott, 1959

ISBN US: 978-0060892999
ISBN UK: 978-1857230147

A CANTICLE FOR LEIBOWITZ

Plot: Following a nuclear holocaust, an engineer named Leibowitz founds an order to try and preserve as much knowledge as possible from a backlash against technology and learning. In the novel's three sections, set some six-hundred-years apart, the Order of Leibowitz continues its task. The new world goes through a Dark Age, a new Renaissance, and eventually rediscovers nuclear power, threatening the Earth with destruction once again.

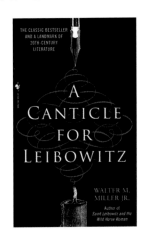

THE CLASSIC BESTSELLER AND A LANDMARK OF 20TH-CENTURY LITERATURE

A CANTICLE FOR LEIBOWITZ

WALTER M. MILLER JR.
Author of
Saint Leibowitz and the Wild Horse Woman

Review: Although Miller converted to Christianity shortly after World War II, his Hugo Award-winning novel is not a religious tract, but a rare example of science fiction successfully dealing with the question of the place theology and technology would have in a post-apocalyptic world.

FURTHER READING: *Saint Leibowitz and the Wild Horses* (completed by Terry Bisson)
SEE ALSO: *Earth Abides* (George R. Stewart); *A Case of Conscience* (James Blish)

★

Writer: Erich von Däniken
Publisher: Souvenir Press, 1969

ISBN US: 978-0425166802
ISBN UK: 978-0285629110

12+

CHARIOTS OF THE GODS?
UNSOLVED MYSTERIES OF THE PAST

Synopsis Pseudo-scientific book in which von Däniken presents his theory that the existence of artifacts like Stonehenge and the pyramids are proof beyond doubt that mankind has been visited by aliens in the past. Ancient tales of visiting gods were actually about beings from the stars, accounts of which can be found in most religious writings, including the Bible.

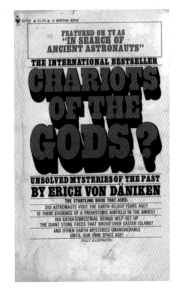

FEATURED ON TV AS "IN SEARCH OF ANCIENT ASTRONAUTS"
THE INTERNATIONAL BESTSELLER

CHARIOTS OF THE GODS?

UNSOLVED MYSTERIES OF THE PAST
BY ERICH VON DÄNIKEN

THE STARTLING BOOK THAT ASKS:
DID ASTRONAUTS VISIT THE EARTH 40,000 YEARS AGO?
IS THERE EVIDENCE OF A PREHISTORIC AIRFIELD IN THE ANDES?
DID EXTRATERRESTRIAL BEINGS HELP SET UP
THE GIANT STONE FACES THAT BROOD OVER EASTER ISLAND?
AND OTHER EARTH MYSTERIES UNANSWERABLE
UNTIL OUR OWN SPACE AGE!
FULLY ILLUSTRATED

Review: While von Däniken did not invent most of the ideas he espouses (many of them date back to the fictional Cthulhu Mythos of H. P. Lovecraft), he popularized them through articles and books that have appeared around the world. Although thoroughly discredited—the evidence in places is illogical, faulty, or simply fabricated—they continue to appear in print.

FURTHER READING: *Gold of the Gods; According to the Evidence: My Proof of Man's Extraterrestrial Origin*
SEE ALSO: *Crash Go the Chariots* (Clifford Wilson); *The Space Gods Revealed* (Ronald Story)

★
★
★
★

Writer: Arthur C. Clarke
Publisher: Ballantine, 1953

ISBN US: 978-0345444059
ISBN UK: 978-0575072633

12+

CHILDHOOD'S END

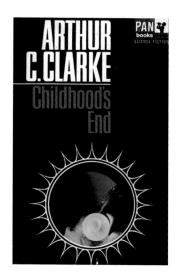

Plot: The Cold War arms race attracts the attention of the Overlords, devil-like aliens who arrive over Earth's biggest cities and announce that they are to become benign overseers of the planet for the benefit of mankind. War ends, but so does man's research into technology, and stifled innovation leads mankind to stagnate. The Overlords, however, have an interest in humanity's children, who evolve to join the Overmind, a cosmic alliance of galactic civilizations.

Review: Although best known as a blue-sky thinker on scientific lines, Clarke's novels occasionally center on spiritual development, most notably here and in *2001*, where mankind transcends to a state where it can be one with the universe. In passing, Clarke created many of the tropes of alien invasion movies (for example, *Independence Day*)—giant spaceships, unrevealed aliens, and humanity united against a common enemy.

FURTHER READING: *2001; Rendezvous with Rama*
SEE ALSO: *Last and First Men* (Olaf Stapledon); *A Mirror for Observers* (Edgar Pangborn); *The Midwich Cuckoos* (John Wyndham)

★
★
★
★

Writer: Charles G. Finney
Publisher: Viking Press, 1935

ISBN US: 978-0803269071
ISBN UK: 978-0803269071

12+

THE CIRCUS OF DR. LAO

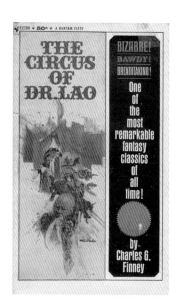

Plot: To the small Arizona town of Abalone comes Dr. Lao's circus of mythical and mystical beasts—a unicorn, a sphinx, a chimera, a satyr—and demigods such as Apollonius of Tyana. The simple townsfolk find it hard to appreciate the exhibits and the spectacle of acts that blur the boundaries of reality. As a finale, the circus vanishes. A "Catalog" at the end of the novel lists characters and creatures, and questions plot holes in the book.

Review: Journalist Finney was inspired by a trip to China while serving in the U.S. Army: reflecting on the scale and beauty of a tiled dragon screen, his contemplation was interrupted by an American sightseer complaining that the artist must have had "the awfulest imagination!" The novel comically appraises American life and culture, but it has an appeal that has lost nothing over the years.

FURTHER READING: *The Unholy City; The Magician Out of Manchuria*
SEE ALSO: *Something Wicked This Way Comes* (Ray Bradbury)

Writer: Jean M. Auel
Publisher: Crown, 1980

ISBN US: 978-0553381672
ISBN UK: 978-0340824429

THE CLAN OF THE CAVE BEAR

Plot: Set roughly 35,000 years ago, a young Cro-Magnon girl, Ayla, is left orphaned by an earthquake and is close to death when she is discovered by a similarly displaced Neanderthal clan. Their medicine woman raises her as her own child, but, as Ayla matures, her physical differences and mindset clash with the traditions of the clan.

Review: Jean Auel conducted extensive research on the prehistoric era and primitive survival skills while writing the first novel of her acclaimed *Earth's Children* series. This attention to detail pays off, as does her ability to write characters that are believably human, no matter what the time period. Although recent archaeological finds have revealed some historical inconsistencies, as a work of fiction this remains a solid, well-crafted novel.

FURTHER READING: *The Valley of Horses;*
The Mammoth Hunters; The Plains of Passage;
The Shelters of Stone
SEE ALSO: *Beyond the Sea of Ice* and sequels
(William Sarabande); *Mother Earth Father Sky*
and sequels (Sue Harrison)

★ **Writer:** Clive Barker   **ISBN US:** 978-0425188934
★ **Publisher:** Sphere, 1985   **ISBN UK:** 978-0751505955
★

18+ THE DAMNATION GAME

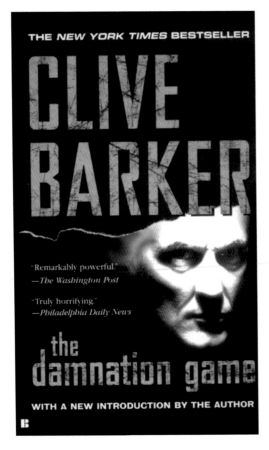

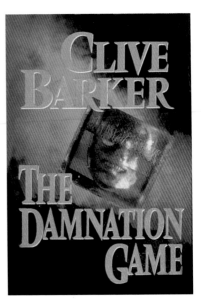

Plot: Marty Strauss, awaiting parole after being imprisoned for armed robbery, is hired as a bodyguard by Joseph Whitehead, a wealthy pharmaceutical company owner. Strauss joins his household, which includes Whitehead's heroin-addicted daughter, and learns that, years before, his new boss gambled with the mysterious Mamoulian, winning money and power. Now Mamoulian is back to collect on his debt.

Review: Barker's *Books of Blood* had already earned comparisons with Stephen King in the horror field. His first novel was a retelling (with a twist) of the legend of Faust and his deal with Mephistopheles, a weaving of gruesome-ness ("He allows no nastiness, cruelty or perversion to go unplumbed," said Chris Morgan) and literary dexterity that propelled it to success beyond the usual horror audience.

FURTHER READING: *The Books of Blood;*
The Great and Secret Show
SEE ALSO: *Necroscope* (Brian Lumley);
Ghost Road Blues (Jonathan Maberry)

★
★
★

Writer: Gustav Meyrink
Publisher: Houghton Mifflin, 1928;
originally in German 1915

ISBN US: 978-1873982914
ISBN UK: 978-0486250250

15+

DER GOLEM (THE GOLEM)

Plot: Inspired by the Jewish legend of Rabbi Judah Loew ben Bezalel's creation of an artificial man from sand and mud. Meyrink's Golem is barely seen: the novel's main focus is Athanasius Pernath (whose tale is retold by an anonymous narrator experiencing Pernath's life through a visionary dream) and his friends and neighbors in the Ghetto of Prague.

Review: Reputedly, the final manuscript was only half its original length, perhaps explaining the jumpy nature of the book. *The Golem* is a creation of the collective psyche of the Ghetto, and it is Meyrink's evocation of a decaying Prague and its inhabitants that elevates the novel; it is a study of the soul of a city, not a soulless supernatural creature.

FURTHER READING: *Walpurgisnacht; The Angel of the West Window*
SEE ALSO: *Frankenstein* (Mary Shelley); *He, She and It* or *Body of Glass* (Marge Piercy)

★
★
★

Writer: W. G. Sebald
Publisher: New Directions, 1996;
originally in German 1992

ISBN US: 978-0811213660
ISBN UK: 978-0099448884

15+

DIE AUSGEWANDERTEN
(THE EMIGRANTS)

Plot: Structured in four sections, each concentrating on the life of a single emigrant who has left Germany and now lives in a foreign land: Henry Selwyn, the homesick retired doctor who at first sight seems typically English but confesses he came to London from Lithuania; Paul Bereyter, school teacher, who returns to Germany from France during the War despite his Jewish background; Ambrose Adelwarth, who stewards the heir of an affluent family around the casinos of Europe; and Max Ferber, a painter based in Manchester, whose paintings evoke the ghettos and death camps that were the fate of his parents.

Review: The specter of war and the past lies heavy on all four as Sebald, the unnamed narrator, explores how each subject has adapted to a life on foreign soil.

FURTHER READING: *Austerlitz; Vertigo*
SEE ALSO: *W.G. Sebald: A Critical Companion* (eds. by J. J. Long and Anne Whitehead); *The Emergence of Memory: Conversations with W. G. Sebald* (Lynne Sharon Schwartz)

ESSENTIAL CULT BOOKS

500

107

INCREDIBLE WORLDS
Best of the Rest

★
★
★
★

Writer: Anne McCaffrey
Publisher: Ballantine, 1968

ISBN US: 978-0345484260
ISBN UK: 978-0552084536

12+

DRAGONFLIGHT

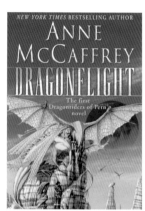

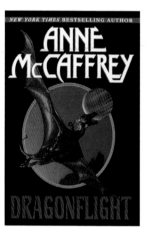

Plot: The planet Pern is home to human colonists whose society is irregularly threatened by "threads" that fall from a neighboring planet. To combat these, riders train with the indigenous, telepathic dragons to destroy the spores before they take root. Centuries can pass between attacks, and defenses can be dangerously weakened as the threat recedes into history. History—the oldriders of four-hundred turns earlier—may be the only resolution to the next attack.

Review: McCaffey's strongest characters have been resourceful and intelligent women and children—as seen here in the shape of Lessa, who becomes a Weyrwoman,

and Kylara, rider of a queen dragon. Some subsequent titles have been aimed at a younger audience; for adults, *Dragonflight* and *Dragonquest* are the most satisfying as they explore for the first time the relationship between the classes, the new and old, and that of rider and dragon.

FURTHER READING: *Dragonquest; The White Dragon*; and eleven others by McCaffrey, plus further titles in collaboration with Todd McCaffrey
SEE ALSO: *The Dragon Masters* (Jack Vance); *Rogue Dragon* (Avram Davidson)

★
★
★
★
★

Writer: Frank Herbert
Publisher: Chilton, 1965

ISBN US: 978-0441013593
ISBN UK: 978-0450011849

15+

DUNE

PART ONE OF THE DUNE TRILOGY

FRANK HERBERT

DUNE

WINNER OF THE HUGO AWARD AND NEBULA AWARD

Plot: In the far future, the universe is ruled by the Emperor of the Imperium, and the most vital resource is the spice melange, created by the spiceworms of the burning desert planet Arrakis. Bedouin-like Fremen live a precarious existence hunting spiceworms. Two noble houses rule Arrakis and the Emperor fears the rise of House Atreides and ferments a war with House Harkonnen. Paul, heir to the House Atreides, undergoes a rite of passage that convinces the Fremen that he is the Maud'Dib, their new messiah.

Review: In Arrakis, Herbert created the most multifaceted and copiously detailed setting SF had to offer, rich in history and complex in political structure. Its ecology and religions add further riches to the novel, as do the characters: Paul Atreides is a flawed messiah who may bring about a holy war.

FURTHER READING: *Dune Messiah; Children of Dune; God Emperor of Dune; Heretics of Dune; Chapterhouse: Dune;* **further sequels have been penned by Brian Herbert and Kevin J. Anderson**
SEE ALSO: *Hyperion* **(Dan Simmons);** *The Rediscovery of Man*

★
★

Writer: Samuel R. Delany
Publisher: Ace Books, 1967

ISBN US: 978-0819563361
ISBN UK: 978-0819563361

12+

THE EINSTEIN INTERSECTION

Plot: In the distant future, still bathed in radiation from wars that all but destroyed mankind, the remains of humanity pick over the remnants in search of human myths and a stable genetic structure. Lo Lobey, our narrator, leaves his village on a journey to find his lost love, Friza. He crosses blasted landscapes in the company of others in search of Kid Death.

Review: Rich in imagery and language, *The Einstein Intersection* is a future-day retelling (in part) of the legend of Orpheus and his quest for Eurydice; however, the various characters (Green-Eye, Dove, Spider, etc.) take on multiple roles, not only mythical but as archetypes from popular culture (Ringo Starr, Jean Harlow, Billy the Kid). The book won Delany his second Nebula Award.

FURTHER READING: *Nova; Triton;*
Stars in My Pocket Like Grains of Sand
SEE ALSO: *A Canticle for Leibowitz* **(Walter M. Miller);**
Some Will Not Die **(Algis Budrys);** *Davy* **(Edgar Pangborn)**

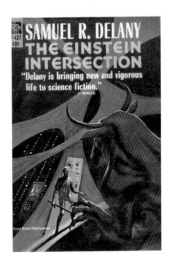

SAMUEL R. DELANY
THE EINSTEIN INTERSECTION
"Delany is bringing new and vigorous life to science fiction."
— ANALOG

First Book Publication

★
★
★

Writer: Orson Scott Card
Publisher: Tor, 1985

ISBN US: 978-0765362438
ISBN UK: 978-1904233022

15+ # ENDER'S GAME

Plot: Six-year-old Andrew "Ender" Wiggin is chosen for military training at an elite Battle School where he proves himself time and again to be the best student. Promoted to Command School, he continues to perform astonishing feats in simulated battles with the Formics, an alien race (nicknamed "buggers") that is threatening mankind. Ender, now aged twelve, faces his final exam: destroying a vast Formic fleet by destroying a planet. He then learns that these have not been simulations but real battles.

Review: *Ender's Game* had a mixed reception, being criticized for its violence and for the fact that Ender is morally in the clear for his act of "xenocide," and praised for his compassion and empathy for the characters. The novel won both the Hugo and Nebula awards (as did its sequel, *Speaker for the Dead*).

FURTHER READING: *Speaker for the Dead; Xenocide;*
Children of the Mind; A War of Gift; Ender in Exile
SEE ALSO: *The Lathe of Heaven* (Ursula Le Guin);
Schismatrix (Bruce Sterling)

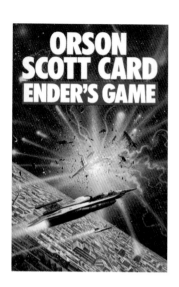

★
★
★
★

Writer: Daniel Keyes
Publisher: Harcourt Brace, 1966

ISBN US: 978-0156030304
ISBN UK: 978-1857989380

12+ # FLOWERS FOR ALGERNON

Plot: Gentle, amiable, and retarded, Charlie Gordon works as a janitor by day and studies at a school for the mentally handicapped by night. Offered a chance to undergo a groundbreaking neurosurgical procedure, successfully performed on a laboratory mouse named Algernon, Charlie becomes increasingly intelligent and sophisticated. But, as his IQ rises, he ponders the implications of his new maturity and of an experiment that he discovers has a critical flaw.

Review: Related through his "Progriss Riport" journal, Keyes credibly follows Charlie's intellectual and emotional changes as Charlie explores the world through new eyes. Charlie finds pleasures he had not imagined but also pain. The old Charlie was happy within his limited world. Exposed to new emotions, new Charlie reassesses the people around him. A touching, sentimental novel, it won both Hugo (in its original short story form) and Nebula awards. Cliff Robertson won an Oscar for his performance in the movie adaptation, *Charly*.

FURTHER READING: *The Touch; The Fifth Sally*
SEE ALSO: *The Minds of Billy Milligan* (Keyes);
Algernon, Charlie and I: A Writer's Journey (Keyes)

Writer: Mary Shelley
Publisher: Lackington, et al, 1818

ISBN US: 978-0743487580
ISBN UK: 978-1853260230

★
★
★
★

15+

FRANKENSTEIN

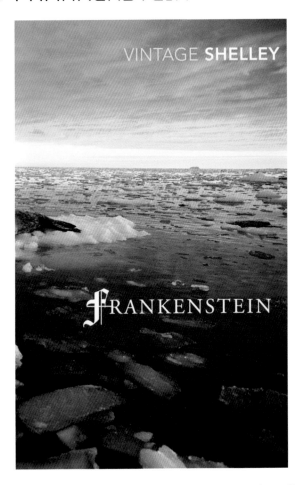

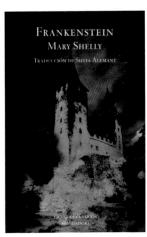

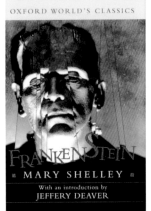

Plot: Dr. Frankenstein of Geneva creates a living Being from human cadavers. Born innocent and good, the "Being" teaches himself about human emotion, but becomes violent as the reality of his situation sinks in.

Review: As with other early examples of the horror genre the story of *Frankenstein* has become distorted by the ravages of time . . . and Hollywood. The Being created by Dr. Frankenstein is twisted and psychotic, yes, but only after being refused a companion by his creator. Flowery language rather muffles the horror of both the plight and actions of the monster. Despite this, *Frankenstein* is a touchstone for both the suspense and horror genres, and as a novel of ideas it more than stands the test of time.

FURTHER READING: *The Last Man*
SEE ALSO: *The Invisible Man* (H. G. Wells); *Strange Case of Dr. Jekyll and Mr. Hyde* (Robert Louis Stevenson)

★
★
★
★

Writer: Terry Pratchett and Neil Gaiman
Publisher: Victor Gollancz, 1990

ISBN US: 978-0060853976
ISBN UK: 978-0552137034

12+ # GOOD OMENS

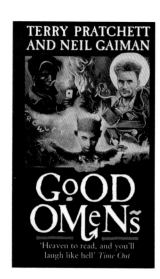

Plot: The Antichrist has been born and the End of Times is near, as prophesied by the seventeenth-century witch Agnes Nutter. The demon Crowley and his angel friend Aziraphale decide to avert the destruction of Earth, not realizing that, owing to a mix-up, the real Antichrist, Adam Young, has been raised as a normal human boy. However, his powers are growing and the Four Bikers of the Apocalypse are riding out . . .

Review: This collaboration by two of Britain's most acclaimed authors could never be less than a match made in Heaven. Pratchett's satirical humor and Gaiman's darker fantasy meshes together so well, it is hard to tell where one begins and the other ends. *Good Omens* parodies the genre of "the Devil's child" hilariously and intelligently, populated with likeable, downright bizarre (and occasionally familiar) characters.

FURTHER READING: *American Gods* (Gaiman); *Mort* (Pratchett)
SEE ALSO: *The Brentford Trilogy* and sequels (Robert Rankin);
The Portable Door and sequels (Tom Holt)

★
★
★
★

Writer: Brian W. Aldiss
Publisher: Faber & Faber, 1962

ISBN US: 978-1600103605
ISBN UK: 978-0141189550

15+ # HOTHOUSE

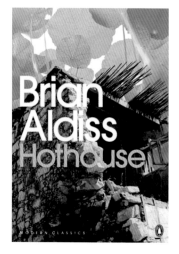

Plot: A Hugo Award-winning collection of interlinked stories, *Hothouse* is set on a far-distant future Earth now locked in its orbit around the sun. The planet is overrun by vegetation, including animal-plant hybrids called traversers that have spun a web between Earth and its moon.

Review: Utterly implausible from a hard science viewpoint, Aldiss uses this vivid landscape to explore the lives of the fragile and almost extinct human race. Much evolved and living in dense tropical jungles and caves, they struggle to survive against giant insects, flymen, parasitic trees, and sentient fungus. Ultimately, they must choose to abandon the doomed planet and escape to the stars or remain behind. Throughout, Aldiss' joy of inventive language shines through.

FURTHER READING: *Non-Stop; The Saliva Tree
and Other Strange Growths; Helliconia Spring* and sequels
SEE ALSO: *The Dying Earth* (Jack Vance); *Against the Fall of Night*
(Arthur C. Clarke); *Catch a Falling Star* (John Brunner)

★
★
★

Writer: Richard Matheson
Publisher: Fawcett/Gold Medal, 1954
ISBN US: 978-0765318741
ISBN UK: 978-1857988093

15+

I AM LEGEND

Plot: Richard Neville is the sole survivor of a virus that turns its victims into vampires. Each night he is besieged by the vampires who try to entice him from his heavily boarded house; by day he seeks out their lairs and destroys them while researching the origins of the virus. Then Neville meets Ruth, who reveals that the infected are adapting to the disease.

Review: Filmed three times (*The Last Man on Earth*, 1964; *The Omega Man*, 1971; *I Am Legend*, 2007), Matheson's novel has also been influential on the zombie movie genre (for example, Romero's *Night of the Living Dead*). The book inverts the usual relationship between human and vampire as Neville realizes that they fear him, and he has become a legend that will be passed down through generations of the infected.

FURTHER READING: *The Shrinking Man*;
Richard Matheson: Collected Stories
SEE ALSO: *The Road* **(Cormac McCarthy);**
One **(Conrad Williams)**

★
★
★

Writer: Robert Shea and Robert Anton Wilson
Publisher: 3 volumes, Dell, 1975
The Eye in the Pyramid,
The Golden Apple, Leviathan
ISBN US: 978-0440539810
ISBN UK: 978-1854875747

15+

THE ILLUMINATUS TRILOGY

Plot: Marketed as science fiction but really a mystery story, the book begins with two detectives investigating the bombing of a magazine's offices and the disappearance of its editor. Meanwhile, a journalist is jailed on trumped up charges and then rescued by a group called the Discordians, who are battling an organization called the Illuminati who secretly rule the world.

Review: Conceived in the late 1960s, when Wilson began creating conspiracy theories that claimed a secret society called the Bavarian Illuminati were plotting to take over the world. Shea and Wilson together penned a meanderingly plotted series linking Atlantis and Adolf Hitler with Cthulhu mythology. Satirical and comic, the books have been treated seriously by some, and they hugely influenced conspiracy fiction.

FURTHER READING: *Schroedinger's Cat*;
Masks of Illuminati; Historical Illuminatus Chronicles **(series)**
SEE ALSO: *The Da Vinci Code* **(Dan Brown);**
Imajica **(Clive Barker)**

ESSENTIAL CULT BOOKS

500

113

INCREDIBLE WORLDS
Best of the Rest

★
★
★
★

Writer: Anne Rice
Publisher: Random House, 1976

ISBN US: 978-0345337665
ISBN UK: 978-0394498218

15+

INTERVIEW WITH THE VAMPIRE

Plot: The compelling confessional of a vampire, Louis, who recounts the tale of his two hundred-year life to a young boy. From his transformation into a vampire at the hands—or rather teeth—of Lestat, to his struggle with the devouring of human flesh, to his flight in search of new companions in the new world, Louis' life story is stirring stuff.

Review: Insatiable head vampire Lestat, the girl-woman Claudia, and the "all-too-human" Louis make for a perverse trio of central characters in the first of Anne Rice's hugely successful vampire series. As unforgettable as these characters are, Rice's plot and setting are equally seductive: a revivification of vampire mythology for a twentieth-century audience.

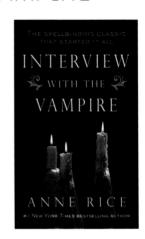

FURTHER READING: *The Vampire Lestat; The Queen of the Damned*
SEE ALSO: *Dracula* (Bram Stoker); *Salem's Lot* (Stephen King); *Lost Souls* (Poppy Z. Brite)

★
★
★
★

Writer: Len Deighton
Publisher: Hodder & Stoughton, 1962

ISBN US: Out of print
ISBN UK: 978-0586026199

15+

THE IPCRESS FILE

Plot: The down-to-earth, nameless protagonist of Deighton's novel works in the unheroic lower levels of the British Secret Service. Against a background of form-filling and report-writing, the narrator is sent to buy back a kidnapped biochemist, whom they eventually have to hijack. These events punctuate a larger narrative as our protagonist discovers a much deeper secret that underlies this operation.

Review: Famously portrayed (and named Harry Palmer) by Michael Caine in the movie adaptation, Deighton's debut novel was perhaps the ultimate "spy procedural." It revels in its technical jargon, acronyms, and cryptonyms, which give the novel a gray, bureaucratic verisimilitude a million miles from James Bond.

FURTHER READING: *Horse under Water; Funeral in Berlin; Billion Dollar Brain*
SEE ALSO: *Epitaph for a Spy* (Eric Ambler); *The Spy Who Came in from the Cold* (John Le Carre)

★
★
★
★
★

Writer: Peter S. Beagle
Publisher: Viking Press, 1968

ISBN US: 978-0451450524
ISBN UK: 978-0285633216

THE LAST UNICORN

Plot: After learning that she is the last of her kind, a unicorn leaves her enchanted forest home in search of others of her kind. She learns from a butterfly that other unicorns are held captive by King Haggard in a distant kingdom. During her journey, she is captured by a witch, freed by an inept wizard, and joined by others.

Review: When originally published, *The Last Unicorn* was praised as a modern fairy tale that combined many characters common to such stories (magical beings, princes, wicked kings) and sent them on an epic quest. While working with many traditional elements of the genre, Beagle's book is both witty and tender, and was rightly—and positively—compared with the works of Lewis Carroll and J. R. R. Tolkien.

FURTHER READING: *A Fine and Private Place; The Innkeeper's Song; The Unicorn Sonata; Giant Bones; The Line Between*
SEE ALSO: *The Little White Horse* (Elizabeth Goudge); *Peter S. Beagle's Immortal Unicorn*

★
★
★

Writer: M. John Harrison
Publisher: Orion, 2002

ISBN US: 978-0553587333
ISBN UK: 978-0575074033

LIGHT

Plot: Michael Kearney, a tormented scientist on the verge of a major mathematical breakthrough, is haunted by a creature known as the Shrander and kills women to alleviate his suffering. In the future, Ed Chianese is a virtual-reality addict on the run from gangsters the Cray Sisters. Seria Mau Genlicher, cybernetically spliced to the ship she pilots, is searching the Kefahuchi Tract—a naked singularity—for ancient alien technology.

Review: An almost throwaway line about "Tate-Kearney transformations" tells the reader that the book's three seemingly unrelated strands must somehow be linked. Harrison weaves three strands into a satisfying whole, although readers will find it is a dark, violent, and disturbing journey of discovery.

FURTHER READING: *The Centauri Device; In Viriconium; Signs of Life; Nova Swing*
SEE ALSO: *Brasyl* (Ian McDonald)

INCREDIBLE WORLDS
Best of the Rest

500 ESSENTIAL CULT BOOKS

115

★
★
★
★
★

Writer: J. R. R. Tolkien
Publisher: George Allen & Unwin Ltd,
1954–55

ISBN US: 978-0618640157
ISBN UK: 978-0261103252

A

THE LORD OF THE RINGS

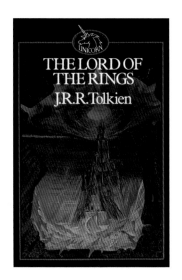

Plot: When hobbit Frodo Baggins inherits a magical ring from his cousin Bilbo, he discovers it is the creation of the fallen Dark Lord Sauron, who seeks it to reclaim his former power. Aided by the wizard Gandalf and a fellowship of men, elves, dwarves, and hobbits, Frodo sets out to destroy the One Ring before Sauron's forces can claim it and enslave Middle-Earth.

Review: Tolkien returns to the world he first introduced to younger readers in *The Hobbit* and develops Middle-Earth into a lushly detailed, epic mythology in the tradition of Norse legends. Inspiring (and frequently imitated by) authors since the 1950s, Tolkien is considered the father of high fantasy writing and *The Lord of the Rings* is often cited as the finest novel published in the twentieth century.

FURTHER READING: *The Silmarillion; The Children of Húrin*
SEE ALSO: *The Return of the Shadow, The Treason of Isengard, The War of the Ring,* and *Sauron Defeated* (Christopher Tolkien)

★
★
★
★

Writer: James Hilton
Publisher: Macmillan, 1933

ISBN US: 978-0692000847
ISBN UK: 978-1840243536

12+

LOST HORIZON

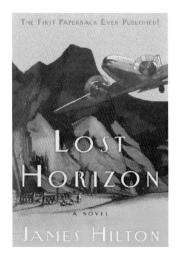

Plot: Hugh Conway, a member of the British consul, and three others—his vice-consul Mallinson, a brash American called Barnard, and Miss Brinkley, a British missionary—are evacuated from Baskul, India, due to an uprising. Their flight, however, takes them over Tibet and crash lands in a remote mountain range. They are saved by the monks of Shangri-La, a lamasery, where Conway meets the High Lama and learns that time stands still in this utopian paradise.

Review: Espousing a philosophy of "everything in moderation," Shangri-La has since become a byword for hidden worlds, peaceful, idyllic, and rich in cultural and spiritual wealth. Famously filmed by Frank Capra in 1937, Hilton's original has hints of a slightly darker side between the philosophizing and pacifist message.

FURTHER READING: *Goodbye, Mr. Chips; Random Harvest*
SEE ALSO: sequels *Messenger* (Frank DeMarco) and *Shangri-La* (Eleanor Cooney and Daniel Altieri)

★
★
★
★

Writer: John Wyndham
Publisher: Michael Joseph, 1957

ISBN US: 978-0899683874
ISBN UK: 978-0141033013

15+

THE MIDWICH CUCKOOS

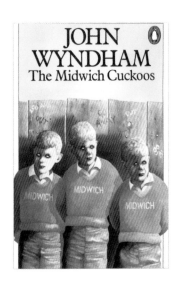

Plot: A picture postcard English country village is cut off from the world for a day and its residents fall into a collective, and temporary, deep sleep. A series of inexplicable pregnancies soon trouble the villagers, then "the Children," are born: golden-eyed and gifted, they quickly develop physically and mentally beyond their years. Their desire, the villagers finally discern, is to "survive and to dominate."

Review: This is accessible sci-fi, what the author himself has labeled "logical fantasy." The prosaic style and everyday dialog cleverly elicit a "what if?" response from the reader, while the dramatic climax has us examining the lengths to which the human race would go to save our own kind. Particularly sinister for those who have ever borne a child.

FURTHER READING: *The Day of the Triffids; The Kraken Wakes*
SEE ALSO: *The Handmaid's Tale* (Margaret Atwood);
The War of the Worlds (H. G. Wells)

★
★
★
★

Writer: Philip Pullman
Publisher: Scholastic Ltd, 1995

ISBN US: 978-0440238607
ISBN UK: 978-1407109428

A

NORTHERN LIGHTS
(THE GOLDEN COMPASS)

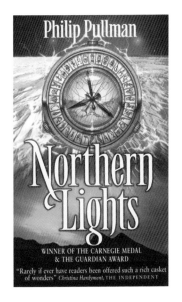

Plot: In a world where the Church holds the greatest power, young orphan Lyra finds herself caught up in a web of intrigue when her friend Roger disappears, and she is taken from her home at Jordan College by the glamorous Mrs. Coulter. But the woman is not what she seems, and Lyra escapes with her daemon Pantalaimon to find Roger; a search that takes her to the North, where armored polar bears, witches, and a terrible secret dwell.

Review: The first book of Pullman's *His Dark Materials* trilogy caused much controversy on its release, with many people interpreting his corrupt alternate-world Papacy as a veiled attack on the Catholic church. *Northern Lights* is a well-crafted, intellectual fantasy filled with delightful concepts and a damning insight on the darker side of humanity.

FURTHER READING: *The Subtle Knife; The Amber Spyglass*
SEE ALSO: *The Ruby in the Smoke* and sequels, *Lyra's Oxford*,
and *Once Upon a Time in the North* (Philip Pullman)

★
★
★

Writer: Charles L. Harness
Publisher: Bouregy & Curl, 1953

ISBN US: 978-0517554333
ISBN UK: 978-0450029967

12+

THE PARADOX MEN
(FLIGHT INTO YESTERDAY)

Plot: Alar, a thief with no memory of who he was, steals jewels to raise money to free slaves in the days of a decadent, Baroque period of future history that is about to come to an end. Caught up in the intrigues of the ruling powers and the Society of Thieves, his escape from the Imperial Police takes him on a journey of discovery, which could end at the heart of the Sun.

Review: *The Paradox Men* bursts with ideas based on Toynbee's theory of cyclical history, Aristotelian/non-Aristotelian logic, theories of evolution, and Einsteinian physics, wrapped up in a colorful, fast-paced, swashbuckling pulp-era space opera. Its intricate plot and dazzling set-pieces has earned the novel high praise from the likes of Brian Aldiss and George Zebrowski.

FURTHER READING: *The Rose; The Ring of Ritornel*
SEE ALSO: *The World of Null-A* (A. E. Van Vogt);
The Stars My Destination (Alfred Bester).

★
★
★

Writer: China Miéville
Publisher: Macmillan, 2000

ISBN US: 978-0345459404
ISBN UK: 978-0330392891

15+

PERDIDO STREET STATION

Plot: The baroque, gas-lit city of New Crobuzon is home to creatures both human and magical. Isaac Dan der Grimnebulin, an eccentric scientist, is approached by a garuda to restore his wings, sawn off by his flock in punishment. In exploring ways to help the mutilated garuda, Isaac is distracted in a direction that releases a citywide threat, which he tries to resolve with his insect-like girlfriend. His actions bring him into conflict with the city's crime lord, Mr. Motley.

Review: Award-winning magical steampunk fantasy with none of the usual fantasy tropes (elves, orcs, etc.). Instead, New Crobuzon is a Dickensian urban sprawl rife with monsters, political corruption, and brutality. Only Miéville's second novel, it set the intellectual, literary, and political tone seen in later books, each of which has been greeted with high praise.

FURTHER READING: *The Scar; Iron Council*
SEE ALSO: *Viriconium* (M. John Harrison);
City of Saints and Madmen (Jeff VanderMeer);
The Etched City (K. J. Bishop)

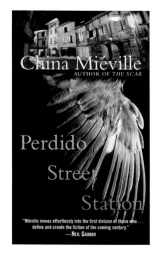

★
★
★

Writer: Christopher Priest
Publisher: Simon & Schuster, 1995

ISBN US: 978-0765317346
ISBN UK: 978-0575075801

15+

THE PRESTIGE

NOW A MAJOR FILM
Starring Hugh Jackman and Christian Bale

THE
PRESTIGE
CHRISTOPHER **PRIEST**

Plot: Two nineteenth-century music hall magicians, Rupert Angier and Alfred Borden, develop a bitter rivalry as each perfects and tries to improve upon an illusion known as "The Transported Man," which allows them to instantly pass from one place to another. Using a multiple-viewpoint technique, the plot is constructed to slowly unveil the truth, using in part the illusionists' techniques—the set-up, the performance, and the *prestige*, the magical finale, the rabbit from the hat where previously there was no rabbit.

Review: As with many of Priest's novels (*The Glamour, The Quiet Woman, The Affirmation*), the overall theme is the search for identity, made explicit here by the surrounding narrative of a descendent who inexplicably believes he has a twin brother. The novel was a well-deserved winner of the James Tait Black Memorial Prize and World Fantasy Award.

FURTHER READING: *The Magic: The Story of the Film*
SEE ALSO: *The Affirmation, The Glamour, The Extremes,*
and *The Separation* (Priest)

★
★
★
★

Writer: Russell Hoban
Publisher: Jonathan Cape, 1980;
expanded, Indiana University Press, 1998

ISBN US: 978-0253212344
ISBN UK: 978-0747559047

12+

RIDDLEY WALKER

Plot: Twelve-year-old Riddley Walker lives in the post-apocalyptic future of two thousand years hence in a corner of "Inland" (England) once called Kent. The citizens eke out a harsh living from the land and by salvaging ancient machinery. They speak a phonetic form of English, and a political system, ruled by the church, conveys its message to the people through puppet theater known as the Eusa Show. Riddley's discovery of a plan to rediscover lost "clevverness" propels him into conflict with authorities.

Review: While the basic plot may echo many stories, the setting, culture, and constant reinvention of the book make it stand out. Better known as a writer and illustrator of children's books, it is little wonder that Hoban creates a believable young protagonist at the center of this exceptionally imagined novel.

FURTHER READING: *Kleinzeit; Fremder*
SEE ALSO: *A Canticle for Leibowitz* (Walter M. Miller);
The Jewels of Aptor (Samuel R. Delany)

Russell Hoban
Riddley Walker

A Twentieth-Anniversary Edition with a new Introduction by Will Self

ESSENTIAL CULT BOOKS

500

119

INCREDIBLE WORLDS
Best of the Rest

★
★
★

Writer: Larry Niven
Publisher: Ballantine, 1970

ISBN US: 978-0345333926
ISBN UK: 978-0575077027

RINGWORLD

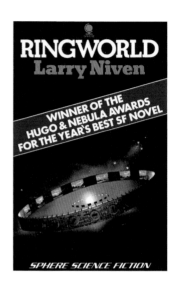

Plot: The Ringworld is an artificial world built around a sun by an ancient, unknown race. The alien discoverers of this artifact put together a team to explore it, including two-hundred-year-old Louis Wu, Teela Brown (genetically bred to be statistically lucky), and aliens Speaker-to-Animals and Neesus. Their ship, attacked by a meteor defense mechanism, crash lands, and the four have to travel vast distances to seek a way off the Ringworld, meeting primitive descendents of its creators along the way.

Review: In *Ringworld*, Niven created one of the most famous artifacts of SF, a world a million miles wide and 3x106 times the surface area of Earth, and his adherence to hard science makes it totally believable. Although speculation on its function and origins dominates the plot, there is more than enough action and adventure to speed the book along.

FURTHER READING: *The Ringworld Engineers;*
The Ringworld Throne; Ringworld's Children
SEE ALSO: *Orbitsville* (Bob Shaw); *Titan* (John Varley); *Eon* (Greg Bear)

★
★
★
★
★

Writer: Cormac McCarthy
Publisher: Alfred A. Knopf, 2006

ISBN US: 978-0307265432
ISBN UK: 978-0307455291

THE ROAD

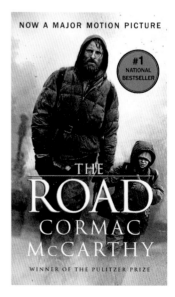

Plot: In a post-apocalyptic America—a land covered in ash where plants do not grow, it's bitterly cold, and food is in desperately short supply—an unnamed father and son head toward the coast in search of, if nothing else, hope.

Review: Superlative upon superlative have rained down on McCarthy's 2007 Pulitzer Prize winner. Small wonder. The book crackles with poetry portending to an uncertain future –"limbless tree trunks" are a recurring image, for instance—and yet the language is spare, which only heightens the tension at the more terrifying and horrific of moments. McCarthy's nightmare vision will have you weeping for father, son, humanity, and for our planet, and yearning for a brighter future for all four.

FURTHER READING: *Blood Meridian; No Country for Old Men*
SEE ALSO: *A Canticle for Leibowitz* (Walter M. Miller);
Star Man's Son (Andre Norton)

★
★
★
★
★

Writer: Neil Gaiman and various artists
Publisher: DC Comics/Vertigo, 1990–91

ISBN US: 978-1563890413
ISBN UK: 978-1852864477

15+

THE SANDMAN SEASON OF MISTS

Plot: Morpheus, Lord of Dreams, travels to Hell to free his former lover Nada, whom he had condemned to eternal torment thousands of years ago. However, Lucifer reveals he has quit, releasing the damned and demons onto Earth. Left in possession of the key to Hell, Morpheus is caught up in a diplomatic struggle as various deities vie to claim it.

Review: Launched as a horror comic, Neil Gaiman's series about Morpheus (or Dream, one of seven anthropomorphic personifications of humanity) evolved into its own mythology, encompassing folklore, legends, and historical fact. *Season of Mists* is a prime example, revealing more about Dream's family, the Endless, and setting in motion key events.

FURTHER READING: *Sandman* collections *Preludes and Nocturnes, The Doll's House, Dream Country, A Game of You, Fables and Reflections, Brief Lives, Worlds' End, The Kindly Ones, The Wake*
SEE ALSO: *Death: The High Cost of Living* and *Death: The Time of Your Life* (Gaiman)

ESSENTIAL
CULT BOOKS
500
INCREDIBLE WORLDS
Best of the Rest
121

★
★
★

Writer: Kurt Vonnegut, Jr.
Publisher: Delacourt Press, 1969

ISBN US: 978-0385333849
ISBN UK: 978-0099800200

15+

SLAUGHTERHOUSE-FIVE

Plot: Billy Pilgrim, having survived capture by the Germans in World War II, is kidnapped by aliens and becomes "unstuck in time." Taken to the planet Tralfamadore, he learns about life and death—when someone dies there, he learns that you shrug and say "so it goes." A mantra that echoes throughout the book, for the body count is high.

Review: Semi-autobiographical, in so far as Vonnegut—like Pilgrim—was a prisoner of war in a meat-locker beneath Dresden as it burned in a firestorm. Not in so far as he was abducted by time-traveling aliens. One suspects. Which is not to make light of the dark themes spoken of in this intelligent, thought-provoking book. A troubling read, but a necessary one.

FURTHER READING: *Cat's Cradle; The Sirens of Titan*
SEE ALSO: *The Good Soldier Svejk* (Jaroslav Hasek);
Birdsong (Sebastian Faulks); *Catch-22* (Joseph Heller)

★
★
★
★

Writer: Neal Stephenson
Publisher: Bantam Spectra, 1992

ISBN US: 978-0553380958
ISBN UK: 978-0140232929

15+

SNOW CRASH

Plot: Hiro Protagonist, computer programmer/hacker, the greatest sword-fighter in the Metaverse, and a pizza delivery boy for the Cosa Nostra, discovers that a new drug, Snow Crash, is being offered to avatars in the virtual world, frying the brains of users in the real world.

Review: One of *Time* magazine's Best 100 Novels, *Snow Crash* was *the* cyberpunk novel of the nineties. Stephenson created a stunning virtual world and a convincing real world, ruled over by corporation-backed franchises and opposed by hackers—now something of a cliché. Religion and ancient Sumerian is woven into the plot, but it's the wildly inventive technology, traffic-dodging high speed courier services, and the one-man nuclear power known as Raven that keep the book moving at breakneck speed.

FURTHER READING: *The Diamond Age; Cryptonomicon; Anathem*
SEE ALSO: *Count Zero* (William Gibson); *When Gravity Fails* (George Alec Effinger); *Islands in the Net* (Bruce Sterling)

'LOOKS SET TO BE TO TECHNO-CULTURE IN THE 1990s
WHAT *NEUROMANCER* WAS IN THE 1980s' – *OBSERVER*

★
★
★

Writer: Harry Harrison
Publisher: Pyramid, 1961

ISBN US: 978-1857984989
ISBN UK: 978-0575081710

12+

THE STAINLESS STEEL RAT

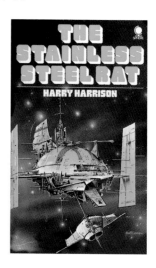

Plot: James Bolivar "Slippery Jim" diGriz is a conman and thief. A charming, accomplished liar, diGriz is a rat in the wainscoting of a future world of concrete and steel whose talents make him the target of a government-backed agency, the Special Corps, led and staffed by former criminals. Tricked into joining—although always looking for a way out—diGriz is assigned to track down Angela, a sociopathic killer with whom he falls in love.

Review: A rare example of humorous science fiction that is well-paced, adventurous, and actually funny. DiGriz has morals, which takes the edge off some of his actions and makes him a character readers can comfortably like.

FURTHER READING: *The Stainless Steel Rat's Revenge;*
The Stainless Steel Rat Saves the World; and seven further sequels
SEE ALSO: *Bill, the Galactic Hero* (Harrison); *Who Goes Here?* (Bob Shaw)

★
★
★
★
★

12+

Writer: Alfred Bester
Publisher: New American Library, 1956

ISBN US: 978-0679767800
ISBN UK: 978-0575079090

THE STARS MY DESTINATION
(TIGER! TIGER!)

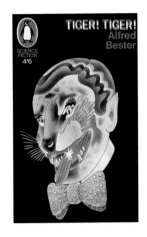

Plot: Trapped in a space wreck for 170 days and refused rescue by a passing spaceship, Gully Foyle is compelled to escape and avenge himself. In a society where teleportation (jaunting) can be taught, Foyle is the one man capable of jaunting across space and wonders whether he should teach this talent to a race he thinks of as a freak show.

Review: Although it uses *The Count of Monte Cristo* for its archetype and draws on the energy and adventure of a straight-forward space opera, *The Stars My Destination* is a pyrotechnic display of sophisticated prose and typographical inventiveness, multilayered, witty, demanding, and rightly recognized as one of the finest SF novels yet published.

FURTHER READING: *The Demolished Man; The Computer Connection*
SEE ALSO: *The Count of Monte Cristo* **(Alexandre Dumas);**
Slan **(A. E. Van Vogt)**

★
★
★
★

12+

Writer: Robert A. Heinlein
Publisher: Putnam, 1961; uncut, 1990

ISBN US: 978-0441788385
ISBN UK: 978-0340938348

STRANGER IN A STRANGE LAND

Plot: Raised on Mars when Earth's first expedition ends in disaster, Valentine Michael Smith arrives on Earth twenty years later only to be held by the government as they try to persuade him to give up a patent for a star drive and, due to a technicality of law, ownership of Mars. Rescued by reporter Ben Caxton and attorney Jubal Harshaw, Smith founds the Martian-influenced Church of All Worlds, to which many people flock after learning of his psychic powers. Naïvely, Smith believes his teachings will benefit humanity, but he is brutally killed.

Review: Notable for introducing the word "grok" into common parlance and inspiring a religious order, Heinlein wanted to write a novel that turned conventional mores on their heads. In fact he argued the case for alternative lifestyle so plausibly that the book was greeted with unabashed fervor by supporters of counterculture.

FURTHER READING: *Double Star; Glory Road;*
The Moon Is a Harsh Mistress
SEE ALSO: *Jesus on Mars* **(Philip Jose Farmer);**
Godbody **(Theodore Sturgeon)**

ESSENTIAL
CULT BOOKS

500

123

INCREDIBLE WORLDS
Best of the Rest

★ **Writer:** Jack Finney
★ **Publisher:** Simon & Schuster, 1970
★

ISBN US: 978-0684801056
ISBN UK: 978-0575073609

12+

TIME AND AGAIN AN ILLUSTRATED NOVEL

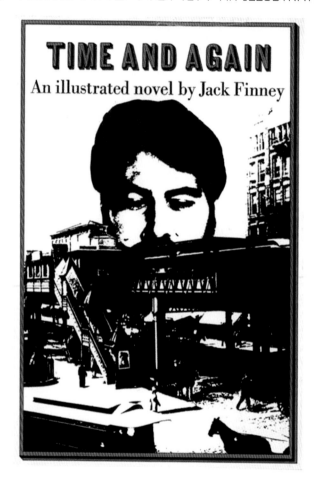

Plot: Simon Morley, a New York advertising sketch artist, participates in a secret government experiment to send him back in time to 1892. Morley wishes to resolve a long-standing mystery relating to Andrew Carmody, an acquaintance of President Grover Cleveland. Morley discovers that he can alter history and avert the Cuban Missile Crisis, but instead he distracts the father of Dr. Danziger, chief scientist behind the time travel project, and as a result Danziger's father fails to meet Danziger's mother, trapping Morley in the past.

Review: Carmody may be a fictional character, but he walks through a meticulously researched and historically authentic New York, illustrated with views and newspaper reports from contemporary sources. The labyrinthine plot is more historical mystery than science fiction.

FURTHER READING: *The Body Snatchers;*
The Woodrow Wilson Dime; From Time to Time
SEE ALSO: *The House on the Strand* (Daphne du
Maurier); *To Say Nothing of the Dog* (Connie Willis)

★
★
★

Writer: Stephen Baxter
Publisher: HarperCollins, 1995

ISBN US: 978-0061056482
ISBN UK: 978-0006480129

15+

THE TIME SHIPS

Plot: An authorized sequel to H. G. Wells' *The Time Machine*, published a century after the original. Traveling to the future to save the Eloi Weena (who died in *Time Machine*), the Time Traveler discovers himself in a different future where Morlocks are far more advanced. The Traveler has changed the future. Returning to 1873 to persuade his younger self to give up researching time travel, he discovers other time lines have been created.

Review: Although Baxter doesn't share the political or social views that Wells seeded throughout his novel, the book stays true to the original while hurling Wells' traveler into distant pasts and futures. The novel deservedly won the John W. Campbell Memorial Award, Philip K. Dick Award, and BSFA Award, and has been called a modern classic.

FURTHER READING: *Voyage* and sequels; "Time's Tapestry" series
SEE ALSO: *The Hertford Manuscript* (Richard Cowper);
The Space Machine (Christopher Priest);
The Man Who Loved Morlocks (David Lake)

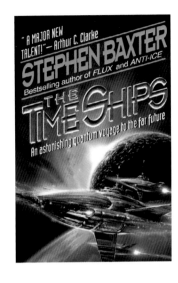

★
★

Writer: E. E. "Doc" Smith
Publisher: Fantasy Press, 1948

ISBN US: 978-0843959499
ISBN UK: 978-1434401014

12+

TRIPLANETARY

Plot: *Triplanetary* introduces the Arisians and Eddorians, alien races of absolute good and utter evil, in a millennia-long conflict. On the side of good are the Lensmen, naturally gifted humans whose powers are enhanced by a ruby lens that allows them to communicate telepathically. Over a series of six novels, the action grows until whole civilizations are wiped out and a new race of super beings emerges as guardians of the universe.

Review: Before Smith, science fiction was bounded by the solar system; with his Lensman series, the scale of action became galactic, then intergalactic, as each successive confrontation with the Eddorians revealed an even greater threat. Read with an eye to historical context, Smith's imagination more than makes up for dry prose.

FURTHER READING: *First Lensman; Galactic Patrol; Gray Lensman; Second Stage Lensmen; Children of the Lens; The Vortex Blaster*
SEE ALSO: *The Legion of Space* (Jack Williamson); *Crashing Suns* (Edmond Hamilton)

AN EPIC TALE OF GALACTIC ADVENTURE

INCREDIBLE WORLDS
Best of the Rest

ESSENTIAL
CULT BOOKS

500

125

★
★   **Writer:** Stephenie Meyer   **ISBN US:** 978-0316015844
★   **Publisher:** Little Brown, 2005   **ISBN UK:** 978-1904233657

15+ TWILIGHT

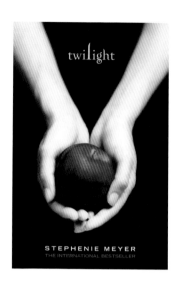

Plot: Bella Swan arrives at a new school, attracting much attention but spurning several boys. When fellow student Edward Cullen saves her life by halting a speeding van with his bare hands, Bella becomes obsessed with discovering his background. Which she does. However, that he and his family are vampires proves no barrier as they fall in love.

Review: Hugely successful and critically praised, *Twilight* uses vampirism as a metaphor for sexual tension for teenagers. Bella is infatuated by moody outsider Edward and wants to be bitten and converted; Edward struggles to remain chaste. It is at the same time satisfying as a romance and packs a lot of suspense into its latter half, which sees a second group of (less benign) vampires arrive in town.

FURTHER READING: *New Moon; Eclipse; Breaking Dawn;*
unpublished, incomplete *Midnight Sun,* available on her website
SEE ALSO: *Dead Until Dark* (Charlaine Harris);
Touch the Dark (Karen Chance)

STEPHENIE MEYER
THE INTERNATIONAL BESTSELLER

★
★   **Writer:** Jeff Noon   **ISBN US:** 978-0312141448
★   **Publisher:** Ringpull, 1993   **ISBN UK:** 978-0330338813

18+ VURT

Plot: Manchester, the near future. Scribble enters the virtual world with his sister, Desdemona, with whom he has an incestuous relationship, to play a game called English Voodoo. He returns to find her replaced by an amorphous creature. With the other members of the Stash Riders, he seeks out the scarce Curious Yellow feather so he can reenter the game and rescue her.

Review: Although it tips its hat at cyberpunk, *Vurt* is more organic than technological: the virtual world is a drug-induced shared reality accessed by sucking on colored Vurt feathers. The novel owes more to Octave Mirbeau's *The Torture Garden* and Orpheus' descent into the underworld than to William Gibson (though Noon acknowledges the latter as an influence). Although it won the 1994 Arthur C. Clarke Award, it is science fiction in the same way that *Alice's Adventures in Wonderland* is science fiction.

FURTHER READING: *Pollen; Nymphomation*
SEE ALSO: *City Come A Walkin'* (John Shirley); *Slaughtermatic* (Steve Aylett); *Dead Girls, Dead Boys, Dead Things* (Richard Calder)

JEFF NOON
Vurt

Writer: Eric Frank Russell
Publisher: Dobson, 1958

ISBN US: 978-1886778337
ISBN UK: 978-0575070950

15+

WASP

Plot: The Sirian Combine outnumbers Terran forces twelve-to-one and Earth's response is to put one man, James Mowry, suitably surgically disguised, onto one of their planets. Mowry begins his war on the aliens simply; he creates a fictitious antiwar movement, *Dirac Angestun Gesept*, distributing stickers and writing to newspapers. As Mowry turns up the pressure with murder, ticking letters, and power cuts, more and more of the enemy police and military resources are tied up dealing with the phantom D.A.G.

Review: "By doing insignificant things in suitable circumstances, one can obtain results monstrously in excess of the effort." Mowry becomes a wasp, a mischievous irritant buzzing around the enemy. Russell's novel may be over fifty years old and exaggerating World War II guerrilla warfare, but it continues to resonate in these days of the War on Terror.

FURTHER READING: *Sinister Barrier; Men, Martians and Machines; Next of Kin; The Great Explosion*
SEE ALSO: *The Best of Eric Frank Russell* (ed. Alan Dean Foster)

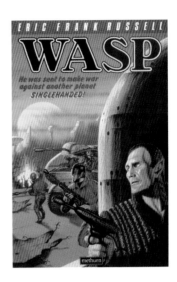

ESSENTIAL
CULT BOOKS

500

127

INCREDIBLE WORLDS
Best of the Rest

Writer: John Christopher
Publisher: Hamish Hamilton, 1967

ISBN US: 978-0689856723
ISBN UK: 978-0689856723

A

THE WHITE MOUNTAINS

Plot: A century has passed since the Earth was enslaved by the Tripods, fifty-foot tall, three-legged alien machines. Two friends, Will and Henry, who are approaching the age where they will be "capped" (via which the Tripods keep the adult population docile), learn of a resistance movement and escape to the continent, where they meet Jean-Paul (Beanpole) and make their way to the Alps and freedom.

Review: The first of a trilogy (later expanded), *The White Mountains* is a fast-paced, entertaining adventure yarn for teenagers, set against a well-realized, almost feudal society background. The Tripods are not the only threat: the caps drive some humans mad, adding to the tension of the journey. Later books in the series reveal more about the invasion and the invaders.

FURTHER READING: *The City of Gold and Lead; The Pool of Fire; When the Tripods Came*
SEE ALSO: *The War of the Worlds* (H. G. Wells); *Sinister Barrier* (Eric Frank Russell)

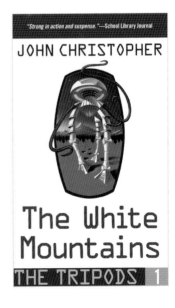

"Strong in action and suspense."—School Library Journal

JOHN CHRISTOPHER

The White Mountains

THE TRIPODS 1

art spiegelman
MAUS
A SURVIVOR'S TALE

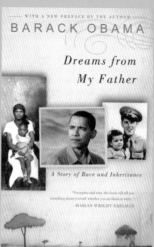
WITH A NEW PREFACE BY THE AUTHOR
BARACK OBAMA
Dreams from
My Father
A Story of Race and Inheritance
"Perceptive and wise, this book will tell you
something about yourself, whether you are black or white."
—MARIAN WRIGHT EDELMAN

ROLLINS
BLACK
COFFEE
BLUES

AUDIO
CONFESS
AN
AUTOBIO
C
NOW A MAJOR

A Million
Little Pieces

James Frey

With Notes from the Author and from the Publisher

PENGUIN
BOOKS

HELL'S ANGELS

HUNTER S. THOMPSON

David B.
Epileptic

PERSE
THE STORY OF A CHILDHOOD

MARJANE

Biography of
MORRISON
O
NE
ERE
ETS
T ALIVE
HOPKINS and DANNY SUGERMAN

#1
BESTSELLER
OVER 2 MILLION
COPIES IN
PRINT

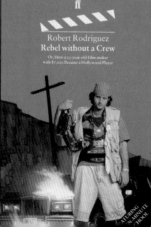
ff
Robert Rodriguez
Rebel without a Crew
Or, How a 23-year-old Film-maker
with $7,000 Became a Hollywood Player

"Stanley Booth's book is the only one I can read and say,
'Yeah, that's how it was.'" —Keith Richards
Stanley Booth
THE TRUE ADVENTURES OF THE
ROLLING
STONES

Adolf
Hit

in Kan

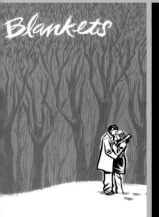

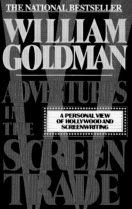

TRUTH IS STRANGER THAN FICTION

Many of the fictional works in this guide could be said to be thinly veiled versions of their authors' lives, but now we have the real deal: the memoirs, biographies, and autobiographies.

From jaw-dropping tales of personal sacrifice and heroism, to hilarious confessions of indiscretion and the occasional self-satisfied life story, the whole gamut of humanity is represented. And it's not always heartwarming—we've included the rantings of the world's most reviled dictator, for instance. But, at the opposite end of the spectrum, a young lawyer's dreams of his father are stirring stuff, and both books show how the memoir can be a useful historical tool in our understanding of the motivations of the great and not so good.

★
★ **Writer:** William Goldman **ISBN US:** 978-0446391177
★ **Publisher:** Warner Books, 1983 **ISBN UK:** 978-0349107059

ISBN US: 978-0446391177
ISBN UK: 978-0349107059

15+

ADVENTURES IN THE SCREEN TRADE
A PERSONAL VIEW OF HOLLYWOOD

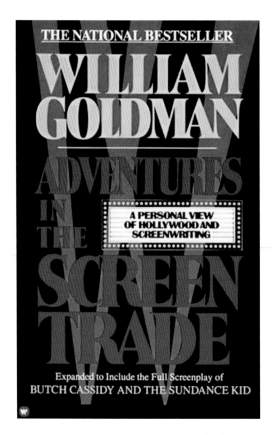

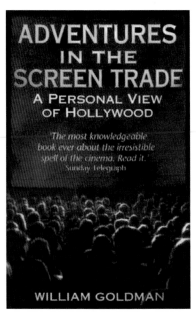

Synopsis: Goldman's "personal view of Hollywood" tells of the connection between the studios, stars, producers, and directors in the movie industry, as well as relaying his experiences of being the scriptwriter for box-office successes such as *Butch Cassidy and the Sundance Kid* and *All the President's Men*.

we don't learn loads about the artistic processes of modern Hollywood too, one of the book's most interesting features being a dissection of Goldman's own screenplay for *Butch Cassidy and the Sundance Kid*. A page-turner.

Review: If you're a lover of tittle-tattle, then you'll feel you've hit the gossip jackpot after reading this hugely engrossing memoir. To whet your appetite: did you know that the original Hollywood actors had to help build sets and do other odd jobs as part of their remit? That's not to say

FURTHER READING: *Boys and Girls Together; Hype and Glory*
SEE ALSO: *Hollywood Babylon* (Kenneth Anger); *Easy Riders, Raging Bulls* (Peter Biskind)

★
★
★
★
★

Writer: Bob Dylan
Publisher: Simon & Schuster, 2004

ISBN US: 978-0743478649
ISBN UK: 978-0743228152

12+

CHRONICLES VOLUME ONE

BOB DYLAN

CHRONICLES
VOLUME ONE

Synopsis: Bob Dylan, whose music and lyrics changed the face of western culture, offers the first volume of his memoirs. The title is misleading, for we don't begin at the beginning and carry on through his career. Rather, Dylan recalls key moments from across the decades: his arrival in New York in 1961; his retreat from the media at the end of that decade; the making of *Oh Mercy* (and a musical rebirth) in 1987; and back to 1961 and his first songwriting deal.

Review: Critically lauded on its release, this memoir managed the remarkable feat of not disappointing the author's legions of fans. Instead of presenting a straightforward history of people, places, dates, and events, Dylan (rightly) assumes that most of his readership know the outline of his career and concentrates on the moments that influenced his creativity. So we are given generous pen-portraits of the musicians he's worked with and creative figures in New York's folk scene; insights into his singing technique; moments when songs poured out of him; stories of difficult recording sessions as well as productive ones; and chance encounters that made him see the world afresh. Related in a conversational, understated, tone, and shot through with a wry humor, this is essential reading for anyone who's been gripped by Dylan's output and wondered where it all came from.

FURTHER READING: *Tarantula;*
Dylan on Dylan
SEE ALSO: *Bob Dylan: The Essential*
Interviews (Jonathan Cott);
The Bob Dylan Encyclopedia
(Michael Gray)

ESSENTIAL CULT BOOKS

500

133

REAL LIVES
Top 10 Classics

★
★
★
★
★

Writer: George Orwell
Publisher: Victor Gollanz, 1933

ISBN US: 978-0156262248
ISBN UK: 978-0140282566

12+

DOWN AND OUT IN PARIS AND LONDON

GEORGE ORWELL DOWN AND OUT IN PARIS AND LONDON

'HE IS A WRITER WHO CAN – AND MUST – BE REDISCOVERED IN EVERY AGE'
IRISH TIMES

Plot: An investigation into poverty in Paris and London, presented as a novel—and Orwell's first literary work. The Paris slums form the first part of the book, and set the scene for the rest—a place of dirty lodgings and "innumerable" bugs, where Orwell's lack of luck and work sees him taking up the seventy-eight hour a week job of a *plongeur* (a dishwasher). In the second part of the novel, Orwell journeys to London on the promise of work. But his employers are away and he must live for a time as a tramp, sleeping in flophouses and surviving on "tea and two slices" (of bread and margarine, or if you're lucky, butter).

One aspect of *Down and Out in Paris and London* is that it is the supporting characters, not the lead down and out, who are the most memorable: there's Boris the alcoholic and lovelorn Russian in Paris who believes that if you have a chessboard you "don't mind being hungry," while Paddy in England is a "typical" tramp from whom Orwell learns that, in London, you have to pay even to sit on a bench. And while we're on the subject of supporting cast, there is also the "disgusting filth" and the bugs in the Paris slums and London flophouses that permeate the book. Indeed, the poverty is so pungently described, it's almost tangible.

Review: In Orwell's sympathetic descriptions of his fellow tramps, down and outs, *plongeurs*, and beggars, we can see an obvious precursor to the socially aware novels *1984* and *Animal Farm*, which would seal his fame. He might not use the precise allegory of those later works here, but the book remains, nevertheless, as *The Nation* puts it, "the most lucid portrait of poverty in the English language."

FURTHER READING: *The Road to Wigan Pier* and *Homage to Catalonia* (the nonfiction); *1984* and *Animal Farm* (the novels)
SEE ALSO: *The People of the Abyss* (Jack London)

★
★
★
★

Writer: Barack Obama
Publisher: Three Rivers Press, 1995

ISBN US: 978-1400082773
ISBN UK: 978-1847670915

12+

DREAMS FROM MY FATHER
A STORY OF RACE AND INHERITANCE

Synopsis: *Dreams from My Father* begins with a telephone call from Nairobi telling a twenty-one year old Barack Obama, Jr. that his father Barack, Sr. has died. This book is the story of what led to that point in Barack, Jr.'s life, and of the soul searching from a man of "divided inheritance" that followed.

Born in Honolulu, Hawaii, to a white mother, Ann Dunham from Kansas, and a black Kenyan, Barack Obama, Sr., Barack, Jr. tells of his formative years after his parent's split when he was two, of his student days at Columbia and Harvard Law School, and of his first job on a church community project. Throughout this journey, Barack becomes increasingly aware of racial tensions in America in the latter part of the twentieth century. Soon he wants more than just family hand-me-down stories about his father, which sees him traveling to Kenya, where the book ends in an emotional finale.

Review: Importantly, *Dreams from My Father* was written when Obama was thirty-three, well before he entered the political arena. As a result there is an honesty and candor to this memoir, which is almost unbecoming in a politician: he makes mistakes, he tells of his anger with the black church leaders of the community center in his first job, he admits to using marijuana and "maybe a little blow." That he analyses such behavior, and applies it as a life lesson, is more than refreshing to hear in a world of politicians who don't seem to learn.

Widely acknowledged as being told with a novelist's eye for detail, an engaging authorial voice, and, above all, a sparky intelligence, this first book from the first African-American President of the United States of America lends him the status of cult legend to his already many-feathered cap.

FURTHER READING: *The Audacity of Hope*
SEE ALSO: *Selected Speeches and Writings*
(Abraham Lincoln)

500 ESSENTIAL CULT BOOKS

135

REAL LIVES
Top 10 Classics

★
★ **Writer:** Art Spiegelman
★ **Publisher:** Penguin, 2003
★

ISBN US: 978-0394747231
ISBN UK: 978-0141014081

15+ # MAUS A SURVIVOR'S TALE, VOLUMES 1 AND 2

Plot: Art Spiegelman, an American cartoonist, speaks to his father Vladek about his experiences as a victim of Nazi Germany's "Final Solution." Following the invasion of their native Poland, Jewish Vladek and his wife Anja struggle to survive; father tells son about the horrendous circumstances of occupied Europe, the ghettos and the concentration camps, in a series of conversations. At the same time, Art and his French wife Françoise have to work out how to deal with the aging, difficult Vladek, and Art has to find a visual way of relating his father's experiences without trivializing them.

Review: This narrative would be compelling in any form, but Spiegelman's stark art—much more accomplished than it seems at first glance—and ruthless honesty make this one of the most memorable testimonies of the long-term effects of the Nazis' crimes. The courageous decision to portray the different peoples of Europe as different animals (Jews are mice, Germans cats, Poles pigs, and so on) works brilliantly, simultaneously establishing a visual shorthand and reminding the reader of the Nazis' crude racial stereotyping, and Vladek's not-quite-perfect English is a convincing voice for witness of the most dreadful crimes.

Comics had addressed serious themes before this, yet the two volumes of *Maus* took the art form to another level of seriousness and complexity. A must-read.

FURTHER READING: *In the Shadow of No Towers*
SEE ALSO: *Persepolis* (Marjane Satrapi)

★

Writer: Adolf Hitler
Publisher: 1925 (first volume);
1927 (second volume)

ISBN US: 978-1593640064
ISBN UK: 978-8172241643

15+

MEIN KAMPF (MY STRUGGLE)

Synopsis: Known to historians as "two volumes and 500-odd pages of repetitive, ranting, dull diatribe," *Mein Kampf* is part autobiography, part summary of Hitler's *Weltanschauung*. It came to being as a result of his imprisonment in 1923 for his failed Munich "Beer Hall Putsch," the time in jail allowing him to dictate its contents to Rudolf Hess.

We learn of his key notion of *Volksgemeinschaft*—that the German race, being superior to the rest of the world, may "someday become lord of the earth." The democratic Weimar Republic, the postwar Treaty of Versaille, and communism all come in for heavy criticism, anticipating Hitler's future foreign policy and election slogans. Meanwhile, "the Jewish question" is a nasty leitmotif running through the book; Hitler's suggestion that Jews be "forced to submit to poison gas," and his outspoken quest to "acquire foreign territory," leave no doubt as to his nefarious aims.

Review: In terms of autobiography, we don't learn much here, other than examples of Hitler's self-glorification. Nor does it become clear just why he came to have such radically abhorrent views. Why read this book, then, you might wonder? For an insight into the mind of the most reviled dictator in history; that is one reason. Second, it's a key cult text (like it or not, cult has many definitions, and *Mein Kampf*'s being favored by a minority of neo-Nazis makes this book so). Thirdly, and most significantly perhaps, we can look back in anger at our forefathers and wonder in stupefied horror at how they missed the warning signs of the blatant anti-Semitic, anti-democratic, warmongering writings contained within this vile tome's pages. Bombastic and racist—but, unfortunately, an important book.

FURTHER READING: Two volumes of drivel
are all the Führer managed
SEE ALSO: *Hitler: The Definitive Biography*
(John Toland)

★ **Writer:** James Frey
★ **Publisher:** Doubleday, 2003

ISBN US: 978-0307276902
ISBN UK: 978-0719561023

18+ A MILLION LITTLE PIECES

A Million
Little Pieces

James Frey

With Notes from the Author and from the Publisher

Synopsis: *A Million Little Pieces* is James Frey's memoir of his time in a drug and alcohol treatment center. "I am an Alcoholic and I am a drug Addict and I am a criminal" repeats through the book like a sort of mantra, giving you an idea of the issues the author endures as he tries to confront his agonizing addictions, which he gives a nickname: "The Fury."

Review: It says a lot about a book that, when you finish it, your first thought is to press it into someone else's hand—it was just such a compulsion by hundreds of thousands of readers that saw *A Million Little Pieces* canonized by the media as an instant cult classic. The memoir was particularly lauded by addicts who admired its gut-wrenching honesty and its potential to change the lives of its readers.

Imagine, then, the rage when two journalists discovered that some, if not much, of Frey's book was a fabrication. The publisher, Doubleday, initially stood by their man. Over time, though, their author was forced to admit that he had written from memory and that several times his memory had failed.

Whatever your feelings about this controversy, it's a dead cert that it will only add to the book's cult status—whether it deserves this label or not. Some would say not. For, even if the book sold massively, there are those who feel the noughties buzzword "overshare" was invented to describe Frey's fictionalized memoir: *A Million Little Pieces* might well, they'd argue, have been best kept to A Thousand.

FURTHER READING: *Bright Shiny Morning*
SEE ALSO: *A Fan's Notes* (Richard Exley)

★
★
★
★

Writer: Ernest Hemingway
Publisher: Scribner, 1964

ISBN US: 978-1416591313
ISBN UK: 978-0099909408

12+

A MOVEABLE FEAST

A Moveable Feast

THE RESTORED EDITION

ERNEST HEMINGWAY

With a personal foreword by Patrick Hemingway
and introduced and edited by Seán Hemingway

A Moveable Feast

Synopsis: *A Moveable Feast* is Ernest Hemingway's post-humously published memoir of the years 1921–1926 when he lived in Paris with his first wife, Hadley, and their young son. It was an exciting time, the city playing host to a constellation of literary expatriates—many of whom were of Hemingway's acquaintance.

The cold and hungry artist living in a foreign city is exquisitely evoked: we observe Hemingway in the garret where he worked, surviving in the daytime on chestnuts roasted on the fire, a glug of Kirsch, and fistfuls of mandarins (which had to be taken home each night or they would freeze). In the evenings Hadley and Ernest eat in the cheapest cafés of their *arrondissement*, pressing their noses to the windows of the fancier bistros, where they spy James Joyce and his family dining in style.

Review: These are the years before Hemingway was a literary star—and we are treated to a unique insight into a man finding his feet in his chosen craft. "Write the truest sentence that you know," he tells himself when attempting a short story. "Cut that scroll work or ornament out." This is good stuff, for aspiring writers in particular, but perhaps more interesting are Hemingway's relationships, particularly with the great and good of the period, including Gertrude Stein, Ezra Pound, James Joyce, and F. Scott Fitzgerald. The picture painted of the latter is not a flattering one—his relationship with Zelda, likewise. But the vignettes of Hemingway's dawning friendship with Fitzgerald are truly fascinating and offer some of the funniest moments of the book. Some say Hemingway is overrated, others that he exaggerated the poverty described in the book. Less cynical readers should, however, find great pleasure in this self-portrait of a writer in the first flushes of a glittering literary career.

FURTHER READING: *For Whom the Bell Tolls*;
A Farewell to Arms
SEE ALSO: *Down and Out in Paris and London*
(George Orwell); *Portrait of the Artist as a Young
Man* **(James Joyce)**

★
★ **Writer:** Howard Marks   **ISBN US:** 978-0749395698
★ **Publisher:** Secker and Warburg, 1996   **ISBN UK:** 978-0749395698

18+ # MR. NICE

Synopsis: The autobiography of one of Britain's most notorious—and self-proclaimed "nicest"—drug dealers, Howard Marks, Mr. Nice being one of the forty-three aliases Marks employed during his reign as a big-time—very big time—dealer in marijuana.

Review: It goes without saying that cannabis smokers will love this book. On the other hand, it might be problematic for those who are in the "just say no" camp, considering Marks' view that he's just a man "transporting beneficial herbs from one place to another." In any case, his "crimes" did not go unpunished: after a massive global operation to hunt him down, he was sentenced to twenty-five years at a state penitentiary in Indiana. He served seven.

FURTHER READING: *Señor Nice:*
Straight Life from Wales to South America
SEE ALSO: *Killing Pablo: The Hunt for the Richest, Most Powerful Criminal in History* (Mark Bowden)

Writer: William Shatner
Publisher: Harper Collins, 1994
ISBN US: 978-0061664694
ISBN UK: 978-0061664694

STAR TREK MEMORIES

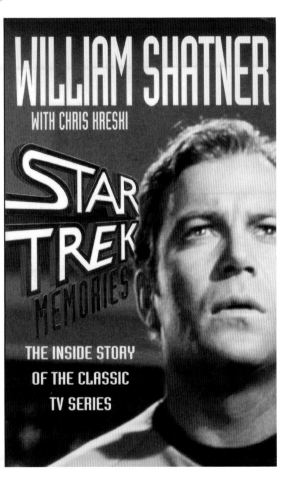

Synopsis: Hard to believe nowadays that the original *Star Trek* series had a painful gestation, a troublesome birth, and a premature, if hard-fought, demise after three seasons in 1969. This life story of the show is recalled here by its top star William Shatner (aka Captain James T. Kirk) with reminiscences and interviews from others in the original cast and crew. The late Gene Roddenberry, the show's creator, gets a starring role, "brilliant, absolutely incontrovertibly brilliant," says Shatner. With a global sci-fi brand success to his name, who are we to argue?

The book is also Shatner's personal journey as he faces up to his own arrogance and acceptance of the fact that, whomever he may be, it is not Captain James T. Kirk. Egoism aside, we become quite fond of Shatner as the book develops; he writes with equanimity, charm, and a liberal dose of good humor. (How much of this comes down to coauthor Chris Kreski is hard to say.)

Review: There are anecdotes aplenty to keep the mildest fan amused, while some tidbits are so juicy that they'll have a catnip like effect on the card-carrying, convention-attending, Vulcan-handshaking Trekkies. Who, for instance, told Shatner during an interview for the book, "I have to tell you why I despise you"? (Clue: they shared television's first interracial kiss in the third season of the original series). Why did Nichelle Nichols, who played Uhuru, receive a fan letter from Dr. Martin Luther King, and, finally, what was Shatner's favorite episode?

That's not to mention details on the show's special effects, stories of backstage squabbles, and the revelation that Shatner's relationship with his colleagues was less than cordial, leading him to be at a loss to understand "how more than twenty-five years worth of shared experiences never quite translated into friendships."

FURTHER READING: *Up Till Now: The Autobiography*
SEE ALSO: *Inside Star Trek* (Robert Justman); *I am NOT Spock* (Leonard Nimoy)

★
★
★

Writer: Janet Frame
Publisher: The Women's Press, 1984

ISBN US: 978-0704346932
ISBN UK: 978-0586085868

15+ AN ANGEL AT MY TABLE

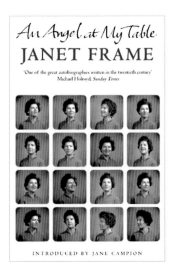

Synopsis: Three volumes of autobiography following the life of New Zealand novelist and poet Janet Frame. The book is perhaps most famous for Frame's account of her time in mental institutions, in one of which she narrowly avoided a lobotomy in 1952 when her first book, *The Lagoon and Other Stories*, won New Zealand's only literary award. A fiercely private individual who shunned publicity, *An Angel at My Table* was Frame's chance to have her "say" about a life of—supposed—mental illness.

Review: Even if you are not keen on autobiography as a genre, there is much to be gotten from Frame's life story. Her journey from childhood to being institutionalized, to being New Zealand's most successful writer is at once engrossing, poignant, and beautifully written.

FURTHER READING: *The Lagoon and Other Stories; Owls Do Cry*
SEE ALSO: *The Bell Jar* (Sylvia Plath)

★
★
★
★

Writer: Charles Mingus and Nel King
Publisher: Knopf, 1971

ISBN US: 978-0679737612
ISBN UK: 978-1841955704

15+ BENEATH THE UNDERDOG
HIS WORLD AS COMPOSED BY MINGUS

Synopsis: Charles Mingus, one of the most important figures in the history of jazz music, tells his life story, from a working-class childhood in Watts, Louisiana, to becoming one of the most important figures in the history of Jazz music. Along the way are digressions about sex, race, music, and love.

Review: Written during one of the most fertile periods of Mingus' career, this is a rollercoaster testament to a life well lived. From the very beginning, it's clear that the erotic is as important to him as the musical, and the book relates his life and (many) loves in vivid detail. Conversational and revealing, this will fascinate jazz fans and lovers of tall tales alike.

FURTHER READING: *More Than a Fake Book*
SEE ALSO: *John Coltrane: His Life and Music* (Lewis Porter)

Writer: Henry Rollins
Publisher: 2.13.61, 1992–2000

ISBN US: 978-1880985557, 978-1880985618, 978-1880985694
ISBN UK: 978-0753510353, 978-0753510407, 978-0753510308

8+

BLACK COFFEE BLUES

Synopsis: Trio of books by the former frontman of hardcore punk band Black Flag. *Black Coffee Blues* (1992), *Black Coffee Blues 2: Do I Come Here Often?* (1996), and *Black Coffee Blues 3: Smile, You're Traveling* (2000). The books mix fiction, poetry, interviews (Jerry Lee Lewis, Isaac Hayes), and essays with travel journals documenting Rollins' trips around the world.

Review: The *Black Coffee* trilogy strips away any misconceptions that touring is glamorous as Rollins charts his progress from 1990 to 1998 and the recording of the Rollins Band's *Come In and Burn*. Rollins is unflinching and uncompromising in everything he writes, even when soul searching, and the volatile writing style has earned his books a strong following.

FURTHER READING: *The Portable Henry Rollins; Solipsist; Unwelcomed Songs: Collected Lyrics 1980–1992*
SEE ALSO: *Our Band Could Be Your Life* (Michael Azerrad); *American Hardcore: A Tribal History* (Steven Blush)

Writer: Craig Thompson
Publisher: Top Shelf, 2003

ISBN US: 978-1891830433
ISBN UK: 978-1891830433

5+

BLANKETS

Plot: Growing up in a Christian fundamentalist family in agricultural central Wisconsin was no joke for the sensitive, artistic author; the young Thompson faces sexual abuse, troubled family relationships, religious intolerance, and his own artistic dilemmas in this graphic autobiography

Review: The first thing that strikes the reader about *Blankets* is the gorgeous monochrome art; Thompson's fluid, elegant lines are the perfect vehicle for this coming-of-age tale, and the eye races across the many pages without tiring. Happily, the story he tells is a deeply moving one—sensitive portraits of his family, and a tender and detailed evocation of first love. Highly recommended, and the perfect book to convince doubters of the potential of the graphic novel form.

an illustrated novel by
CRAIG THOMPSON

FURTHER READING: *Good-bye, Chunky Rice; Carnet de Voyage*
SEE ALSO: *Epileptic* (David B.); *Fun Home* (Alison Bechdel)

★ **Writer:** Chuck Barris
★ **Publisher:** St. Martin's Press, 1984

ISBN US: 978-0786888085
ISBN UK: 978-0091890377

15+

CONFESSIONS OF A DANGEROUS MIND
AN UNAUTHORIZED AUTOBIOGRAPHY

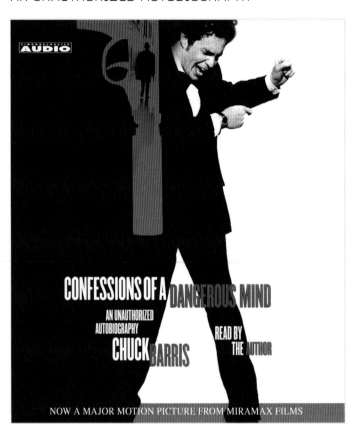

Synopsis: After writing a couple of hit records, Chuck Barris created and produced *The Dating Game* for ABC, followed it with *The Newlywed Game* and several others before he created and hosted the *The Gong Show*, which lasted only two seasons. At a low in the 1980s, Barris penned an auto-biography in which he claimed that he had been leading a double life, using trips abroad on behalf of his shows as cover for assassinating enemies of the United States on behalf of the CIA.

Review: While the book sank on its original release and his later autobiography failed to mention that he was a hitman,

Barris kept up the myth of his CIA connections, even when it was patently a fabrication. Treated as a novel, it's a reasonably entertaining piece of fiction, although not as good as his earlier fictionalized biographical novel *You and Me, Babe*.

FURTHER READING: *The Game Show King: A Confession; Bad Grass Never Dies: More Confessions of a Dangerous Mind*
SEE ALSO: *Killing Hope* (William Blum); *Legacy of Ashes: The History of the CIA* (Tim Weiner)

★
★
★
★
Writer: Yoshihiro Tatsumi
Publisher: U.S. Edition,
Drawn & Quarterly, 2009

ISBN US: 978-1897299746
ISBN UK: 978-1897299746

12+

A DRIFTING LIFE

Synopsis: Narrated by Hiroshi Katsumi, a vaguely disguised version of the author, *A Drifting Life* is Tatsumi's visual memoir of his artistic evolution from boyhood manga obsessive to one of the creators of the "Gekija" group. In the foreground, both plot-wise and graphically, are Japan's changing history and culture during the fifteen years covered by the book (1945 to 1960).

Review: The eight-hundred-plus pages here may deter non-manga lovers, but it shouldn't: this snapshot of Tatsumi's life is fascinating, and the insight into the darker, more adult side of manga, which he named Gekija, is enlightening. Non-comic-book lovers need not fear the illustrations either; simple black and white lines draw the reader in and don't detract from Katsumi/Tatsumi's engaging text.

FURTHER READING: *The Push Man and Other Stories;*
Abandon the Old in Tokyo; Good-Bye
SEE ALSO: *Astro Boy Volumes One and Two* (Osamu Tezuka)

★
★
★
★
Writer: David B.
Publisher: L'Association, 2003

ISBN US: 978-0375714689
ISBN UK: 978-0224079204

15+

EPILEPTIC

Synopsis: 1960s France is the setting for this autobiographical memoir of a family life overshadowed by the severe epilepsy of the author's older brother. The boys play out all the normal rivalries of brotherhood, but find it difficult to fit in with their contemporaries; meanwhile, their parents, increasingly desperate and isolated, seek a cure for their son—falling victim to an unsympathetic medical establishment and ineffective alternative practitioners.

Review: David B.'s memoir is notable for its ruthless honesty; he is scathing in his treatment of the various healers to whom his parents turned in their quest for a cure for his brother, and he doesn't attempt to cover up his own less-than-supportive behavior either. The monochrome art is similarly uncompromising, with nightmarish imagery inspired by his brother's condition dominating the page and invading the characters' lives. This is a simple tragedy—of an isolated family trying to do the right thing—uniquely told.

FURTHER READING: *Babel*
SEE ALSO: *Persepolis* (Marjane Satrapi); *Fun Home* (Alison Bechdel)

★
★
★

Writer: Stephen Davis
Publisher: William Morrow, 1985

ISBN US: 978-0425182130
ISBN UK: 978-0330438599

18+ # HAMMER OF THE GODS

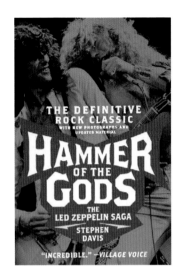

Synopsis: Led Zeppelin—fronted by a Satanist, and with a chaotic alcoholic on drums—were the biggest rock draw of the mid 1970s, and their U.S. tours became notorious for anarchic behavior. Davis draws heavily on the account of Richard Cole, the band's ex-road manager, and tells tales of stupendous drinking, life-threatening drug abuse, orgies, hotel room trashing . . . and indoor motorcycling.

Review: It's worth pointing out that all of the surviving members of the band have gone on the record to criticize the book's lack of accuracy, and that Cole himself has reputedly admitted that he embroidered many of the stories he told Davis. Who cares? The stories are great, the myth lives on; this was the rock book that fed a million teenaged dreams of stardom and bad behavior.

FURTHER READING: *Walk This Way: The Autobiography of Aerosmith*
SEE ALSO: *I'm with the Band* (Pamela Des Barres)

★
★
★
★

Writer: Hunter S. Thompson
Publisher: Random House, 1966

ISBN US: 978-0679603313
ISBN UK: 978-0141187457

18+ # HELL'S ANGELS
THE STRANGE AND TERRIBLE SAGA
OF THE OUTLAW MOTORCYCLE GANGS

PENGUIN BOOKS

HELL'S ANGELS

HUNTER S. THOMPSON

Synopsis: The original Hell's Angels grew out of the motorcycle gangs of ex-servicemen that sprang up in California after World War II. Inspiring fear in settled communities, they were an object of fascination to a young Hunter S. Thompson. Over the course of a year, he managed to become close to the Angels and their leader Sonny Barger, describing their rituals and lifestyle in vivid fly-on-the-wall prose. But it ended badly . . .

Review: This was Thompson's first published book and shows all of the virtues that would make him one of the most notorious cult authors. He writes himself into the story, is frequently drunk, is fascinated by his subjects' outlaw mystique, and offers a fascinating, at times repellent, insight into one of the most important countercultural movements.

FURTHER READING: *Fear and Loathing in Las Vegas*
SEE ALSO: *Hell's Angel* (Sonny Barger)

★
★
★
★

Writer: David Simon
Publisher: Houghton Mifflin, 1991

ISBN US: 978-0805080759
ISBN UK: 978-1847673121

15+

HOMICIDE
A YEAR ON THE KILLING STREETS

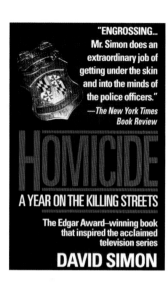

"ENGROSSING...
Mr. Simon does an
extraordinary job of
getting under the skin
and into the minds of
the police officers."
—The New York Times
Book Review

HOMICIDE
A YEAR ON THE KILLING STREETS

The Edgar Award–winning book
that inspired the acclaimed
television series
DAVID SIMON

Synopsis: A month-by-month portrait in the life of the Baltimore homicide department, warts and all. Simon is a fly on the wall, following fifteen homicide detectives, three sergeants, and a lieutenant in their attempts to solve the 234 murders that took place in the city in 1988.

Review: At once eye-opening, tragic, and darkly funny, this is an inspiration for all writers of police procedurals. Winner of the 1992 Edgar Award in the Best Fact Crime category, it is now hailed by many as a true crime classic, and is an essential document of urban America in the twentieth century.

FURTHER READING: *The Corner:*
A Year in the Life of an Inner-city Neighborhood
SEE ALSO: Anything by George Pelecanos,
perhaps starting with *The Big Blowdown*

★
★

Writer: Toby Young
Publisher: Little Brown, 2001

ISBN US: 978-0306812279
ISBN UK: 978-0349114859

15+

HOW TO LOSE FRIENDS
AND ALIENATE PEOPLE

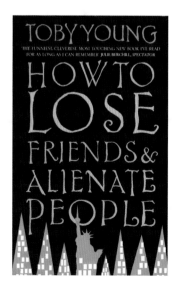

TOBY YOUNG
THE FUNNIEST, CLEVEREST, MOST TOUCHING NEW BOOK I'VE READ
FOR AS LONG AS I CAN REMEMBER' JULIE BURCHILL, SPECTATOR

HOW TO
LOSE
FRIENDS &
ALIENATE
PEOPLE

Synopsis: After the collapse of *Modern Review* (which he founded and co-edited) in 1995, Toby Young moved to New York and joined the staff of *Vanity Fair*. Instead of taking Manhattan by storm as he'd intended, he was plunged into the superficial social whirl where the only important things are who you are dating and which celebrities you know. Young failed dismally to fit into the status-obsessed world of American publishing.

Review: Julie Burchill dubbed Young a "spoiled child" but admired his writing greatly. Young does not hold back on his own failings: he is pushy, desperate, acts inappropriately at work, tries to chat up uninterested models, crashes parties, puts the wrong questions to actors, and drinks excessively. The book survives its unappealing hero by packing in anecdotes both scathing and funny.

FURTHER READING: *The Sound of No Hands Clapping*
SEE ALSO: *Seemed Like a Good Idea at the Time* (David Goodwillie);
That's Me in the Corner (Andrew Collins)

★ **Writer:** Orhan Pamuk
★ **Publisher:** Knopf, 2005 (originally in Turkish
★ as Istanbul: Hatiralar ve Sehir, 2003)
★

ISBN US: 978-1400033881
ISBN UK: 978-0571218332

12+

ISTANBUL MEMORIES AND THE CITY

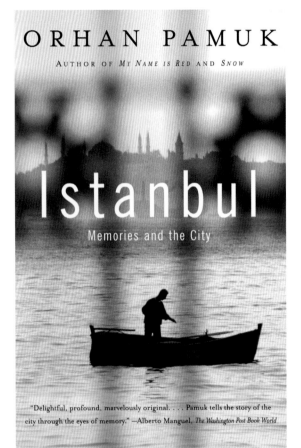

Synopsis: Born in Istanbul into a secular family, Pamuk studied architecture briefly before taking a degree in journalism. His first novel was published in 1982, although the first English language translations of his work did not appear until 1990. *Istanbul* is a memoir of Pamuk's early life, embedded in an extended essay about his perception of the city he grew up in, a city with a rich cultural and artistic history now filled with a melancholy.

Review: Multiple award-winning author, winner of the Nobel Prize for Literature in 2006, Pamuk is feted internationally while being seen as a controversial writer in his native Turkey for discussing the country's checkered history. *Istanbul* is a revealing and insightful study of both the city and the author, with personal memories interspersed with essays on writers and artists connected with the city.

FURTHER READING: *The Black Book*;
My Name Is Red; Snow
SEE ALSO: *Istanbul: The Imperial City* (John Freely);
The Rough Guide to Istanbul (Terry Richardson)

★
★
★
★
★

15+

Writer: Ernesto "Che" Guevara
Publisher: First edition in English, Verso, 1995

ISBN US: 978-1920888107
ISBN UK: 978-0007172337

THE MOTORCYCLE DIARIES

Synopsis: Before Cuba, before Bolivia, before the T-shirts, posters, and baseball caps, before, that is, the iconic image, was the young Ernesto "Che" Guevera and his road trip by motorcycle with a friend across Latin America in 1952. This—part travelogue, part memoir, part political awakening—is the record of that nine-month trip.

Review: "*Das Kapital* meets *Easy Rider*" is how the book was marketed by the original publisher. It's a fair assessment: we have on the one hand the messy awakening of a Marxist hero as he comes into "close contact with poverty, hunger and disease." On the other, there is the squalor and smelly clothes of the rough life on the road. It's not a stylistically rewarding book, but it is a fascinating one. A must read and one that explains Guevara's powerful appeal.

FURTHER READING: *Guerilla Warfare*
SEE ALSO: *Das Kapital* (Karl Marx)

★ **Writer:** Kevin Smith
★ **Publisher:** Titan Books, 2007 (revised 2009)
★

ISBN US: 978-1848564978
ISBN UK: 978-1848564978

18+ # MY BORING-ASS LIFE

THE UNCOMFORTABLY CANDID DIARY OF KEVIN SMITH

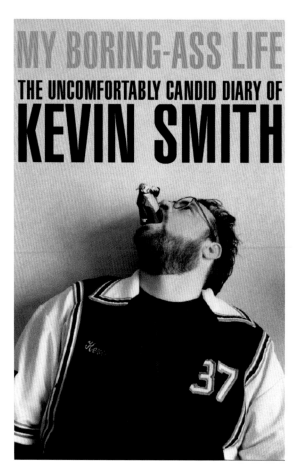

Synopsis: An askew Dear Diary look at the life of film-director and actor Kevin Smith between 2005–2007 as he works on *Clerks II*, a follow-up to his cult hit debut movie, guests in *Die Hard 4.0*, watches TV, goes to the bathroom, has sex, and runs into various Hollywood celebrities. Smith has a comparatively large income, a family he loves, a successful career, and a life that is far from boring.

Review: Densely packed with detail and humor, Smith's book offers plenty of insight into his working method and revisits some of his movies (*Mallrats* in particular) to take a critical look at their failures (not always Smith's fault). The strongest section deals with Jason Mewes, Smith's regular costar (Jay to Smith's Silent Bob), whose drug addiction almost destroys their long friendship.

FURTHER READING: *Silent Bob Speaks: The Collected Writings of Kevin Smith; Shootin' the Sh*t with Kevin Smith*
SEE ALSO: *An Askew View: The Films of Kevin Smith* (John Kenneth Muir); *The Dueling Personas of Kevin Smith* (Matthew Miller)

Writer: Jerry Hopkins and Danny Sugerman
Publisher: Warner Books, 1980

ISBN US: 978-0446697330
ISBN UK: 978-0859651387

★★★★

■5+

NO ONE HERE GETS OUT ALIVE

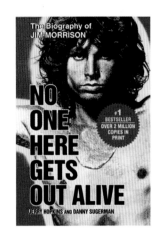

Synopsis: Jim Morrison, poet, lyricist, and singer, was the charismatic frontman of The Doors, founded in 1965. They released a number of hugely successful albums, of which *The Doors*, *Strange Days*, and *L.A. Women* are considered classics. From the third album (*Waiting for the Sun*) on, Morrison became more unpredictable onstage and in the studio due to drug and alcohol dependency. Morrison moved to Paris where he died in July 1971, aged twenty-seven.

Review: If anyone had the inside track on rock band The Doors it was Danny Sugerman, who began working for the group at the age of twelve, answering fan mail. Jerry Hopkins was already a leading writer of rock history and the two produced what is perhaps the definitive rock biography.

FURTHER READING: *The Lizard King: The Essential Jim Morrison* (Hopkins); *The Doors: The Illustrated History* (Sugerman)
SEE ALSO: *The Lords and The New Creatures* (Jim Morrison); *Riders on the Storm* (John Desmore); *Light My Fire* (Ray Manzarek)

Writer: Marjane Satrapi
Publisher: Jonathan Cape, 2003

ISBN US: 978-0224080392
ISBN UK: 978-0375422300

★★★★

■12+

PERSEPOLIS

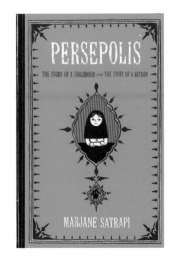

Synopsis: *Persepolis* is Marjane Satrapi's graphic autobiography. Her bourgeois childhood in Tehran is depicted against the background of the Iranian revolution and bitter ideological conflicts; later, she studies in Austria while Iran and Iraq are at war. Her family is a constant source of inspiration and encouragement, but eventually the oppressive religious regime forces Marjane to consider emigration to the west.

Review: This monochrome graphic memoir achieved more mainstream critical acclaim than any other comic since *Maus*. Like Spiegelman's, Satrapi's art initially seems naïve—although it displays a mastery of composition, pacing, and characterization—and the book tackles similar themes of loss, oppression, exile, and filial bonds. Above all, *Persepolis* successfully opens an Iranian experience—complicated, passionate, human—to a world used to stereotypes of fundamentalism and repression.

FURTHER READING: *Persepolis 2: The Story of a Return*
SEE ALSO: *Maus* (Art Spiegelmann); *American Born Chinese* (Gene Luen Yang)

★
★
★
★

Writer: Robert Rodriguez
Publisher: Dutton, 1995

ISBN US: 978-0452271876
ISBN UK: 978-0571178919

15+

REBEL WITHOUT A CREW

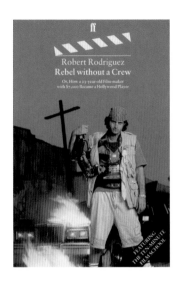

Synopsis: Independent filmmaker Robert Rodriguez relates—through the journal he kept at the time—how he created the movie *El Mariachi*, shot for $7,000, the money mostly raised by subjecting himself to medical experimentation at a research hospital. To keep within budget, Rodriguez was his own cameraman, special-effects creator, and editor, and he shot the whole movie in just twenty-one days. The book also includes the film's script with a running commentary.

Review: From concept through production to selling the movie in Hollywood, Rodriguez records his experiences in this witty, straight-from-the-hip guide to making movies on the cheap, with plenty of tricks of the trade offered along the way. Since he was his own crew, he can offer views on every aspect of the filmmaking process.

FURTHER READING: *Roadracers; Grindhouse* (with Quentin Tarantino)
SEE ALSO: *Microbudget Hollywood: Budgeting (and Making) Feature Films for $50,000 to $500,000* (Gaines and Rhodes)

★
★
★

Writer: Antonio Gramsci
Publisher: First edition of edited selections in English, Lawrence Wishart, 1970

ISBN US: 978-0717803972
ISBN UK: 978-0853152804

12+

SELECTIONS FROM THE PRISON NOTEBOOKS

Synopsis: Antonio Gramsci was a founding member of the Communist Party in Italy and also once its leader. While confined in prison for eight years from 1926 at the behest of Mussolini, Gramsci wrote his notebooks: a collection of Marxist writings about Italian history, philosophy, politics, and culture, and the role of the intellectual. The collection recommended includes his most famous notebooks, *The Modern Prince* ("brief notes on Machiavelli's politics") and *Americanism and Fordism*.

Review: A scholarly book, vast in its intellect as well as its page length, this should only be approached if you are seriously interested in Marxist or cultural theory.

FURTHER READING: If you are left undaunted by Volume One of the *Notebooks*, try Volumes Two and Three
SEE ALSO: *The Communist Manifesto* (Karl Marx)

★
★
★
★

Writer: Philip Norman
Publisher: Elm Tree Books, 1981

ISBN US: 978-0684830674
ISBN UK: 978-0743235655

12+

SHOUT!
THE BEATLES IN THEIR GENERATION

Synopsis: In the summer of 1957, fifteen-year-old Paul McCartney joined John Lennon in a band called The Quarrymen in their native Liverpool. George Harrison subsequently joined, then bass player Stuart Sutcliffe and, shortly before taking up a residency in Hamburg, drummer Pete Best. By then they had changed their name to The Beatles. Spotted and signed by Brian Epstein, massive success ensued . . . and eventually a messy break-up.

Review: Elegantly written and meticulously researched, Norman is particularly good on how it must have felt for the band to be at the center of a media and fan frenzy. A vibrant chronicle of sixties pop and culture.

FURTHER READING: *The Road Goes on Forever; Symphony for the Devil: The Rolling Stones Story; John Lennon: The Life*
SEE ALSO: *The Beatles* (Hunter Davies); *Revolution in the Head: The Beatles' Records and the Sixties* (Ian MacDonald)

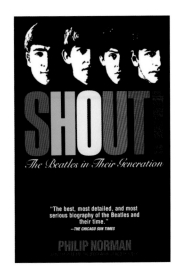

"The best, most detailed, and most serious biography of the Beatles and their time."
—*THE CHICAGO SUN TIMES*

PHILIP NORMAN

500 ESSENTIAL CULT BOOKS

153

REAL LIVES
Best of the Rest

★
★

Writer: Giacomo Casanova
Publisher: Brockhaus, 1822–1828

ISBN US: 978-0140439151
ISBN UK: 978-0140439151

15+

THE STORY OF MY LIFE

Synopsis: Rampant with amorous activity, the reminiscences of the world's most infamous Lothario don't disappoint, detailing countless cavortings with, among others, nuns, prostitutes, and noblewomen. However, it would be unfair to reduce Casanova's story to that of his libido: he also details a string of adventures, from his youth in Venice to his time in, and escape from, prison, and his many encounters with European writers and intellectuals.

Review: "Economy in pleasure is not to my taste," Casanova writes. Economy in writing wasn't either; even the abridged version of this lengthy memoir is overlong. Still, it's the kind of book you can dip in and out of, and you can be assured that at every perusal, you will find a yarn, opinion, or remark of interest.

FURTHER READING: With twelve volumes of autobiography under his belt, you might be surprised Casanova wrote plays, essays, and a novel, but it's the memoirs that remain of interest
SEE ALSO: *Henry and June* (Anaïs Nin)

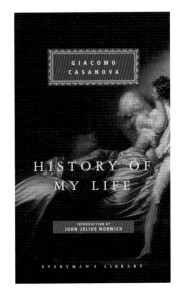

GIACOMO CASANOVA

HISTORY OF MY LIFE

INTRODUCTION BY
JOHN JULIUS NORWICH

EVERYMAN'S LIBRARY

★
★ **Writer:** Robert F Kennedy   **ISBN US:** 978-0393318340
★ **Publisher:** W.W. Norton, 1969   **ISBN UK:** 978-0393098969

12+ THIRTEEN DAYS
A MEMOIR OF THE CUBAN MISSILE CRISIS

Synopsis: The Cold War lasted fifty years, but the short span of the Cuban missile crisis was undoubtedly the point at which the peace between the USSR and U.S. held most tenuously. For that period (the "thirteen days" of the book's title) the world held its breath.

Review: The Kennedy brothers—John, President of the United States, and Robert, Attorney General and perhaps John's closest adviser—were at the very heart of the crisis. Told by some of their advisors that a "limited" nuclear war was the way to avert the threat posed by Soviet missiles on Cuba, they held firm to pursuing other solutions. Kennedy's memoir, written only a few years after the event, is a vivid testament to the tension the men, and the military, were under, and the agonizing moral choices faced by those in command.

FURTHER READING: *The Enemy Within*
SEE ALSO: *The Week the World Stood Still* (Sheldon M. Stern)

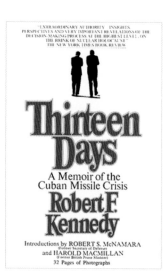

★
★ **Writer:** Deborah Curtis   **ISBN US:** 978-0571239566
★ **Publisher:** Faber & Faber, 1995 **ISBN UK:** 978-0571239566
★

15+ TOUCHING FROM A DISTANCE

Synopsis: Ian Curtis was the front man of Joy Division, one of the most important bands of the post-punk era, which has a legion of fans to this day. He was a troubled man suffering from epilepsy and the side-effects of his medication; he was also uncomfortable with his growing star-status and prone to depression. *Touching from a Distance* is his widow Deborah's memoir of their life together.

Review: Deborah Curtis writes with a clear idea of her late husband's cultural importance (his lyrics are reprinted at the end of the book), and although she is not the person to turn to for a fully rounded analysis, she tells the sad story of their relationship, vividly evokes Curtis' magnetic presence as a performer, and gives a gripping insight into the difficulties of life with such an intensely creative personality.

FURTHER READING: *This is Deborah Curtis' only book*
SEE ALSO: *Joy Division: Piece by Piece* (Paul Morley)

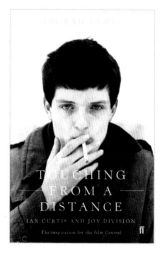

Writer: Christopher Hitchens
Publisher: Verso, 2001

ISBN US: 978-1859843987
ISBN UK: 978-1859843987

15+

THE TRIAL OF HENRY KISSINGER

Synopsis: In this passionately argued polemic, Hitchens accuses Henry Kissinger, U.S. Secretary of State for much of the 1970s, of a series of crimes, both against the people of Laos, Cambodia, Chile, and elsewhere—and against the U.S. constitution. Following his policies, U.S. forces and agents committed war crimes and murder on a massive scale, supplying arms to oppressive regimes and condemning millions to dictatorship and chaos. Hitchens argues that Kissinger should face trial for his part in these atrocities.

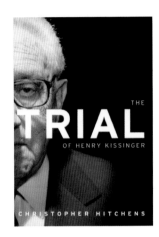

Review: This book is, of course, misnamed, for it consists of the case for the prosecution. It doesn't contain anything in the way of new research or startling new findings: Hitchens is a commentator, not an investigative journalist. But in its synthesis of matters of public record and Kissinger's own arrogant, unconvincing, and evasive rebuttals, it presents a compelling picture of amoral superpower *realpolitik* out of control. Shocking and eye-opening.

FURTHER READING: *Love, Poverty, and War: Journeys and Essays*
SEE ALSO: *Kissinger: A Biography* (Walter Isaacson)

Writer: Stanley Booth
Publisher: Chicago Review Press, 1984

ISBN US: 978-1556524004
ISBN UK: 978-1556524004

15+

THE TRUE ADVENTURES OF THE ROLLING STONES

Synopsis: In the fall of 1969 the Rolling Stones embarked on a coast-to-coast U.S. tour that would come to symbolize the end of the sixties era of peace and love. At the height of their musical powers, and freely taking advantage of the perks of their fame, they allowed Booth, a young journalist, to document the tour from the inside.

Review: Southerner Booth knew and loved black American music as much as the Stones did (he had been in the studio when Otis Redding recorded "Dock of the Bay"), was an incisive observer of human nature, and understood the extraordinary effect their music had on American youth, riven as it was by the stresses of culture clash, racism, and war. Brilliantly evoking the fevered atmosphere of their concerts and the chaos behind the scenes, he draws the narratives toward the twin tragedies of Altamont and Brian Jones' premature death. Perhaps the best book about rock 'n' roll ever written.

FURTHER READING: *Rythm Oil*
SEE ALSO: *Exile on Main Street* (Robert Greenfield)

★
★
★
★

Writer: Cyril Connolly
Publisher: 1944

ISBN US: 978-0892550586
ISBN UK: 978-0892550586

12+

THE UNQUIET GRAVE
A WORD CYCLE BY PALINURUS

Synopsis: Connolly was one of the leading men of letters of his time: as a book reviewer, he was hugely influential, he was well connected, and he wrote a popular memoir. But he never completed the great novel that he—and others—believed he was capable of, and never established himself as an artist in his own right. This is his response to that situation; a collection of thoughts, quotations, aphorisms, and memoir.

Review: This is a book that stays with the reader and inspires the same devotion that a close friend does. As a companion, it's funny, wise, kind, and philosophical, resigned to fate: "Life is a maze in which we take the wrong turning before we have learnt to walk." Hemingway called it "A book which, no matter how many readers it will ever have, will never have enough."

FURTHER READING: *Enemies of Promise*
SEE ALSO: *Cyril Connolly: A Life* (Jeremy Lewis)

The Unquiet Grave
A Word Cycle by Palinurus
(Cyril Connolly)

"It is a book which,
no matter how many readers it will ever have,
will never have enough."
—ERNEST HEMINGWAY

★
★
★

Writer: Art Linson
Publisher: Bloomsbury, 2002

ISBN US: 978-0802143389
ISBN UK: 978-0747562054

15+

WHAT JUST HAPPENED?
BITTER HOLLYWOOD TALES
FROM THE FRONT LINE

Synopsis: Linsom, the producer of *Car Wash*, *Fast Times at Ridgemont High*, and *The Untouchables* recounts the behind-the-scenes spats and stupidity from some of his less successful movies. *The Edge* comes in for particular study as it lost its first choice of star, Robert De Niro, and hired an overweight, bearded Alec Baldwin to play a svelte fashion photographer.

Review: Anecdotal, comic, and occasionally blunt, Art Linson's tell-all is an entertaining look at Hollywood from an insider who has had both production successes and failures on his resume.

FURTHER READING: *A Pound of Flesh:*
Perilous Tales of How to Produce Movies in Europe
SEE ALSO: *Adventures in the Screen Trade* (William Goldman)

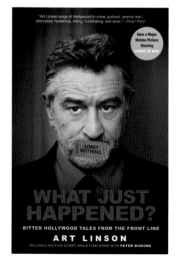

"Art Linson sings of Hollywood in a low, guttural, animal wail, alternately hysterical, biting, humiliating, and wise."—Sean Penn

Now a Major
Motion Picture
Starring
ROBERT DE NIRO

ADMIT
NOTHING

WHAT JUST
HAPPENED?
BITTER HOLLYWOOD TALES FROM THE FRONT LINE
ART LINSON
INCLUDES HIS FILM SCRIPT AND A FOREWORD WITH PETER BISKIND

★
★
★

Writer: Julia Phillips
Publisher: Random House, 1991

ISBN US: 978-0451205339
ISBN UK: 978-0571216239

8+

YOU'LL NEVER EAT LUNCH IN THIS TOWN AGAIN

Synopsis: Hollywood producer Julia Phillips had worked on blockbuster movies *The Sting*, *Taxi Driver*, and *Close Encounters* before cocaine dependency caused her to fall from favor; she was fired from the latter. François Truffaut (one of the film's stars) described her as incompetent.

Review: A "573-page primal scream" was the view of *Newsweek*. Phillips was ostracized when the book was published, but it spent thirteen weeks on the *New York Times'* bestseller chart. Although heavily edited before publication, her memoirs mercilessly chart her own addiction, the drug culture, and the "boy's club" mentality of the movie industry, as well as the foibles of the Hollywood elite around her.

FURTHER READING: *Driving under the Affluence*
SEE ALSO: *Adventures in the Screen Trade* (William Goldman);
Easy Riders, Raging Bulls (Peter Biskind)

★
★
★
★

Writer: Robert Graysmith
Publisher: St. Martin's Press, 1986

ISBN US: 978-1845765316
ISBN UK: 978-0425212189

18+

ZODIAC

Synopsis: One of America's most notorious serial murderers, "Zodiac" killed at least five people in and around San Francisco in the late 1960s and 1970s; the police, though, were unable to find the killer, and the investigation lapsed. The book tells the story of how Graysmith, cartoonist on the *San Francisco Chronicle*, became obsessed with the case, working on the teasing messages that the killer sent, burrowing through old police files, and eventually deducing that one of the main suspects was the probable killer.

Review: This true-life detective story has all the ingredients of a classic crime novel: a crusading, obsessed amateur detective; a ruthless killer; mysterious clues; narrow escapes; police incompetence; everything, in fact, except the final confession from the unmasked killer. Graysmith's prime suspect died in 1992, so that will never come, but this remains a gripping read.

FURTHER READING: *Zodiac Unmasked: The Identity of America's Most Elusive Serial Killer Revealed*
SEE ALSO: *This is the Zodiak Speaking* (Michael D. Kelleher);
In Cold Blood (Truman Capote)

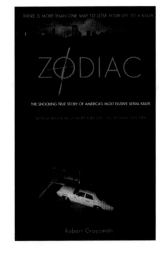

Yann Martel
Life of Pi
A NOVEL

quite
ugly
one
morning
christopher
brookmyre

CARTER
BEATS
THE
DEVIL
'Addictive' Guardian
'Electrifying' Independent
Glen David Gold

T

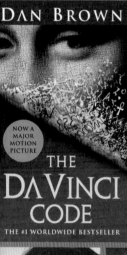

DAN BROWN

NOW A
MAJOR
MOTION
PICTURE

THE
DA VINCI
CODE
THE #1 WORLDWIDE BESTSELLER

jim THOMPSON

"Probably the most chilling and believable
first-person story of a criminally warped mind
I have ever encountered." —Stanley Kubrick

the KILLER

INSIDE ME

John Ball

PAN
books
X 711

IN THE HEAT
OF THE NIGHT

THE NEW YORK T

THE
Eyre

"I think it's CLEVER, wordplay,
LITERARY allusion and
BIBLIOPHILIC. The Eyre Affair
combines elements of
MONTY PYTHON, HARRY
POTTER, STEPHEN
HAWKING and BUFFY THE
VAMPIRE SLAYER...
but its quirky charm..."

THE
NEXT

Jas

A MAJOR TV SERIES
RKLY DREAMING

DEXTER

"Super-ingenious, super-lethal. . . . Parker is super-tough!"
—New York Times Book Review

RICHARD STARK

THE
HUNTER

A PARKER
NOVEL

NEW YORK TIMES BESTSELLING AUTHOR OF MYSTIC RIVER

DENNIS
LEHANE

"HIS VOICE IS AN ORIGINAL." Michael Connelly

A DRINK BEFORE THE WAR

WEAPO
OF CHOI

Worl
a sta

JOHN BIRMIN

Norman Mailer

The Naked and the Dead

A MODERN LIBRARY BOOK

ll the
s of a
assic'
ornby

ch
AND

"What's your name?"

"Fletch."

"What's your full name?"

"Fletcher."

"What's your first name?"

"Irwin. Irwin Fletcher. People call me Fletch."

"Irwin Fletcher, I have a proposition to make to you. I will give you a **thousand dollars** for just listening to it. If you decide to reject the proposition, you take the thousand dollars, go away, and never tell anyone we talked."

"Is it criminal?"

"Of course."

"Fair enough. For a thousand bucks I can listen. What do you want me to do?"

"I want you to murder me."

Fletch said, "Sure."

Fletch

Gregory Mcdonald

NEW YORK TIMES BESTSELLING AUTHOR

Carl Hiaasen

TOURIST SEASON

"WONDERFUL....LIVELY...FUN."
—Tony Hillerman, *New York Times Book Review*

George P.
PELECANOS

"Pelecanos brilliantly captures
debonair ambience of...
perfect of its kind...

the Big
BLOWDOV

WORLD WAR Z

INSTANT
W YORK TIMES
BESTSELLER

AN ORAL HISTORY OF THE ZOMBIE WAR

MAX OOKS

Wilkie Collins

the Woman in White

'One of the best plots in English literature'

GUNSLINGERS, PRIVATE EYES, AND THE ODD GHOST OR TWO

Since time immemorial, storytelling has had the power to shock, excite, and amaze. Consider that in 1719 *Robinson Crusoe*, the first novel in the English language, is an adventure story, and that thrilling tales of derring-do on sea, land, and, eventually, in space have followed it onto book shelves every year.

As time has gone on, the adventure genre has become an increasingly fertile ground for new subgenres: war, westerns, and the ubiquitous crime novel all counting among its literary offspring. Sure, on the surface a book about gunslingers in the Wild West may not seem to have much in common with police procedurals, horror tomes, or spy-thrillers, but in fact they are united by fast-moving plots, plucky heroes, action aplenty, and, of course, they're all thrilling tales—which is why they feature together in this chapter.

the KILLER

THRILLING TALES

★
★
★
★

Writer: John Buchan
Publisher: William Blackwood and Sons, 1915
ISBN US: 978-1842327937
ISBN UK: 978-1853260803

15+

THE 39 STEPS

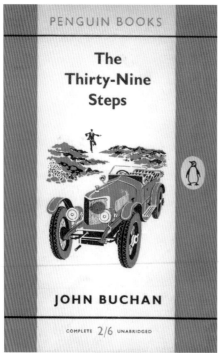

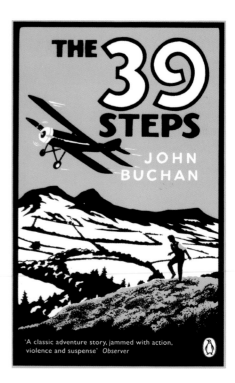

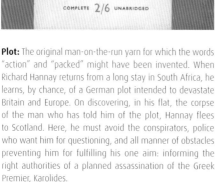

Plot: The original man-on-the-run yarn for which the words "action" and "packed" might have been invented. When Richard Hannay returns from a long stay in South Africa, he learns, by chance, of a German plot intended to devastate Britain and Europe. On discovering, in his flat, the corpse of the man who has told him of the plot, Hannay flees to Scotland. Here, he must avoid the conspirators, police who want him for questioning, and all manner of obstacles preventing him for fulfilling his one aim: informing the right authorities of a planned assassination of the Greek Premier, Karolides.

Review: The Scots have a word for that damp, chilly weather peculiar to their country, "dreich"; it's superbly evoked here and, together with the wild Scottish topography with which Hannay has to contend, serves to increase his sense of isolation and panic. This dramatic tension is one of the best aspects of the novel.

Nitpickers might find the Jerry-bashing and xenophobia uncomfortable, but it would be surprising if a novel to come out of Britain during World War I were anything but. Beyond the realms of credibility is another criticism that might well be levied at the book, to which you have to remember to suspend your disbelief: it's fiction, people!

Hannay went on to have further spying adventures, but *The Thirty-Nine Steps* was the most successful. It's also the most enduring, was hugely influential (anticipating the spy novels of Deighton, Fleming, Le Carré, and that ilk), and comes highly recommended.

FURTHER READING: *Greenmantle* and the other Hannay adventures
SEE ALSO: *The Riddle of the Sands* (Erskine Childers); *Bulldog Drummond* (Herman Cyril McNeile); *The Spy Who Came in from the Cold* (John Le Carré)

★
★
★
★
★

Writer: Stephen King
Publisher: Doubleday, 1974

ISBN US: 978-0385086950
ISBN UK: 978-0450025174

15+

CARRIE

Plot: A high school outcast, Carrie, becomes increasingly aware of her telekinetic powers. Tormented by her peers at school, violently repressed by her religiously zealous mother, she unleashes a terrible revenge in a memorably destructive moment at the high school prom.

From the bloody opening scene set in the school showers, to the punishments doled out by Carrie's mother, to the eerily portentous ending, the book is a succession of alternately realistic and supernatural crises.

Review: Hands up if you were a teenager in the 1970s or 1980s? Hands down if you didn't read Stephen King. Thought so. A universal show of hands is nothing less than the master of horror and suspense deserves.

Carrie is arguably the best of King's early novels. The characterizations of her religious nut of a mother, the bitchy teens, and the terrified, increasingly alienated Carrie are spot on. The latter is remarkable considering we have here a male writing about a young woman's dawning sexuality—and the hormonal ups and downs that go with it. The character of Carrie, King's website says, is "a composite of two girls" he knew during high school, while the anger Carrie feels at being a misfit stems from his own "angry, energetic" youthful feelings. "I know how outsiders feel," he has said.

As if this perfect evocation of adolescent angst weren't enough, *Carrie* is, it perhaps goes without saying, goose-bump inducingly frightening too. If you've seen the film, do still read the book—the narrative, which includes newspaper clippings, scientific reports, and journals, has added bite.

FURTHER READING: *The Stand;*
Pet Sematary; The Shining
SEE ALSO: *The Fury* (John Farris)

ESSENTIAL CULT BOOKS

500

163

THRILLING TALES
Top 10 Classics

★
★ **Writer:** Ian Fleming   **ISBN US:** 978-0142002025
★ **Publisher:** Jonathan Cape, 1953   **ISBN UK:** 978-0141028309
★
★

12+ CASINO ROYALE

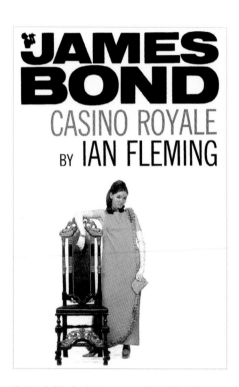

Plot: The early 1950s and the height of the Cold War. James Bond, an agent of Britain's Secret Intelligence Service, is sent on a mission against the villainous le Chiffre—a key member of SMERSH, a secret organization dedicated to the downfall of the western world. His task is to bankrupt le Chiffre by outplaying him at the baccarat tables of Royale-les-Eaux in France, and the contest is played out in tense detail. But this is only the start of the life-and-death struggle between the men and Bond's assistant, the alluring, mysterious Vesper Lynd.

Review: The plot is—like all Fleming's Bond scenarios— deeply implausible and bears no relation to the realities of the Cold War. It is, though, this lack of realism that has proved to be the secret of the continued fascination of *Casino Royale*, for it allows this drama of the crudest emotions— lust, fear, violence, the thrills of luxury and power—to be played out on a timeless stage.

The Bond of the books is more complicated than his screen incarnations; he feels fear, for one thing, and there is a strong misogynist streak in his make-up. But the riches, the fetishistic love of weapons and cars, the beautiful women of ambivalent loyalties, even the horrifying torture scene, come together in a brew as powerful as one of Bond's signature Martinis. "Three measures of Gordons, one of Vodka, half a measure of Kina Lillet. Shake it very well until it's ice cold . . ."

FURTHER READING: *Diamonds Are Forever; Thunderball; The Spy Who Loved Me*
SEE ALSO: *The Thirty-Nine Steps* (John Buchan); *The Spy Who Came in from the Cold* (John Le Carré)

★
★
★

Writer: Horace Walpole
Publisher: W. Bathoe and T. Lowndes, 1765

ISBN US: 978-0199537211
ISBN UK: 978-0199537211

15+

THE CASTLE OF OTRANTO

Plot: Here is a study of Prince Manfred of Otranto, a man obsessed by status, and his castle, along with his fear of losing both. His fear stems from a prophecy pertaining to the castle which says that it "should pass from the present family, whenever the real owner should be grown too large to inhabit it." His only son is promptly killed by a giant helmet, so Manfred dumps his wife and resolves to marry his late son's betrothed to ensure the family line. Further mysteriousness follows, as Walpole animates the imposing medieval castle, adorns it with a host of spooky occurrences, and adds a brutal ghost. By the end, he has scared the living daylights out of Manfred, as well as the petrified reader.

Review: Even the modern reader will stay awake all night to finish *The Castle of Otranto*. It was one of the first Gothic novels and was an immediate success. Success turned to public outrage, however, when a year later it was discovered the story was not based on a 1592 manuscript about a thirteenth-century castle, as Walpole had claimed, but was

in fact born of the author's imagination. An overactive imagination, if the book is anything to go by. The outrage must have dampened down at some point because, 115 editions later, *The Castle of Otranto* is still raising goose-bumps on most of its readers.

The characterization of the tyrannical Manfred is one of the main reasons for the book's popularity, but it's also memorable for the castle itself, considered the archetype of the Gothic tradition: the winding passages, the secret doors, and the eerie giant objects that appear therein all haunt the memory of each and every new reader who nervously turns its pages.

FURTHER READING: This was Walpole's first and only novel
SEE ALSO: *Frankenstein* (Mary Shelley); *Vathek* (William Beckford); *The Tales of Hoffmann* (E. T. A. Hoffmann)

★
★
★
★
★

Writer: James M. Cain
Publisher: Knopf, 1943
(first separate edition Avon Books, 1943)

ISBN US: 978-0679723226
ISBN UK: 978-0752864273

15+

DOUBLE INDEMNITY

784
SIGNET BOOKS
By the author of "Serenade"
JAMES M. CAIN
DOUBLE INDEMNITY
SIGNET BOOKS
Complete and Unabridged

Plot: Seduced by femme fatale Phyllis Nirdlinger, Walter Huff, an insurance guy, bumps off one of his wealthy clients so that Phyllis can claim "double indemnity" on his insurance policy, the aforementioned wealthy client also happens to be Phyllis' husband.

The drama as the pair attempt to escape detection is nail-biting enough, but matters complicate further as Huff falls for Phyllis' stepdaughter Lola. It's a light-bulb moment when he realizes the differences between the two women: his love for Phyllis, it dawns on him, had been "some kind of unhealthy excitement" whereas he feels "sweet peace" with Lola. Spurred on by this epiphany, Huff resolves to settle the whole sorry affair for once and for all—unfortunately, somebody else, somebody female, has had the same idea.

Review: The resolution—if you can call it that—only serves to complicate the ambiguous feelings we've experienced for Huff throughout. In fact, Cain does such a good job of painting a picture of an ordinary Joe caught in the web of a black widow that you almost forget Huff is a criminal several times over. The ending, without spoiling things, is therefore frustrating and satisfying in equal measure.

Okay, you might think you've read it all before, but let's not forget that crime fiction pre-Cain was all black and white in terms of the moral compass: the good guys were squeaky clean, and the baddies always got their comeuppance. In short, James M. Cain reinvented crime fiction, and he did it with a great panache—*Double Indemnity*, his masterwork, is a gripping classic.

FURTHER READING: *Mildred Pierce;*
The Postman Always Rings Twice
SEE ALSO: *The Maltese Falcon*
(Dashiell Hammett); *The Big Sleep*
(Raymond Chandler)

★
★
★
★

Writer: Alan Moore
Publisher: Top Shelf Productions, 1989

ISBN US: 978-0958578349
ISBN UK: 978-0861661411

8+ FROM HELL

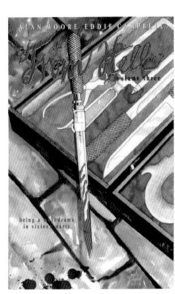

Plot: London, 1888. Believing himself to be simultaneously carrying out Queen Victoria's orders and fulfilling divine will, Doctor William Gull embarks on a series of grisly murders of women in the poverty-stricken East End. Detective Abberline of the Yard comes closest to unearthing the secret that binds the victims together, but the murderer is never caught and goes down in history as "Jack the Ripper."

Review: Forget the feeble movie adaptation: this is dark, complicated, absorbing, and wonderful stuff, which will chill you through the first reading and on subsequent returns will amaze you with the wealth of ideas and period detail. Often called a horror comic, it's really beyond genre; Alan Moore's writing is—as ever—bursting with life, and Eddie Campbell's monochrome art, scratchy and utterly distinctive, perfectly evokes the smoke and grime of Victorian London.

Moore's take on the case is complicated, winding together two conspiracies—one at the highest level of society, one at the lowest—with Masonic ritual, the cynical framing of an innocent suspect, pre-Christian mysticism, sex, drugs, and a lot of gore. As such, it's probably a much more involved story than the truth of what happened on those few ghastly nights: Moore takes the known facts and runs with them freely (and in doing so, happily joins the ranks of the "Ripperologists" whom he satirizes in a laugh-out-loud epilogue). In its combination of historical research and fictional imagination, and its powerfully humane voice, this is an awesome achievement.

FURTHER READING: *The League of Extraordinary Gentlemen; The Lost Girls*
SEE ALSO: *Portrait of a Killer: Jack the Ripper— Case Closed* (Patricia Cornwell)

★
★
★
★

Writer: Shirley Jackson
Publisher: Viking Press, 1959

ISBN US: 978-0143039983
ISBN UK: 978-0141191447

15+

THE HAUNTING OF HILL HOUSE

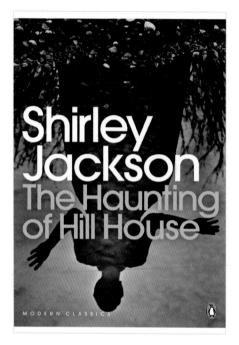

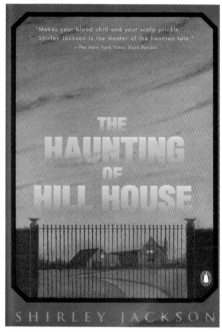

Plot: It's the kind of invitation that does not drop through the letterbox every day. Dr. John Montague, an investigator of the supernatural, invites a collection of people who have experienced paranormal phenomena to spend a summer with him at Hill House. This is not any old country pile; it is an eighty-year-old mansion with a ghostly reputation. Sensibly, most of the invitees decline. Two young women accept: Theodora, Montague's assistant, and Eleanor, a solitary figure who has spent much of her life caring for her invalid mother and experiencing visits by poltergeists. Also joining the fun is Luke, the future heir of Hill House, who plays host to the quartet of ghost-botherers and the uncanny proceedings that envelop them during their stay.

Review: It takes a helluva story to scare the living daylights out of a reader through the printed word alone, and a helluva writer who conveys the fear of their protagonists and imparts it skillfully, as if through osmosis, to the reader. *The Haunting of Hill House* is just such a book, and Jackson is just such a writer.

The economical scariness of the haunting makes the flesh creep, and the implied horrors make the hair stand on end. Much of the action takes place behind closed doors: things go bump in the night, blood is left splattered on walls and clothing, and uninvited guests of the spirit variety are heard but not seen.

Ultimately, it is left to our imaginations as to whether Eleanor is a woman haunted by a house or simply freaking herself out. That's a nice touch to a story that, despite the sensory invasion, despite the bloodshed, despite the traumatic ending, is surprisingly subtle.

FURTHER READING: *The Lottery*
SEE ALSO: *The Private Memoirs and Confessions of a Justified Sinner* (James Hogg); *The Turn of the Screw* (Henry James); *The Woman in Black* (Susan Hill)

★
★
★
★
★

Writer: Jim Thompson
Publisher: Lion Books, 1952

ISBN US: 978-0752879581
ISBN UK: 978-0752851433

18+

THE KILLER INSIDE ME

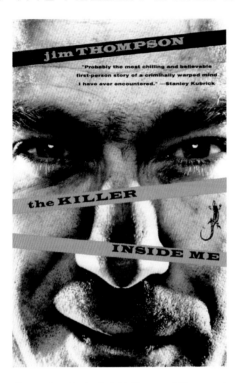

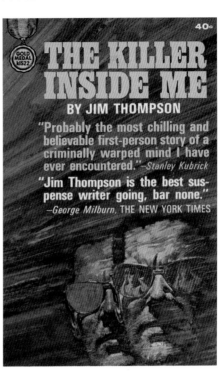

THRILLING TALES
Top 10 Classics

169

500

ESSENTIAL
CULT BOOKS

Plot: Stanley Kubrick called this "the most chilling account of a criminally warped mind" he had ever encountered.

First appearances, though, show Lou Ford, the central character of *The Killer Inside Me*, as a dim deputy Sheriff in Central City, Texas, a regular guy prone to cheesy one-liners and too soft to carry a gun. But Ford has a secret. He suffers from a "sickness," a psychopathic propensity for violence that began in childhood but has not been acted upon since he was fourteen. A violent and sexually charged scene with a female hustler sees the sickness returning with a vengeance. Ford, it seems, is a man trapped in an endless cycle of sadism: from casual acts of violence to cold-blooded murder, and finally to the planned destruction of the entire town.

Review: Thompson has a gift for shaping his characters through dialog—much of what we learn of Ford is through the words he speaks. Thompson's prose is no less effective,

though: short, snappy sentences hit the reader like they're a punch bag, leaving you gasping for breath, and intensifying the effect of the crimes depicted.

This was Thompson's breakthrough novel, a novel that stunned America by subverting the wholesome folksiness of 1950s small town life. Ultimately, Thompson's serial killer could not enjoy impunity, and Ford's fall is inevitable. The thrill is not in his downfall, though, but watching the mask of decency slip as he slides inexorably toward it. Kubrick was right on the money.

FURTHER READING: *The Grifters*
SEE ALSO: *Red Dragon* (Thomas Harris);
Darkly Dreaming Dexter (Jeff Lindsay)

★
★
★
★
★

Writer: Agatha Christie
Publisher: Collins, 1926

ISBN US: 978-0425173893
ISBN UK: 978-0007141340

12+

THE MURDER OF ROGER ACKROYD

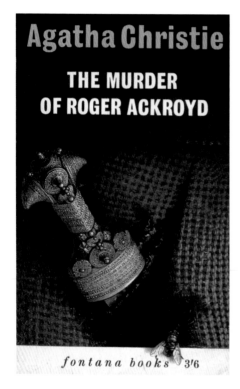

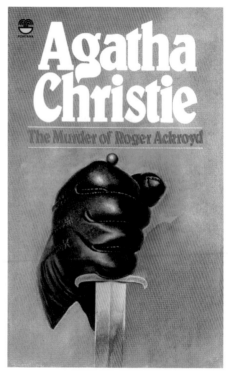

Plot: Belgian detective Hercule Poirot comes out of retirement to investigate murder in the sleepy English village of King's Abbot. The suspects are numerous, the secrets and lies of the villagers manifold, and there are possible motives aplenty, ranging from drug addiction to blackmail and a secret marriage. The local doctor, Dr. Sheppard, narrates the story, acting as a sidekick to the aging Poirot. "It was just a few minutes after nine," the book begins, which is an opening of which you'd do well to take note.

Review: She's the original Queen of Crime, whose mysterious disappearance in the very year of publication of this book only adds to her legendary status. Christie had written the rules for crime fiction. In this, her sixth novel, she broke them, to the delight of her fans and the consternation of the critics. There was a visceral reaction to the denouement from contemporary critics, and even as late as 1998 a French

intellectual, Pierre Bayard, wrote the "true ending" to the book in *Who Killed Roger Ackroyd?: The Mystery Behind the Agatha Christie Mystery*.

What readers will want to know, though, is not whether the heated debated about the plot is justified, but if the book still thrills eighty years after it was first published. The answer is a nail-biting and heart quickening "yes." As with all Christie novels the pace picks up as the novel progresses, and there is a frenzied quickening of the heartbeat as it is revealed whodunnit at the climax. And—as with most other Christie novels—villain-spotting is nigh on impossible, though here she takes her plot-crafting cunning to extremes. A crime fiction masterpiece.

FURTHER READING: *Death on the Nile*
SEE ALSO: *Whose Body?* (Dorothy L. Sayers)

★
★
★
★
★

Writer: Patricia Highsmith
Publisher: Coward McMann, 1955

ISBN US: 978-0393332148
ISBN UK: 978-0099282877

15+

THE TALENTED MR. RIPLEY

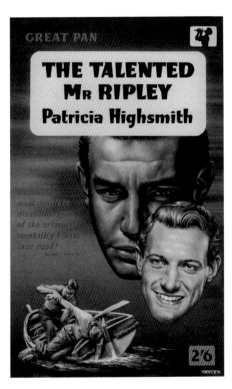

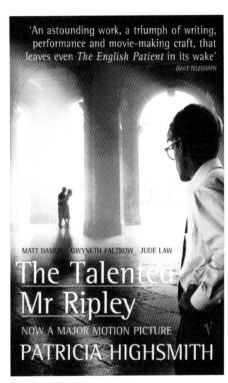

Plot: Tom Ripley—cultured, educated, young, and American—finds himself in Italy alongside the rich and glamorous Dickie Greenleaf and his lover Marge. At once fascinated and repelled by Greenleaf, Ripley takes the drastic step of killing him and assuming his identity.

Review: Literary villains fascinate us; that much is undeniable. Think of Fagin, Dracula, Iago, Moriaty . . . the list is endless. However, they are rarely at center stage, even if their actions drive the plot and give the heroes, the leads, their motivation. With *The Talented Mr. Ripley* and its sequels, Patricia Highsmith bravely made the central protagonist of the book a villain of such self-interest and amoral cynicism that he should, by rights, be impossible to sympathize with. And yet Ripley not only engages but drags the reader into situations of unbearable tension. We should be willing his downfall—but we end up rooting for him.

The book is sometimes called a pulp, but it's much more complicated than that label implies, for the game of empathy and morality built into the narrative technique also relates to the novel's themes. Ripley's genius for becoming another man, as casually as if he were putting on a suit of clothes, raises questions of sexuality, mental health, class, and identity—as does the relationship between the moneyed Americans and their Old World playgrounds. Nasty, but in a very good way, and gripping for anyone who has ever thought about class, sex, or committing a terrible crime. Which is all of us, right?

FURTHER READING: *Strangers on a Train;*
Ripley Under Ground; Ripley's Game;
The Boy Who Followed Ripley; Ripley Under Water
SEE ALSO: *Butterfly* (James M. Cain);
Tales of the Unexpected (Roald Dahl)

★
★
★
★

Writer: Elmore Leonard
Publisher: Delacorte Press, 1974

ISBN US: 978-0753819623
ISBN UK: 978-0753819623

15+

52 PICK UP

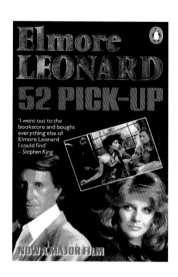

Plot: Detroit in the 1970s, and businessman Harry Mitchell is being black-mailed over secret trysts with a young woman. The blackmailers have picked the wrong guy to mess with, however, and Mitchell will make them pay, big time.

Review: "After writing 23 novels, Elmore Leonard has been discovered," *The New York Times* wrote in 1983. A year later *Newsweek* called him, "The Dickens of Detroit." His status as a novelist, both cult and in mainstream, was assured. What makes him stand out in the mystery suspense genre is his ear for dialog, the convincing characterization, and here, in *52 Pick Up*, the omission of the private eye—a brave and welcome twist on the conventions of the crime formula.

FURTHER READING: *Get Shorty; Rum Punch; Freaky Deaky*
SEE ALSO: *The Postman Always Ring Twice* (James M. Cain);
A Rage to Live (John O'Hara)

★
★
★
★

Writer: Alex Garland
Publisher: Viking, 1996

ISBN US: 978-1573226523
ISBN UK: 0-140-25841-8

15+

THE BEACH

Plot: When a map leading to a mysterious beach falls into a back-packer's hands, he begins an adventure that sees him finding paradise on Earth . . . as well as its opposite number.

Review: "All the makings of a cult classic," cites Nick Hornby on the back cover of early editions of *The Beach*. Sure, it is full of drugs and a troubled central protagonist—it defines the back-packing drop-out culture of the 1990s, even. The thing is, although "beaucoup bad shit" happens, and there is much in the way of plot, the writing feels self-conscious, and has little to offer by way of writerly experimentation. If you back-packed round Thailand in the 1990s you will probably derive much pleasure from this book. The opposite, however, also applies.

FURTHER READING: *The Tesseract*
SEE ALSO: *The Magus* (John Fowles);
Lord of the Flies (William Golding)

Writer: Philip Kerr   **ISBN US:** 978-0140231700
Publisher: Penguin, 1993   **ISBN UK:** 978-0140231700

★
★
★
★

15+

BERLIN NOIR

Plot: A trilogy of novels featuring the adventures of hardboiled ex-cop Bernhard Gunther. *March Violets* begins in 1936, involving the death of a lawyer investigating corruption in the SS; *The Pale Criminal*, set two years later, sees Gunther looking into the blackmailing of a homosexual and tracking down a serial killer; *A German Requiem* is set in postwar Vienna, with ex-Nazis, Russians, and Americans complicating Gunther's investigation into the death of an American soldier.

Review: Kerr's Gunther has been described as a German Philip Marlowe, a tarnished knight errant in Berlin's mean streets. The backgrounds are vivid and authentic, and the plots unfold with many layers, made all the more compelling by our knowledge of events that were soon to follow.

FURTHER READING: *The One from the Other;*
A Quiet Flame; If the Dead Rise Not
SEE ALSO: *The Bridge of Sighs* (Olen Steinhauer);
Zoo Station (David Downing)

Writer: George Pelecanos   **ISBN US:** 978-0312242916
Publisher: St. Martin's Press, 1996   **ISBN UK:** 978-1852427382

★
★
★
★

18+

THE BIG BLOWDOWN

Plot: Pete Karras and Joey Recevo used to be friends, but, after returning from war, they fall out when working for Mr. Burke's protection racket. When Karras tries to go straight, their paths cross again, with hard and potentially fatal consequences.

Review: Pelecanos excels at depicting the sticky urban landscape of Washington D.C., whether here, a period piece set in the 1940s, or in his later work in a contemporary setting. Another unifying theme is the humanity and the social conscience of his protagonists and their fragile masculinity. Whether you go for the D.C. Quartet, or the later Derek Strange novels, one thing is for sure: if you want to read the best in modern crime writing, make sure it's a Pelecanos.

FURTHER READING: *Hell to Pay; Drama City*
SEE ALSO: *Homicide: A Year on the Killing Streets*
(David Simon); *Clockers* (Richard Price)

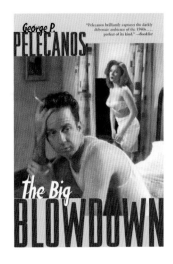

THRILLING TALES
Best of the Rest

173

500 ESSENTIAL CULT BOOKS

★
★
★
★
★

Writer: Graham Greene
Publisher: William Heinemann, 1938

ISBN US: 978-0142437971
ISBN UK: 978-0142437971

12+ # BRIGHTON ROCK

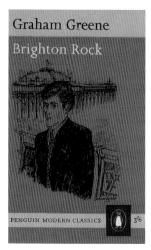

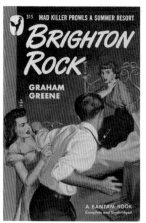

Plot: A thrilling page-turner that exposes the violent under-world of British seaside town Brighton in the 1930s. The murder of newspaperman Fred Hale (in Brighton to distribute cards for a newspaper competition) is the trigger for a game of cat and mouse between the dangerously capricious teenaged gangster Pinkie and life-loving Ida Arnold. After sharing a fleeting moment with Hale on Brighton seafront, Ida "the sticker" Arnold turns amateur sleuth to get to the truth behind his death.

Review: Although Greene's obsession with his Catholicism can bore in his other work, here the picture of retribution bearing in on the Catholic Pinkie in the person of nonbeliever Ida is as riveting as it is unsettling. A *tour de force* of twentieth Century literature.

FURTHER READING: *The End of the Affair;*
The Power and the Glory; The Heart of the Matter
SEE ALSO: *Night and the City* (Gerald Kersh)

★
★
★

Writer: Glen David Gold
Publisher: Hodder & Stoughton, 2001

ISBN US: 978-0786886326
ISBN UK: 978-0340794999

15+

CARTER BEATS THE DEVIL

Plot: A fictionalized account of the career of Charles Carter, a magician in the 1920s. The story opens with a magic trick in which President Warren G. Harding is a volunteer from the audience. When Harding dies soon afterward, Carter is propelled into a series of adventures and illusions, and falls in love with a blind woman.

Review: This is a fast-paced, colorful yarn that reinvented the historical novel genre, and reveled in a cast of crazy characters including cameos from the Marx Brothers (albeit in disguise), the inventor of television, and many other 1920s grandees inbetween. Some may argue that the "ta-da!" climax ruins the spectacle, but others may find this could be the only possible conclusion to a book that cherishes the era of vaudeville.

FURTHER READING: *Sunnyside*
SEE ALSO: *The Amazing Adventures of Kavalier and Clay* (Michael Chabon); *Drood* (Dan Simmons)

★
★
★

Writer: P. D. James
Publisher: Faber and Faber, 1992

ISBN US: 978-0307279903
ISBN UK: 978-0571233779

12+

THE CHILDREN OF MEN

Plot: The future is bleak. The future, in *The Children of Men*, is a sterile land, where humanity is suffering a "universal infertility," national porn shops have been opened, and the infirm are encouraged to commit suicide. Theo Faren, an Oxford historian, plays by the dehumanizing rules of this dystopia before a chance meeting sees him joining a group of dissidents, "the Five Fishes."

Review: The philosophical bent to P. D. James' detective novels is applied to full effect here (she is perhaps better known as a Queen of Crime); equally so, her mastery of suspense. À propos which, don't be fooled by the plodding start: the pace picks up in part two, and then some.

FURTHER READING: *Cover Her Face; A Taste of Death; An Unsuitable Job for a Woman*
SEE ALSO: *The Handmaid's Tale* (Margaret Atwood); *Brave New World* (Aldous Huxley)

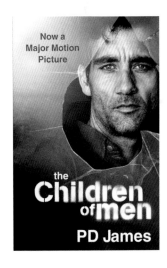

★
★
★
★

Writer: Desmond Barry
Publisher: Little, Brown & Co, 2000

ISBN US: 978-0316120845
ISBN UK: 978-0099285427

15+ # THE CHIVALRY OF CRIME

Plot: A fictionalized account of gunslinger Jesse James' and his murderer Robert Ford's life stories. An imaginary personage, fifteen-year-old Joshua Benyon, is at the book's heart. After accidentally shooting his father dead, Benyon is visited in prison by Ford, who then recounts to the boy, and us, his version of the Jesse James legend.

Review: In equal parts historical novel and whip-cracklingly good tale, *The Chivalry of Crime* should delight those gagging for detail on the wilder aspects of the Wild West, as well as those who insist on historical accuracy in their novels. The trial scenes with young Joshua add a human aspect to the story, which otherwise might have been lost among the historical carnage.

FURTHER READING: *A Bloody Good Friday*
SEE ALSO: *Blood Meridian* (Cormac McCarthy); *Little, Big Man* (Thomas Beger); *Warlock* (Oakley Hall)

★
★
★

Writer: Richard Price
Publisher: Houghton Mifflin, 1992

ISBN US: 978-0060934989
ISBN UK: 978-0747598206

18+ # CLOCKERS

Plot: When a model citizen puts his hands up to a murder, veteran homicide cop Rocco Klein's suspicions are aroused. Could it be that the confessor's half-brother—a known hoodlum nicknamed Strike—is the real culprit? The fire of justice that had gone out in Klein's belly is relit, and he makes it his mission to get to the truth.

Review: This is a stunning depiction of the urban jungle, where self-defense takes on a new meaning: you're a "survivor" if you make it to thirty-seven, and it's the angriest of young men who have the "power." The language and mores of the streets ring true, anticipating the stunning and gritty realism of cult TV show, *The Wire*, on which Price was a lead writer.

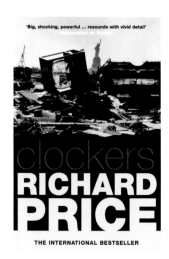

FURTHER READING: *The Wanderers; Freedomland*
SEE ALSO: *Homicide: A Year on the Killing Streets* (David Simon); *The Big Blowdown* (George Pelecanos)

Writer: Charles Willeford   **ISBN US:** 978-0679734710
Publisher: Chicago Paperback House, 1962   **ISBN UK:** 978-0887390265

8+

COCKFIGHTER

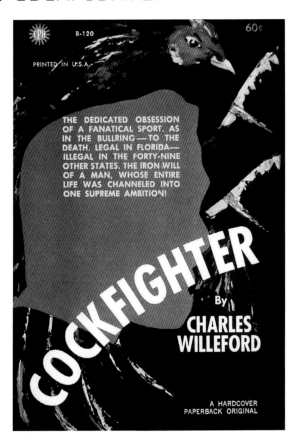

Plot: An unblinking look at the "sport" of cock-fighting via the story of Frank Mansfield, whose "one supreme ambition" is to win the champion's medal at the Southern Conference Cock-fighting Tournament. Stranger still, he's taken a vow of silence until he does so.

Review: Animal lovers, look away now: breaking cocks' beaks, cock training, and bloody pit fights are typical of the animal cruelty used by Willeford to paint a depressing picture of the rural south and its criminal classes. As nasty as this might all sound, Willeford handles the plot tightly and the overall effect is actually one big adrenaline rush.

FURTHER READING: *The Burnt Orange Heresy*
SEE ALSO: *Killshot* (Elmore Leonard); *The Hunter* (Richard Stark)

★ **Writer:** Dan Brown
★ **Publisher:** Doubleday Company, 2003

ISBN US: 978-0385504201
ISBN UK: 9780552159715

ISBN US: 978-0385504201
ISBN UK: 9780552159715

15+ # THE DA VINCI CODE

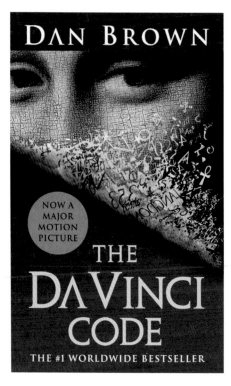

Plot: Symbologist Robert Langdon is called to assist in the investigation of a murder committed in the Louvre, in which the victim seems to have used the museum's famous artworks as clues to his killer's identity. However, the mystery is soon revealed to be a game for far higher stakes as Langdon finds himself seeking the Holy Grail; by way of the history of Christianity, the origins of the Bible, and even the blood line of Jesus Christ.

Review: Reviled by critics but outsold in 2004 only by *Harry Potter*, Brown's thrilling tale has the literary world divided. On the one hand, his prose is notoriously flat and his characters merely tools to drive on his merciless plot. He gets around these handicaps by deploying cheap tricks to keep the pages turning: cliff-hangers, short chapters, and action-packed plot lines. On the other hand, as protests from the church show, the book offers a surprisingly subversive tale.

FURTHER READING: *Angels and Demons; The Lost Symbol*
SEE ALSO: *Kiss the Girls* (James Patterson); *The Name of the Rose* (Umberto Eco); *The Holy Blood and the Holy Grail* (Baigent, Leigh, Lincoln)

Writer: Jeff Lindsay
Publisher: Doubleday, 2004

ISBN US: 978-0307277886
ISBN UK: 978-0752866758

18+ # DARKLY DREAMING DEXTER

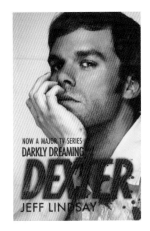

Plot: A police lab technician, Dexter Morgan, who is a serial killer, must decide whether to help, catch, or make friends with a new serial killer on the scene in his native Miami.

Review: "A serial killer to fall in love with," so the strap line goes. Kept down your coffee so far? Then suspend your disbelief yet further and read on for a transgressive rollercoaster ride of vivisection, dismembered limbs, and the like. The prose works better than the dialog, even if Lindsay is over-fond of alliteration, but I guess fans (and there are many) are not in this for the quality of the writing: blood and gore is what this is all about.

FURTHER READING: The four other Dexter titles if you have the stomach
SEE ALSO: *The Silence of the Lambs* and *Hannibal* (Thomas Harris)

NOW A MAJOR TV SERIES
DARKLY DREAMING
DEXTER
JEFF LINDSAY

Writer: Robert Stone
Publisher: Secker & Warburg, 1975

ISBN US: 978-0395860250
ISBN UK: 978-0395860250

15+ # DOG SOLDIERS

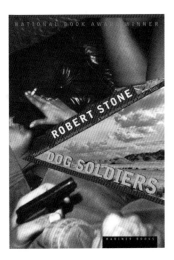

Plot: It's the tail-end of the Vietnam War and morality has gone out the window. John Converse, "a journalist of sorts," persuades an old pal, Merchant Marine Ray Hicks, to smuggle two kilos of heroin from Vietnam into the United States. Needless to say the result is a snafu: crooked Feds, a manhunt, and a drug-addled climax add to the whole sorry mess.

Review: Told with a scathing tone, *Dog Soldiers* is the work of a man troubled by a changing America as the euphoric sixties counterculture gave way to the heavier mood of the 1970s. As one character notes, "in a world where flying men hunt elephants people are just naturally going to want to get high."

NATIONAL BOOK AWARD WINNER
ROBERT STONE
DOG SOLDIERS
MARINER BOOKS

FURTHER READING: *A Hall of Mirrors; A Flag for Sunrise*
SEE ALSO: *Dispatches* (Michael Herr)

★ **Writer:** Bram Stoker **ISBN US:** 978-0451523372
★ **Publisher:** A. Constable & Co. 1897 **ISBN UK:** 978-0140620634
★
★

15+ DRACULA

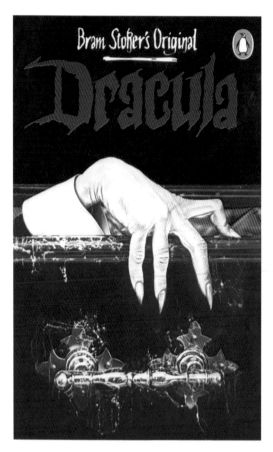

Plot: Solicitor Jonathan Harker's visit to Castle Dracula on legal business does not go as planned: his host, the Transylvanian nobleman Count Dracula has, it transpires, vampiric tendencies. Finding insufficient prey in his native land, Dracula comes to England, where he unleashes a bloodthirsty plan to spawn new legions of the Un-Dead. But he has not reckoned on the intervention of Professor Abraham Van Helsing.

Review: You may think you know *Dracula* from its many cinematic and literary imitators, but this is truly a case of the original being the best. Stoker's tale is creepy and atmospheric and is lent an air of verisimilitude by its composition of journal entries and letters from multiple narrators. Studies by academics have looked for subtexts in the book, but who needs them when themes such as the supernatural, sexuality, and the occult simmer on the surface in all their horrific glory?

FURTHER READING: Stoker was a prolific novelist, but *Dracula* is his only work that you'll want to get your teeth into . . .
SEE ALSO: *The Vampire Lestat* (Anne Rice); *Lost Souls* (Poppy Z. Brite)

★
★
★

Writer: Dennis Lehane
Publisher: Harcourt, 1994

ISBN US: 978-0156029025
ISBN UK: 978-0553818222

5+

A DRINK BEFORE THE WAR

Plot: Lehane's debut novel introduced Patrick Kenzie and Angel Gennaro, partners in a detective agency based in Boston. Hired to find a missing cleaning woman—or, more importantly, some papers that have also gone missing—the pair find themselves the targets of a vicious gang boss. The action escalates when they discover what they have really been chasing: photographs that implicate the man who hired them, a top official, in child abuse.

Review: Lehane doesn't flinch in the telling of a dark and nasty tale, although a tendency to soapbox interrupts the flow of the story. Kenzie, abused by his father, and Gennaro, trapped in a violent marriage, are compelling characters. The book picked up a well-deserved Shamus Award.

FURTHER READING: *Darkness, Take My Hand*; *Sacred*; *Gone, Baby, Gone*; *Prayers for Rain*
SEE ALSO: *The Monkey's Raincoat* (Robert Crais); *The Neon Rain* (James Lee Burke); *Right as Rain* (George Pelecanos)

★
★
★

Writer: Jasper Fforde
Publisher: Penguin, 2001

ISBN US: 978-0142001806
ISBN UK: 978-0340733561

5+

THE EYRE AFFAIR

Plot: Having kidnapped Mr. Quaverley from the pages of *Martin Chuzzlewit*, Acheron Hades, Britain's Third Most Wanted criminal, is contriving to steal Jane Eyre. Only Thursday Next, "literary detective," can save the day (with the help of her uncle's Prose Portal) before Hades changes the ending to one of literature's most famous novels.

Review: Equal parts alternate history, literary character spotter's guide, and kooky mystery, the first of Fforde's Thursday Next books is as cult as they come. But while some authors might relish this label, Fforde prefers the term "enthusiastic following." Well, whatever he'd like to call it, the highly original and entertaining Thursday Next books deserve a manically obsessive readership, and you should make it your job to belong.

FURTHER READING: *Something Rotten*
SEE ALSO: *The Vesuvius Club* (Mark Gatiss); *Aberystwyth Mon Amour* (Malcolm Pryce)

★
★
★

Writer: Robert Harris
Publisher: Century Hutchinson, 1992

ISBN US: 978-0061006623
ISBN UK: 978-0099263814

15+

FATHERLAND

Plot: Imagine that Hitler has won World War II, the world is unaware of the Holocaust, and America and Germany are on the cusp of something approaching an *Entente Cordiale*. The year is 1964, the place Berlin. A police detective, Xavier March, and his American sidekick, Charlotte Maguire, are slowly uncovering the terrible truth: can they tell the world abut the murder of Europe's Jews before President Kennedy meets Hitler?

Review: Police procedural, nail-biting thriller, or chilling alternate history? Why not all three? Accusations of tastelessness have been levied at Harris, whose plot centers around the sensitive subject of the Holocaust. We think not. Rather, we'd call this a well thought through and necessary reminder that the good guys "won."

FURTHER READING: *Enigma; Pompeii; The Ghost*
SEE ALSO: *Rogue Male* **(Geoffrey Household)**

★
★
★
★

Writer: Sarah Waters
Publisher: Virago Press, 2002

ISBN US: 978-1573229722
ISBN UK: 978-0571245642

18+

FINGERSMITH

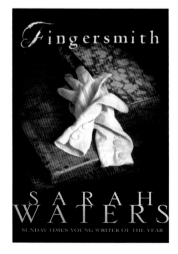

Plot: A suspenseful tour de force that links the lives of two orphaned girls in Victorian London: one spends her growing years among a gang of "fingersmiths" and petty criminals, the other lives a strange existence in a nearby mansion. Themes of insanity, double-crossing, and fraud emerge as their stories begin to intertwine.

Review: Classic storytelling, a lesbian love story, and a vivid patchwork of characters and plots make this a ripping and substantial yarn. To repeat oft-cited comparisons with Dickens is not to be hackneyed, but to remind you of just how good Sarah Waters is. That *Fingersmith* was shortlisted for both the Orange and Man Booker prizes is testament to its brilliant, page-turningly good writing. Historical fiction to tempt even those who hate the genre.

FURTHER READING: *Tipping the Velvet; The Little Stranger*
SEE ALSO: **Any novel by Charles Dickens**

Writer: Gregory McDonald
Publisher: Bobbs-Merrill, 1974

ISBN US: 978-0375713545
ISBN UK: 978-0375713545

★★★★

15+

FLETCH

Plot: Irwin M. Fletcher—Fletch to his colleagues—is in California, wandering the beaches, talking to junkies, trying to break a story on the drug trade. Mistaken for a bum, he is approached by a businessman, who offers him a contract to kill a man. The victim is to be the businessman himself, Alan Stanwyk. Suicide would invalidate his insurance, but he cannot face the slow agonizing death from terminal cancer. Accepting the deal, Fletch investigates Stanwyk and discovers all is not what it seems.

Review: An egotistical opportunist, Fletch has only one interest: his own wellbeing. He stumbles on clues rather than arriving at conclusions from investigation. However, as a character he is funny, acerbic, and engaging, and the book deserved the Edgar for First Novel it was awarded.

FURTHER READING: *Eight sequels and two spin-offs featuring Fletch's son*
SEE ALSO: *The Hunter (Richard Stark); Tourist Season (Carl Hiaasen)*

Writer: Joe Haldeman
Publisher: St. Martin's Press, 1974
(restored edition 1997)

ISBN US: 978-0312536633
ISBN UK: 978-1857988086

★★★

15+

THE FOREVER WAR

Plot: William Mandella is conscripted into the U.N. Exploratory Force to seek out an aggressive alien species, the Taurans. Interstellar distances can be traveled via collapsars, but while months seem to pass for the soldiers, years—sometimes centuries—pass on Earth. Returning soldiers barely recognize the planet or the people they have sworn to protect, often reenlisting.

Review: Haldeman's experiences in Vietnam inform his award-winning novel. The technology, weapons, and relativistic effects of near-light-speed travel are carefully worked out, but the core of the book is its narrator and his attempts to cope with future shock. Mandella endures centuries of war's horror, disconnected from humankind, whose evolution makes his connections ever more tenuous.

FURTHER READING: *Forever Peace; Forever Free; War Year; 1968*
SEE ALSO: *Starship Troopers (Robert A. Heinlein); Hyperion (Dan Simmons); Old Man's War (John Scalzi)*

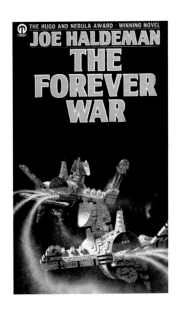

★
★
★
★

Writer: Kinky Friedman
Publisher: Beech Tree Books, 1986

ISBN US: 978-0970238306
ISBN UK: 978-0571191345

18+ GREENWICH KILLING TIME

Plot: In which we are introduced to Friedman's fictional alter-ego, the whisky-drinking, cat-loving, New York City-dwelling, Jewish cowboy detective Kinky Friedman. So to Greenwich Village, where a corpse is discovered clutching eleven pink roses, and the first of many Kinky Friedman crime-solving adventures.

Review: This violently funny debut is everything you'd expect from a country musician-cum-writer of detective fiction: it's kooky, has a wonky beat, and has a dazzling cast of supporting characters who wouldn't be out of place in the lyrics to a country ballad. As to whether it's worth reading: if you like country music, you'll like Kinky Friedman. If you don't like country music, you'll still like Kinky Friedman. Capiche?

FURTHER READING: Kinky is available in a variety of bind-up editions—why not buy all of them?
SEE ALSO: It's hard to say; could it be that Kinky's Jewish cowboy detective alter-ego defies comparison?

★
★
★
★

Writer: Jim Thompson
Publisher: Regency, 1963

ISBN US: 978-0679732488
ISBN UK: 978-0752879598

18+ THE GRIFTERS

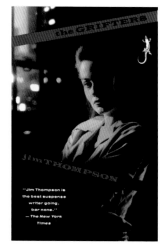

Plot: For a handsome, personable con man, Roy Dillon has a heck of a problem handling his women. Not least his lover Moira and his youthful mother Lilly—who share an uncanny physical resemblance. Roy lives on "uneasy street," a place where petty crooks make a buck from "short con grifts" and weigh up the odds of the advantages of "going straight."

Review: As with so many cult novelists, Thompson was overlooked in his lifetime, gaining posthumous fame via his novels and their film adaptations. His 1963 *The Grifters* may not be the hippest, most lyrical, or grittiest, depiction of 1950s lowlife but the plot—in particular the climax—socks it to you with suspense and aplomb, nevertheless.

FURTHER READING: *The Killer Inside Me; A Hell of a Woman*
SEE ALSO: *Double Indemnity* (James M. Cain);
LA Confidential (James Ellroy)

Writer: Richard Stark
Publisher: Pocket Books, 1962

ISBN US: 978-0226770994
ISBN UK: 978-0226770994

★
★
★
★

18+

THE HUNTER

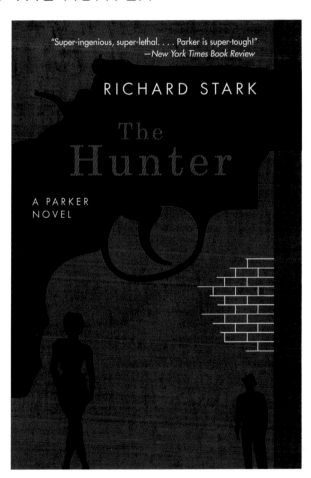

"Super-ingenious, super-lethal. . . . Parker is super-tough!"
—*New York Times Book Review*

RICHARD STARK

The Hunter

A PARKER
NOVEL

THE TABLES WERE TURNED NOW—SUDDENLY THE HUNTED HAD BECOME THE HUNTER

RICHARD STARK

Plot: Betrayed, and left for dead, by his wife and his partner, Parker wants revenge. But don't feel sorry for him. He's the rough, tough criminal antihero of Stark's punchy creation, coming to New York where he unleashes a terrible angry violence with big hands "born to slap with": it's payback time.

Review: The short, snappy sentences pack a punch, the dialog fizzes, the characters are delightfully repellent. It's a pivotal text in the noir genre, which had perhaps never been so stomach-churningly violent before. When Stark tells his wife Lynn his plans to peel the skin off, rip the veins from, and chew up the heart of his ex-partner, you know he really ain't kidding.

FURTHER READING: Any of the other twenty-three Parker novels
SEE ALSO: *Cockfighter* (Charles Willeford); *The Hunter* (Darwyn Cooke), a recent graphic-novel version of the Parker stories

Writer: John Ball
Publisher: Harper and Row, 1965

ISBN US: 978-0786708833
ISBN UK: 978-0881848878

15+

IN THE HEAT OF THE NIGHT

Plot: August, the 1960s, the Southern town of Wells, and a murder has been committed. Virgil Tibbs, a Californian homicide detective passing through the town, is taken in for questioning about the killing by local police; it's no coincidence that Tibbs is black. Police chief Bill Gillespie and arresting officer Sam Wood get their come-uppance, however, when the victim's family call on Tibbs to help catch the killer.

Review: *In the Heat of the Night* employs all the techniques of the classic whodunnit, with the requisite red herrings, numerous suspects, and a twist in the tale. What sets it apart is the racial tension, making it not only a gutsy thriller, but a thoughtful study of the prejudices of a bygone era.

FURTHER READING: The others in the Virgil Tibbs series including *Johnny Get Your Gun*
SEE ALSO: *A Rage in Harlem* (Chester Himes)

Writer: William Kennedy
Publisher: Viking Press, 1983

ISBN US: 978-0140070200
ISBN UK: 978-0140070200

15+

IRONWEED

Plot: A one-time major baseball league player, hobo Francis Phelan's life changes forever when he drops his thirteen-day-old son while changing his diaper. During the next two decades his life spirals downwards, haunted by the ghosts of others whose deaths he has been implicated in. Eventually he returns home, ostensibly for a voting scam to earn a little money, but it gives him the opportunity to put his ghosts to rest.

Review: Kennedy creates a grueling tale against the authentic background of Depression-era Albany. Phelan struggles to retain any sort of identity as he suffers humiliation and degradation; the one thing left to him is his determination to survive. Kennedy struggled for years to find a publisher, but the book went on to win the National Critics Award and the Pulitzer Prize.

FURTHER READING: *Legs; Billy Phelan's Greatest Game; Quinn's Book; Very Old Bones; The Flaming Corsage*
SEE ALSO: *Tobacco Road* (Erskine Caldwell); *A Summons to Memphis* (Peter Taylor)

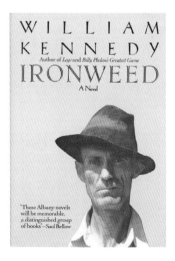

★
★ **Writer:** H. Rider Haggard **ISBN US:** 978-0141439525
★ **Publisher:** Cassell & Co, 1885 **ISBN UK:** 978-0140621235
★

12+

KING SOLOMON'S MINES

Plot: In which we are first introduced to boy's own adventure legend Allan Quartermain. Here we see him journeying to the heart of the "dark continent," with two blustering, yet brave, sidekicks to search out a lost adventurer and the fabled diamond mines of King Solomon.

Review: Not only is *King Solomon's Mines* one of the most successful adventure stories of all time, it is also one of the most enduring (dodgy imperialist tendencies aside). If you can forgive Rider Haggard those, pick up a copy and discover for yourself three heroes of derring-do battling the elements, out-smarting—understandably—unfriendly tribesmen, and risking death to find King Solomon's lost treasure, all with the help of a mysterious map.

FURTHER READING: *She*
SEE ALSO: *The League of Extraordinary Gentlemen* (Alan Moore), in which Quartermain is reincarnated in graphic novel form alongside other literary legends such as Edward Hyde and Captain Nemo

★
★ **Writer:** Choderlos de Laclos **ISBN US:** 978-0199536481
★ **Publisher:** Durand, 1782 **ISBN UK:** 978-0199536481
★

15+

LES LIAISONS DANGEREUSES
(DANGEROUS LIAISONS)

Plot: De Laclos weaves a tangled web of plots, sexual intrigue, and deception through the fictional letters of aristocrats in prerevolutionary France. It centers on the correspondence between the libertine Vicomte de Valmont and his ex-lover, the Marquise de Merteuil, revealing their rivalry and cynical attempts to turn seduction into a game. A game in which—it transpires—there are only losers.

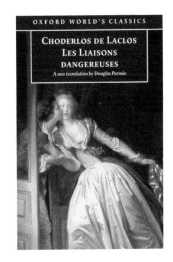

Review: A deliciously damning portrait of the French aristocracy of the ancien régime, De Laclos presents us with characters so idle that they have little other option but to descend into moral turpitude—just to pass the time. Wickedly appealing, the evermore malicious plots and schemes of the Comte and his arch-rival Merteuil will enthrall readers to this day.

FURTHER READING: De Laclos never came close to these literary heights again, though he did invent the artillery shell
SEE ALSO: *Clarissa/Pamela* (Samuel Richardson); *La Nouvelle Heloise* (Jean-Jacques Rousseau)

THRILLING TALES
Best of the Rest

500 ESSENTIAL CULT BOOKS

187

★ **Writer:** Jean-Christophe Grangé
★ **Publisher:** Harvill Press, 1999;
★ originally in French 1998

ISBN US: 978-1860466595
ISBN UK: 978-0099449027

 18+

LES RIVIÈRES POURPRES
(BLOOD RED RIVERS)

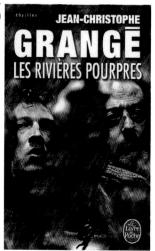

Plot: Abrasive cop Pierre Niémans, removed from Paris after a violent attack on an English football fan, is assigned to investigate a murder after a mutilated corpse is found in the French Alps near the university town of Guernon. In Nanterre, Karim Abdouf is investigating the desecration of a child's grave and the break-in at a primary school. The two threads of the story eventually unite the two officers as more corpses are discovered.

Review: Gritty French police procedural, better known to English-language fans as *The Crimson Rivers*, under which title the movie adaptation was released. The pace is furious, the characters complex and driven, and the background—the silent halls of the university and the expanse of Alpine glaciers—a welcome break from urban America.

FURTHER READING: *The Flight of the Storks; The Empire of the Wolves*
SEE ALSO: *The Laughing Policeman* **(Maj Sjöwall and Per Wahlöö)**

★ **Writer:** Yann Martel
★ **Publisher:** Knopf Canada, 2001
★
★

ISBN US: 978-0156027328
ISBN UK: 1-84195-392-X

15+ # LIFE OF PI

Plot: Noah's ark but not as you know it. This is the story of young Pi Patel and a Royal Bengal tiger named Richard Parker who are the sole survivors of a sunken cargo ship. Together they drift in a lifeboat for 227 days, with Pi surviving on his zoological knowledge, and on storytelling, where fact and fiction meld in a hallucinatory blur.

Review: *Life of Pi*'s success lies in Martel's ability to take a fantastical situation and make it seem as real as the hand in front of you—though never as unremarkable. For this inventiveness and breathing new life into the dusty literary form of the novel, he is celebrated by numerous other writers: small wonder this mesmerizing fable won the 2002 Man Booker Prize for Fiction.

FURTHER READING: *Self; We Ate the Children Last*
SEE ALSO: *Gulliver's Travels* **(Jonathan Swift);**
Robinson Crusoe **(Daniel Defoe)**

Writer: Thomas Berger
Publisher: Dial Press, 1964

ISBN US: 978-0385298292
ISBN UK: 978-1860466410

LITTLE, BIG MAN

"An epic such as Mark Twain might have given us . . . a delicious, crazy, panoramic enlargement . . . " —Henry Miller

LITTLE
BIG
MAN

THOMAS
BERGER

WITH AN INTRODUCTION BY BROOKS LANDON

Plot: Evoking the lawlessness and battles of the American West in the 1850s, *Little Big Man* is the reflections of 111-year-old Jack Crabbe. The sole white survivor of the Battle of Little Big Horn, he is raised by Cheyenne Indians only to perform an astonishing volte-face when he joins Custer's Seventh Cavalry.

Review: Berger's genius is in presenting the ways of life of both sides of the American Frontier through the eyes of just one man. His scintillating presentation of the Wild West is all the more remarkable considering he is no specialist on the subject (his other books deal with all manner of different genres and themes). *Little, Big Man's* success on publication was immense, and it has been enjoyed by generations ever since.

FURTHER READING: *Killing Time; Crazy in Berlin*
SEE ALSO: *The Chivalry of Crime* (Desmond Barry)

Writer: Raymond Chandler
Publisher: Hamish Hamilton, 1953

ISBN US: 978-0394757681c
ISBN UK: 978-0140108958

THE LONG GOODBYE

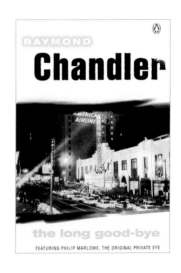

RAYMOND
Chandler
the long good-bye
FEATURING PHILIP MARLOWE, THE *ORIGINAL* PRIVATE EYE

Plot: Trouble is private dick Philip Marlowe's business. In *The Long Goodbye* his troubles are many: there's the drunken and disfigured Terry Lennox, Lennox's very beautiful and very dead wife, and the nightstick-wielding cop Captain Gregorious. Not to mention another drunk, author Roger Wade, his femme fatale wife, and the headache they, and their high-society world, give Marlowe.

Review: Dilys Powell has described Chandler's writing as "backstreet poetry." Who can argue when Marlowe's wisecracks and pithy dialog sear onto the page with such conviction? Chandler wrote *The Long Goodbye* at the height of his fame, and, some would argue, when he was at the top of his game. Another point we can't contest, considering this brilliantly plotted and entertaining gumshoe story.

FURTHER READING: *Farewell My Lovely;*
The Big Sleep; The High Window
SEE ALSO: *The Maltese Falcon* (Dashiell Hammett)

★ **Writer:** Poppy Z. Brite
★ **Publisher:** Delacorte Press, 1992
★

ISBN US: 978-0440212812
ISBN UK: 978-0440212812

15+ # LOST SOULS

Plot: Nothing, a mixed-up teenaged orphan, runs away from home. This is not your usual misplaced teenaged angst, however. Unbeknown to Nothing, his father is Zillah, a hard-drinking, hedonistic vampire who, with his sidekicks Molocahi and Twig, raise merry hell from North Carolina to New Orleans.

Review: Strong on character and mood, weak on plot, Brite nonetheless set a new benchmark for the vampire novel with her 1992 cult hit, dragging the genre biting and screaming to the modern age; drugs, sex, and booze dominate the action. This is not your usual genre fiction language-wise either: *Lost Souls* drips in metaphor that, although sometimes overplayed, gives Brite top marks for effort, especially considering she was only nineteen when she wrote it.

FURTHER READING: *Wormwood* (short stories); *Drawing Blood*
SEE ALSO: *The Lost Boys* (Craig Shaw Gardner); *Interview with the Vampire* (Anne Rice)

★
★
★

Writer: Richard Condon
Publisher: McGraw-Hill, 1959

ISBN US: 978-0965931540
ISBN UK: 978-1874061083

15+

THE MANCHURIAN CANDIDATE

Plot: A richly plotted and chilling political thriller, *The Manchurian Candidate* is the story of Sgt. Raymond Shaw, winner of the Congressional Medal of Honor, who was brainwashed by the Chinese during the Korean War in the 1950s. On returning to the U.S., Shaw becomes an unwitting assassin for the Communist Party at the behest of a close family member.

Review: Complex and riveting, Condon's Cold War thriller was controversial at the time of publication—the 1962 movie adaptation of the book had to be pulled from theaters when JFK was assassinated. In truth, the Cold War paranoia seems a bit silly now, but the book remains a powerful reminder of the fears and tensions of the era.

FURTHER READING: *Winter Kills; An Infinity of Mirrors*
SEE ALSO: *The Last Supper* (Charles McCarry);
The Day of the Jackal (Frederick Forsyth)

★
★
★
★

Writer: Herman Melville
Publisher: Harper, 1851

ISBN US: 978-0451526991
ISBN UK: 978-1853260087

12+

MOBY DICK

Plot: A sea captain, Ahab, swears revenge on the white whale (known as Moby Dick) that "reaped" his leg, driving his ship, the Pequod, and his crew to destruction in its pursuit. Our narrator, Ishmael, is an ordinary seaman on board the Pequod, a schoolmaster who's left his post for the drama of the high seas.

Review: Melville drew on his experience of years at sea to write this boy's own adventure, and we are treated to numerous encyclopedic digressions on the bloody art of whaling throughout the book. From one of the most oft-cited opening lines in literature ("Call me Ishmael") to an unforgettably ironic last image, this is a masterpiece—as well as a bona fide blueprint for experimental cult classics to follow.

FURTHER READING: *Bully Budd; Redburn*
SEE ALSO: *The Island of Doctor Moreau* (H. G. Wells);
Life of Pi (Yann Martel)

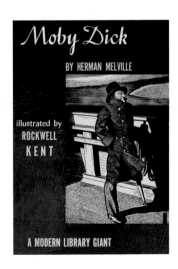

ESSENTIAL
CULT BOOKS

500

191

THRILLING TALES
Best of the Rest

★ **Writer:** Paul Theroux   **ISBN US:** 978-0140060898
★ **Publisher:** Houghton Mifflin, 1982   **ISBN UK:** 978-0140060898

15+ THE MOSQUITO COAST

Plot: Family misadventure in the Honduran jungle. Charlie Fox, the fourteen-year-old son of inventor Allie Fox, narrates a thrilling tale of his father's mission to uproot their family in order to start a new civilization in central America.

Review: If you ever dreamed of upping sticks and turning your back on the consumerist, capitalist hell of modern life, this book might appeal, although it's probably best you don't read it if you want to keep your fantasy alive. That said, Theroux's red mist at, and descriptions of, the "dope taking, door locking, ulcerated danger zone of scavengers," (that is, modern Americans) might just spur you on. Oh and there's a top tip for all you would be adventurers: ice-making machines in the jungle are not a good idea.

FURTHER READING: *The Great Railway Bazaar* (non-fiction)
SEE ALSO: *Lord of the Flies* (William Golding); *Robinson Crusoe* (Daniel Defoe)

Writer: Norman Mailer
Publisher: Rinehart and Company, 1948

ISBN US: 978-0312265052
ISBN UK: 978-0007204953

★
★
★

5+

THE NAKED AND THE DEAD

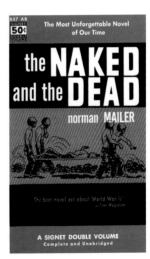

Plot: A graphic and brutal war novel that changed the public's perception of the glories of World War II. Following a platoon of soldiers fighting their way across a South Pacific island, *The Naked and the Dead* depicts the combat of war in forensic detail, while also focusing on the inner struggles of the fourteen-man infantry platoon.

Review: Written when he was only twenty-six years of age, this was the book that made Mailer's name. The novel made a huge impact at the time of publication—a time when the U.S. and her Allies were trumpeting victory from pillar to post. There are faults, but the writing's raw and gripping, and the "time machine passages," which relate the characters' pre-war lives, are a key to understanding their various flaws, as well as the unit's dynamics.

FURTHER READING: *The Fight*
SEE ALSO: *Slaughterhouse Five* (Kurt Vonnegut); *Catch-22* (Joseph Heller)

★
★
★
★
★

Writer: Umberto Eco
Publisher: Bompiani, 1980

ISBN US: 978-0156001311
ISBN UK: 978-0099466031

15+

THE NAME OF THE ROSE

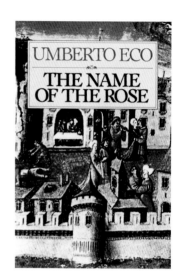

Plot: Eco uses a contemporary framing device to lend veracity to the manuscript that makes up the main text of *The Name of the Rose*. In it a novice monk, Adso of Melk, describes his adventures with Brother William of Baskerville and their investigations, firstly for heresy, then for murder, in a medieval Italian monastery.

Review: Something for everyone here. Those with academic leanings will appreciate the signs and codes that William and the reader must decipher, as well as Eco's intellectual jokes. History buffs, meanwhile, will savor the exacting details of the medieval setting. Fret not if you are a simple lover of a good whodunnit though. Eco himself said he wrote the book because he "felt like poisoning a monk." Above all then, this is a murder mystery, and one which not only lovers of genre detective fiction will lap up.

FURTHER READING: *Foucault's Pendulum*
SEE ALSO: *My Name Is Red* (Orhan Pamuk);
The Club Dumas (Arturo Pérez-Reverte)

★
★
★
★

Writer: Gerald Kersh
Publisher: Michael Joseph Ltd, 1938

ISBN US: 978-0743413046
ISBN UK: 978-0955185137

15+

NIGHT AND THE CITY

Plot: *Night and the City*'s central character is Harry Fabian, a con man who lives on immoral earnings. Can Harry get together £100 to become London's top wrestling promoter, or will the police arrest him before it's too late?

Review: Back in the 1930s, during the Depression, London was not a safe place to be: razor gangs roamed the streets, pickpockets were a dime-a-dozen, and roughnecks like Harry Fabian hung out in clip-joints, pubs, and in sleazy all-night cafés. Kersh had a bird's eye view of London lowlifes, stemming from his poor upbringing and a Bohemian lifestyle; he draws them to perfection here, in this, a 500 lb. gorilla of an "East End novel."

FURTHER READING: *Selected Stories*
SEE ALSO: *They Drive by Night* (James Curtis);
Hangover Square (Patrick Hamilton)

74

Writer: Edgar Allan Poe
Publisher: Periodical publication, 1842

ISBN US: 978-0385074070
ISBN UK: 978-1840220520

5+ THE PIT AND THE PENDULUM

Plot: An unnamed prisoner is sentenced to death by the Spanish Inquisition. He is flung into a darkened room, blacks out, and, on awakening, discovers there is a deep pit at its center; awakening from a second bout of unconsciousness he becomes aware of a pendulum that threatens to swing and slice through his chest.

Review: A tale of the unexpected that gives new meaning to the expression, "stuck between a rock and a hard place." Poe serves up a feast for the senses here, arousing our innate human fears of the dark, confined spaces, and rats—fears shared by the narrator with his gasping anxiety at the molten dangers offered by the room. Chilling and macabre, this is Poe at his best.

FURTHER READING: *The Masque of the Red Death; The Murders in the Rue Morgue*
SEE ALSO: *The Call of Cthulhu: And Other Weird Stories* (H. P. Lovecraft)

75

Writer: Christopher Brookmyre
Publisher: Little Brown and Co, 1996

ISBN US: 978-0802138613
ISBN UK: 978-0349108858

8+ QUITE UGLY ONE MORNING

Plot: In Edinburgh, Scotland, Jack Parblane, investigative journalist, wakes up to the familiar agonies of a hangover and the unfamiliar problem of a grisly and vomit-soaked murder scene in a neighboring apartment. Parblane, initially a suspect, investigates and uncovers political misdeeds in Edinburgh's local National Health Service.

Review: Brookmyre, when asked, told us that for him cult means a book that some readers would be keen to share with their friends, but that others just won't "get." In writing this novel for himself, he says, he knew he would alienate certain people. In this reviewer's opinion, he will only alienate those who don't appreciate the powers of a clever satirist and brilliant storyteller, for *Quite Ugly One Morning* is a political satire and crime romp of unrivalled dark fun.

FURTHER READING: The best of the other Parblane titles is *The Attack of the Unsinkable Rubber Ducks,* while *Pandaemonium*, Brookmyre's latest, is a contemporary take on the sci-fi/ horror genre
SEE ALSO: *Tourist Season* (Carl Hiaasen)

★
★
★

Writer: Chester Himes
Publisher: Gallimard, 1958

ISBN US: 978-1841950242
ISBN UK: 978-1841950242

A RAGE IN HARLEM

Plot: It's not hip to be square on the mean streets of 1950s Harlem, a lesson which our main protagonist "Jackson" learns to his cost. Beguiled by the scamming Isabelle, desperate to make easy money, he spirals into a vortex of petty crime. Step up detectives Coffin Ed Johnson and Gravedigger Jones, characters appearing in nine Himes novels, and touchstones for all future fictional African-American cops.

Review: Himes is perhaps best known for nailing the nuance of the precarious race relations of postwar America. All the more impressive considering he wrote this first novel in the un-Harlemesque *milieu* of a Parisian apartment. Incarnated previously as an armed robber, it's not surprising that the cops and crooks are so perfectly nailed down as well. Who says crime doesn't pay?

FURTHER READING: *Cotton Comes to Harlem*;
The Real Cool Killers; *If He Hollers Let Him Go*
SEE ALSO: *The Native Son* (Richard Wright)

★
★
★
★
★

Writer: Daphne du Maurier
Publisher: Victor Gollanz, 1938

ISBN US: 978-0380778553
ISBN UK: 978-1844080380

REBECCA

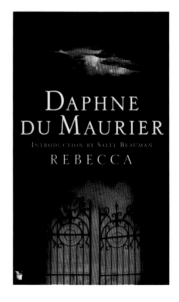

Plot: While working as a lady's companion, a mousy young woman has a whirlwind romance with the charming and wealthy widower Maxim de Winter. Two weeks later they are married and head home to Maxim's country estate, Manderley. The new Mrs. de Winter becomes possessed by the notion that Maxim still loves his first wife—Rebecca—a notion inflamed by the meddlings of Manderley's housekeeper, the vile and eerie, Mrs. Danvers.

Review: Two images loom over this story: the sprawling, foreboding estate of Manderley, and the captivating adulteress Rebecca. Thusly du Maurier skillfully entwines the reader in the fears haunting her unnamed narrator: what she suffers, we suffer, all the way to the novel's heart-stopping and thrilling conclusion. Small wonder that the book has inspired writers, film-makers, and readers ever since its first publication.

FURTHER READING: *Jamaica Inn*
SEE ALSO: *Mrs. de Winter* (Susan Hill);
The Key to Rebecca (Ken Follet)

Writer: Zane Grey
Publisher: Harper & Brothers, 1912

ISBN US: 978-0486424569
ISBN UK: 978-1404328945

5+ RIDERS OF THE PURPLE SAGE

Plot: "Seven Mormons all packin' guns, an' a gentile tied with a rope, an' a woman who swears by his honesty! Queer, ain't that?" Lassiter, "a gunman in black leather," describes the punishment of cattle-rancher Jane Withersteen for her friendship with a gentile. Set in Utah in 1871, *Riders of the Purple Sage* is Lassiter's and Jane's story as they stand up to the Mormons for entirely different reasons, at first, but, eventually, with a commonality borne of love.

Review: Zane Grey has long since been regarded as the progenitor of the fictional Wild West as we know it. Some might be deterred by the melodramatic tone of the piece, but see past this and lovers of a good old-fashioned cowboy story won't be disappointed.

FURTHER READING: Grey was a prolific writer, so plenty to choose from, but you could try *The Vanishing American* next
SEE ALSO: *Last of the Mohicans* (James Fenimore Cooper); *Shane* (Jack Schaefer)

Writer: Geoffrey Household
Publisher: Chatto and Windus, 1939

ISBN US: 978-1590172438
ISBN UK: 978-0752851396

5+ ROGUE MALE

Plot: An unnamed protagonist stalks an evil European dictator (modeled on Hitler). His intention is not, he tells himself, to kill the leader, but to see how close he can get to his prey. But before this resolve can be put to the test, our hero is caught by the dictator's guards and tortured. He escapes with his tormentors in hot pursuit—the hunter has become the hunted and is forced to go underground in the English countryside.

Review: Gripping and thought-provoking, *Rogue Male* is a well-constructed psychological thriller and an early classic of that genre. The fear and claustrophobia of living underground has gripped generations of readers since the book's publication in 1939. And, of course, the image of the dictator in the hunter's sights is a very powerful one.

FURTHER READING: *Rogue Justice; Rough Shoot; Watcher in the Shadows*
SEE ALSO: *The Third Man* (Graham Greene); *The Thirty-Nine Steps* (John Buchan); *Fatherland* (Richard Harris)

★
★
★

Writer: Mark Billingham
Publisher: Little, Brown, & Co., 2001

ISBN US: 978-0066212999
ISBN UK: 978-0751531466

18+

SLEEPYHEAD

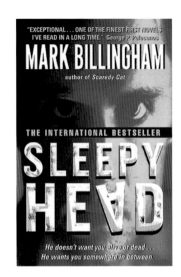

"EXCEPTIONAL... ONE OF THE FINEST FIRST NOVELS
I'VE READ IN A LONG TIME." George P. Pelecanos

MARK BILLINGHAM
author of *Scaredy Cat*

THE INTERNATIONAL BESTSELLER

SLEEPY
HEAD

He doesn't want you alive or dead . . .
He wants you somewhere in between.

Plot: A criminal is on the loose. His first three victims die, a fourth is in a coma state known as "locked-in syndrome." Detective Inspector Tom Thorne must use all his wiles to discover not just whodunnit but whydunnit before the benzodiazepine-happy lunatic strikes again.

Review: It's a bold person who would attempt a new take on the police procedural—an overpublished genre if ever there was one. Billingham, however, takes on the genre, and brings to it, as writer George Pelecanos has said, a "rare and welcome blend of humanity, dimension, and excitement." High praise from a high priest of crime fiction, and something echoed by this reviewer. Read Billingham, and find out why for yourself.

FURTHER READING: *Buried; Scaredy Cat*
SEE ALSO: *Lonely Hearts* (John Harvey);
The Rebus novels (Ian Rankin)

★
★
★
★
★

Writer: Andrey Kurkov
Publisher: Alterpress (Kiev), 1996

ISBN US: 978-1860469459
ISBN UK: 978-1860469459

15+

SMERT POSTORONNEGO
(DEATH AND THE PENGUIN)

Death and
the Penguin
Andrey Kurkov

HARVILL
PANTHER

"A black comedy of rare distinction, and the penguin
is an invention of genius" JOHN DE FALBE, Spectator

Plot: Be careful what you wish for. Viktor, an aspiring short story writer who makes a living penning obituaries, yearns to see his name in print, yet the subjects of his obituaries seem to cheat death. When finally they do start dropping off, Viktor is drawn into a shady world of Ukrainian gangsters and dodgy politicians. Not good news for him, or the depressed pet penguin, Misha, with whom he shares an apartment in "complimentary lonelinesses."

Review: A satirical look at Ukranian life in the post Soviet era. Laconic third person narration, together with the silent Misha, creates a bleak and darkly comic atmosphere. Despite the feeling of emptiness, this is a touching story, and it would be a stone-hearted person who would not care deeply for the unlikely duo . . . especially as the body count starts to rise.

FURTHER READING: *Penguin Lost; A Matter of Death and Life*
SEE ALSO: *Absurdistan: A Novel* (Gary Shteyngart)

Writer: Robert Louis Stevenson
Publisher: Longmans, Green and Co, 1886

ISBN US: 978-0451528957
ISBN UK: 978-0140620511

12+

STRANGE CASE OF DR. JEKYLL AND MR. HYDE

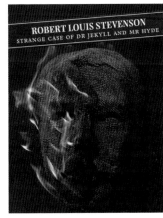

Plot: When a lawyer, Mr. Utterson, discovers that his friend Dr. Henry Jekyll has willed his estate to the malevolent Edward Hyde, he fears there may be some "disgrace." A letter from Dr. Jekyll finally reveals the truth: as the result of an experiment gone wrong, Jekyll and Hyde are one and the same person. When Jekyll can no longer suppress Hyde, "the child of hell" becomes the more dominant of his two natures.

Review: A gothic page-turner that is a black-and-white portrayal of man's potential for good and evil. Corny lines such as, "If he shall be Mr. Hyde . . . I shall be Mr. Seek" abound. Yet, the book's cultural impact and its allegorical ideas on the dualism of human nature make it essential reading.

FURTHER READING: *Treasure Island; Kidnapped*
SEE ALSO: *Frankenstein* (Mary Shelley);
The Invisible Man (H. G. Wells)

500 ESSENTIAL CULT BOOKS

199

THRILLING TALES Best of the Rest

Writer: E. T. A. Hoffmann
Publisher: 1814–1817

ISBN US: 978-1409955399
ISBN UK: 978-0140443929

12+

TALES OF HOFFMANN

Synopsis: Reality and the supernatural coincide in Hoffmann's hugely influential stories from the German Romantic period of literature. The most famous, perhaps, is "The Sandman," a horror story about a young boy whose childhood fears of a grotesque figure haunt him into adulthood, eventually driving him mad. Or do they?

Review: Though written many moons ago, these tales of horror and the uncanny are so unnerving they might have you checking under the bed for the boogeyman. In fact, the antiquated tone and language, far from dating the stories, imbue them with a spookily dark atmosphere. Since different editions vary in their selection, make sure you get hold of one that includes "The Sandman," "The Golden Pot," and "Master Flea."

E. T. A. HOFFMANN
Tales of Hoffmann

FURTHER READING: *The Devil's Elixirs* (a novel in two volumes)
SEE ALSO: The stories of Edgar Allen Poe

★
★
★
★

Writer: James Curtis
Publisher: Jonathan Cape, 1938

ISBN US: 978-0955185144
ISBN UK: 978-0955185144

15+

THEY DRIVE BY NIGHT

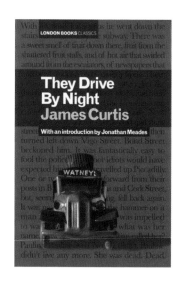

Plot: *They Drive By Night* begins in the manner of a Hitchcockian thriller as Shorty Matthews, fresh from spending time at Her Majesty's Pleasure (in other words, in jail), stumbles across the corpse of an ex-girlfriend. His instinct is to flee, heading for the Great North Road, leaving behind a clutch of suspicious coppers and a murderer on the loose.

Review: Within this fast-moving novel's pages you will find a nail-gripping thriller, a glimpse into the poverty suffered in 1930s Britain, and an unlikely love story. The slang used by Curtis' deadbeats may seems dated, idiosyncratic even, but dig deeper and you should be impressed by a socially aware novel with real heart.

FURTHER READING: *The Gilt Kid; There Ain't No Justice*
SEE ALSO: *Night and the City* (Gerald Kersh);
Hangover Square (Patrick Hamilton)

★
★
★
★

Writer: Carl Hiaasen
Publisher: G.P. Putnam's Sons, 1986

ISBN US: 978-0446695718
ISBN UK: 978-0330322362

18+

TOURIST SEASON

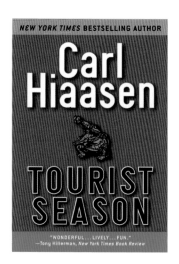

Plot: A blackly comic crime caper involving perhaps the strangest murder weapon in history: a rubber toy alligator. Private dick and one-time journalist Brian Keyes investigates this murder, and other strange goings on, which have him wondering if someone is trying to kill off the South Florida tourist season.

Review: Fans of Hiaasen dig his absurdist take on the machinations of politicians, developers, and bureaucrats, as well as the ecological preoccupations of his books. Hiaasen cherishes South Florida's natural eccentricities and swamps, and this appreciation might just be *Tourist Season*'s biggest strength. His comic take on the private eye formula comes a close second, however.

FURTHER READING: *Basket Case; Double Whammy; Sick Puppy*
SEE ALSO: *A Snowball in Hell* (Christopher Brookmyre);
Last Tango in Aberystwyth (Malcolm Pryce)

★
★
★

Writer: Gil Scott-Heron
Publisher: World Publishing Co, 1968

ISBN US: 978-0862415280
ISBN UK: 978-0862415280

8+

THE VULTURE

Plot: *The Vulture* is the story of a murder victim, John Lee, told in the words of four men who knew him in childhood.

Review: Yes, it's *that* Gil Scott-Heron, "the godfather of rap," much better known for his musical output. A shame, that, since there is certainly much to admire here. The scenario for the plotting is highly original, the language of the streets sweet and sharp, and Scott-Heron's political voice is put to good use with the nervous race relations of the streets of Lower Manhattan permeating the novel and raising it above the level of potboiler. Scott-Heron has only written one further novel—it seems that musical success has robbed fans of crime fiction of a first-rate talent.

FURTHER READING: *The Nigger Factory;*
Now and Then: The Poems of Gil Scott-Heron
SEE ALSO: *Black Skin, White Masks* (Frantz Fanon)

★
★
★
★

Writer: Oakley Hall
Publisher: Viking, 1958

ISBN US: 978-1590171615
ISBN UK: 978-1590171615

5+

WARLOCK

Plot: Something ain't right in Warlock—a silver mining town in the Wild West—and its citizens want order restored. Step up gunslinger Clay Blaisedell, a trigger-happy lawman who—against the backdrop of a miner's strike and political struggles—must attempt to clean up the town.

Review: For some the words "Wild West" might be synonymous with cartoon goodies and baddies and a one-dimensional morality. Blaisedell, though, is not your archetypal lawman, and *Warlock* is not your archetypal tale of right and wrong. If you don't believe us, then we're sure you'll take it from cult hero Thomas Pynchon, who said, "it is the deep sensitivity to abysses that makes *Warlock* one of our best American novels."

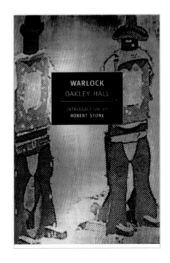

FURTHER READING: *The Badlands; Apaches*
SEE ALSO: *Blood Meridian* (Cormac McCarthy);
Little, Big Man (Thomas Berger)

★ **Writer:** John Birmingham **ISBN US:** 978-0345457134
★ **Publisher:** Macmillan, 2004 **ISBN UK:** 978-0141029115
★

18+

WEAPONS OF CHOICE

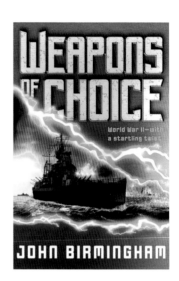

Plot: In the year 2021, an American-led CI taskforce is about to attack the Indonesian islands. The multinational force also includes a scientific group who are experimenting with wormholes, which cause most of the ships to travel back in time to 1942. Here, the CI encounter an American taskforce sent to protect Midway from an attack by the Japanese navy and all but wipe them out.

Review: While playing fair to readers looking for a fast-paced alternative history adventure, Birmingham creates a series that has more going for it than futuristic missiles versus WWII bombs by contrasting attitudes of the wartime American soldiers to the future multinational forces. The centerpiece is still the old standard time paradox: how will the arrival of technology from the future alter the future the taskforce arrived from?

FURTHER READING: *Designated Targets; Final Impact*
SEE ALSO: *1901* (Robert Conroy); *Island in the Sea of Time* (S. M. Stirling)

★ **Writer:** James Hawes **ISBN US:** 978-0679776154
★ **Publisher:** Jonathan Cape, 1996 **ISBN UK:** 0-099-59151-0

15+

A WHITE MERC WITH FINS

Plot: Central to this cinematic novel is "the plan." A plan, that is, to perform a heist at Michael Winner's bank (allegedly) with the help of a plastic gun, a sultry Scot, the IRA, and a white Merc with fins.

Review: Pastiche but in a good way, this gripping heist story acknowledges its major influence, Quentin Tarantino, on page two. Hawes successfully transports the filmmaker's snappy dialog to the darkest reaches of Shepherd's Bush, in a London akin to "a mincing machine, where people go in one end and money comes out the other." This book will not change your life, but it will certainly have you canceling all other engagements until you have puzzled and chortled your way to its satisfying climax.

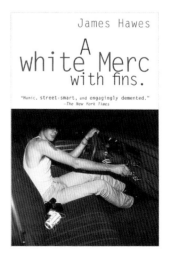

James Hawes
A
white Merc
with fins.
"Manic, street-smart, and engagingly demented."
—The New York Times

FURTHER READING: *Rancid Aluminium*
SEE ALSO: *Get Carter* (Ted Lewis)

★
★
★
★

Writer: Wilkie Collins
Publisher: S. Low, Son & Co, 1859

ISBN US: 978-0486440965
ISBN UK: 978-0140620245

15+

THE WOMAN IN WHITE

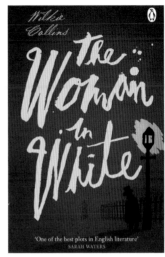

'One of the best plots in English literature'
SARAH WATERS

Plot: Dark secrets lie at the heart of Collins' suspenseful tour de force. When a teacher of drawing, Walter Hartright, espies a mysterious woman on Hampstead Heath, he becomes involved in a mystery involving identity theft, a nefarious husband, and doppelgangers. The tale is presented by "more than one pen," a narrative technique that lends credence, intrigue, and drama as events unfold.

Review: Although *The Woman in White* is a stunning example of the sensation novel so popular in the 1860s (a genre full of melodrama and improbability), it is nonetheless free of heavy Victorian values. As such it more than stands the test of time.

FURTHER READING: *The Moonstone*
SEE ALSO: *The Castle of Otranto* **(Horace Walpole);**
The Turn of the Screw **(Henry James);**
Lady Audley's Secret **(Mary Braddon)**

★
★

Writer: Max Brooks
Publisher: Crown, 2006

ISBN US: 978-0307346612
ISBN UK: 978-0715637036

15+

WORLD WAR Z
AN ORAL HISTORY OF THE ZOMBIE WAR

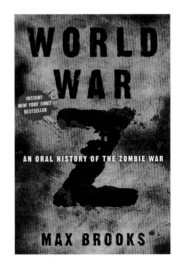

Plot: A follow-up to *The Zombie Survival Guide: Complete Protection from the Living Dead* (2003), in which Brooks created a manual for dealing with outbreaks of zombies as well as chronicling documented accounts dating back to 60,000 BC. *World War Z* continues the conceit with an oral account taken from many dozens of recollections about the worldwide zombie pandemic that sweeps the world in the not-too-distant future.

Review: Does what it says on the tin but in a politically savvy way. Brooks has used historical events from which to posit how nations would react to an infectious zombie virus outbreak. Thus China stays silent (as it did with bird flu), and America ignores it, then reacts poorly (as with Hurricane Katrina).

FURTHER READING: *The Zombie Survival Guide;*
The Zombie Survival Guide: Recorded Attacks
SEE ALSO: *Day by Day Armageddon* **(J. L. Bourne);**
Plague of the Dead **(Z. A. Recht);** *Dying to Live* **(Kim Paffenroth)**

ESSENTIAL CULT BOOKS

500

203

THRILLING TALES
Best of the Rest

TOVE JANSSON

FINN FAMILY MOOMINTROLL

A Puffin Book

THE OUTSIDERS

S. E. HINTON
Now a Major Film

WINNER OF THE WHITBREAD
BOOK OF THE YEAR

MARK HADDON

THE CURIOUS INCIDENT

of THE DOG
in THE NIGHT-TIME

'OUTSTANDING...A stunningly
good read' INDEPENDENT

ALICE'S ADVENTURES IN WONDERLAND

'Precise,
dream-like,
subversive'
Quentin Blake,
Independent
on Sunday

LEWIS CARROLL

HERGÉ
LES AVENTURES DE TINTIN

L'ÎLE NOIRE

casterman

THE MAGIC FARAWAY TREE

Enid Blyton

MELVIN BURGESS

JUNK

winner
of the
Guardian
Fiction Award
and the
Carnegie
Medal

Forever

#1
NEW YORK TIMES
BESTSELLING
AUTHOR

JUDY
Blume

There i

NANCY DREW MYSTERY STORIES 1

THE SECRET
OF THE
OLD CLOCK

CAROLYN KEENE

read by
LAURA
LINNEY

Piccolo

the little prince

Antoine de Saint-Exupéry
Now filmed by Stanley Donen for Paramount Pictures

TOLKIEN
The Hobbit

FLAT STANLEY

Jeff Brown

HANS
CHRISTIAN
ANDERSEN

THE COMPLETE FAIRY TALES AND STORIES

TRANSLATED FROM THE DANISH BY
ERIK CHRISTIAN HAUGAARD

WITH A FOREWORD BY VIRGINIA HAVILAND

"The best English edition of Andersen in three decades."
—Psychology Today

WHERE THE WILD THING

STORY AND PICTURES BY

A Series of
Unfortunate Events
by Lemony Snicket

BOOK THE FIRST

The Bad Beginning

THE No.1 INTERNATIONAL BEST

MARKUS ZUSA

The
Book Thie

"A novel of breath-taking scope, masterfully
Guardian

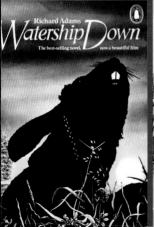

Richard Adams

Watership Down

The best-selling novel, now a beautiful film

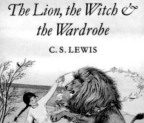

The Lion, the Witch &
the Wardrobe

C. S. LEWIS

A Puffin Book

CHAPTER 5

YOUNG CULT

REMEMBRANCE OF THINGS PAST

You might not remember much about your childhood, but we'll bet you can recall page-for-page, word-for-word, and picture-for-picture some of the books you read or which were read to you from that time; books that, like acne or your first kiss, are such a big part of your formative years they will never be forgotten. We've included some of those titles in this selection, but we've also included that special kind of children's book that would not have you flushing with embarrassment if you were caught reading it on the train—the crossover books that appeal to both adults and children alike.

You might be browsing this chapter to get inspired for your own reading matter, or, more likely, to see what books might be suitable for your kids. In the latter case, don't forget to look at our age ratings to get the best out of the Young Cult recommendations that follow.

★
★
★
★
★

Writer: Lewis Carroll
Publisher: Macmillan, 1865

ISBN US: 978-0451527745
ISBN UK: 978-0141439761

A

ALICE'S ADVENTURES IN WONDERLAND

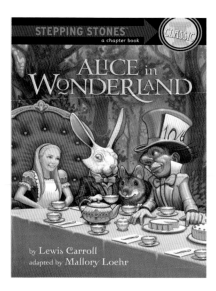

Plot: Under a sweltering summer sun, young Alice of the title spies a White Rabbit who is in a terrible hurry. Her curiosity piqued, she follows the fully clothed mammal "down, down, down" a rabbit-hole into the Wonderland of the title. In this dream-world she variously: gets advice from a caterpillar; attends a most unusual tea party; plays croquet with a (live) flamingo; and encounters all manner of creatures—from the extinct (a Dodo), to the fantastic (a Gryphon), to a menagerie of anthropomorphic animals who, together, distract Alice from finding her way home.

Review: An intoxicating mix of riddles and rhymes, a cascade of word play, and the above-mentioned cast of characters make this a surreal experience. But not one which alienates children. On the contrary, in Alice, Carroll captures the very essence of childhood: Alice's curiosity, her muddle-headedness, and her forthrightness being features that most children will identify with.

There may be some of you who've known the nonsense rhymes in Alice off-by-heart since childhood—"Speak roughly to your little boy and beat him when he sneezes" will be forever ensconced in my brain—there may be others who read the story first as an adult, and there may be a few who only know the story from the faithful, if underwhelming, Disney movie (shame on you). Whichever you are, it's probably been some time since you read Alice in full. In which case it's time to dust off a copy and delight in its episodic whimsy . . . And if you've a child to read and enjoy it with, better still.

FURTHER READING: *Through the Looking Glass*; *The Hunting of the Snark* (nonsense verse)
SEE ALSO: *Harry Potter* series (J. K. Rowling)

★
★
★
★
★

Writer: Anne Frank
Publisher: Contact Publishing, 1947;
new edition - Doubleday, 1995

ISBN US: 978-0553296983
ISBN UK: 978-0141182759

(A)

HET ACHTERHUIS
(ANNE FRANK: THE DIARY OF A YOUNG GIRL)

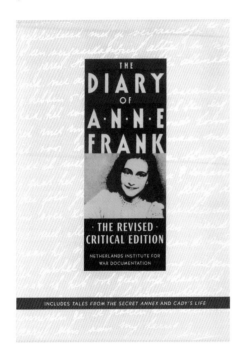

500 ESSENTIAL CULT BOOKS

YOUNG CULT
Top 10 Classics

Synopsis: Perhaps the most important personal record of World War II, Jewish teenager Anne Frank's diary covers the last 25 months of her life—the period over which she and her family were forced to go into hiding in an Amsterdam warehouse, in Nazi-occupied Holland.

In the diaries, Anne recounts both the usual teenage anxieties—friendships, boys, and family squabbles—as well as the growing horrors of living in confinement: the lack of sanitation and food, the arguments among her fellow refugees, and the terror of being discovered.

Review: Anne Frank's extraordinary diary is not without its critics. People read it to learn about the Holocaust, Professor Lawrence Langer has written, but what they are getting is a "safe and sanitized version." Others argue that universalizing Anne detracts from the fact she died because she was a Jew. Well, maybe. But as a primary source of information

for children learning about the horrors of anti-Semitism in the 1940s—especially the new generation of children for whom Nazism is such a remote concept—its value cannot be overstated.

In any case, the cult of Anne Frank lives on (by 2007 one million people had visited the museum dedicated to her life), and both the adult and child reader should not fail to be moved by Anne's passions and human spirit, as well as her remarkable skill as a writer, given her number of years; Anne died at Bergen-Belsen just before her sixteenth birthday.

FURTHER READING: The 1947 edition of the Diary, for comparison's sake.
SEE ALSO: *The Boy in the Striped Pyjamas* (John Boyne); *The Book Thief* (Markus Zusak)

★
★
★
★
★

Writer: J. R. R. Tolkien
Publisher: George Allen & Unwin, 1937

ISBN US: 978-0618968633
ISBN UK: 978-0261102217

A

THE HOBBIT

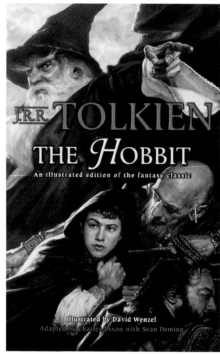

Plot: Bilbo Baggins, a conservative hobbit who loves his home comforts, has his life changed forever when, one evening, his wizard friend Gandalf brings thirteen dwarves uninvited to his home for supper. This group are on a quest to reclaim their ancestors' treasure, which was stolen by the evil dragon, Smaug, and Bilbo is stunned when Gandalf reveals he has been chosen to join them, as their "burglar." Though he seems an unlikely hero at first, the hobbit soon discovers a taste for adventure, plus a ring of invisibility that proves useful when dealing with goblins, giant spiders, and the sinister Gollum.

Review: Long before *Harry Potter*, children and adults alike have been enthralled by *The Hobbit*, a well-crafted fantasy that does not talk down to its readers. The origin of the story was a scribbled note: while marking school certificates, Tolkien was struck by inspiration and jotted down the sentence that would become the opening line of the story: "In a hole in the ground there lived a hobbit."

Prior to this, Tolkien had already published a number of children's poems and had been developing his own mythology and accompanying eleven languages since 1917. Although the latter were only published posthumously, they provided the foundations for *The Hobbit*, which was also inspired by the epic Anglo-Saxon poem *Beowulf*. Tolkien created a rich, dazzling, often terrifying world in Middle-Earth, populated by fantastical beings, yet *The Hobbit* also conveys powerful messages about responsibility, maturity, and the terrible cost of war, based upon his own experiences of battle in World War I. In response to popular demand for a sequel, Tolkien wrote *The Lord of the Rings*, not only drawing upon certain elements from *The Hobbit* (such as the ring discovered by Bilbo), but even revising it to fit the events that would follow.

FURTHER READING: *The Lord of the Rings*; *Adventures of Tom Bombadil; Unfinished Tales*
SEE ALSO: *Chronicles of Narnia* series (C. S. Lewis)

★
★
★
★

Writer: Hergé
Publisher: Casterman, 1943

ISBN US: 978-1405206181
ISBN UK: 978-1405206181

A

L'ILE NOIRE

(THE BLACK ISLAND)

Plot: The seventh all-action comic-strip adventure to feature Hergé's instantly recognizable boy-detective, Tintin. Here, returning from South America, Tintin embarks on a breath-taking British adventure after stumbling across a gang of international counterfeiters, led by the nefarious Dr. Müller. His investigations soon take him across the channel, firstly to the South Coast of England, and eventually to a remote Scottish island, said to be terrorized by an evil beast. But is the monster real and, if so, why is it there?

Review: Planes, trains, and automobiles feature in abundance in this, the only Hergé title to have been published in three editions. For the, now ubiquitous, 1966 edition Hergé fastidiously overhauled the graphics, having sent his assistant Bob de Moor to England on a research mission. So, all in Hergé's trademark ligne claire style, we have accurate sign posts, authentic rocky landscapes of the Black Island (based on the west coast Isle of Arran), and

picture perfect policeman's uniforms of the early 1960s—all sketched by Moor and transferred in pen and ink by the master craftsman of comic strips himself. It is this attention to detail, together with nail-biting stories, witty and pithy dialog, and a certain je ne sais quoi besides, which has kept adults and children alike entertained by *The Adventures of Tintin* for generations.

The Black Island, our personal favorite, is a fantastic introduction not only to this series, but to the detective genre in general, whose motifs Hergé follows with both aplomb and an exciting originality here.

FURTHER READING: All the other Tintin stories:
The Seven Crystal Balls **and** *Explorers on the Moon*
come a close second and third to *The Black Island*.
SEE ALSO: *Lucky Luke* **series (Goscinny/Morris);**
Asterix **series (René Goscinny)**

★
★
★
★
★

Writer: Antoine de Saint-Exupéry
Publisher: Gallimard, 1943

ISBN US: 978-0749707231
ISBN UK: 978-0749707231

A THE LITTLE PRINCE

Plot: Our narrator is a pilot who crash-lands in the Sahara Desert. Here he encounters the little prince, a lonely boy who has a wealth of stories about the asteroid he has recently deserted, where he lived with a coquettish rose and three volcanoes. He also tells of its surrounding planets, which are inhabited by—among others—a despotic king, a tippler, and a conceited man.

Review: A moving parable which teaches us that imagination and the search for friendship should not be the sole preserve of children. If there's one criticism of the book, however, it's that adults do come in for a pasting, with each of the little prince's encounters (apart from with the narrator) highlighting a negative aspect of the grown-up world. "The grown-ups are certainly extraordinary," the little prince says, after meeting a particularly greedy businessman. The result is that the innocence of childhood is glorified, and this can seem overplayed. But, in the context that de Saint-Exupéry was writing at a time of what he called "spiritual decay" in the immediate postwar period, it's hardly surprising.

Simple drawings both complement and are integral to the story: It is a picture of a boa-constrictor digesting an elephant that allows the narrator to find a kindred spirit in the little prince, when he (the narrator) is able to identify the drawing. It's these images we recall from childhood, while the allegorical element was perhaps lost on us. Regardless, the friendship between the little prince and the narrator certainly did strike a chord, even back then, and is known as one of the most unusual in literary history. The influence of *The Little Prince* cannot be underestimated.

FURTHER READING: *The Little Prince* is de Saint-Exupery's only work of fiction
SEE ALSO: *Fairy Stories* (Oscar Wilde)

★
★
★
★
★

Writer: S. E. Hinton
Publisher: The Viking Press, 1967

ISBN US: 978-0140385724
ISBN UK: 978-0141314570

12+ THE OUTSIDERS

Plot: A moving drama set in 1950s America, which tells of Ponyboy Curtis, an orphan living with his elder brothers Sodapop and Darry. Ponyboy and his brothers are (or have been) members of the teenaged "Greasers" gang— outsiders with "long greased back hair" who live on their wits, and on the wrong-side-of-the-tracks. When he and best-friend Johnny get in a rumble with rival (right-side-of-the-tracks) gang, the "Socs" (short for socials), and a boy is killed, Ponyboy and Johnny are forced to go on the run, precipitating an exciting, but ultimately tragic, chain of events.

Review: Sentimental, but not saccharine, Hinton's novel perfectly conjures up the deeply felt teenaged pain of not belonging. The grown-up mantra that echoes through the book, that is, to "stay gold," is based on Robert Frost's poem "Nothing Gold Can Stay"; a lament to the inevitability of the destructive force of nature. This emotion reaches a tear-jerking apogée at a key point in the story—which we won't spoil for you by describing here.

Other references from literature are peppered through the book. You might even say (without giving away the ending) that literature or writing is Ponyboy's savior, something which Hinton doubtless intended her young readers to absorb. "*The Outsiders* is definitely my bestselling book," she has said, "but what I like most about it is how it has taught a lot of kids to enjoy reading." By kids, she means both sexes, and that's what's so interesting about *The Outsiders*: it has both boy appeal (fightin', boozin', and cussin'), as well as girl (romance, tragedy, and emotion). Or if you prefer not to consider young adult fiction in such a pink-and-blue hued way, suffice to say *The Outsiders* will get right to the heart of the reader, regardless of gender. Or, for that matter, age.

FURTHER READING: *Rumble Fish*
SEE ALSO: *The Bully* (Paul Langan); *Scorpions* (Walter Dean Myers)

★ **Writer:** Caroyln Keene
★ **Publisher:** Grosset & Dunlap, 1930,
★ revised 1959
★

ISBN US: 978-1557091550
ISBN UK: 978-1557091550

A

THE SECRET OF THE OLD CLOCK

Plot: The first in the hugely successful *Nancy Drew Mysteries* series, ghost-written under the umbrella pseudonym of Carolyn Keene. Here, flame-haired Nancy ("an attractive girl of eighteen") rescues a little girl, a puppy, and old woman, and—as if all that wasn't enough—goes on a search for a missing will, and the old clock of the title. Along the way she displays her trademark heroism, and uses her innate ability to combine feminine wiles and masculine strength, in order to foil crooks twice her age and size.

Review: I was unpleasantly surprised when I reread the *The Secret of the Old Clock* for this review. It struck me as dated and cliché-ridden, whereas when I read it as a pre-teenaged girl (a tweenie you might call it nowadays), in my eyes, Nancy could have done no wrong: beautiful, intuitive and, I hate to say it, rich, she was my role model; I wanted so much to be her. Now, I'd be alarmed if my daughter expressed such a fantasy.

But, as the plot thickened (to the consistency of wallpaper paste: there's a lot going on), and I tried to adopt tweenie-tinted spectacles, I remembered all the things I loved about Nancy. She's just so, for want of a better word, nice, and really, what more could you want your daughter to aspire to? That, and the mystery element (there are genuinely scary moments) is probably what has helped the Nancy Drew brand go from strength-to-strength. Indeed, parents searching for tough, sassy, and intelligent role models for their daughters in days of pink princesses and Pop Star mania could do worse than adding Nancy Drew to her book shelves.

FURTHER READING: *Nancy Drew: All New Girl Detective* series
SEE ALSO: *The Hardy Boys* (Franklin W. Dixon); *Harriet the Spy* (Louise Fitzhugh)

★
★
★
★

Writer: Tove Jansson
Publisher: Ernest Benn, 1950
(originally in Swedish as
Trollkarlens hatt (1948))

ISBN US: 978-0374423070
ISBN UK: 978-0140301502

A

TROLLKARLENS HATT
(FINN FAMILY MOOMINTROLL)

Plot: Isolated in a secret valley in Finland, the Moomins are small, happy trolls unlike any in Scandinavian folklore (in Jansson's illustrations they look like hippos). Other creatures inhabit the valley, friends and neighbors of the Moomins. When Moomintroll, Sniff, and Snufkin wake up one spring, they decide to go to the mountain and make a pile of stones to prove they were the first there. There they find a tall, black hat, which has the power to change anything placed in it.

The Moomintroll family travel to the Hattifatteners' Island, where the Hemulen looks for samples for his botanical collection, and to the Lonely Island where they discover a Wooden Queen. Back at home, Snufkin discovers that the Hobgoblin—who spends his days looking for the King's Ruby, a jewel the size of the head of the flying black panther he uses for transport—may be the owner of the magical hat. The hat, meanwhile, turns the Moominhome into a jungle while Moomintroll is away on a Mameluke hunt. Thingumy and Bob arrive, bringing with them a suitcase that seems to be of great interest to the nasty Groke. In the ensuing court case, the Groke accepts the hat in exchange for the contents of the suitcase, soon revealed to be the King's Ruby. Its light attracts the Hobgoblin, who offers a wish to each of the inhabitants of Moomin Valley.

Review: *Finn Family Moomintroll*, the third book in the series by Finnish artist and writer Jansson, was the first to be translated into English. Jansson's books are inhabited by a broad range of creatures that live closely together in Moomin Valley and the stories are about friendship, acceptance, and tolerance—simple, universal themes that have made the books widely read in many different languages. While the landscapes can be harsh and occasional natural disasters (from thunderstorms to the arrival of a comet) may throw the Valley into turmoil, the warmth and kindness of its close-knit community always win out. Moominland is freshly minted each spring with countless possibilities for adventure, each as delightful as the last.

FURTHER READING: Many further adventures of the Moomins
SEE ALSO: *La Flûte à six Schtroumpfs* (Peyo); *Barbapapa* (Annette Tison and Talus Taylor)

★ **Writer:** Richard Adams
★ **Publisher:** Rex Collings, 1972

ISBN US: 978-0380002931
ISBN UK: 978-0140306019

A # WATERSHIP DOWN

Plot: "We've got to go away before it's too late." Fearing the bloody destruction of their warren, Fiver, a rabbit, and his brother Hazel, search for a new home on Watership Down. Along their perilous journey, they face danger at the hands of Man, do battle with the totalitarian leader of another warren, and come to the realization that the future of any new warren is in doubt—they forgot to bring any does with them on their odyssey.

Adams' writing style intertwines detailed natural description (the landscape is that of Berkshire, his home for many years), a didactic call for Man not to destroy the environment, mythological lore, and an abundance of allegory; all the time employing what has been called a "sorrowfully optimistic" style.

Review: Split into four parts, and weighing in at a lengthy four-hundred-plus pages, this might not be the first book of choice for the couch potato "Wii," generation. The quotes from classic texts at the beginning of each chapter might also be off-putting for young readers, more familiar with *America's Got Talent* than the talents of Aeschylus, among others. Moreover, for a book written in the feminist era of the 1970s, Adams' gender politics are a bit iffy—Much has been made of this over the years, with numerous articles and essays appearing deriding his limited portrayal of female rabbits.

Despite these faults, however, *Watership Down's* cautionary message about the man-made destruction of the natural world ("Men will never rest till they've spoiled the earth and destroyed the animals") lives on, and has made the book a cult classic since its first publication in 1972.

FURTHER READING: *Tales from Watership Down*
SEE ALSO: *Call of the Wild/White Fang* (Jack London); *Tarka the Otter* (Henry Williamson)

★
★
★
★
★

Writer: Maurice Sendak
Publisher: Harper & Row, 1963

ISBN US: 978-0060254926
ISBN UK: 978-0099408390

Ⓐ WHERE THE WILD THINGS ARE

500 ESSENTIAL CULT BOOKS

YOUNG CULT
Top 10 Classics

Plot: The night Max wears his wolf suit he "makes mischief" of the kind that has him sent to bed without any supper. Max's mother calls him "wild thing," inspiring him to sail away to a land where a group of monsters, in awe of his rambunctious behavior, make him their king.

Review: A much-loved picture book classic, which explores a child's imagination as he works through his feelings at being chastened by his mother. Rhythmic language encourages even the youngest child to join in when the book is read aloud, while the artwork is the perfect accompaniment to the underlying dark mood of the story. And with only ten lines of text in the whole book, it is the artwork that really makes the story—Sendak used watercolor, pen, and ink, to create the scratchy, scary, yet endearing paintings of Max, the monsters, and the striking landscape of the land of the wild things—to see them once is to want to see them over and over again.

Max's anti-hero status was something of a revolution in 1963, a time when children's books, in the main, were a celebration of the innocence of childhood. In contrast Sendak wished to depict the full gamut of childhood emotion. His books, he has said, are "all variations on the same theme: how children master various feelings." It's that daring to be different, that originality, which gives *Where the Wild Things Are* its edge, and an enduring cult appeal.

FURTHER READING: *In the Night Kitchen; Outside over There; Higglety Pigglety Pop!; Or There Must Be More to Life*
SEE ALSO: Few picture books contain the ominous presence in Sendak's work but try *The Tiger Who Came to Tea* (Judith Kerr)

★
★ **Writer:** Françoise Sagan   **ISBN US:** 978-0066211695
★ **Publisher:** Juillard, 1954   **ISBN UK:** 978-0140278781

 12+

BONJOUR TRISTESSE

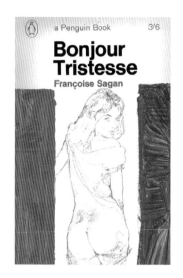

Plot: The Côte D'Azur, France, the early 1950s: a feisty seventeen-year-old girl, Cécile, is holidaying with her widowed and womanizing father, Raymond, when he surprises them both by falling in love. Jealousy, plots, and ultimately tragedy ensue.

Review: Since its publication in the 1950s, reading *Bonjour Tristesse* has been nothing short of a rite-of-passage for teenage girls. It's fashionably French—that's one reason. Melancholy pervades the book like the ever-present French sun—that's two. A frisson of scandal surrounded its publication—that's three. As if all this weren't enough, Sagan perfectly captures that precarious step from adolescence to adulthood. Overall effect? Teenage fiction par excellence.

FURTHER READING: *A Certain Smile*
SEE ALSO: *Le Grand Meaulnes* (Alain-Fournier);
Ghost World (Daniel Clowes)

★
★ **Writer:** Markus Zusak   **ISBN US:** 978-0375831003
★ **Publisher:** Pan Macmillan Australia, 2005   **ISBN UK:** 978-0552773898

12+

THE BOOK THIEF

Plot: This is the story of Liesel, who is sent away to live with foster parents during World War II. Just before her arrival, Liesel steals her first book, "The Grave-Digger's Handbook," and develops a compulsion that sees her pilfering further books from all manner of sources (book-burnings, bomb shelters, and the mayor's library, for instance). All the while the shadow of death—who narrates the story—looms, as well as the everyday struggles of life in Nazi Germany.

Review: At 500 pages and with unusual digressions, the novel is perhaps challenging for the young adult market for which it was published in the U.S. Not the definitive World War II novel, but definitely the most experimental—full of black humor and grim historical detail.

FURTHER READING: *I Am the Messenger; Getting the Girl*
SEE ALSO: *The Boy in the Striped Pyjamas* (John Boyne)

★
★
★
★

Writer: Mark Haddon
Publisher: Jonathan Cape, 2003

ISBN US: 978-1400032716
ISBN UK: 978-0099450252

12+

THE CURIOUS INCIDENT OF THE DOG IN THE NIGHT-TIME

Plot: Christopher Boone, our fifteen-year-old narrator, likes timetables, arithmetic, and his pet rat; he does not like being touched, strangers (except policemen), liars, or the colors brown and yellow. Christopher suffers from Asperger's syndrome, a condition that does not stop him turning amateur sleuth when his neighbor's dog is killed. Could the dog's murder provide a clue as to the cause of his mother's death as well?

Review: Mark Haddon successfully reached out to both an adult and child audience with this universally appealing story of a boy who makes sense of the world through numbers. It is heartbreaking, intelligent, and unusual all at once. Small wonder it won the 2003 Whitbread Book of the Year.

FURTHER READING: *A Spot of Bother*
SEE ALSO: *Holes* (Louis Sachar)

WINNER OF THE WHITBREAD
BOOK OF THE YEAR

MARK HADDON

The
CURIOUS
INCIDENT
of THE DOG
IN THE NIGHT-TIME

'OUTSTANDING...A stunningly
good read' *INDEPENDENT*

★
★
★
★

Writer: Hans Christian Andersen
Publisher: C. A. Reitzel, 1835

ISBN US: 978-0385189514
ISBN UK: 978-1435362352

A # FAIRY TALES

Plot: A collection of well-known and not so well-known tales, dating from 1835 onwards. Andersen drew on folklore for many of his tales; other, later stories sprang from the bowels of the humiliation and poverty of his childhood. Among his band of misfit and unerringly tragic figures, we have a mermaid who wants to join the human world, a snowman that becomes besotted with a stove, and a steadfast tin solider.

Review: If you want to cosset your children in the paranoid bubble of twenty-first century living, stick to Disney. If you would like them to learn something about the sorrow of the human condition, you will do no better than reading them this collection of sentimental, but not mawkish, and anarchic, but not dangerous, tales.

FURTHER READING: The fairy tales are Andersen's life's work—different collections offer different tales, so check which edition you're buying
SEE ALSO: *The Complete Fairy Tales* (Brothers Grimm);
Fairy Tales (Oscar Wilde)

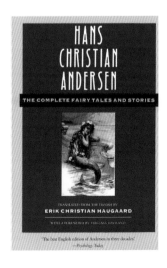

HANS
CHRISTIAN
ANDERSEN

THE COMPLETE FAIRY TALES AND STORIES

TRANSLATED FROM THE DANISH BY
ERIK CHRISTIAN HAUGAARD

WITH A FOREWORD BY VIRGINIA HAVILAND

'The best English edition of Andersen in three decades'
—*Psychology Today*

★
★
★

Writer: Jeff Brown
Publisher: Harper Collins, 1964

ISBN US: 0-06-009791-4
ISBN UK: 978-0060097912

A FLAT STANLEY

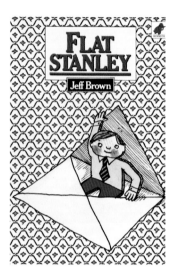

Plot: Stanley Lambchop is just like any other boy until one day a bulletin board falls on him, squashing him to half an inch thick. The story tells of Stanley's adventures as he makes excellent use of his new flat shape: sliding under doorways, being posted in an envelope to California, and even helping catch a pair of sneak-thieves.

Review: That the writing is nothing special should not deter *Flat Stanley* neophytes. A hugely original and inspiring story, coupled with quirky, friendly drawings by Tomi Ungerer, make it a fun read for younger children. The Flat Stanley Project, started by a Canadian teacher in 1995 to encourage letter writing by kids, is testament to the enduring appeal of the book.

FURTHER READING: The other Stanley books do not quite hit the spot, but the picture book version is nice enough for the 3–6 age group
SEE ALSO: *Danny, Champion of the World* (Roald Dahl)

★
★
★

Writer: Judy Blume
Publisher: Bradbury Press, 1975

ISBN US: 978-1416934004
ISBN UK: 978-0330397803

12+ FOREVER

Plot: Katherine is a senior in high school getting to grips with the first flushes of her sexuality. She meets Michael and their relationship soon develops sexually. When their love is consummated they both deem it will last "forever."

Review: When a book is deemed unsuitable for the classroom, what is the first thing adolescents will do? Right. They will go all out to get their raging hormones and hands on it. But censoring of this book and the scandal surrounding its publication should not be the focus here. Instead, let's celebrate its sensitive frankness toward teenage sexuality, which makes it the original and best of the genre.

FURTHER READING: *Just as Long as We're Together; Deenie*
SEE ALSO: *Doing It* (Melvin Burgess); *Love Lessons* (Jacqueline Wilson)

Writer: Melvin Burgess
Publisher: Andersen Press, 1996

ISBN US: 978-0413738400
ISBN UK: 978-0140380194

★
★
★
★

12+

JUNK

Plot: Gemma is a runaway who joins her boyfriend Tar in Bristol and is forced into prostitution after they become addicted to heroin—the "junk" of the title.

Review: A cynic might say Burgess was courting controversy in presenting all parents' worst fears—drink, sex, and drugs—in one teen-novel-shaped package. The more open-minded would argue that in 1996, the time was right for a book that addressed these issues for the most vulnerable age group in society. Burgess himself says the book was a "real experiment," coming at a time when few books were directly aimed at teenagers. The experiment paid off. *Junk* was an international bestseller and won a Carnegie medal in 1997.

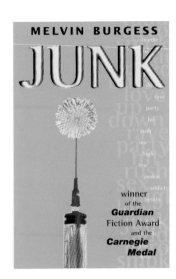

winner
of the
Guardian
Fiction Award
and the
**Carnegie
Medal**

FURTHER READING: *Doing It*
SEE ALSO: *Forever* (Judy Blume);
The Other Side of Truth (Beverly Naidoo)

Writer: C.S. Lewis
Publisher: Geoffrey Bles, 1950

ISBN US: 978-0060765484
ISBN UK: 978-0007115617

★
★
★

A

THE LION, THE WITCH AND THE WARDROBE

Plot: A snowy white wonderland, Narnia, is discovered via a portal in an old wardrobe by Lucy Pevensie, the youngest of four siblings. The land is ruled by an evil Queen, the White Witch, whom Lucy and the other Pevensie children (Edmund, Peter, and Susan) must defeat with the help of a lion, Aslan, "Lord of the whole wood."

Review: Fantasy, adventure, and spellbinding storytelling synchronize in perfect unison in this classic children's tale (the second book in the *Chronicles of Narnia* but the first to be published). Christian allegory is admittedly rammed down the reader's throat—sacrifice, redemption, and the seven deadly sins are all explored here. But if those of other (or no) faiths can overlook this, it is a delightful book for the 8–12 age group.

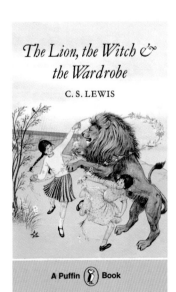

The Lion, the Witch & the Wardrobe

C. S. LEWIS

A Puffin Book

FURTHER READING: The remaining *Chronicles of Narnia* titles
SEE ALSO: *The Hobbit* (J. R. Tolkien); *Harry Potter* series (J. K. Rowling)

ESSENTIAL
CULT BOOKS
500

221

YOUNG CULT
Best of the Rest

★
★
★
★

Writer: William Golding
Publisher: Faber and Faber, 1954

ISBN US: 978-1573226127
ISBN UK: 978-0571191475

12+ # LORD OF THE FLIES

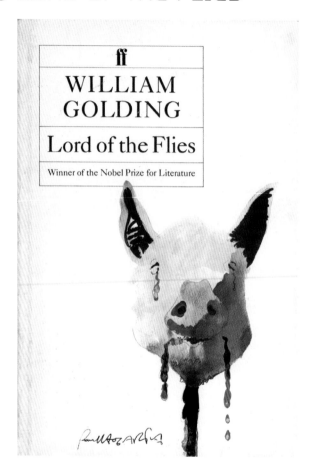

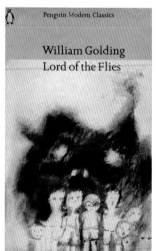

Plot: A group of boys are stranded on a desert island after their plane crashes during World War II. Co-operation is their first impulse, but without the restraints of the adult world, they soon revert to savagery.

Review: More allegory and conflict than you can shake a stick at, but a thrilling tale nonetheless. The common good versus selfish individualism, order versus chaos, and civilized society versus savagery are all explored through the person-alities of the main protagonists. For some such a close inspection of the dark reaches of the human soul is too much, and the book remains on the list of most frequently challenged books of the last century. Thought-provoking stuff, though.

FURTHER READING: *Rites of Passage*
SEE ALSO: *The Mosquito Coast* (Paul Theroux);
The Beach (Alex Garland)

Writer: Enid Blyton
Publisher: Newnes, 1943
ISBN US: 978-0749748029
ISBN UK: 978-1405230285

Ⓐ THE MAGIC FARAWAY TREE

Plot: Three children, Joe, Beth, and Frannie (so-named in modern editions of the book), take their cousin Rick on a magical adventure to the Faraway Tree, introducing him to a host of unusual characters such as Silky the Fairy, Moon-Face, and Saucepan Man.

Review: The *Faraway Tree* stories have legions of devoted fans, incensed by updates to modern editions of the books. Others may feel the publishers have not gone far enough: "Good old Mother" and the "Land of Goodies" being phrases that particularly grate on the nerves of this reviewer. On the plus side, where contemporary storytelling for ages 5–7 can tend towards the prosaic, this is undoubtedly good fantasy fun to spark young imaginations.

FURTHER READING: *The Magic Wishing Chair*
SEE ALSO: *The Hobbit* (J. R. Tolkien); *Narnia* series (C. S. Lewis)

Writer: Lemony Snicket
Publisher: Harper Collins, 1999
ISBN US: 978-0064407663
ISBN UK: 978-1405208673

Ⓐ A SERIES OF UNFORTUNATE EVENTS
THE BAD BEGINNING

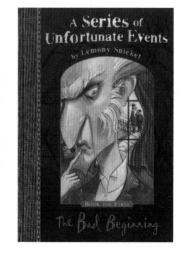

Plot: The first of thirteen volumes featuring the Baudelaire children: Violet, a whizz at inventing; Klaus, a bookworm with a thirst for knowledge; and baby Baudelaire, Sunny, a sharp-toothed toddler. In chapter one, Mr. Poe announces the children's parents are dead, unleashing the unfortunate events of the title, and sees the children living for a spell with the nefarious Count Olaf. The story is related by a world-wise (and world-weary) narrator whose occasional synonymizing will please pedagogically inclined parents.

Review: This "book the first" in a long series throws up more questions than it does answers, whetting the appetite for the misfortunes of the Baudelaire orphans to come. Snicket (aka Daniel Handler) may overegg the portentous pudding but—as any child will tell you—unpleasantness is a far better kiddy-crowd pleaser than happiness every time.

FURTHER READING: Twelve adventures of the Baudelaire children
SEE ALSO: *Harry Potter* series (J. K. Rowling);
Alex Rider series (Anthony Horowitz)

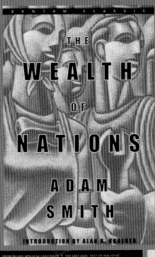

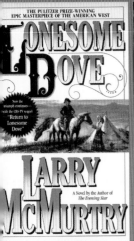

RACES
NTIETH CENTURY

CUS

THIS STORY IS ABOUT WHAT HAPPENED WHEN A SMALL GROUP OF MEN—HIGHLY
PLACED WITHIN THE UNITED STATES MILITARY, THE GOVERNMENT, AND
THE INTELLIGENCE SERVICES—BEGAN BELIEVING IN VERY STRANGE THINGS

NOW A
MAJOR
MOTION
PICTURE

THE MEN
WHO STARE
AT GOATS

JON RONSON
FROM THE BESTSELLING AUTHOR OF THEM: ADVENTURES WITH EXTREMISTS

HERODO

The

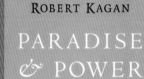

ROBERT KAGAN

PARADISE
& POWER

AMERICA AND EUROPE
IN THE NEW WORLD ORDER

MODERN CLASSICS

Sigmund Freud
Interpreting Dreams

OVER 1 MILLION IN PRINT 75¢

THE YEAR'S MOST
CONTROVERSIAL
BESTSELLER
The
Feminine
Mystique
BETTY FRIEDAN

*The book we have been waiting for
.. the wisest, sanest, soundest, most
understanding and compassionate
treatment of contemporary American
woman's greatest problem, a triumph."*

3055 D A PERENNIAL CLASSIC 75¢

Native Son
RICHARD WRIGHT

CHAPTER 6
REBELLIOUS VOICES

SHOUT, SHOUT, LET IT ALL OUT

In our selection of 500 cult books we felt it was important not to limit ourselves to fiction. And we're glad we didn't, because of all our recommendations these might just be the ones that will resonate with you most. There are cries for justice, books that have awakened the public to race or gender inequality, and authors who dared to speak the unspeakable. Oh, and a woman who calls for all men to be killed.

Needless to say, you might not agree with the politics or ideology in certain of these books, but if you want an insight into some of the most powerful rebel yells of the past two hundred years, then you need look no further than perusing our top ten "rebellious voices."

★
★ **Writer:** Stephen W. Hawking
★ **Publisher:** Bantam, 1988
★

ISBN US: 978-0553380163
ISBN UK: 978-0553175219

15+

A BRIEF HISTORY OF TIME
FROM THE BIG BANG TO BLACK HOLES

showed, first, that black holes could exist in the physical universe, then that singularities (points of infinite density in zero volume) of all sizes could have been created during the Big Bang, and, finally, that they could in fact emit particles, previously thought impossible.

In tackling the origins of the universe, Hawking theorized (far more eloquently over three chapters and a conclusion than in one sentence) that a universe with no boundaries but with finite time potentially implies that the universe had no beginning and therefore no need for a creator.

Hawking admits this is a hypothesis-in-progress and famously concludes that to unify physics in one complete theory would be the ultimate triumph of humanity, "for then we would know the mind of God."

Review: Desiring to write a popular science book on the cosmology and quantum theory of space and time, Stephen Hawking was warned that every time he included an equation in the book, he would halve the sales. The resulting book, *A Brief History of Time*, dealt with the birth of the universe and cutting-edge theoretical physics without using language and equations incomprehensible to the layman. The book is clearly written, informative, and thought provoking to anyone whose knowledge of physics begins and ends with E=mc2.

Synopsis: The book opens with a number of questions: "What do we know about the universe, and how do we know it? Where did the universe come from, and where is it going? Did the universe have a beginning, and if so, what happened *before* then? What is the nature of time? Will it ever come to an end?"

In trying to answer some of these, theoretical physicist Stephen Hawking has pushed the boundaries of what is known about the universe, taking a step toward the Grand Unified Theory that will reconcile general relativity, quantum mechanics, and general thermodynamics. Physically frail and wheelchair-bound due to a degenerative neuromuscular disease, Hawking was able to apply his full attention to theoretical questions, often surprising himself with the results. His work on black holes—derived from Einstein's theories and developed by Schwartzchild and others—

FURTHER READING: *Black Holes and Baby Universes and Other Essays; Stephen Hawking's A Brief History of Time: A Reader's Companion; The Nature of Space and Time* (with Roger Penrose)
SEE ALSO: *The First Three Minutes* (Steven Weinberg)

★
★
★
★

Writer: Doctor Benjamin Spock
Publisher: Pocket Books, 1946
ISBN US: 978-0671537623
ISBN UK: 978-0671690540

15+

THE COMMON SENSE BOOK OF BABY AND CHILD CARE

Synopsis: A classic reference work outlining practical advice for parents, covering everything from toilet training to medical problems and illness, from developmental issues to the all-important issue of sleep (Baby's, not yours). The no-nonsense bullet-pointed style allows stressed out parents to easily access information—handy when you are leafing, bleary-eyed, through the book's pages at 2am in the morning.

At the heart of the book is Spock's mantra to parents "you know more than you think you do." On its first publication in the 1940s such a stance was deemed rebellious, dangerous even, by pedantic paediatricians who thought they knew best. But it was this breaking with tradition that had Spock adored by parents, who were heartened to hear that cuddling and kissing your baby should be encouraged—believe it or not, such loving kindness toward babies and children had been hitherto frowned upon.

Review: Fifty million copies sold worldwide, forty-two foreign language editions, and an eighth edition published in recent years. Can this bestselling how-to manual really be considered a cult book? Well, yes. We'd said we'd include books here that strike a chord with the reader, that resonate with them, that change their lives, even. And, if there is one area of life where empathy between reader and author is most required, it is the minefield of diapers, broken sleep, and constant crying that is the lot of the first-time parent.

That for over sixty years these first-time parents have found as much comfort from Dr. Spock's *Baby and Child Care* as their baby does from his comfort toy explains the continued cult following of Spock as well as his perennial mainstream appeal.

FURTHER READING: *Spock on Spock*
(Dr. Benjamin Spock)—the autobiography
SEE ALSO: *The Contented Little Baby* (Gina Ford);
Secrets of the Baby Whisperer (Tracy Hogg).
Parenting comes full circle in these books,
which suggest you leave your baby to cry it out:
Spock would be turning in his grave

★
★
★

Writer: Karl Marx
Publisher: Verlag von Otto Meissner, 1867

ISBN US: 978-0140445688
ISBN UK: 978-0140445688

15+

DAS KAPITAL (CAPITAL)

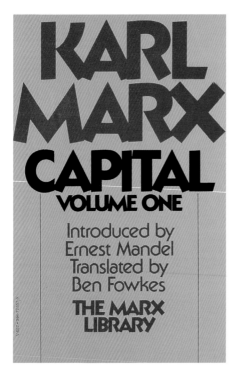

Review: Marx believed in the materialist conception of history, that politics, class, and religion were an outgrowth of the changes caused by economic development. The world progressed because of the clash of ideas—the conflict of thesis and antithesis creating a synthesis—and moved inevitably toward perfection: the overthrowing of capitalism. With *Das Kapital* Marx hoped to offer a scientific basis for his theories. It is a dense historical, mathematical, and philosophical study of the economics of capitalism, the exploitation of the work force, the production of commodities, and the creation of surplus value.

Marx theorized that capitalist societies would create history's last class of people, the oppressed proletariat. They would rise up in violent revolution, creating firstly a proletarian dictatorship that would evolve into communism. In this classless society, there would be no exploitation or inequality. Marxism, as it has subsequently been practiced, has usually been in name only; in most communist countries, the revolutions were not initiated by disaffected workers of advanced industrial societies but by political (Lenin in Russia) or military (Mao in China) leaders, and Marxist philosophy gave way to Bolshevism and Maoism, with which it is often mistaken.

Synopsis: Prussian-born Karl Marx studied philosophy at the University of Berlin but neglected his studies in favor of debating with the Young Hegelians, who drew on the works of philosopher Georg Wilhelm Hegel to attack religion and the Prussian political system. Marx began working for a liberal newspaper, moving to Paris when the paper was suppressed by the government.

He was expelled from France after three years and moved to Brussels where he founded the German Workers' party and was active in the Communist League. For the latter he wrote the infamous *Manifesto of the Communist Party* in 1848. Hounded around Europe for his radicalism, Marx settled in London in 1849, where he remained the rest of his life. Most of his time was spent in revolutionary politics and researching *Das Kapital*. Only one volume was published in his lifetime; two further volumes were completed by Marx's lifelong friend, Friedrich Engels.

FURTHER READING: *The Communist Manifesto* (Marx and Friedrich Engels);
The Portable Karl Marx (ed. Eugene Kamenka)
SEE ALSO: *Discourse on the Origin of Inequality* (Jean-Jacques Rousseau); *The General Theory of Employment, Interest, and Money* (John Maynard Keynes)

★
★
★
★
★

Writer: Doris Lessing
Publisher: Michael Joseph, 1962

ISBN US: 978-0061582486
ISBN UK: 978-0007247202

15+

THE GOLDEN NOTEBOOK

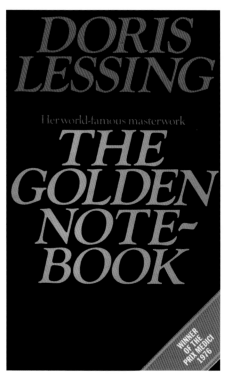

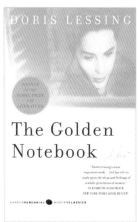

Plot: The novel, like its heroine, is split into parts, reflecting fragmented aspects of her personality at various times of her life. Anna Wulf's story is told through four differently colored notebooks she has kept: one recording her life in Africa, a second her experiences with the Communist Party, a third the thinly veiled autobiographical novel she has been writing, and, lastly, a journal where she records her thoughts and emotions. *The Golden Notebook* interweaves extracts from these notebooks with sections of her published novel, *Free Women*, and a main narrative as Anna tries to make sense of her life.

Review: Born Doris May Taylor in Persia, Lessing grew up in Southern Rhodesia where her father ran a large but unsuccessful farm in the district of Banket. Her education was cut short by recurrent eye trouble, although she gained employment as a typist and secretary in Salisbury and, later, as a typist in Cape Town, South Africa. Married and divorced twice, Lessing came to London in 1949 and published her first novel in 1950. She was considered a colonial writer during the 1950s, *The Golden Notebook* being her first successful novel set in her adopted homeland.

In *The Golden Notebook* she explored, she later said, "certain political and sexual attitudes that have force now; it is an attempt to explain them, to objectivize them, to set them in relation with each other. So in a way it is a social novel, written by someone whose training—or at least whose habit of mind—is to see these things socially, not personally."

For many, the book is Lessing's best, although the author has said that, while she likes the novel, she believes it to be a failure hinting at complexity. It established her as a leading contemporary novelist from which foundation she has built a remarkable career.

FURTHER READING: *The Grass is Singing; Memoirs of a Survivor; The Good Terrorist*
SEE ALSO: *Under My Skin and Walking in the Shade, two volumes of autobiography by Lessing*

★
★
★
★

Writer: Edward S. Herman and Noam Chomsky
Publisher: Pantheon Books, 1988

ISBN US: 978-0375714498
ISBN UK: 978-0099533115

15+

MANUFACTURING CONSENT
THE POLITICAL ECONOMY OF THE MASS MEDIA

foreign policy, where similar events are given dissimilar coverage: there was a media outcry against massacres in (Communist) Cambodia but similar massacres in (American-backed) Indonesia made little impression. Rather than respond to news, the mass media colludes with governments to create public opinion and silence dissenting voices.

Review: Chomsky, a leading researcher in linguistics and an outspoken political activist, and former professor of finance Herman turn their attention to the mass media as a political tool with firsthand experience of its effects: their book *Counterrevolutionary Violence*, published by a subsidiary of Warner Communications, was pulped on the orders of a Warner executive. *Manufacturing Consent* received no reviews in major media outlets.

The "propaganda model" developed by Herman and Chomsky has been applied numerous times in the intervening years, proving its usefulness in comparing similar events and the way they are reported. Even in the supposedly liberal media examples continue to be found; for instance, Kevin Young's brief study of reports covering the closure of a TV station critical to (U.S. antagonist) Hugo Chavez's government in Venezuela and a similar move by (U.S. friendly) Alvaro Uribe in Columbia: the former was strongly condemned, the latter not mentioned once.

Synopsis: Herman and Chomsky argue that the control of the media by a handful of large corporations has a pernicious effect on what and how things are reported. The desire for profit (primarily from advertising and sponsorship) means that news is filtered and controls are in place before anything is seen or read by the audience. Of over 25,000 media outlets (everything from newspapers to movies) over half were (in the 1980s) owned by some two dozen companies and many others relied on those companies for material (for example, wire services for anything but local news).

Companies of that size require the support of government and advertisers, both of whom are major suppliers of an endless stream of news and money. The media thereby becomes the propaganda arm of government and big business who can exert control over the content and coverage. This is particularly noticeable in issues of American

FURTHER READING: *The Global Media:*
The New Missionaries of Corporate Capitalism
(Herman and Robert W. McChesney);
Media Control: The Spectacular Achievements
of Propaganda (Chomsky); *The Essential Chomsky*
SEE ALSO: *Chronicles of Dissent: Interviews with*
Noam Chomsky (David Barsamian); *Noam Chomsky:*
On Power, Knowledge, and Human Nature
(Peter Wilkin)

★
★
★
★
★

Writer: Naomi Klein
Publisher: Knopf Canada, 2000

ISBN US: 978-0312421434
ISBN UK: 978-0006530404

15+

NO LOGO

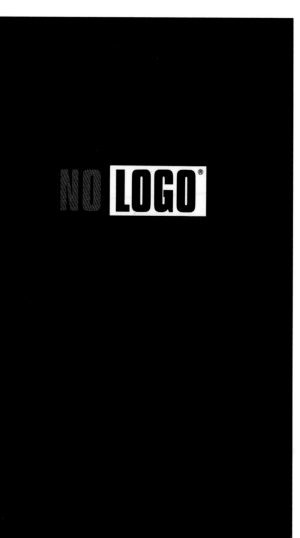

Synopsis: *No Logo* reveals a world in which brand is king, image is value, and the biggest, glossiest, and richest corporations span the globe. Brands are everywhere, in the media, in the high street: part of the advertising-saturated landscape we all inhabit. The book's four sections—No Space, No Choice, No Jobs, and No Logo—cover the history of big brands and trace their power and sweep across the globe, from sweatshops in the developing world to the minimum-wage McJobs of North America, by way of their huge media presence everywhere. Klein's book exposes the way brands control which products reach consumers, the disproportionate voice they have when it comes to censorship, their abuse of copyright laws, and, perhaps most shockingly, who is really profiting from it all.

Review: With its focus on the power and tactics of big brands, *No Logo* is the bible of the anti-globalization movement, which the book itself, in part, predicted. Klein's groundbreaking work masterfully exposes how, for the big name brands, image is everything and real integrity and responsibility mean nothing. The message can be bleak at times and the sheer ruthlessness of big-brand's behavior will anger most readers.

But there is hope too. Klein explains how resistance is growing. Larger and larger numbers of people are getting wise to the smokescreen of benevolence big brands operate behind. This resistance movement is, of course, furthered by the success of the book itself, which, along with the freshness of the writing and the message, means it is still as relevant as ever ten years on.

FURTHER READING: *The Shock Doctrine*
SEE ALSO: *PopCo* (Scarlett Thomas); *Shopped: The Shocking Power Of British Supermarkets* (Joanna Blytheman); *Manufacturing Consent* (Noam Chomsky)

500 ESSENTIAL CULT BOOKS

233

REBELLIOUS VOICES
Top 10 Classics

★
★
★

Writer: Colin Wilson
Publisher: Victor Gollancz, 1956

ISBN US: (out of print)
ISBN UK: 978-0753814321

THE OUTSIDER

12+

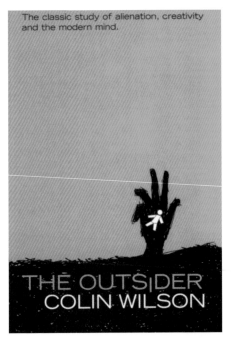

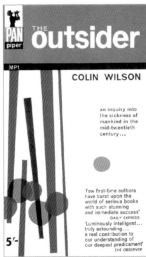

Synopsis: Considered at first to be the work of a prodigy, Colin Wilson's *The Outsider* reflected the youthful writer's eclectic and extensive reading habits—he lists his influences as Eliot, Joyce, Sartre, and Camus—and the writing of his first novel, *Ritual in the Dark*, the central theme of which was alienation from modern society. In *Ritual* (completed some years), the hero finds his answer in a kind of mysticism. "*The Outsider* was simply an attempt to spell out the issues more clearly," Wilson has said. He looked to the work of Camus, Sartre, Barbusse, Hemingway, Hesse, Kafka, Dostoyevsky, and others to study the theme of alienation in the heroes of literature. These outsiders, as Wilson dubs them, have a greater insight and awareness of the ills of the world around them; they can successfully navigate the pessimistic world (as in Sartre's *Nausea*) or allow the world to engulf them.

Review: With *The Outsider*, Wilson, alongside with a number of other new writers, found themselves categorized as the "Angry Young Men." As early as 1958, critic Kenneth Allsop had dubbed the 1950s "The Angry Decade," seeing cultural revolt all around him. In literature the revolt was led by John Wain's *Hurry on Down* and Kingsley Amis' *Lucky Jim* and *That Uncertain Feeling*, all more comically frustrated and irreverent than angry, and published only a few years earlier. John Osborne's *Look Back in Anger* (1956) and John Braine's *Room at the Top* (1957) were definitive texts. Attempts to bring writers together as if they were some anti-establishment protest group (for example, the Tom Maschler-edited *Declaration*, 1957) failed to generate any real sparks.

Wilson's *The Outsider* was critically lauded and, in the dizzying high that followed, its twenty-four-year-old author was interviewed, photographed, and generally turned into an overnight literary celebrity. Headlines like "My Genius" didn't endear him to the critics, who—perhaps realizing they had over-praised his first outing—turned on his second (*Religion and the Rebel*) and tore it to shreds.

The Outsider has subsequently been reassessed as a somewhat middling book deserving neither the unqualified praise nor unreserved hostility it received in the past. It remains Wilson's best-known book of literary exploration.

FURTHER READING: *Religion and the Rebel*; *The Age of Defeat*
SEE ALSO: *Emerging From Chaos* (Stuart Holroyd); *The Divine and the Decay* (Bill Hopkins)

★
★ **Writer:** Aristotle
★ **Publisher:** c. 340 BC

ISBN US: 978-0521484008
ISBN UK: 978-0199538737

5+ # POLITICS

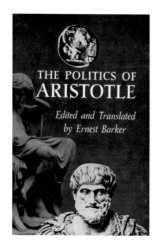

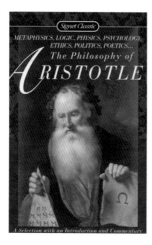

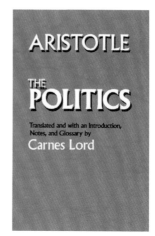

Synopsis: Aristotle is regarded as one of the greatest philosophers of the ancient world; his influence in the organization and classification within sciences as diverse as physics and zoology still resonates today, millennia after his death. The son of a doctor to the royal court of Macedonia, Aristotle was trained by Plato at the Academy in Athens. He developed an absorbing fascination with what things existed and how they existed and interacted rather than the more philosophical question of why they existed.

After setting up an academy at Assos, he began work on his *Historia Animalium*, describing the physical and behavioral habits of every animal, demonstrating his remarkable talent for observation and description. He moved to Lesbos where he worked on *Politics*, and subsequently to Athens where he set up the Lyceum academy. *Politics* attempted to bring together Aristotle's thoughts on the nature of political systems and constitutions, and how these systems affected its citizens and could be affected by its citizens. Originally published in eight volumes, the final two are concerned with Aristotle's speculations on the ideal state.

Review: *Politics* has a greater scope than the title implies as it studies not only the ruling body, but the part played by citizens and even slaves in the modern society. The city (or state) is made up of households, each with their own economy and internal ruling structure. The larger city/state is dependent on the wellbeing of individual households and communities and the wellbeing of citizens depends on sufficient goods, health, and virtue. Everyone should agree on this, says Aristotle, while admitting that the jury is still out on what people consider sufficient wealth, money, power, and reputation.

Some feminist critics have attacked the books for phrases like, "The male is by nature fitter for command than the female," and implying the husband should have "over his wife a constitutional rule." His arguments against the absolute rule of a single monarch and his disapproval of imperialism had little impact on his most famous student, Alexander, the son of Phillip II of Macedonia, whom Aristotle taught for three years. Alexander the Great (as he became known) went on to conquer most of the known world.

FURTHER READING: *The Nicomachean Ethics*;
Commentary on Aristotle's Politics
(Thomas Aquinas)
SEE ALSO: *The Republic* (Plato);
On the Republic (Cicero)

★
★
★
★

Writer: Richard Dawkins   **ISBN US:** 978-0192860927
Publisher: OUP, 1976   **ISBN UK:** 978-0192860927

15+

THE SELFISH GENE

Synopsis: Since Darwin's publication of *The Origin of Species*, it has been widely accepted that species change over time, random mutations being steered by the pressures of survival and reproduction to give rise to new forms of life. While Darwin's theory and insights remain unchallenged by serious scientists, it was later discoveries (in particular DNA, chromosomes, and the operation of genes) that explained the nuts and bolts of how evolution works. Distilling research from many fields, Dawkins explains that it is not individual organisms that are the units of evolution, but their genes, and sets out the important consequences—especially as they relate to understanding human behavior.

Review: One of the most important books of science published in the twentieth century. While genetics themselves were not revolutionary at the time of writing, Dawkins' accomplishment was to allow any reader to grasp the elegant science of evolution and to recognize its mani-festations—not only in the varied forms of plants and animals but in everyday human relations. Tragically, it's widely misunderstood and misquoted, especially by religious activists keen to demonstrate that Dawkins' worldview is immoral; perhaps the title is partly responsible for this (the author later commented that he could have entitled the book "The Selfless Gene" without significant alterations), but it remains as relevant today as ever, and is one of the essential books of the modern age.

FURTHER READING: *The God Delusion*
SEE ALSO: *The Origin of Species* (Charles Darwin);
The Naked Ape: A Zoologist's Study of the Human Animal (Desmond Morris)

★
★
★
★
★

Writer: E. F. Schumacher

Publisher: Harper, 1973

ISBN US: 978-0060916305

ISBN UK: 978-0099225614

12+

SMALL IS BEAUTIFUL

Synopsis: Schumacher began sounding warnings of economic and conservation issues in the early 1960s, noting, for instance, that developing countries were not growing with the appropriate technology that would make full use of the workforce. Instead, investment was being made in the latest Western developments in automated systems (such as the car assembly line), which would inevitably lead to great debt abroad, and underemployment and social disruption locally.

Schumacher set up the Intermediate Technology Development Group to study the implications of this problem and encourage the use of an adequate level of technology that would grow an economy in a slower but more sustainable way.

As a former advisor to the National Coal Board, he also stressed the problems that the demand for energy would bring in the future, arguing against the quest for size, consumption, and profits. Bigger is not always better.

In *Small Is Beautiful*, he championed the need for a decentralized, non-energy, non-capital intensive society, taking a somewhat Buddhist approach to economics and consumerism: selling products to consumers, he argued, was the sole aim of businesses, where it should be to "obtain the maximum of well-being with the minimum of consumption."

Review: Man is small, and, therefore, small is beautiful, Schumacher said. At first, his views were described as Utopian, but the book's release shortly before the 1973 oil crisis and the stock market crash, which led to recession in the UK in 1974, raised its profile and turned it into a bestseller. The book was subsequently translated into fifteen languages and received worldwide attention in places as diverse as the White House and the Vatican. It was named among the one hundred most influential books published since World War II by the *Times Literary Supplement* in 1995. Schumacher's concerns for ecological sustainability and arguments against the blind pursuit of profit by inefficient industries made the writer a popular figure with the environmental movement.

FURTHER READING: *A Guide for the Perplexed*;
This I Believe and Other Essays
SEE ALSO: *Limits to Growth* (Donella Meadows,
Jorgen Randers, and Dennis Meadows);
The Principals of Sustainability (Simon Dresner)

★
★
★

Writer: Sid Jacobson and Ernie Colon

Publisher: Hill & Wang, 2006

ISBN US: 978-0809057399

ISBN UK: 978-0670916733

15+

THE 9/11 REPORT
A GRAPHIC ADAPTATION

Synopsis: The National Commission on Terrorist Attacks—more commonly known as the 9/11 Commission—produced a final report in 2004, which was a surprisingly lucid and readable account of the attacks on the World Trade Center. Here it is translated into graphic form, abridged but faithful to the final report, for those who found the six-hundred pages of the original too daunting.

Review: Intended as a clear and concise version of *The 9/11 Commission Report*, Jacobson and Colon's comic strip version was criticized from the moment it was announced as an inappropriate vehicle to record such a tragic event. The book was, however, well received on publication: Colon's artwork, visually dramatic and occasionally quite graphic, and the depth and detail in Jacobson's captions, make this 130-page adaptation accessible to everyone.

FURTHER READING: *After 9/11: America's War on Terror*
SEE ALSO: *In the Shadow of No Towers* (Art Spiegelman)

★
★
★

Writer: James Gleick

Publisher: Viking, 1987

ISBN US: 978-0143113454

ISBN UK: 978-0749386061

15+

CHAOS MAKING A NEW SCIENCE

Synopsis: Chronicles the development of chaos theory and theoretical models of complex systems from the quantum level to the order and disorder of the universe. Along the way, readers are introduced to Mandelbrot sets, Lorenz attractors, and, now in common parlance, the Butterfly Effect.

Review: As a journalist with the *New York Times*, Gleick made his name writing highly researched features about science and technology, honing a writing style that is detailed yet engages the layman audience by showing how often complex theoretic concepts could have an impact in the real world. In *Chaos*, Gleick brought together work from diverse sciences—mathematics, physics, biology—and explored how understanding chaotic systems could have practical implications, such as a better understanding of weather patterns.

FURTHER READING: *Faster: The Acceleration of Just About Everything; What Just Happened*
SEE ALSO: *Does God Play Dice? The Mathematics of Chaos* (Ian Stewart); *The Essence of Chaos* (Edward Lorenz)

Writer: Henry David Thoreau
Publisher: Aesthetic Papers, 1849

ISBN US: 978-1573922029
ISBN UK: 978-0140390445

CIVIL DISOBEDIENCE

Synopsis: In 1846, Thoreau refused to pay his poll taxes as a protest against government support for slavery. He was marched to jail where, despite the tax being quickly paid, he was not released until the next day. The incident inspired the essay, originally published as "Resistance to Civil Government" in the *Æsthetic Papers* magazine in 1849, in which he championed the notion of passive resistance.

Review: Famously the source of the aphorism, "The government is best which governs least," Thoreau's essay expressed the opinion that, if the actions of a government—whether democratic or not—conflict with the higher moral law, they should be disobeyed. Little noticed at the time of publication, the essay became highly influential in the twentieth century when applied by Mahatma Gandhi and Martin Luther King.

FURTHER READING: *A Yankee in Canada, with Anti-Slavery and Reform Papers*; *Thoreau in Our Season* (Martin Buber)
SEE ALSO: *The Story of My Experiments with Truth* (Gandhi)

REBELLIOUS VOICES
Best of the Rest

ESSENTIAL
CULT BOOKS

500

239

Writer: Carl Sagan
Publisher: Simon and Schuster, 1985

ISBN US: 978-0671004101
ISBN UK: 978-1857235807

CONTACT

Plot: Astronomer Ellie Arroway works at a S.E.T.I. station in New Mexico, seeking communication from the stars. A repeating signal proves to be first contact. A series of messages follow that describe how to construct a device that transports Ellie and four others to Vega where they learn that the aliens they encounter have seen the hand of the creator in the universe.

Review: One imagines that alien contact was number one on Sagan's wish list of things that would happen in his lifetime and *Contact* his means of seeing it happen. Heavy on scientific detail and philosophical/religious discourse on what extraterrestrial contact might mean to mankind, *Contact* is fascinating as a novel about science and scientists but slow-paced. Nevertheless, Sagan was a great communicator of ideas and his novel is brimming over with them.

FURTHER READING: *The Cosmic Connection; Cosmos; Pale Blue Dot: A Vision of the Human Future in Space*
SEE ALSO: *A for Andromeda* (Fred Hoyle and John Elliot); *The Listeners* (James Gunn)

★
★ **Writer:** Sigmund Freud
★ **Publisher:** Allen & Unwin, 1913
(originally in German, 1899)

ISBN US: 978-8562022487
ISBN UK: 978-1853264849

DIE TRAUMDEUTUNG
(THE INTERPRETATION OF DREAMS)

Synopsis: In practicing various techniques to treat his patients, neurologist Freud created what we now call psychoanalysis. He interpreted the spontaneous responses of patients to images and ideas, believing they revealed hidden obsessions and phobias. These revived memories struck Freud as resembling dreams, which he then studied. Dreams, he believed, fulfill the desires of the unconscious mind.

Review: Critics have argued the validity of Freud's ideas: some argue that the usefulness of dreams is not the initial unconscious wish but the elaborate way it is disguised in dream content. Later editions of the book include many of Freud's notes on the text as well as revisiting subjects such as nightmares in the light of his later model of the psyche: the id, the ego, and the superego.

FURTHER READING: *Beyond the Pleasure Principal*
SEE ALSO: *Dreams* (Jung); *The Innocence of Dreams* (Rycroft)

MODERN CLASSICS

Sigmund Freud
Interpreting Dreams

★
★ **Writer:** Michael Herr
★ **Publisher:** Knopf, 1977
★

ISBN US: 0-67-973525-9
ISBN UK: 978-0330255738

DISPATCHES

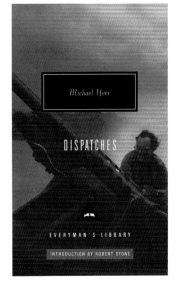

Synopsis: Michael Herr was a war correspondent, traveling widely in Vietnam at the height of the conflict there. Mixing mostly with junior ranks—and deeply skeptical about the officer classes—he wrote about soldiers and how the war affected them. A long chapter set at Khe Sanh evokes the strains of siege warfare; other, more impressionistic, sections throw together diverse recollections of conversations and encounters from all corners of the theater.

Review: Based on Herr's experiences between 1967 and 1969, *Dispatches* was not published until 1977, years after the last U.S. soldiers had left Vietnam. Most of these soldiers had been reluctant—or unable—to talk about what they had seen, and Americans often only had a very limited idea of their experiences. *Dispatches*, with its evocation of the strains of war and its keen ear for the rhythm, fatalism, and humor of the servicemen's language, changed all that: Herr's account was widely read, and the author went on to contribute to the screenplays for both *Platoon* and *Full Metal Jacket*.

FURTHER READING: *Kubrick*
SEE ALSO: *Generation Kill* (Evan Wright)

Michael Herr

DISPATCHES

EVERYMAN'S LIBRARY

INTRODUCTION BY ROBERT STONE

Writer: Søren Kierkegaard
Publisher: 1939 (originally in Danish, 1843)

ISBN US: 978-1448638390
ISBN UK: 978-0141023939

5+

FRYGT OG BÆVEN: DIALEKTISK LYRIK
(FEAR AND TREMBLING: A DIALECTICAL LYRIC)

Synopsis Originally published under the pen-name Johannes de Silentio (John the Silent), *Fear and Trembling* uses the biblical story of Abraham to argue whether faith requires Abraham to put aside all ethical thoughts when God asks him to sacrifice his son, Isaac, and, in resigning himself to God, if Abraham believes that Isaac will be returned to him.

Review: In *Fear and Trembling* Kierkegaard explores the concept of utter, passionate faith, which demands the suspension of ethics, and the paradox that to do so may result in actions unethical to human society and ungodly. Kierkegaard is regarded by some (for example, Karl Popper) as a reformer of Christian ethics but by others (Emmanuel Levinas) as an egocentric.

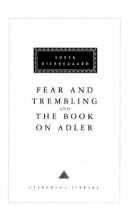

FURTHER READING: *Christian Discourses; The Sickness Unto Death*
SEE ALSO: *Existentialism Is a Humanism* (Jean-Paul Sartre)

Writer: Eric Schlosser
Publisher: Houghton Mifflin Co., 2001

ISBN US: 978-0060938451
ISBN UK: 978-0141006871

5+

FAST FOOD NATION

Synopsis: Investigation, research, and historical anecdotes combine for a damning exposé of the American fast food industry and its impact on the world. In part one we learn how eating "junk" food has become engrained in American culture so as to create a "hamburger hegemony," while in part two food production and manufacture are given a thorough pasting.

Review: Immensely readable stuff that neither preaches nor judges—it's left up to you whether to have it "your way." What's interesting, though, is whether the zeitgeist, with its credit-crunch headlines, will render the debate moot: can we, in fact, afford *not* to risk our health as the price of healthy foodstuffs rises? Time and the impact of the 2009 global recession will tell if this book remains cult for long.

FURTHER READING: *Reefer Madness: Sex, Drugs, and Cheap Labor in the American Black Market*
SEE ALSO: *The Jungle* (Upton Sinclair)

★
★
★
★

Writer: Germaine Greer
Publisher: MacGibbon & Kee, 1970

ISBN US: 978-0061579530
ISBN UK: 978-0007205011

15+

THE FEMALE EUNUCH

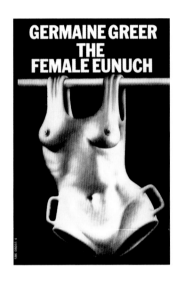

Synopsis: Greer's seminal work of the second wave of feminism, which ignited the British feminist movement in the 1970s and 1980s. Shocking, loud—at times misguided—Greer delivers a withering assault on the misogyny of the patriarchy. Revolution, in the form of intellectual and sexual autonomy, is the only answer, she cries.

Review: There is no doubting that Greer had one of the most powerful rebel yells of the twentieth century. Her blueprint for change was not, however, universally taken up: abandon your families, she urges women (your children as well as your men), taste your own menstrual blood (in so doing you will find sexual emancipation, we're told). Angry, erudite, accessible . . . and just the right side of sane.

FURTHER READING: *The Whole Woman*
SEE ALSO: *SCUM Manifesto* (Valerie Solanas); *Backlash* (Susan Faludi); *The Feminine Mystique* (Betty Friedan)

★
★
★

Writer: Betty Friedan
Publisher: W.W. Norton, 1963

ISBN US: 978-0393322576
ISBN UK: 978-0140136555

15+

THE FEMININE MYSTIQUE

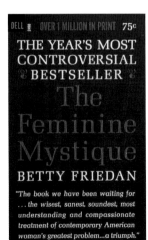

Synopsis: Betty Freidan's analysis of women's position in postwar society in the U.S., which blew sky-high the notion that a woman's place is in the home. On the contrary, argues Friedan, the lot of the housewife is boring and unfulfilling, and she urges women to become educated and find paid work.

Review: Although this is a well-researched and strongly argued polemic, there are limitations to its relevance for the modern reader, including its narrowness of scope (middle-class women of the postwar period), and its lack of solutions for the problems posed (who will look after the kids?). Still, the present-day housewife may still lay in bed awake at night, troubled by the simple, yet depressingly resonant, question evoked by Friedan: "Is this all?"

FURTHER READING: *Fountain of Age*
SEE ALSO: *Backlash* (Susan Faludi);
Female Chauvinist Pigs (Ariel Levy)

★ **Writer:** Herodotus
★ **Publisher:** c. 420 BC

ISBN US: 978-0140449082
ISBN UK: 978-0199535668

2+

THE HISTORIES

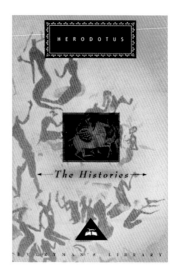

Synopsis: Classical Greek record of the ancient traditions, geography, politics, and battles in various parts of the Mediterranean and Asia in the period around 450–420 BC. Herodotus made a lengthy study of the rise of the Persian Empire and the reasons behind the Greco-Roman Wars, including the famous Battle of Marathon. *The Histories* also had a broader interest in the culture, religion, and fauna of other lands.

Review: Herodotus is sometimes called the "father of history." Historical writings existed before him, but Herodotus was more systematic in the gathering of information for his "inquiries." He traveled widely, interviewed many, and gathered stories firsthand as well as noting his own observations. In *The Histories*, he presented as true an account as he could, rather than give events a favorable political or religious interpretation.

FURTHER READING: *Travels with Herodotus* (Ryszard Kapuscinski)
SEE ALSO: *History of the Peloponnesian War* (Thucydides);
Hellenica: History of My Time (Xenophon)

★ **Writer:** Robert Bly
★ **Publisher:** Addison-Wesley, 1990

ISBN US: 978-0306813764
ISBN UK: 978-0712610704

5+

IRON JOHN A BOOK ABOUT MEN

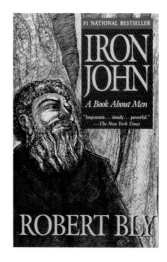

Synopsis: Poet and activist Bly began running seminars and workshops urging men to reclaim their masculinity in the 1980s. In *Iron John*, Bly studies the fairy-tale character created by the Brothers Grimm and discovers lessons meaningful to men who, he says, have lost touch with what it means to be a man. Rituals, ceremonies, and everyday contact with older men have disappeared from modern life leaving today's male disconnected from his emotions and feelings.

Review: A cross between self-help book, anthropology, and literary study, Bly tries to restore the male spirit rather than the obvious traits of manliness. Some saw it as anti-feminist, although Bly emphasized courage, strength, and wisdom over machismo as the positive traits of what he calls the mythopoetic man.

FURTHER READING: *The Light Around the Body; The Sibling Society*
SEE ALSO: *King, Warrior, Magician, Lover: Rediscovering the Archetypes of the Mature Masculine* (Robert Moore and Douglas Gillette); *Fire in the Belly: On Being a Man* (Sam Keen); *Backlash: The Undeclared War Against American Women* (Susan Faludi)

★
★
★

Writer: Upton Sinclair
Publisher: Doubleday, 1906

ISBN US: 978-0743487627
ISBN UK: 978-0140390315

12+

THE JUNGLE

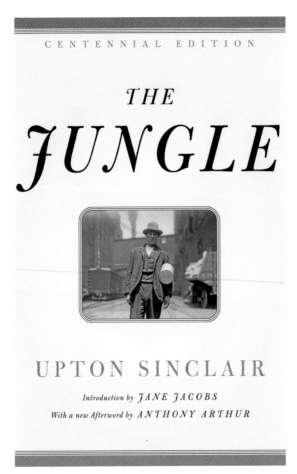

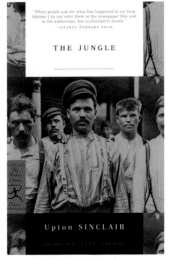

Plot: Jurgis Rudkus, a Lithuanian man, comes to Chicago with his wife Ona in search of the American dream. Instead he must live a hand-to-mouth existence and suffer the iniquities of working in the American meat-packing industry.

Review: "I aimed for the public's heart, and by accident I hit it in the stomach." So said Upton Sinclair when the public reacted angrily to his moving account of the working conditions of the wage slaves of the early twentieth century. Though socialism is presented as the answer, the book is more muckraking than propaganda. And if this all sounds too worthy, rest assured that the novel has a Zola-esque vigor in its presentation of human behavior, which makes it a universally appealing read.

FURTHER READING: *Oil!*
(basis for the film *There Will Be Blood*)
SEE ALSO: *The Road to Los Angeles* (John Fante);
David Copperfield (Charles Dickens)

Writer: Thomas Hobbes
Publisher: Andrew Crooke, 1651

ISBN US: 978-0140431957
ISBN UK: 978-0199537280

LEVIATHAN

Synopsis: Tutor, secretary, translator, poet, author, and philosopher Thomas Hobbes, set down his thoughts on political philosophy at a time when politics was being tested to its limit by the English Civil War. In the book, he set out the doctrine of a strong central authority; to live without any form of control would, he said, lead inevitably to war. More controversial was his belief that religious power must be subordinate to civil power.

Review: Often described as one of the greatest works of political philosophy in English, in *Leviathan* Hobbes tried to analyze society—beginning with man himself—from which analysis he concluded that the only solution is a social contract with the leviathan of the title, a form of government to whom power was given, which, in turn, would ensure that the social contract was not broken, thus preventing anarchy.

FURTHER READING: *Elementa philosophica de cive; De Corpore*
SEE ALSO: *A Compendium of the Art of Logick and Rhetorick; Reason and Rhetoric in the Philosophy of Hobbes* (Skinner)

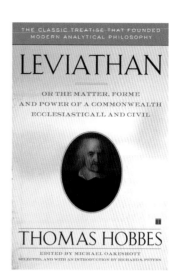

Writer: Greil Marcus
Publisher: Harvard University Press, 1989

ISBN US: 978-0674535817
ISBN UK: 978-0571232284

LIPSTICK TRACES
A SECRET HISTORY OF THE TWENTIETH CENTURY

Synopsis: The history of popular music meets Left Bank intellectualism via a cultural analysis of punk and various avant-garde art movements. Told through anecdotes, confessions, and a large dose of history, Marcus explores how the Sex Pistols transformed pop music with "Anarchy in the UK," and how the song crudely distilled the ideas of various countercultural movements.

Review: Nine years in the writing, Marcus, an author and editor at *Rolling Stone* in the 1970s, had originally planned to write a book about punk, especially the British bands of the mid-1970s, but his study of the origins of punk led him to the situationists and Dadaists of the Left Bank in the fifties and sixties. The book flips between the Sex Pistols and the surrealists, Marcus later explaining that the "explosive, noisy, confused, rushed journey through the decades" demanded it.

FURTHER READING: *Mystery Train*
SEE ALSO: *England's Dreaming* (Jon Savage); *Rip It Up and Start Again* (Simon Reynolds)

★
★
★
★

Writer: Larry McMurtry
Publisher: Simon & Schuster, 1985

ISBN US: 978-0684871226
ISBN UK: 978-0330317542

15+

LONESOME DOVE

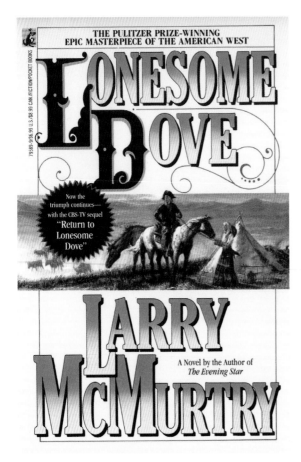

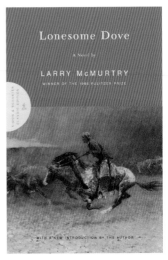

Plot: In the south Texas border town of Lonesome Dove, loquacious womanizer Augustus McCrae and emotionally cut-off workaholic Woodrow Call run the Hat Creek Cattle Company. The arrival of one-time comrade Jake Spoon with stories of the new wild frontier persuades the two former Texas Rangers to drive their cattle three thousand miles north to Montana.

Review: McMurtry deals with fairly standard characters of the Wild West (even prostitutes with hearts of gold) but humanizes them; on the cattle drive, McCrae and Call face many equally standard tribulations, from natural disasters to attacks by renegades and Indians, but at no time does the novel, which won the Pulitzer Prize, feel hackneyed. Although he has done much to demythologize the Wild West, the landscape and characters are still mythic, and the novel has rightly been praised as epic.

FURTHER READING: *Streets of Loredo; Dead Man's Walk; Comanche Moon*
SEE ALSO: *The Time It Never Rained* (Elmer Kelton); *Blood Meridian* (Cormac McCarthy)

Writer: C. G. Jung
Publisher: Doubleday, 1964

ISBN US: 978-0440351832
ISBN UK: 978-0330253215

5+

MAN AND HIS SYMBOLS

Synopsis: Popular presentation of the essential ideas of Jungian psychology. Jung writes on the unconscious, while others tackle the growth of personality and how it may be distorted, ancient myths and their meaning, symbolism, analysis, and the relationship between Jungian theory and science.

Review: Published following Jung's death in 1961, with a number of sections of the book written by other hands under Jung's supervision, *Man and His Symbols* was intended to be an introduction to Jung's theories for the general audience. Overall, the book is written in an easy to understand style, although this reveals some shaky ground, especially in areas such as comparing Jungian psychology with quantum physics.

FURTHER READING: *The Psychology of the Unconscious;*
Psychological Types; Memories, Dreams, Reflections
SEE ALSO: *Man's Search for Meaning* (Viktor E. Frankl);
A Primer of Jungian Psychology (Calvin S. Hall)

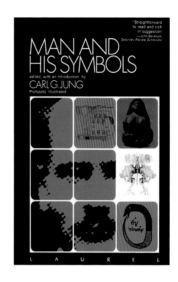

Writer: Oliver Sacks
Publisher: Summit Books, 1985

ISBN US: 978-0684853949
ISBN UK: 978-0684853949

2+

THE MAN WHO MISTOOK HIS WIFE FOR A HAT

Synopsis: Case histories about patients with little-known visual, emotional, cognitive, and auditory disorders. Dr. P, for instance, was only able to see objects as abstracts. As a result, he greeted parking meters thinking they were people, and once grabbed his wife's head, thinking it was his hat. Other essays concern lost senses of perception and memory, and heightened senses and talents.

Review: Although clearly suffering from some handicapping maladies, neurologist Sacks observes that in many ways his patients live fulfilling lives, and he tries to understand the worldview of his patients rather than just the clinical manifestations of their inability to comprehend reality. The book proved so successful that it inspired a play by Peter Brook and an opera (*Hat*) by composer Michael Nyman.

FURTHER READING: *Awakenings; An Anthropologist on Mars*
SEE ALSO: *Time and Myth* (John S. Dunne); *Newton's Madness*
(Harold L. Klawans)

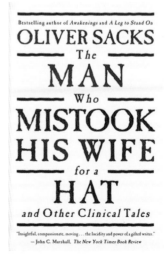

★
★
★
★

Writer: Jon Ronson
Publisher: Picador, 2004

ISBN US: 978-1439181775
ISBN UK: 978-0330375481

15+

THE MEN WHO STARE AT GOATS

Synopsis: Ronson assures his readers "This is a true story" in his opening line. In 1995, the CIA declassified documents relating to experiments in E.S.P. and telepathy. A secret Black Ops unit—the First Earth Battalion—was set up to explore the military possibilities of psychic powers: would it be possible for a soldier to walk through walls or kill a goat by simply staring at it?

Review: Dry wit and nightmare meet head on, though unlike many of Ronson's documentary subjects (white supremacists, militants, conspiracy theorists), the interviewees involved are neither mad nor evil. Ronson traces the history of seemingly bizarre programs back to MK-ULTRA in the 1950s and explores how psychological tactics have been used in recent situations, from playing children's TV theme songs at cult hideaways to the excesses of Abu Ghraib.

FURTHER READING: *Out of the Ordinary; What I Do*
SEE ALSO: *The Manchurian Candidate* (Richard Condon); *Psychic Warrior* (David Morehouse)

★
★

Writer: Martin Amis
Publisher: Jonathan Cape, 1986

ISBN US: 978-0140127195
ISBN UK: 978-0099461869

15+

THE MORONIC INFERNO AND OTHER VISITS TO AMERICA

Synopsis: A collection of interviews, essays and reviews gathered primarily from the pages of the London *Observer*, linked by their American connections and through which Amis reflects on the character of contemporary America. Amis' America is peopled by its great novelists, some now gone (Truman Capote, Joseph Heller, Norman Mailer), some still active when the book was published (Gore Vidal, Philip Roth, Paul Theroux), filmmakers (Steven Spielberg, Brian de Palma), legends (Elvis Presley, Hugh Hefner), and presidential candidates (Ronald Reagan).

Review: Anticipating reaction to his somewhat disdainful attitude toward America, Amis said in his introduction that cultural decline was not "a peculiarly American condition. It is global and perhaps eternal." Painting New Yorkers as materialist, politicized, and surprisingly thin, some critics (certainly in New York) thought his generalizations sweeping and his America unlike the real thing.

FURTHER READING: *Money: A Suicide Note; The War Against Cliché*
SEE ALSO: *Love, Poverty and War* (Christopher Hitchens)

Writer: Richard Wright
Publisher: Harper and Brothers, 1940

ISBN US: 978-0791096253
ISBN UK: 978-0099282938

NATIVE SON

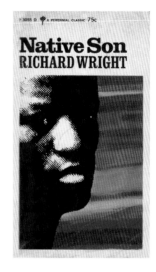

Plot: In 1930s Chicago, Bigger Thomas lives in abject poverty. His relationships fail, he can't get into the property game, and the only work he can get is menial labor. Bigger's life goes from bad to worse when, after being offered a job as a chauffeur with a white family, he accidentally kills their daughter, Mary Dalton. The remainder of the book deals with the effects of his crime on the wider black community and on Bigger himself, as his life becomes a self-fulfilling prophecy.

Review: An undisguised assault on the racism of prewar American society. Shocking and powerful, *Native Son* was highly successful, and with its publication Wright became the first bestselling black writer in America.

FURTHER READING: *The Outsider*
SEE ALSO: *Go Tell It on the Mountain* (James Baldwin)

Writer: Robert Kagan
Publisher: Knopf, 2003

ISBN US: 978-1400034185
ISBN UK: 978-1843541783

PARADISE AND POWER

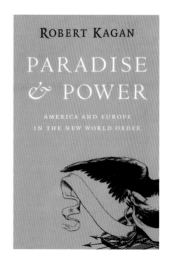

Synopsis: Political advisor and foreign policy commentator Kagan argues that there has been a growing disparity between American and European views of the ways to keep peace and order in the post-Cold War world. Both are financially strong, but Europe is comparatively weak militarily and favors diplomacy over America's use of force.

Review: Expanding on ideas from his 2002 *Policy Review* essay "Power and Weakness," Kagan eloquently reasons that the creation of the League of Nations and the United Nations has led to a policy in Europe of avoiding war at all costs. As Kagan says, a man with a knife will lie low rather than tackle a bear; a man with a gun is less cautious in seeking it out.

FURTHER READING: *Warrior Politic;*
The Return of History and the End of Dreams
SEE ALSO: *The Shield of Achilles: War, Peace and the Course of History* (Philip Bobbitt); *Soft Power: The Means to Success in World Politics* (Joseph Nye)

★
★
★
★
★

Writer: Joe Sacco
Publisher: Fantagraphics, 1996

ISBN US: 978-1560974321
ISBN UK: 978-0224069823

15+

PALESTINE

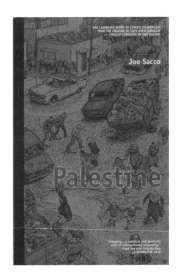

Synopsis: In the late 1980s/early 1990s, cartoonist-journalist Sacco journeyed across Europe and the Middle East, recounting his stay in Israel and the Palestinian territories in *Palestine*. The resulting comic strip mixes his own detailed observations of everyday life with interviews, flashbacks, and accounts of experiences of Palestinians living under occupation in Jerusalem, and of citizens and refugees in the West Bank and Gaza Strip.

Review: Although he tries to remain a detached reporter of events, Sacco's sympathies for the Palestinians can't help but come through as he documents abuses and deprivations; in the end, even he has to admit that this is a one-sided view of the conflict. The book's black-and-white images give it a feeling of a historical documentary.

FURTHER READING: *Safe Area Gorazde: The War in Eastern Bosnia, 1992–1995; The Fixer: A Story from Sarajevo*
SEE ALSO: *Maus* (Art Spiegelman); *Deogratias: A Tale of Rwanda* (Jean-Philippe Stassen)

★
★
★

Writer: Brian K. Vaughan and Niko Henrichon
Publisher: DC Comics, 2006

ISBN US: 978-1401203153
ISBN UK: 978-1845763756

15+

PRIDE OF BAGHDAD

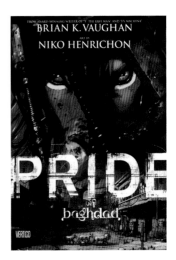

Plot: Based on a true incident, the pride of the title were four lions that escaped from Baghdad Zoo following a bombing raid by American forces in 2003. Zill, the leader, must protect his pride (one-eyed Safa, his mate, Noor, and Noor's cub Ali) as they seek freedom and the safety of a new home in the bombed-out landscape of Baghdad.

Review: Vaughan's allegorical story works on two levels: as a straightforward adventure story for the younger audience and as a commentary and meditation on the war in Iraq for older readers. As outsiders caught up in the war (somewhat like the noncombatant citizens of Baghdad), the lions discuss what it means to be free and the morality of the situation that surrounds them. The watercolor artwork by Henrichon is beautiful.

FURTHER READING: *Y: The Last Man; Ex Machina; Runaways*
SEE ALSO: *Amazing Adventures of The Escapist* (Michael Chabon)

★
★
★
★
★

Writer: Virginia Woolf **ISBN US:** 978-0156787338
Publisher: Hogarth Press, 1929 **ISBN UK:** 978-0141183534

2+

A ROOM OF ONE'S OWN

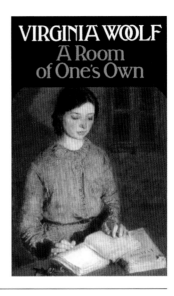

Synopsis: Virginia Woolf gave a series of lectures about female creativity at Cambridge University in 1928. In 1929 the lectures were published as a book, giving us one of the most brilliant feminist polemics of all time. In it Woolf takes an imaginary walk around "Oxbridge" and visits the British Museum, where she seeks out works by women, or written about them, powerfully exposing the rampant sexism surrounding the arts in western society.

Review: In lamenting the fate of the hypothetical sister of Shakespeare in an evocative "what if?" scenario, Woolf will leave all female creative geniuses paralysed with fear. The horrible truth about her most famous work is that the central premise—that "intellectual freedom depends on material things"—remains a stark reality for women nearly 100 years later.

FURTHER READING: *Mrs Dalloway; To the Lighthouse*
SEE ALSO: *The Second Sex* (Simone de Beauvoir)

★
★
★

Writer: Daniel Ellsberg **ISBN US:** 978-0142003428
Publisher: Viking, 2002 **ISBN UK:** 978-0142003428

5+

SECRETS
VIETNAM AND THE PENTAGON PAPERS

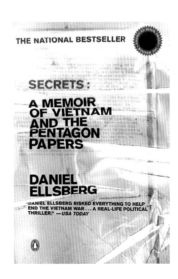

THE NATIONAL BESTSELLER

SECRETS :

A MEMOIR OF VIETNAM AND THE PENTAGON PAPERS

DANIEL ELLSBERG

"DANIEL ELLSBERG RISKED EVERYTHING TO HELP END THE VIETNAM WAR... A REAL-LIFE POLITICAL THRILLER." — USA TODAY

Synopsis: On June 13, 1971, the *New York Times* began a series of articles based on government research leaked by Daniel Ellsberg, a contributor to the original report, to *Times* journalist Neil Sheehan. The study—marked "Top Secret"—revealed that four administrations had involved the U.S. far deeper in Southeast Asia than they had made public.

Review: Ellsberg's hope was that publication and discussion of the Pentagon papers would bring an end to the Vietnam War, but attention was sidetracked as the debate turned instead to one of constitutional (especially First Amendment) rights when the Nixon administration successfully filed for an injunction against the *Times*, although it was soon lifted after a Supreme Court ruling. The publication of Ellsberg's carefully researched memoirs benefitted from his waiting until certain documents were declassified.

FURTHER READING: *The Pentagon Papers* (Neil Sheehan)
SEE ALSO: *The Papers and the Papers: An Account of the Legal and Political Battle over the Pentagon Papers* (Sanford J. Ungar)

★
★
★
★

Writer: Primo Levi
Publisher: Orion Press, 1959
(originally in Italian, 1947)

ISBN US: 978-0349100135
ISBN UK: 978-0349100135

15+

SE QUESTO E UN UOMO
(IF THIS IS A MAN OR SURVIVAL IN AUSCHWITZ)

Synopsis: Levi, an Italian Jew, was fighting with the partisans when he was captured and sent to Fossoli internment camp and subsequently to Auschwitz in February 1944. Using bread to pay for German lessons, and surviving on smuggled-in soup, Levi (a former chemist) worked in the laboratories of I. G. Farben. Ill with scarlet fever, he was left behind when the camp was hurriedly evacuated as the Russian Army approached in January 1945. Levi was one of only twenty survivors from the 650 Italian Jews he arrived with.

Review: Levi was inspired to write his memoirs of Auschwitz so that the wider world would know what had happened, making it as detailed an account of the conditions and history of his internment as he could. He writes of the senseless violence and humiliation but also of the bonds formed by those held in the camp.

FURTHER READING: *The Reawakening; Moments of Reprieve*
SEE ALSO: *Five Chimneys* (Olga Lengyel)

★
★
★

Writer: Joan Didion
Publisher: Simon & Schuster, 1968

ISBN US: 978-0374531386
ISBN UK: 978-0007115228

15+

SLOUCHING TOWARDS BETHLEHEM

Synopsis: After a childhood and education disrupted by constant moves, Didion worked for *Vogue* in New York before relocating to Los Angeles in 1964 to write essays and screenplays. *Slouching Towards Bethlehem* features interviews with John Wayne, Joan Baez, Marxist-Leninist Michael Laski, as well as more personal essays about the fading of the American Dream, reflected in everything from vulgar wedding chapels in Nevada to disintegrating subcultures in California.

Review: Twenty essays in three sections culled from the pages of some of America's leading magazines, Didion was praised for her eye for detail. In places the book is warm, in others nihilistic and bleak as Didion looks for new folk heroes in a country that is becoming morally empty. The title is derived from a poem by W. B. Yeats.

FURTHER READING: *The White Album; The Year of Magical Thinking; We Tell Ourselves Stories in Order to Live*
SEE ALSO: *Polaroids from the Dead* (Douglas Coupland)

Writer: Michael Moore

Publisher: Regan Books, 2002

ISBN US: 978-0060987268

ISBN UK: 978-0141019994

★
★
★

15+

STUPID WHITE MEN
AND OTHER SORRY EXCUSES FOR
THE STATE OF THE NATION

Synopsis: From the "stolen" 2000 election, through the demonizing of African-Americans to politicians in the pockets of big business, Moore skewers the Bush administration, right wing media, poor education, and greedy corporations with facts, figures, and humor.

Review: With a 50,000-copy printing already in hand, the events of 9/11 caused publisher Regan Books to reconsider the Bush-bashing book, asking Moore for extensive rewrites, which he refused. Anti-censorship groups spearheaded the campaign to get the book published, which it duly was, spending a year on the *New York Times* bestseller list.

FURTHER READING: *Downsize This!*; *Dude, Where's My Country?*
SEE ALSO: *Lies and the Lying Liars Who Tell Them* (Al Franken)

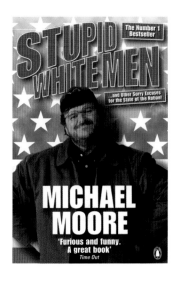

Writer: Friedrich Nietzsche

Publisher: T. F. Unwin, 1908
(originally in German, 1883–85)

ISBN US: 978-0521602617

ISBN UK: 978-0199537099

★
★
★

2+

THUS SPOKE ZARATHUSTRA
(ALSO SPRACH ZARATHUSTRA)

Plot: After ten years of isolation and contemplation in the mountains, Zarathustra (based on the Persian sage Zoroaster) descends into the lowlands to enlighten the world. He meets a hermit and tells him that God is dead, having been rendered redundant in a skeptical, scientific world. Without God, man can now strive to rise above what he has and is until he can enjoy the repetition of all events in an endlessly recycling universe.

Review: In *Thus Spoke Zarathustra*, Nietzsche voices his philosophical views as a series of prophetic revelations, including most of the famous elements of the Nietzschean philosophy: the Übermensch, as far above man as man is above the ape; eternal recurrence, the notion that all events have happened before and will infinitely repeat themselves; and the will to power (ambition, aggrandizement, control), which is the driving force of man.

FURTHER READING: *Beyond Good and Evil*; *Ecce Homo*
SEE ALSO: *Being and Time* (Martin Heidegger); *Nietzsche: Philosopher, Psychologist, Antichrist* (Walter Kaufmann)

PENGUIN CLASSICS

NIETZSCHE
Thus Spoke Zarathustra

★
★
★
★

Writer: Adam Smith
Publisher: W. Strahan & T. Cadell, 1776

ISBN US: 978-0553585971
ISBN UK: 978-0199535927

12+ # THE WEALTH OF NATIONS

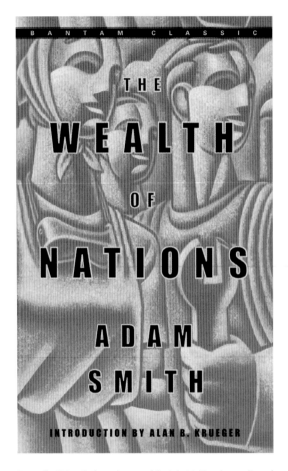

Synopsis: Written in the early years of the Industrial Revolution, *Wealth of Nations* was a study of economics and what makes a nation prosperous. In it, Smith looked at manufacturing, pricing, stocks, and shares; the movement of labor to cities and towns; and how the government had passed restrictive laws or applied tariffs that hindered free trade.

Review: *An Inquiry into the Nature and Causes of the Wealth of Nations*, to give it its full title, gave us the still familiar phrase that Britain is a nation of shopkeepers. The book had a degree of impact at the time in improving the lives of some of the workforce through minimum wages and better conditions. Over the years, many of his ideas (such as a more specialized workforce to increase efficiency in production) have become commonplace.

FURTHER READING: *The Works of Adam Smith;
Adam Smith and the Wealth of Nations:
1776-1976* (ed. Fred R. Ghahe)
SEE ALSO: *Report on Manufactures*
(Alexander Hamilton)

Writer: Charlotte Perkins Gilman
Publisher: Small Maynarad, 1899
(as Charlotte Perkins Stetson)

ISBN US: 978-0199538843
ISBN UK: 978-0199538843

5+

THE YELLOW WALLPAPER

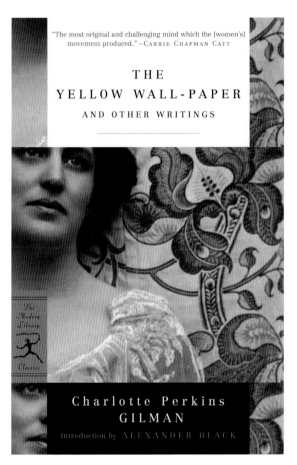

"The most original and challenging mind which the [women's] movement produced."—CARRIE CHAPMAN CATT

THE
YELLOW WALL-PAPER
AND OTHER WRITINGS

The Modern Library Classics

Charlotte Perkins
GILMAN

Introduction by ALEXANDER BLACK

BANTAM CLASSIC

The Yellow
Wallpaper and
Other Writings

Charlotte Perkins Gilman

With an Introduction by Lynne Sharon Schwartz

Plot: A disturbing, autobiographical novella inspired by Gilman's profound depression following the birth of her daughter. A neurologist recommended bed-rest and minimal intellectual stimulation, and in the story the heroine narrator is at first melancholic. Taken by her husband to a country house, she is confined to a room. Staring at the dirty yellow wallpaper, she descends into madness, convinced that there are women concealed behind the wallpaper.

Review: Gilman wrote the story in order to convince her neurologist, Dr. S. Weir Mitchell, that his "cure" for nervous prostration (now more commonly known as postpartum depression) was precisely what she did not need. Gilman later revealed in her autobiography that she sent a copy of *The Yellow Wallpaper* to Mitchell and he subsequently changed his treatment.

FURTHER READING:
The Living of Charlotte Perkins Gilman; Herland
SEE ALSO: *The Awakening* (Kate Chopin); *The Bell Jar* (Sylvia Plath)

feuchtgebiete

CHARLOTTE ROCHE
ROMAN

ullstein

TIMOTHY LEARY, Ph.D.

THE POLITICS OF

ECSTASY

ENGLAND'S
DREAMING

*Sex Pistols
and Punk Rock*

Jon Savage

'A hole-in-one, grand-slam knockout
of a book.' *Charles Shaar Murray*

W

Last EXIT to
BROOKLYN

UBERT SELBY JR

WITH AN INTRODUCTION BY Anthony Burgess

minjo
IN CLASSIC

HUNTER S. THOMPSON
AUTHOR OF THE GREAT SHARK HUNT

FEAR AND LOATHING
in LAS VEGAS

A Savage Journey to the
Heart of the American Dream

"Ever since *Naked Lunch* . . . William S. Burroughs has been ordained
America's most incendiary artist."—*Los Angeles Times*

NAKED
the restored text
LUNCH

william s. burroughs

edited by
james grauerholz and barry miles

Panther

J. G. B

CRA

A brutal, er

Ryū Murakami

ALMOST
TRANSPARENT
BLUE

LOCAS

I DON'T WANNA
GO TO WORK!
I HATE WORK!
WORRY WORRY
ME?

BESTSELLING AUTHOR OF THE BONFIRE OF THE VANITI

TOM
WOLFE

THE
ELECTRIC
KOOL-AID
ACID
TEST

CAND

'An American Classic'

The novel by
Terry Southern & Mason H

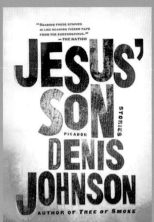

JESUS' SON
STORIES
PICADOR
DENIS JOHNSON
AUTHOR OF *TREE OF SMOKE*

HOLLYWOOD BABYLON
KENNETH ANGER

Simon Reynolds
Author of
RIP IT UP AND START AGAIN
Energy Flash

New updated 20th anniversary edition
A Journey Through Rave Music and Dance Culture

Wonderland Ave
TALES OF GLAMOUR AND EX

DANNY SUGERMAN
author of No One Here Gets Out A

THE CLASSIC BESTSELLER
MY SECRET
GARDEN
WOMEN'S SEXUAL FANTASIES

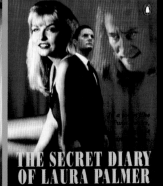

THE SECRET DIARY OF LAURA PALMER

SEX, DRUGS, AND TABOO-BUSTING

The boundaries of taste and decency have changed since the nineteenth century, when John Cleland, the author of *Fanny Hill*—a novel of euphemistic, but not graphic, rudeness—was put on trial for obscenity. As we drift further along the twenty-first century, literature still has the power to shock: take the example of Charlotte Roche's *Wetlands*, which depicts certain paraphilias no other writer had hitherto dared to touch.

In this chapter you'll find eyebrow-raisers from both now and then: chemical confessions and sexual transgressions of authors past and present, which express the wilder side of human nature that has long since been associated with the cult book.

TOP 10

WALK ON THE WILD SIDE

★ **Writer:** Terry Southern and Mason Hoffenberg
★ **Publisher:** Olympia Press, 1958 (suppressed);
★ then 1962
★

ISBN US: 978-0802134295
ISBN UK: 978-0747530886

18+ CANDY

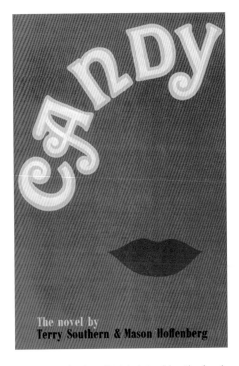

"Terry Southern is the most profoundly witty writer of our generation."
—Gore Vidal

Terry Southern
and Mason Hoffenberg

Plot: A satirical update of Voltaire's *Candide* with a female protagonist, Candy, and owing its plotline to the eighteenth-century work. Candy Christian, born on Valentine's Day, is naïve and pretty. Naturally, perhaps, all men want to have sex with her. Unnaturally, perhaps, she obliges, thinking it her duty to fulfill men's needs, a perspective which propels her into all manner of ridiculous sexual misadventures. Her suitors include her father's gardener, her uncle, a hunchback, and a spiritual guru. In the end her naivety takes her to India, where an earthquake brings about a surprise ending.

Review: Let's firstly tackle what might be considered *Candy*'s fatal flaw: satirizing a satire of *Candide*'s stature is hugely ambitious and Southern and Hoffenberg don't seem quite up to the job. Indeed, instead of deflating this or that modern fad, the writers all too often galumph into burlesque. Moreover, with her litany of "darn daddy anyways," Candy does not comes across as naïve (like her counterpart Candide) so much as dim.

On another level, though, *Candy* is enormous fun. Farce and graphic sex is a mix that has been around since the Ancient Greeks. And why not? It's one that works. Be warned, though: the sex is as dirty as it is funny—so "blue" is it, in fact, that the British censor said the novel would have to undergo a "pornectomy" to spare the blushes of the public before it could be published. Happily this literary operation has now been reversed, and we can enjoy Candy's farcical sexual shenanigans in all their intended glory. Just make sure you have your tolerance level set to high.

FURTHER READING: *The Magic Christian; Blue Movie*
SEE ALSO: *Candide* (Voltaire); *The Candy Men: The Rollicking Life and Times of the Notorious Novel Candy* (Nile Southern)

★
★
★
★

Writer: Thomas De Quincey
Publisher: London Magazine, 1821

ISBN US: 978-0140439014
ISBN UK: 978-0199537938

15+

CONFESSIONS OF AN ENGLISH OPIUM EATER

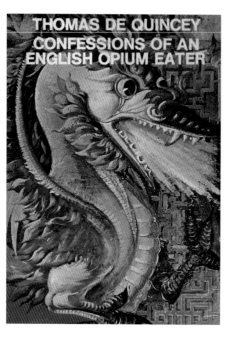

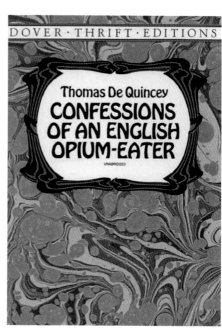

Synopsis: De Quincey's meandering and dream-like auto-biography will certainly enlighten those who thought that drug abuse was a strictly modern-day phenomenon. This nineteenth-century memoir recounts the author's addiction to opium: from his first experiences taking the drug to fight a headache, to becoming a daily user, to the point, eight years later, when the pains begin to outweigh the pleasures, the whole gamut of the opiate experience is revealed.

Review: What's fascinating here is that the book tells you what scientific and clinical trials wouldn't—what it is actually like taking opium. The state of the mind, body, and soul of the author is so authentically described that it's almost as if we experience a collective trip with him. That De Quincey is unapologetic about his drugs use may perturb some readers, but let's not forget this is not a polemic arguing for or against, but the highly subjective and personal account of one man's experiences. And it's not like he doesn't paint a bleak picture of the dark truth of addiction: "How came

any reasonable being subject himself to such a yoke of misery, voluntarily to incur a captivity so servile?" he asks out of bitter experience. Contrariwise, the author is seductive in the "pleasures" section, "the abyss of the divine enjoyment" of opium being temptingly described.

Whether or not you are fascinated by all this self-induced misery, it can't be denied that De Quincey was the founding father of an entire genre of literature: the confessional drugs memoir. Without him, it is said, we would not have Huxley's essays, we would not have Burroughs, we would not, perhaps, have fictional works like *Trainspotting* and *Fear and Loathing in Las Vegas*. And if anything should convince you to read *Confessions of an English Opium Eater*, it's that.

FURTHER READING: *Suspiria de Profundis;*
The English Mail-Coach
SEE ALSO: *High Priest* (Timothy Leary); *Opium* (Jean Cocteau); *Junkie* (William Burroughs)

★
★
★
★

Writer: J. G. Ballard
Publisher: Jonathan Cape, 1973

ISBN US: 978-0312420338
ISBN UK: 978-0099334910

18+ CRASH

Plot: James Ballard, the narrator, meets Dr. Robert Vaughn, former TV scientist, when they are involved in an automobile incident at an airport. Vaughn is the ring-leader of a group who re-enact the car-crashes of celebrities for a sexual thrill—his ultimate goal being to die in a head-on collision with the actress Elizabeth Taylor. Though Ballard has us looking full face, with an almost cinematic view, at the man-meets-metal action, a detached clinical tone (mercifully) disengages the reader somewhat from what might otherwise be too shockingly perverted a read.

Review: If there is a formula for cult fiction, J. G. Ballard is its progenitor. Here, controversy plus graphic sex with the open wounds of car crash victims plus post-modern narration from a man with the same name as the author equals a benchmark against which future cult novels would be set.

Crash wasn't and isn't without its critics. Some have called it pornography for mechanophiliacs. Others have gone further. A more generous reading is that Ballard is looking to teach us something about how human sexuality is an organic being, changing with new technologies. Car crashes are, narrator Jim Ballard says, "the keys to a new sexuality born from a perverse technology."

If Ballard, the writer, had not died in 2009, perhaps he might have developed this idea to write the story of man's sexual interaction with the internet. Budding cult fiction authors, might, however, look to the formula above, replace "car crash" with "internet porn," and be sure of a cult hit.

FURTHER READING: *Cocaine Nights; The Unlimited Dream Company; Empire of the Sun*
SEE ALSO: *My Idea of Fun* (Will Self); *A Clockwork Orange* (Anthony Burgess)

★
★
★
★

Writer: John Cleland
Publisher: G. Fenton, 1748/49

ISBN US: 978-1840224177
ISBN UK: 978-1840224177

15+

FANNY HILL MEMOIRS OF A WOMAN OF PLEASURE

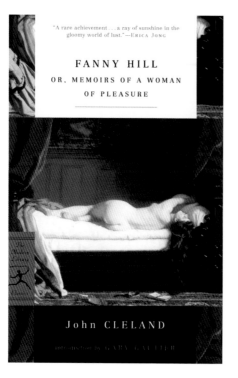

Plot: When she is orphaned at fourteen, Fanny, née Frances, Hill "seeks her fortune" in London. It doesn't end badly for her—we know, from the preface, that before her confessions end she will be a wealthy woman. However, en route she is tricked into working in a brothel, and her lover, Charles, is shipped overseas by his father, which sees her ending up back in the "unhappy profession" of prostitution.

Along the way Fanny's memoirs are resplendent with the lurid glories of her sex life, creatively described by Cleland with a wealth of euphemisms and imagery.

Review: The author himself denounced his book when it saw him on trial for obscenity in England in 1761, saying it was "a book I disdain to defend, and wish, from my Soul, buried and forgot." Across the pond, the American censors were no less lenient, and the prospective publisher there was called a "scandalous and evil disposed person." The book was finally published in the U.S. in 1966.

After this teasing foreplay, you are probably burning to know if it is really all that naughty. Well, despite the name, which might conjure up visions of lame Benny Hill-esque romps, it's actually pretty filthy. The physiological detail, and the reactions of both men and women to sex, are vividly depicted—variously heterosexuality, homosexuality, fetishes, flagellation, and masturbation don't escape Fanny's notice or involvement.

However, Fanny's moral outrage at such sexual doings, even as she is in the midst of them, is disappointing. Also, the language often raises a titter, rather than titillates, and feminists may bemoan Fanny's penis-focused adventures. Still, that *Fanny Hill* has endured two-hundred years of censure, ridicule, and debate means it has a well-deserved place in the annals of erotic cult literature.

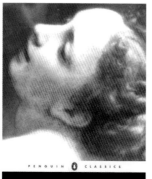

FURTHER READING: None of Cleland's other work compares to the fun romp that is *Fanny Hill*
SEE ALSO: *Shamela* (Henry Fielding); *Moll Flanders* (Daniel Defoe); *Justine* (Marquis de Sade)

★
★
★
★
★

Writer: Hunter S. Thompson
Publisher: Random House, 1971
ISBN US: 978-0679785897
ISBN UK: 978-0007204496

`18+` # FEAR AND LOATHING IN LAS VEGAS

HUNTER S. THOMPSON
AUTHOR OF **THE GREAT SHARK HUNT**

Fear and Loathing in LAS VEGAS

A Savage Journey to the
Heart of the American Dream

PALADIN

Plot: Raoul Duke and his companion, his attorney Dr. Gonzo, are journeying to Las Vegas, ostensibly for Duke to cover the annual Mint 400 desert race for a "fashionable sports magazine." In their rental car, however, is a trunkful of drugs akin to a "mobile police narcotics lab," which they are making fast work of consuming. Their trip is, Duke suggests, actually "a savage journey to the heart of the American dream," which also happens to be the book's subtitle.

Choosing Las Vegas as the most appropriate site for this experiment, the pair set up residence in a hotel and embark on a series of hallucinations and drug-fuelled adventures, almost destroying themselves in the process.

Review: Funny, outrageous, psychedelic, yes. But what does it mean? If it's a quest for the American dream, then unfortunately the drugged-up duo are unsuccessful. Though at one point two waitresses inform them that it's around here somewhere, but they cannot point our heroes in the right direction.

Who needs meaning though? *Fear and Loathing in Las Vegas* is like a legalized version of consuming mind-altering substances, so deftly does it describe their effects: dementedly funny, paranoid and hallucinatory, self-indulgent, and at times just very, very silly. All this and one of the most memorable opening lines in cult fiction: "We were somewhere around Barstow on the edge of the desert when the drugs began to take hold." Duke and Dr. Gonzo's road trip—both meanings to the word "trip" here—goes all downhill from there.

FURTHER READING:
The Rum Diary (novel);
Hell's Angels (journalism);
The Great Shark Hunt (journalism)
SEE ALSO: *Naked Lunch*
(William Burroughs)

Writer: Charlotte Roche

Publisher: DuMont Buchverlag, 2008

ISBN US: 978-0802118929

ISBN UK: 978-0802118929

18+

FEUCHTGEBIETE (WETLANDS)

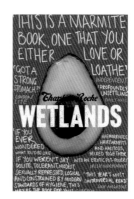

Plot: An incident with a Ladyshave sees eighteen-year-old Helen Memel laid up in hospital recovering from an intimate operation. Left enduring the agonies of an anal fissure, she contemplates her lot, obsessing over her bodily functions and secretions. There's an incident with a used tampon left in an elevator, she pops zits, remembers visits to prostitutes, masturbates under her hospital bed, and enjoys wearing dirty knickers. And in the midst of these scatological and biological preoccupations, she grows avocado trees. You get the picture: Helen is not your average eighteen-year-old girl.

Review: Feminist manifesto against female body-image and hygiene fascism, literary porn, or gross-out novel of the century? Which, if any, of these labels given to Charlotte Roche's 2008 monster hit are deserved?

Feminism-wise, Roche intended to present "a heroine that has a totally creative attitude towards her body . . . A real free spirit." On this level, it works. However, the plot line and climax may trouble some feminists, as the central conflict of the book—Helen's attempts to reunite her parents—is only resolved by the rather conventional route of . . . you guessed it, the help of a man.

Accusations of gross-out and porn have been levied at Roche, and this taboo-busting aspect will certainly be too much for some. This is not just political incorrectness, it is anatomical incorrectness and then some: flatulence, scatology, urination, and blood all feature highly. And—needless to say—the language is not as politely reserved as we've used here.

This said, if you go in for dirty books, you'll delight in a corporeal adventure that has enough muck to start a small-holding. Or possibly an entire farm. If you don't go in for hemorrhoids, anal wounds, anal sex, hairy armpits, and periods, best avoid.

FURTHER READING: Roche has not yet unleashed another novel on the world
SEE ALSO: *The Story of O* (Pauline Réage); *Girl with a One Track Mind* (Abby Lee); *The Story of the Eye* (Georges Bataille)

★ **Writer:** Marquis de Sade
★ **Publisher:** J. V. Girouard, 1791

ISBN US: 978-0802132185
ISBN UK: 978-0007300440

18+ # JUSTINE

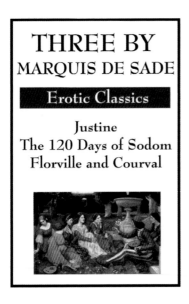

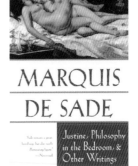

Plot: Born in 1740 to a privileged family, the Marquis de Sade was well educated and served with the infantry and cavalry, fighting in the Seven Years' War. Discharged in 1763, he married (an arrangement made by his father) but was soon imprisoned for scandalous behavior in a brothel. The next few years saw many other brief imprisonments, liaisons, and an affair with his wife's sister. His mother-in-law applied for a *lettre de cachet*, a royal order under which he could be imprisoned without trial for an indefinite period, after Sade was accused of sexually and physically abusing a young woman.

Imprisoned in 1772 for poisoning prostitutes and sodomy with a manservant, de Sade escaped to Italy. Back in France in 1776, he was accused again of abusing servant girls and arrested, remaining in prison until 1790.

Justine, written during this period of incarceration, was originally a short novel entitled *The Misfortunes of Virtue* (this version not published until 1930). It was expanded (and published in 1791) and expanded again (as *La Neuvelle Justine*, 1797–1801), each revision becoming progressively more explicit. Napoleon ordered the arrest of the anonymous author, reputedly calling *Justine* "the most abominable book ever engendered by the most depraved imagination." Sade

was imprisoned again, declared insane in 1803, and moved to an asylum where he remained until his death in 1814.

Review: *Justine* was Sade's answer to *Pamela; or, Virtue Rewarded* by Samuel Richardson, in which the heroine suffers greatly but is rewarded with happiness and prosperity in the end. Twelve-year-old Justine, instead, suffers at the hands of everyone she meets or turns to, is raped and tortured endlessly, and her search for virtue goes unrewarded. Parallel with his revisions, Sade also penned *Juliette*, about Justine's sister, who embraces vice and prospers through it.

Neither book saw wide circulation until the twentieth century, when critics began to reassess Sade's work: his novels were seen as a precursor to modern existentialist and psychological works, while surrealists embraced his philosophy of no limits. To others he remains a writer of misogynistic torture porn of the most vile kind.

FURTHER READING: *Histoire de Juliette, ou les Prospérités du vice; Les Crimes de l'amour, Nouvelles héroïques et tragiques*
SEE ALSO: *Venus in Furs* (Leopold von Sacher-Masoch); *Ice and Fire* (Andrea Dworkin)

★
★
★
★
★

Writer: William Burroughs
Publisher: Olympia, 1959

ISBN US: 978-0802132956
ISBN UK: 978-0007204441

8+

NAKED LUNCH

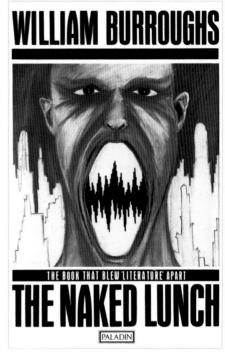

Plot: Fragmented text and random episodes provide an account of the surreal, nightmarish, and existential nature of a drug addict's life. We begin in the realms of reality as our protagonist, William Lee, is on the run from police in New York. He will later return to the U.S. (and some semblance of normality), but not before being assigned the strange quack, Dr. Benway, in Mexico, and providing a hallucinatory account of his time in the orgy and drug-filled world of "Interzone," a fictional version of Tangiers.

Along the way Lee encounters the myriad characters who orbit the drug-addicted: the pushers, dealers, and fellow addicts who help him get his next fix, and the narcotics police who are hell-bent on stopping him.

Review: A friend of the "Beats," even if a few years older than others in the ultra-cool literary movement of the 1950s, Burroughs is your archetypal counterculture icon. If that's not

a contradiction in terms. It was a fellow Beat, Jack Kerouac, who rescued the handwritten embryonic draft of *Naked Lunch*, typed it, and persuaded Burroughs to send it to a publisher.

Burroughs claims to have written this literary mash-up, which pioneered the "cut-up" technique, in order to expel the demons of his middle-class background, aiming to write "the most horrible, dirty, slimy, awful, niggardliest posture possible." He succeeded, and *Naked Lunch* went on trial for obscenity in 1962. Burroughs lost that case but a later 1966 ruling saw the ban on his counterculture tour de force lifted, paving the way for other previously banned works to be published.

FURTHER READING: *Junkie*
SEE ALSO: *Fear and Loathing in Las Vegas*
(Hunter S. Thompson); *Howl* **(Allen Ginsberg)**

★
★ **Writer:** Pauline Réage **ISBN US:** 978-0345301116
★ **Publisher:** Jan-Jacques Pauvert, 1954 **ISBN UK:** 978-0552089302

18+ # STORY OF O

Story of O
by Pauline Réage

Synopsis: "O," a Parisian photographer, is taken by her lover René to the mysterious chateau of Roissy. Here, she consents to being treated as a sexual slave by René and other, unknown, men, obeying strict rules enforced by beatings and living as a silent submissive. Later, back in Paris, René presents O as a gift to his friend Sir Stephen; her subjugation deepens as she is dispatched to Samois, another country house—this time solely inhabited by women. Her friend Jacqueline cannot understand her willingness to subjugate herself, but O sees it as an expression of love.

Review: The many elements of fantasy and dream (with luxurious chateaus, bestial man-servants, and a pervading atmosphere of unreality) have helped *Story of O* become a key text for anyone interested in S&M—and one of the most important books about sexuality since de Sade. It's remarkable for the contrast between the extreme sex and violence presented and the neutral, almost unnaturally calm language Réage uses; there are no four-letter words, no detailed depictions of sex acts, but the parade of encounters is nonetheless unrelentingly pornographic.

The book is related from O's point of view (it's made clear that she's a willing participant in the many tortures and torments) and, unusually for one this explicit, it dwells as much on her emotional state as her erotic bondage. Of real literary interest—it won one of France's most prestigious literary awards, the *Prix des Deux Magots*, on publication. This is not for everyone, but it is unique.

FURTHER READING: Réage (aka Anne Desclos) didn't pen another book—in fact, she didn't even own up to writing this one for forty years
SEE ALSO: *The Torture Garden* (Octave Mirbeau); *120 Days of Sodom* (Marquis de Sade); *Confessions of O* (Régine Deforges)

Writer: Radclyffe Hall
Publisher: Jonathan Cape, 1928

ISBN US: 978-0385416092
ISBN UK: 978-1844085156

5+ THE WELL OF LONELINESS

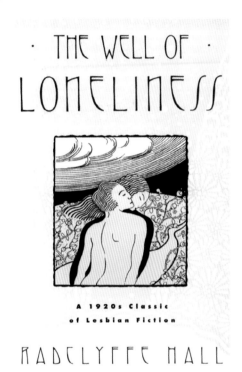

Plot: The biography of a fictional woman, Stephen Gordon, whose life bears a strong resemblance to that of her creator's. Born to English upper-class parents who yearn for a son, Stephen is given a boy's name and grows up resembling her father: "Narrow-hipped and wide-shouldered," she is anything but feminine. As she grows older she increasingly shuns female pursuits and realizes that she craves the love of a woman, eventually finding it, if briefly, with Mary Llewellyn.

The book is considered Hall's plea for acceptance of "sexual inversion"—an idea of the prewar period that homosexuality was a medical condition and therefore "couldn't be helped."

Review: Let's get down to brass-tacks: *The Well of Loneliness* is not the wildly explicit depiction of Sapphic love you might expect. For its time, though, it was highly controversial. Hall bravely defended her novel in public when it was labeled

obscene, even sending it to the British Government in the hope they'd allow it past the censors. Her plan backfired, and *The Well of Loneliness* was banned—not for its sexual content, but because of Hall's argument for the acceptance of sexual inversion.

This argument has meant the book became unfashionable over the years—after all, sexual inversion is an unpalatable concept for some. Still, as the argument, whether rightly or wrongly, over nature or nurture rages on, Hall's book will continue to engage readers, but not necessarily for its literary merits.

FURTHER READING: *The Unlit Lamp*
SEE ALSO: *Orlando* (Virginia Woolf)

★
★
★
★

Writer: Ryu Murakami
Publisher: Kodansha, 1976

ISBN US: 978-4770029041
ISBN UK: 978-4770029041

18+

ALMOST TRANSPARENT BLUE

Plot: *Almost Transparent Blue* is a brutal antidote to the Western view of Japan as a land of soft cherry blossoms and quiet tradition. In it Murakami paints a wild and episodic portrait of a group of friends immersing themselves in drugs and sex, and not forgetting rock 'n' roll, as they come of age in the 1970s.

Review: He's the enfant terrible of Japanese literature of whom Irvine Welsh has said, "his strongest suit as a writer is how he portrays tripped-out, hallucinogenic sex and violence." There's certainly a lot of that here. The style is all "panties . . . spread legs . . . and good asses," which might annoy you, but hey, the book has sold about a squillion copies in Japan, so it would be churlish not to give it a look.

FURTHER READING: *In the Miso Soup; Audition; Piercing*
SEE ALSO: *The Woman in the Dunes* (Kobo Abe)

★
★
★

Writer: Mary Gaitskill
Publisher: Poseidon Press, 1988

ISBN US: 978-0679723271
ISBN UK: 978-0340494837

18+

BAD BEHAVIOR

Synopsis: Nothing much happens in this collection of short stories, famous for its taboo-busting sex scenes. It doesn't matter, really: Gaitskill's punctilious depiction of the harrowing nature of sexual relationships and close friendships renders this lack of diagenesis of little import.

Review: New York City provides the backdrop for Gaitskill's disenfranchised and lonely souls, while an almost photographic capturing of the styles of the 1980s provides the mood. In interviews the author can come across as shy and retiring, relating how she was unsure how to deal with the attention that this, her first collection of short stories, brought her. The writing is anything but unassured, though—bold and savvy, erotic but not overly explicit, this collection is sure to strike a chord with those who over-think their close relationships.

FURTHER READING: *Don't Cry; Because They Wanted To* (stories);
Two Girls, Fat and Thin (a novel)
SEE ALSO: *Slaves of New York* (Tama Janowitz)

Writer: Stuart Maconie
Publisher: Ebury Press, 2005

ISBN US: 978-0091897451
ISBN UK: 978-0091897451

CIDER WITH ROADIES

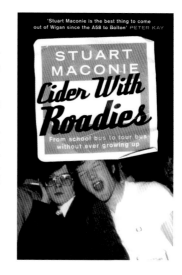

'Stuart Maconie is the best thing to come out of Wigan since the A58 to Bolton' PETER KAY

STUART MACONIE

Cider With Roadies

From school bus to tour bus without ever growing up

Synopsis: The memoirs of an obsessive music fan who wrote for popular British music newspaper *NME* and currently resides as a pop-picker on the BBC's Radio 2.

Review: Maconie takes us by the hand and leads us with cheeky good humor through his journey from pop-music fan to well-known music journalist. Equally at home describing his first frisson of musical pleasure in his auntie's bedroom in Swindon (at the age of three) or on a tour bus with extreme-metalers Napalm Death, his down-to-earth and jaunty style will have universal appeal. Yes, the finer details of Maconie's Northern English back-ground might be a befuddlement for some, but that's part of this joyful biography's obscure charm.

FURTHER READING: *Adventures on the High Teas: In Search of Middle England; Pies and Prejudice: In Search of the North*
SEE ALSO: *That's Me in the Corner: Adventures of an Ordinary Boy in a Celebrity World* (Andrew Collins); *High Fidelity* (Nick Hornby)

Writer: J. G. Ballard
Publisher: Harper Collins, 1996

ISBN US: 978-1582430171
ISBN UK: 978-0006550648

COCAINE NIGHTS

JG Ballard

Cocaine Nights

Plot: Club Nautico is a gated enclave for retired Brits in Estrella da Mar, Spain. It is also a hotbed of cocaine, sex, and criminal activity. Into the midst of these geriatric misdeeds stumbles Charles Prentice on a mission to rescue his arsonist brother, Frank, from jail. But does Frank want to be rescued?

Review: Transgression by numbers. It's what literary shock jock and avant-garde guru Ballard does best, but the excesses wear a little thin here. Although the nightmare vision of a society with too much time for leisure is realistic, the mystery element does not quite ring true. In fact it seems almost ludicrous. We forgive Ballard, of course, because what lies beneath is the genius of a truly original writer.

FURTHER READING: *The Unlimited Dream Company; Crash; Empire of the Sun*
SEE ALSO: *Fight Club* (Chuck Palahniuk); *Atomized* (Michel Houellebecq)

★
★
★
★

Writer: A. C. Weisbecker
Publisher: Vintage, 1986

ISBN US: 978-0451203069
ISBN UK: 978-0451203069

18+

COSMIC BANDITOS

A CONTRABANDISTA'S QUEST
FOR THE MEANING OF LIFE

Plot: Mr. Quark, a dope smuggler, takes a "Sherlock Holmesian" interest in a book about quantum physics after one of the titular banditos steals it from an American tourist. Soon the pair are setting off to confront the book's owner about the meaning of life, leading to a heady mix of tequila, enlightenment, and scientific instruction.

Review: Quite the cult figure, Weisbecker: surfer, ex-drugs runner, writer, and, now, book publisher. (In 2007 he launched his own publishing company, Bandito Books.) In this, his only novel to date, his life experience is taken to absurd fictional extremes. A crazy freewheeling novel you won't forget.

FURTHER READING: *In Search of Captain Zero*
SEE ALSO: *Fear and Loathing in Las Vegas* (Hunter S. Thompson)

★
★
★
★

Writer: Anaïs Nin
First Published in Britain: Allen Lane, 1978
First Published in USA: Harcourt Brace, 1977

ISBN US: 978-0156029032
ISBN UK: 978-0141182841

15+

DELTA OF VENUS

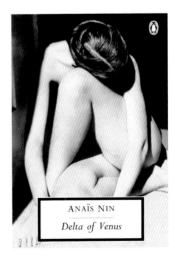

Synopsis: Erotic stories, written as an antidote to the phallocentric scribblings of centuries previous and taking us into a realm of mostly feminine sensuality. Nin offers fifteen stories of lovers, including the veiled woman who enjoys sex with strangers, the Hungarian adventurer who seduces, then steals from, rich women, and a hat-maker who ditches her husband to languish in the opium dens of Peru.

Review: Current writers of sexual fiction and memoir might well look to Nin's work for something of the beautiful frankness that makes her work an exotic, provocative, and exciting cut above the rest. All the senses are stimulated and every sexual taste catered for, so there is no excuse other than prudishness not to read this extraordinary collection.

FURTHER READING: *Little Birds; Henry and June*
SEE ALSO: *The Story of O* (Pauline Réage);
Tropic of Cancer (Henry Miller)

★
★

Writer: Aleister Crowley
Publisher: W Collins Sons & Co, 1922

ISBN US: 978-1585092451
ISBN UK: 978-1585092451

15+

DIARY OF A DRUG FIEND

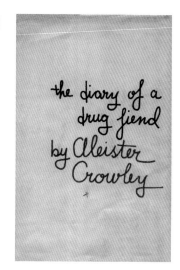

Synopsis: A young serviceman, Peter Pendragon, falls prey to the lure of cocaine and an attractive young woman, Louise Laleham, and together they make a drug-fueled trip across Europe. Running dry of supplies, they encounter King Lamus, a magician who teaches them how to combat their addiction with "True Will."

Review: Perhaps better known—and loved by many—for his writings on the occult, Crowley was once called the "wickedest man in the world." As to whether he can write fiction, the answer is probably no. At the book's offset Crowley resorts to the blunderbuss of drugs glorification, while the downfall of the lovers is no less subtly handled. There are many successful depictions of the pleasures and pitfalls of hard drugs; this, sadly, is not one of them.

FURTHER READING: *Book of Lies*
SEE ALSO: *Confessions of an English Opium Eater*
(Thomas De Quincey); *Rock Salt and Glissandos* (Steve Fisher)

★
★
★
★

Writer: Arthur Schnitzler
Publisher: First Published 1926

ISBN US: 978-1931243483
ISBN UK: 978-0141182247

5+

DREAM STORY

Plot: Following a row with his wife and a visit to the deathbed of an elderly patient, Fridolin, a doctor, embarks on a sexually charged nocturnal adventure. On his return home, his wife recounts an erotic dream of a Danish military man she had encountered on their last summer holiday. A cathartic conversation ensues and the couple fall into a dreamless sleep.

Review: Set over two days in fin de siècle Vienna, *Dream Story* is an intriguing exploration of sexual relations in a marriage. If you are looking for porn on a plate, though, think again; Schniztler's novella is an evocative journey through the erotic landscape of one man's mind which informs, rather than ignites, the flames of passion.

ARTHUR SCHNITZLER
Dream Story

FURTHER READING: *Anatol; Fräulein Else*
SEE ALSO: *The Interpretation of Dreams* (Sigmund Freud);
Le Grand Meaulnes (Alain Fournier)

★
★
★

Writer: Nicholas Saunders
Publisher: Self Published, 1993

ISBN US: 978-0950162881
ISBN UK: 978-0950162881

18+ E IS FOR ECSTASY

Synopsis: The late Nicholas Saunders' comprehensive investigation into Ecstasy, the recreational drug associated with rave culture. Saunders examines the drug's origins, its chemical make-up, the dangers, and its vilification by the media, as well as his own experiences of using the drug.

Review: As interest in the rave movement as a twentieth-century subculture increases, Saunders' 1993 book should become increasingly important. Granted the book glorifies Ecstasy use, and can, sometimes, yield to hyperbole—for example when it suggest that "for people with an intense and speedy lifestyle, Ecstasy can provide as much relaxation in two days as a week on a tropical island." But E was also for enthusiasm, so we can forgive an otherwise fascinating study its foibles.

FURTHER READING: *Ecstasy and the Dance Culture* (the follow up title with more detailed information and interviews from the rave scene)
SEE ALSO: *Generation Ecstasy* (Simon Reynolds); *E, The Incredibly Strange History of Ecstasy* (Tim Pilcher)

★
★
★
★

Writer: Tom Wolfe
Publisher: Farrar, Strauss, & Giroux, 1968

ISBN US: 978-0553380644
ISBN UK: 978-0552993661

15+ THE ELECTRIC KOOL-AID ACID TEST

Synopsis: D'you think you could pass the acid test? That is, could you survive the trip that follows drinking Kool-Aid spiked with LSD? Ken Kesey and his roving band of Merry Pranksters sure can—and then some—in this multicolored account of hippies tripping out in San Francisco in the late 1960s.

Review: *The Electric Kool-Aid Acid Test* is a founding example of "new journalism," a technique that dovetails journalistic reporting with fictional devices. Wolfe's subjects, Bay Area hippies and drop-outs, were likewise trying to create something new. It's hard to resist their innocent wide-eyed idealism, and not to be disgusted by the squalor they found themselves living in. But it's not just hippies who will enjoy this magical mystery tour through one of popular culture's more psychedelic moments.

FURTHER READING: *The Right Stuff; The Bonfire of the Vanities*
SEE ALSO: *Hell's Angels* (Hunter S. Thompson);
The Doors of Perception (Aldous Huxley)

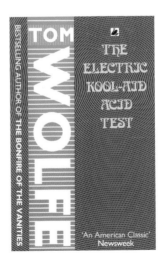

Writer: Simon Reynolds   **ISBN US:** 978-0330350563
Publisher: Pan Macmillan, 1998 **ISBN UK:** 978-0330350563

5+ # ENERGY FLASH
A JOURNEY THROUGH RAVE MUSIC AND DANCE CULTURE

Synopsis: *Energy Flash* shows how the rave scene burst to life on the streets of Chicago and Detroit in the late eighties and later found its way to the fields orbiting England's M25 highway. The drug Ecstasy, an integral part of rave culture, is discussed, as well as the music: interviews with Paul Oakenfold, Derrick May, Jeff Mills, and the like, being a welcome inclusion.

Review: This is a sterling evaluation of a cultural phenomenon that Reynolds, a respected music journalist, describes as "weirdly poised between idyllic and apocalyptic." It's nice to see that he mentions "happy hardcore," the perhaps less well-regarded little brother of house and techno, an inclusion that makes *Energy Flash* not only an entertaining book, but a comprehensive one.

FURTHER READING: *Rip It Up and Start Again; Bring the Noise*
SEE ALSO: *E is for Ecstasy* (Nicholas Saunders)

Writer: Jon Savage   **ISBN US:** 978-0571167913
Publisher: Faber & Faber, 1991 **ISBN UK:** 978-0312288228

5+ # ENGLAND'S DREAMING
SEX PISTOLS AND PUNK ROCK

Synopsis: Punk rock—fast, simple songs, played by misfits on electric guitars—was an American invention, but it was in the UK that it had the greatest impact, inspiring a frustrated generation to contemptuously reject the conventions of its elders. At the center of punk were the Sex Pistols, endlessly confrontational, cynical, violent, intellectual, doomed . . . and one of the greatest rock acts ever.

Review: Not only was this the first book to seriously take on the confusing, complicated story of punk, it was one of the first to take the tools, and scholarship, previously reserved for analysis of "high" art and apply them with the same seriousness to pop music. At once a brilliant dissection of British society and the music industry, and a fascinatingly detailed account of the Sex Pistols' continual conflicts, *England's Dreaming* raised the bar for writing about pop culture, or rock music, to new heights of intelligence and insight.

FURTHER READING: *Teenage: The Prehistory of Youth Culture*
SEE ALSO: *Rip it Up and Start Again* (Simon Reynolds)

★ **Writer:** Kingsley Amis
★ **Publisher:** Originally published: Jonathan
★ Cape, 1972; bind-up: Bloomsbury, 2008

ISBN US: 978-1596915282
ISBN UK: 978-1596915282

18+ EVERYDAY DRINKING (ON DRINK)

Synopsis: A bind-up edition of three nonfiction books from British novelist Kingsley Amis (father of Martin), highlighting the delights—and how to combat the effects—of alcohol.

Review: Fizzing with sparkling humor (but not wine—Amis was not much of a wine drinker), delightfully irreverent advice (such as "drink sangria—you can drink a lot of it without falling down"), and handy recipes, this is a welcome kick in the teeth to those who suggest that Great Britain's binge-drinking culture is a modern phenomenon. The liquid measures for the recipes and other practical tips may be out of date, but no matter: some of the material, such as the metaphysical torpor brought on by hangovers, is both timeless and hilarious.

FURTHER READING: *The Green Man; New Maps of Hell; What Became of Jane Austen and Other Questions*
SEE ALSO: *The Book of Bond: or Every Man His Own 007* (Lt. Col. William "Bill" Tanner)

★ **Writer:** J. P. Donleavy
★ **Publisher:** Olympia Press, 1955
★
★

ISBN US: 978-0802137951
ISBN UK: 978-0349108759

18+ THE GINGER MAN

Plot: Rebellious, greedy, cruel, and egocentric, Sebastian Dangerfield, an American in postwar Ireland, studies at Trinity College and lives his life to excess: drinking and womanizing with no thought to others, especially his wife and child, who are also resident with him in Dublin. The tone moves between slapstick and melancholy as Dangerfield's irresponsible actions constantly undermine his desire for money and status.

Review: Critics have argued the place of *The Ginger Man* in literature for years, although few now disagree that it is a classic. Its lusty, scatological content, shocking at the time of publication, earned it a ban in Ireland and the U.S. on publication, but its qualities earned it an underground following—and not many books can claim to have inspired a chain of pubs.

FURTHER READING: *The History of the Ginger Man; J. P. Donleavy's Ireland*
SEE ALSO: *At Swim-Two-Birds* (Flann O'Brien); *Borstal Boy* (Brendan Behan)

Writer: Abby Lee
Publisher: Ebury Press, 2006

ISBN US: 978-0091912406
ISBN UK: 978-0091912406

8+ GIRL WITH A ONE TRACK MIND
DIARY OF A SEX FIEND

Synopsis: *Girl with a One Track Mind* follows the sexploits of a latter-day female Casanova as she romps her away across London, chronicling a succession of one-night stands, a lesbian clinch, group romps, and many "self-fulfilling" moments, all with a sticky frankness.

Review: An on-again, off-again relationship with a fellow blogger is the sum total of the plot in Lee's memoir, but as one of the first examples of confessional writing that made the transition from blogosphere mega-hit to print bestseller, plot was never meant to be at its heart. A brave and bold account of one woman's enjoyment of sex.

FURTHER READING: Nothing in book form yet; the blog is still live
SEE ALSO: *Belle de Jour* (Anonymous); *Story of O* (Pauline Réage)

Writer: Georges Bataille
Publisher: Gallimard, 1928

ISBN US: 978-0872862098
ISBN UK: 978-0141185385

8+ HISTOIRE DE L'OEIL
(STORY OF THE EYE)

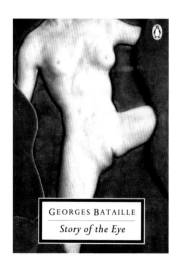

Plot: The story depicts the sexual relations between an unnamed boy and his lover (using the term loosely) Simone. Together they partake in a urine fetish, a lewd use of eggs, the deflowering and driving to insanity of a friend, and, finally, an unspeakable misdeed on a priest.

Review: Susan Sontag suggests that in *Story of the Eye* Bataille is more "potent and outrageous" than de Sade because he possesses "a finer and more pronounced sense of transgression." In other words, this panoply of erotica contains more filth, sacrilege, perversion, and plain weirdness than you can shake a stick at. This is not your usual boy-meets-girl story, and those who are easily offended won't make it past the second page: be warned!

FURTHER READING: *Literature and Evil* (essays)
SEE ALSO: *A Lover's Discourse* (Roland Barthes);
The Torture Garden (Octave Mirbeau)

★
★ **Writer:** Kenneth Anger   **ISBN US:** 978-0440153252
★ **Publisher:** J. J. Pauvert, 1959   **ISBN UK:** 978-0440153252

15+

HOLLYWOOD BABYLON

Synopsis: Hollywood's "darkest and best kept secrets" are laid bare in underground filmmaker Anger's notorious exposé. Taking D. W. Griffith's 1916 movie *Intolerance* as his starting point, Anger dishes the dirt on the degenerate lifestyles of the Hollywood stars of the silent movie era through to the late 1950s.

Review: *Hollywood Babylon* is a fine example of a book that battered its way to cult status despite the odds: it took over eighteen years for an unabridged version to go on general sale in Anger's native country after its 1959 publication in France, only for reviewers to be, well, angry at his "keyhole" style of journalism. But it's exactly his tattle-telling, veraciously vague approach that earned *Hollywood Babylon* more than a chorus line of fans and has it coming highly recommended.

FURTHER READING: *Hollywood Babylon 2*
SEE ALSO: *Day of the Locust* (Nathanael West);
Adventures in the Screen Trade (William Goldman)

★
★ **Writer:** Pamela Des Barres   **ISBN US:** 978-1556525896
★ **Publisher:** Chicago Review Press 1987   **ISBN UK:** 978-1900924610

18+

I'M WITH THE BAND
CONFESSIONS OF A GROUPIE

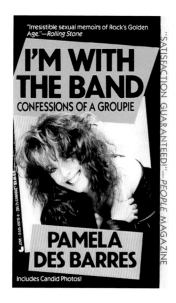

Synopsis: A girl meets boys (many of them) story which goes: girl is a "boy-crazy" teen. Girl heads to Sunset Strip and becomes a groupie, bedding, among others, Mick Jagger, Jim Morrison, and Keith Moon. Girl gets married, waters down her previous hedonistic hijinx, and writes a memoir.

Review: That the chapters have titles such as "Let Me Put It In" and "Every Inch of My Love" should give you some indication of the book's racy content. It's a dazzling insight into the hotel bedrooms of the rich and famous and is so much the better for being told by a woman of obvious warmth and intelligence. When the fairytale marriage to a rock star happens, we are happy for Des Barres, even if her happiness cannot last forever.

FURTHER READING: *Take Another Little Piece of My Heart:*
A Groupie Grows Up
SEE ALSO: *Wonderful Tonight: George Harrison, Eric Clapton,*
and Me (Pattie Boyd)

Writer: Anthony Swofford
Publisher: Simon and Schuster, 1997

ISBN US: 978-0743287210
ISBN UK: 978-0743275378

JARHEAD

Synopsis: "Welcome to the Suck." Here are first Gulf War veteran Anthony Swofford's reminiscences about the frustrations of being a "Jarhead," a member of the United States Marine Corps, at a time when combat operations were more about smart bombs from the air than bullets on the ground.

Review: Swofford brilliantly captures the absurdist nature of war and shows that combat is not all about firing weapons—there is the interminable waiting, the constant loneliness, the cleaning of sand from weapons, the letters to and from the unfaithful girlfriends and wives back home, and the "trouser-pissing horror" at what's to come. Humanity breaks through when an especially tough marine demands a hug before they go out on a dangerous patrol. Which is not to say blood and guts don't feature—this is a war memoir, after all.

FURTHER READING: *Exit A* (a novel)
SEE ALSO: *Dispatches* (Michael Herr);
Black Hawk Down (Mark Bowden)

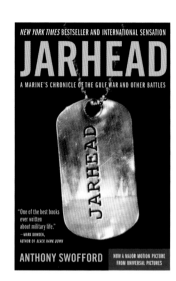

Writer: Denis Johnson
Publisher: Farrar, Strauss, Giroux, 1992

ISBN US: 978-0060975777
ISBN UK: 978-0312428747

JESUS' SON

Synopsis: This collection of eleven stories, loosely connected by an unnamed male narrator, are set in the contemporary American Midwest among lonely folk who drink, take drugs, and steal to support habits—and also merely to pass the time.

Review: *The New Yorker* has described *Jesus' Son* as the only book written under the influence of drugs that isn't mediocre. Johnson denies being high when he wrote the stories, even if they're based on things people would do or say when he was "using and drinking." There's no denying the authenticity, then, but that doesn't make the barren view of human relations depicted here any more palatable. Quite the opposite, in fact.

FURTHER READING: *Train of Dreams; Tree of Smoke*
SEE ALSO: *Fear and Loathing in Las Vegas*
(Hunter S. Thompson); *Naked Lunch* (William S. Burroughs)

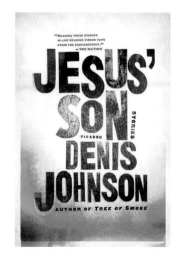

★
★
★

Writer: D. H. Lawrence
Publisher: Self-published, 1928

ISBN US: 978-1604596168
ISBN UK: 978-1840224887

15+

LADY CHATTERLEY'S LOVER

Plot: A sexually charged love affair between Lady Connie Chatterley and her gamekeeper, Mellors, forms the basis for what D. H. Lawrence called, "a very pure and tender novel" but also "the most improper novel in the world."

Review: This book, though tame to modern eyes, was pretty radical for 1928 when it was published privately in Florence: the "F" word was used by a mainstream author for the first time, the curious blend of narrative voices broke away from traditional novelistic forms, and the subject was a rejection of the mores of the time. It was over thirty years before the book was published legally in the UK. Since then it has been a symbol of free expression and sexual liberation.

FURTHER READING: *Women in Love; The Rainbow; Sons and Lovers*
SEE ALSO: *The Lover* (Marguerite Duras); *The Thorn Birds* (Colleen McCullough)

★
★
★
★
★

Writer: Hubert Selby, Jr.
Publisher: Grove Press, 1957

ISBN US: 978-0802131379
ISBN UK: 0-586-08588-2

15+

LAST EXIT TO BROOKLYN

Plot: Pimps, hookers, rapists, junkies, transvestites. Yes, these colorful characters could fill a police cell on a Saturday night, but they are also the principals in this, Hubert Selby, Jr.'s vivid view of the sordid and uncivilized goings-on in his native Brooklyn in the 1950s.

Review: Creative writing tutors tell aspiring writers: have your manuscripts properly punctuated; DON'T USE SHOUTY CAPITAL LETTERS; employ a minimal use of the vernacular. Thankfully Selby eschewed this advice and then some, along with the skewed notion that representations of the sexual act should be cosseted in the fluffily romantic. Okay, so we are left with an unflinchingly brutal, violent, and pessimistic world view in this series of six united stories, but a more truthful exposé of urban 1950s America would be hard to find.

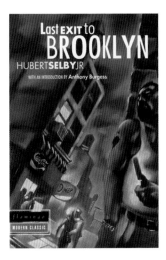

FURTHER READING: *Requiem for a Dream*
SEE ALSO: *City of Night* (John Rechy)

★
★
★

Writer: John O'Brien
Publisher: Watermark Press, 1990

ISBN US: 978-0802134455
ISBN UK: 978-0330351799

8+ LEAVING LAS VEGAS

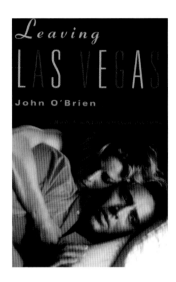

Plot: The bitter-sweet story of a romance that was doomed from the start. Ben is a broken man in the mire of alcohol addiction, come to Las Vegas for one last all-out drinking binge. On Las Vegas Boulevard, "The Strip," he meets Sera, a prostitute, and, for a very short time, they console one another.

Review: A clinical, almost pathological style sees us finding a humanity in a story that in a lesser writer's hands could have wound up sentimental. Yes, it's a humanity tied up in the seamier aspects of American life, but that doesn't stop *Leaving Las Vegas* exuding an honesty at once shocking, harrowing, and moving. Read it, but don't weep.

FURTHER READING: *Stripper Lessons; The Assault on Tony's*
SEE ALSO: *Last Exit to Brooklyn* (Hubert Selby, Jr.)

★
★
★

Writer: Michel Houellebecq
Publisher: Flammarion, 1999

ISBN US: 978-0434007936
ISBN UK: 978-0099283362

8+ LES PARTICULES ÉLÉMENTAIRES
(ATOMISED OR THE ELEMENTARY PARTICLES)

Plot: Two half-brothers grow up to middle age without having known one another. Bruno, an unappealing libertine, letches his way through life, spending time at New Age camps and swingers' clubs. Michel is a biologist who has trouble forming sexual relationships. Their stories are told amid a series of digressions attacking various elements of modern society.

Review: There are two schools of thought when it comes to Houellebecq's worldview. His detractors say *Atomised* is a vehicle for his racism and misogyny. Fans argue he is an existential hero, perfectly evoking the schisms and pessimisms of our epoch. That the book is immensely readable should encourage you to give it a go and decide in which camp you lie.

FURTHER READING: *Platform; Lanzarote*
SEE ALSO: *The Ogre* (Michel Tournier)

★
★
★
★
★

Writer: Jaime Hernandez
Publisher: Fantagraphics, 2004

ISBN US: 978-1560976110
ISBN UK: 978-1560976110

15+

LOCAS THE MAGGIE AND HOPEY STORIES

Plot: In the Southern California community of Barrio Huerto, or Hoppers 13, Maggie is a mechanic repairing robots and rockets. Her lover, the abrasive Hopey, plays in a punk band. *Locas* gathers together many of their misadventures as the two grow up, grow apart, find and lose friends, enter relationships, and endure tragedies.

Review: Los Bros Hernandez, the brothers Jaimie, Gilbert, and Mario, launched *Love and Rockets* in 1982, each issue an anthology of stories each was writing, drawing, and lettering. The title rapidly gained international acclaim. With a keen ear for dialog, the stories range from comedy to bittersweet. Jamie's clean line and naturalistic figurework (Maggie gains weight as the years go by) add to the reality.

FURTHER READING: *Love and Rockets; Locas II*
SEE ALSO: *Heartbreak Soup, Palomar* (Gilbert Hernandez)

★
★
★
★
★

Writer: Venedikt Yerofeev
Publisher: 1970 (Originally published in Samizdat)

ISBN US: 978-0571190041
ISBN UK: 978-0810112001

15+

MOSCOW STATIONS

Moscow Stations
Venedikt Yerofeev

An elegy for once-hopeful twentieth-century systems, quite wrong that's as daunting and moving as could be.
Observer

Plot: Yerofeev's autobiographical novel is an alcohol-soaked tour of the thirty stops on the Moscow to Petushki underground line by his fictional alter ego, Venya. The 125km journey is enlivened by Venya's alcoholic pink elephants and confusions, as well as his inventive urge to create cocktails with names such as "Dog's Giblets."

Review: "Then I promptly had a drink," says Venya in the chapter entitled "Hammer and Sickle to Karacharovo." These words would not, however, be out of place in any chapter of this dissolute and entertaining book. But Yerofeev's Venya is as erudite as he is plastered, and readers will also enjoy a liberal dose of quotations and cultural references throughout. Distributed originally in Samizdat to defeat the censors, *Moscow Stations* was finally published in Yerofeev's native Russia in 1989. A wittier record of the Brezhnev era has not been published since.

FURTHER READING: Nothing, he died of drink before he could write anything else
SEE ALSO: *Babylon* (Viktor Pelevin);
Death and the Penguin (Andrey Kurkov)

ff

★
★
★
★

Writer: Nancy Friday
Publisher: Simon and Schuster, 1973

ISBN US: 978-0671019877
ISBN UK: 978-0704332942

8+ MY SECRET GARDEN

Synopsis: *My Secret Garden* casts a dazzling light on the sexual fantasies of real women, hundreds of whom were either interviewed by, or wrote to, Friday during her extensive research for this collection.

Review: When twenty-first century bookstore shelves are weighed down with explicit female confessionals, you might wonder whether *My Secret Garden* is not out of date. Certainly, the book's primary assertion—that women's fantasies can be every bit as outré as men's—might seem a little quaint. However, in its time, this was an extraordinary, revolutionary book that redefined women's sexuality. Even now, the smorgasbord of sexual imaginings presented—from incest to rape, S&M, and bestiality—may be too much for the mainstream. The presentation, though, is never titillating, but meant as a comfort for females who fantasize. Powerfully stirring stuff.

FURTHER READING: *Women on Top*
SEE ALSO: *Little Bird* (Nin); *The Butcher, The Baker, The Candlestick Maker: An Erotic Memoir* (Portnoy)

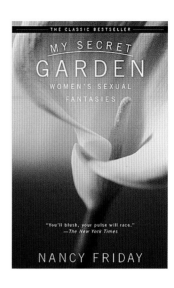

★
★
★
★

Writer: Robert Crumb
Publisher: Last Gasp, 2000

ISBN US: 978-0867193749
ISBN UK: 978-0867193749

8+ MY TROUBLES WITH WOMEN

Synopsis: Sexual confession in comic book form from the most influential underground cartoonist of the 1960s. *My Troubles with Women* is a series of short stories (originally written in the 1980s) that honestly and explicitly detail Crumb's sex life from the "terrible impossible sexual longing" of his youth to the "hot sex" he's still enjoying with his wife and partner, Aline Kominsky-Crumb. Aline, incidentally, adds to the proceedings with three stories done in collaboration with her husband.

Review: Unadulterated and unapologetic in its style and content, readers of *My Troubles with Women* looking for fun and filth will hit paydirt. Feminists might not feel similarly rewarded, but Crumb knows he's "cutting his own throat" in that regard—women will "despise me," he acknowledges in one of the stories.

FURTHER READING: *Weirdo; The Book of Genesis*
SEE ALSO: *American Splendor* (Harvey Pekar); *Asterios Polyp* (David Mazzucchelli)

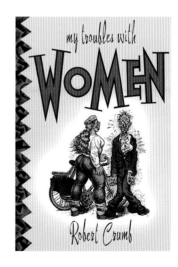

★
★ **Writer:** Michael Azerrad   **ISBN US:** 978-0316787536
★ **Publisher:** Little Brown & Co, 2001   **ISBN UK:** 978-0316787536
★

15+ OUR BAND COULD BE YOUR LIFE

Synopsis: *Our Band Could Be Your Life* is an involving panorama of the U.S. indie music scene in the 1980s, which arose from the dying embers of punk. Starting with hardcore punk's "godfathers" Black Flag, Azerrad covers thirteen bands in thirteen chapters, including Mudhoney, Dinosaur Jr., and hardcore punk legends Fugazi.

Review: Remember mosh pits? Remember slam-dancing? Remember the straight-edge movement? Azerrad does, and fondly so, in a well-researched survey of the era that led up to the "grunge" explosion in the 1990s. The strength of the book is its focus on the scene's key players: Henry Rollins, Ian Mackaye, Steve Albini, and Bob Mould; they're all vociferous eccentrics, and they recall a time when musicians had something meaningful to say. A good read and not just for musos.

FURTHER READING: *Come as You Are: The Story of Nirvana*
SEE ALSO: *Trapped in a Scene: UK Hardcore, 1985–1989*
(Ian Glasper); *Rip it Up and Start Again* (Simon Reynolds)

★ **Writer:** Timothy Leary   **ISBN US:** 978-1579510312
★ **Publisher:** G. P. Putnam, 1968   **ISBN UK:** 978-1579510312

18+ THE POLITICS OF ECSTASY

Synopsis: An at times scholarly, at times belligerent, at times rambling extolment of the effects of LSD from hippy guru Timothy Leary via his essays, thoughts, and speeches. The book covers the period when Leary was first turned on to magic mushrooms while at Harvard through to the cultural and political rebellion that was the Summer of Love in 1967.

Review: This is a tangled web of ideas: scientific, political, and sociological, which unite in a pro-drugs chorus, what we might call psychedelic-babble. Yes, it is all as esoteric as it sounds. That said, taken as a whole, the book should give you a better understanding of that period in the 1960s that is characterized by Leary's own legendary catchphrase "turn on, tune in, drop out."

FURTHER READING: *High Priest* (Leary's autobiography)
SEE ALSO: *The Road of Excess* (Brian Barritt);
The Doors of Perception (Aldous Huxley);
The Long Trip: A Prehistory of Psychedelia (Paul Devereux)

★
★
★
★
★

Writer: Philip Roth
Publisher: Random House New York, 1969

ISBN US: 978-0679756453
ISBN UK: 978-0099399018

5+

PORTNOY'S COMPLAINT

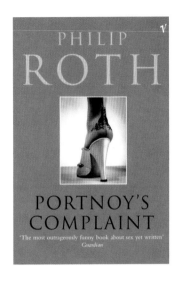

PHILIP
ROTH

PORTNOY'S
COMPLAINT

'The most outrageously funny book about sex yet written'
Guardian

Plot: Roth's most commercially successful book explores themes of sexual desire, self, mother-son relations, and Jewishness. The main focus is the "complaint" of his narrator Alexander Portnoy; that is, the paraphiliac "extreme sexual longings that go against his ethical and altruistic impulses." Continuous confessional monologue is split into sections, with candid headings such as "Whacking Off" and "Cunt Crazy."

Review: "Unabashedly sexually explicit" is the best description of this novel from the swinging sixties. The adolescent Portnoy lives half his "waking life spent locked behind the bathroom door," and steps things up a notch as he grows older to "chase cunt." Although the book is unlikely to shock now, it nevertheless remains a clever and comic portrayal of a man driven by abundant and insatiable sexual urges.

FURTHER READING: *Goodbye Columbus; The Human Stain*
SEE ALSO: *Couples* (John Updike); *The Elementary Particles* (*Atomised*) (Michel Houellebecq)

★
★
★
★

Writer: Hunter S. Thompson
Publisher: Simon and Schuster, 1988

ISBN US: ISBN US: 978-0684856476
ISBN UK: ISBN UK: 978-0747574576

5+

THE RUM DIARY

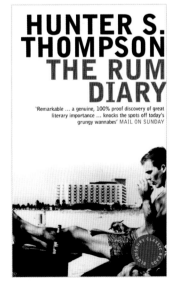

HUNTER S.
THOMPSON
THE RUM
DIARY

'Remarkable ... a genuine, 100% proof discovery of great literary importance ... knocks the spots off today's grungy wannabes' MAIL ON SUNDAY

Plot: In San Juan of the 1950s the rum flows freely and the sun sweats its residents into a sweltering pool. Into this soporific atmosphere a young newspaperman, Paul Kemp, arrives "half-drunk" to work on *the Daily News*. A love triangle ensues, featuring a colleague, Yeamon, and a beautiful woman.

Review: Written when Thompson was twenty-two, *The Rum Diary* finally found its way onto bookshelves in 1998. While fans of his "gonzo journalism" and later work might be disappointed with this comparatively straight-laced story, there is a pace and intensity in the narrative which anticipates that later work. For the most part, though, this can be recommended quite simply—as Thompson himself said—because "It's a good story."

FURTHER READING: *Fear and Loathing in Las Vegas*
SEE ALSO: *Jules et Jim* (Henri Pierre Roche)

★
★
★

Writer: Jennifer Lynch
Publisher: Penguin, 1990

ISBN US: 978-0671735906
ISBN UK: 978-0140149449

15+ # THE SECRET DIARY OF LAURA PALMER

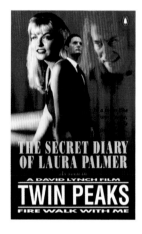

Plot: Who killed Laura Palmer? What are this troubled teen's secrets? Are the owls what they seem? This diary may not solve these puzzles of the first season of David Lynch and Mark Frost's cult TV show, *Twin Peaks*, but it does go some way to offering clues. The diary form allows intimate access into the hopes, dreams—and nightmares—of the double life of the victim at the heart of the show, Laura Palmer.

Review: TV tie-in publishing at its best, and written by Lynch's daughter Jennifer. The book might only have enjoyed an ephemeral success during the heyday of the TV show and movie *Fire Walk with Me*, but nevertheless remains essential reading for all David Lynch and *Twin Peaks* devotees.

FURTHER READING: *The Autobiography of FBI Special Agent Dale Cooper* (Scott Frost)
SEE ALSO: *Full of Secrets: Critical Approaches to Twin Peaks* (David Lavery)

★
★
★

Writer: Camille Paglia
Publisher: Vintage, 1992

ISBN US: 978-0679741015
ISBN UK: 978-0679741015

18+ # SEX, ART, AND AMERICAN CULTURE

Synopsis: Twenty-one essays from scholar, teacher, and *enfant terrible* of American culture Camille Paglia. In them she celebrates her devotion to cultural icons Madonna and Elizabeth Taylor, as well as commentating on issues such as date rape and the decline of American schools.

Review: Feminists and religious conservatives are, Paglia states here, "an illuminating alliance of contemporary puritans." It's pithy remarks like those that saw her crowned queen of contentious prose. But would she say the same now? And that's one problem reading this collection in the 2000s—it's a product of its time. Still, long may she reign her strong opinions over us, for a more provocative commentator on American culture would be hard to find.

FURTHER READING: *Sexual Personae; Break, Blow, Burn: Vamps and Tramps*
SEE ALSO: *The History of Sexuality* (Michel Foucault)

Writer: Catherine Millet
Publisher: Editions du Seuil, 2001

ISBN US: 978-1852428112
ISBN UK: 978-0552771726

THE SEXUAL LIFE OF CATHERINE M.

Plot: The erotic memoirs, or "quest for the sexual grail," of the art-historian Catherine Millet. The more memorable of her many sexual trysts include an alfresco orgy in the beautiful Parisian park the Bois de Boulogne, another orgy in a famous Paris restaurant, and what we might call "drive-by gang bangs" where drivers have sex at agreed locations across Paris.

Review: There is something different about Millet from other writers of the confessional erotic memoir—the love of sex is lost here, the intimate dialog with the reader vanished. The opposite of titillation, the cold, ritualistic nature of Catherine M.'s sexual life will interest those who see sex as a curiosity rather than as the physical manifestation of love or even, simply, desire.

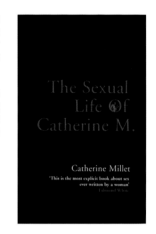

FURTHER READING: *Dali and Me*
SEE ALSO: *The Story of O* (Pauline Réage);
Girl with a One Track Mind (Abbey Lee)

Writer: Henry Miller
Publisher: Obelisk Press, 1934

ISBN US: 978-0802131782
ISBN UK: 978-0007204465

TROPIC OF CANCER

Plot: An exploration of the Paris demimonde of the 1930s by the struggling expatriate writer Henry Miller. The book is best known for the graphic depiction of his plentiful sexual encounters, though Miller also includes aspects of the more mundane happenings of his everyday life.

Review: Banned for obscenity in the U.S. and the UK until the early 1960s, Miller's semiautobiographical work throbs with erotic tension and is one of the most explicit serious novels to have come out of the prewar period. But Miller is not your run-of-the-mill pornographer—*Tropic of Cancer* also has a mint of philosophical ideas, even if this, his most famous, book's literary merits remain in question.

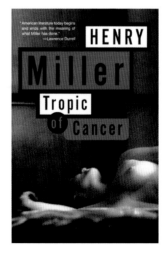

FURTHER READING: *Tropic of Capricorn*
SEE ALSO: *Henry and June* (Anaïs Nin);
Story of O (Pauline Reage)

★
★ **Writer:** Marie Darrieussecq   **ISBN US:** 978-1565844421
★ **Publisher:** Editions P.O.L., 1996   **ISBN UK:** 978-0571193721
★

18+ TRUISMES (PIG TALES)

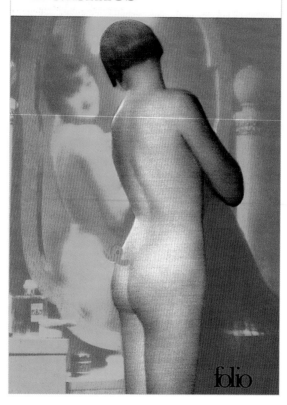

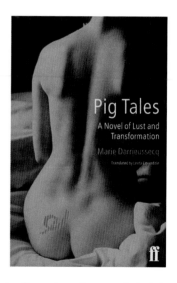

Plot: In the Paris of the near future a young woman is excelling in her job as a masseur at Perfumes Plus, but there's a problem: why are her thighs so "pink and firm," what is this sudden aversion to ham, and, eugh, where did that third breast come from? There is a slow but sure transformation taking place—our heroine is metamorphosing into a pig. clients fall into her "barnyard ways." However, think a little deeper, and you'll discover a compelling parable about body and health fascism in the modern age, which only the (ahem) pig ignorant won't enjoy.

Review: A brilliantly disgusting book that acknowledges how much "distress and confusion" it may cause on its very first page. You might think the same as the pig-woman's

FURTHER READING: *My Phantom Husband*
SEE ALSO: *Metamorphosis* (Franz Kafka)
Wetlands (Charlotte Roche)

Writer: Danny Sugerman
Publisher: Sidgwick & Jackson, 1989

ISBN US: 978-0349101750
ISBN UK: 978-0349101750

8+ WONDERLAND AVENUE
TALES OF GLAMOUR AND EXCESS

Synopsis: As befits someone who entered the music industry as a teenaged manager to The Doors, Sugerman's memoir is as sex, drugs, and rock 'n' roll laden as they come. He begins with his privileged childhood in Beverly Hills, takes us through the degenerate eight years of his music industry career, and ends just past his twenty-first birthday, when the consequences of his rock 'n' roll lifestyle become all too tangible.

Review: If ever there was a bird's eye view of the trials and rewards of life in the music biz, this is it. Of course, Sugerman's definition of the word "glamour" might perturb lexicographers: since when was performing fellatio on your heroin dealer for a fix "glamorous," they might well ask? Funny, horrible, mind-boggling. And utterly believable.

FURTHER READING: *Nobody Gets Out of Here Alive*
SEE ALSO: *I'm With the Band* (Pamela Des Barres)

Writer: Alexander Trocchi
Publisher: Olympia Press, 1954

ISBN US: 978-0802139771
ISBN UK: 978-1847490421

3+ YOUNG ADAM

Plot: In a detached, spare prose style we learn of Joe, a barge-hand on the River Clyde, Scotland, in the early 1950s. At the book's opening he and the barge owner, Leslie, discover the corpse of a young woman floating in the river. As the book develops we realize Joe and the dead woman had an affair—but was he involved in her death?

Review: An intriguing book that has you wondering why Trocchi isn't better known. There are two good reasons why he should be. Firstly, Joe's alienation and passivity, in the face of both Cathie's death and his (many) sexual conquests, are an expression of existentialism up there with the likes of Camus. Secondly, the graphic sexual content leaves an indelible impression on the reader. Remarkable, but bleak.

FURTHER READING: *Cain's Book*
SEE ALSO: *Trainspotting* (Irvine Welsh);
How Late It Was, How Late (James Kelman)

The Young Man's Guide
(Large Print Edition)

William A. Alcott

JAMES LOVELOCK

GAIA

A NEW LOOK AT LIFE ON EARTH

WITH A NEW PREFACE BY THE AUTHOR

OXFORD

ILLUSTRATED EDITION WITH
EXCLUSIVE NEW MATERIAL

THE HOLY BLOOD AND THE HOLY GRAIL

MICHAEL BAIGENT
RICHARD LEIGH
& HENRY LINCOLN

James Redfield

THE CELESTINE PROPHECY
MANUSKRIP CELESTINE

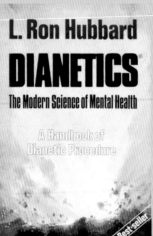

L. Ron Hubbard

DIANETICS®

The Modern Science of Mental Health

A Handbook of Dianetic Procedure

Best-seller

The teachings of Don Juan:
a Yaqui way of knowledge
Carlos Castaneda

R. D. LAING

THE DIVIDED SELF

'Dr Laing is saying something very important

PENGUIN CLASSICS

DANTE
THE DIVINE COMEDY • 1
HELL

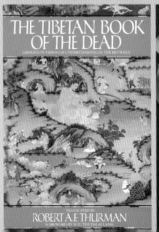

THE TIBETAN BOOK OF THE DEAD
LIBERATION THROUGH UNDERSTANDING IN THE BETWEEN

TRANSLATED BY
ROBERT A. F. THURMAN
FOREWORD BY H. H. THE DALAI LAMA

THE DOORS
OF PERCEPTION
AND
HEAVEN AND HELL
ALDOUS HUXLEY

THE COMPLETE
I CHING

The Definit

Taoist Mas

MUNSON

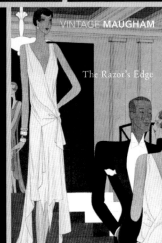

VINTAGE **MAUGHAM**

The Razor's Edge

WHAT IT
TAKES TO
BE
#1

*VINCE
LOMBARDI
ON
LEADERSHIP*

VINCE LOMBARDI, J

A PENGUIN BOOK

ZEN
FLESH,
ZEN
BONES:

A
COLLECTION
OF
ZEN AND
PRE-ZEN
WRITINGS

COMPILED BY
PAUL REPS

The
Medium
is the
Massage

Marshall
McLuhan

Quentin
Fiore

CHAPTER 8

INNER SPIRITS

MIND, BODY, AND SPIRIT

As holy books go these might not be the biggest hitters (the Bible and the Qur'an don't get a look in), but they are the ones that have touched deep among certain sections of society, sparking a flicker of enlightenment or spiritual awakening in even the most pragmatic of readers. Like so many subgenres of cult books, these titles are neatly tied up with the mood of their epoch. We have everything from the transcendental tomes that inspired the hippies up to the self-help manuals of the late twentieth century. Indeed, as time has gone the line between spirituality and psychology has perhaps become blurred, but in common these books all have the power to change lives, or at the very least, outlooks on life.

TOP 10

INNER SPIRITS

★
★
★
★

Writer: Alfred Huang
Publisher: Inner Traditions, 1998

ISBN US: 978-0892811458
ISBN UK: 978-0892811458

12+

THE COMPLETE I CHING

Synopsis: Commonly known as The Book of Changes, at its simplest the *I Ching* is a divination system based on eight trigrams (or kua), a trigram being a grouping of three lines, either complete or broken (to represent Yin or Yang), one above the other for which there are eight possible variations. Two trigrams (one above the other) create sixty-four possible hexagrams. Each hexagram and trigram has a name and a variety of associations with aspects of the natural world and the nature of those seeking enlightenment. These added associations mean that the sixty-four hexagrams are open to tens of millions of different interpretations.

The origins of the *I Ching* remain a scholarly detective mystery, although tradition (dating from long after the event) puts its genesis in the hands of mythical Chinese emperor Fu Xi (or Hsi) in around 3000 BC, who is said to have had the eight trigrams revealed to him, although some scholars now believe the sixty-four hexagrams pre-date the trigrams. Commentary and interpretation has been added over the thousands of years the symbols have existed. The *I Ching* existed in many forms until the Confucian era when it was standardized and became the most significant book of Chinese society.

Review: Probably the most widely read book outside of the Koran and the Bible, the *I Ching* is far more than a selection of feel-good fortune cookie quotes. Its influence in the English-speaking West only began in the 1950s with the translation by Cary F. Baynes of a German version by Richard Wilhelm. Huang's translation addressed what he saw as a problem in earlier Western editions that did not fully appreciate the Confucian commentaries. Although it alters the names of some hexagrams from that established by Wilhelm/Baynes, it is generally considered a good translation with an eye to the spiritual truth of the original.

FURTHER READING: *The Numerology of the I Ching*
SEE ALSO: *The I Ching* (Richard Wilhelm); *I Ching: An Annotated Biography* (Hacker, Moore, and Patsco)

Writer: L. Ron Hubbard
Publisher: Hermitage House, 1950
ISBN US: 978-0884046325
ISBN UK: 978-8779897717

DIANETICS
THE MODERN SCIENCE OF MENTAL HEALTH

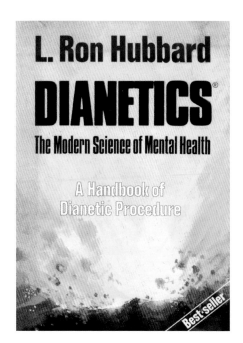

Synopsis: In its simplest terms, Dianetics is a science, or pseudoscience, which promises to help the mind to recall hidden memories, edit them out, and thus cure psychosomatic ills. Within the reactive (subconscious) mind are stored "engrams" (traces of painful memories), which can be uncovered and "audited" by revealing traumatic events to a trained auditor. By reliving these events, the engrams lose their power. Once all engrams are removed, the newly "clear" patient will have greatly improved mental and physical health. The ability to audit, to a limited degree, is available to all after only a few hours study and training.

Review: In 1950, John W. Campbell, editor of *Astounding Science Fiction*, announced the publication of a 16,000-word article, "Dianetics . . . an Introduction to a New Science," which he said, "will, I believe, cause one full-scale explosion across the country." Campbell's words echo down the years: the magazine received two thousand letters in the first two weeks after publication and, when Hubbard's full-length book appeared shortly after, its publisher reported sales of one thousand copies a day.

Dianetics was received with mostly hostile reviews but positively by readers. Hubbard, with almost twenty years experience writing articles and fiction for magazines, was a capable and inventive author. His own assessment was that "The creation of Dianetics is a milestone for man comparable to his discovery of fire and superior to his invention of the wheel and the arch." Most critics paint another picture—that Dianetics was nothing more than a cobbled-together mish-mash of Freud, regression-therapy, Eastern philosophy, and the occult.

For all the complaints, readers liked the breezy style and confidence with which Hubbard introduced his new science. Within months, the Hubbard Dianetic Research Foundation had offices in six major cities and began spending money vigorously. Rather too vigorously: the last office filed for bankruptcy in February 1952. Hubbard resigned from the board and set up the Hubbard College. Shortly after he replaced the "science of mental health" with the "science of knowledge," Scientology.

FURTHER READING: *Dianetics:*
The Evolution of a Science; New Era Dianetics
SEE ALSO: *A Doctor's Report on Dianetics* (Dr. Joseph Winter); *Bare-Faced Messiah* (Russell Miller)

★
★ **Writer:** R. D. Laing
★ **Publisher:** Quadrangle Books, 1960

ISBN US: 978-0415198189
ISBN UK: 978-0140135374

15+

THE DIVIDED SELF

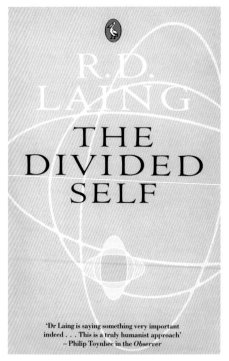

'Dr Laing is saying something very important indeed . . . This is a truly humanist approach' – Philip Toynbee in the *Observer*

a Pelican Book

The Divided Self

R.D.Laing

Synopsis: Exposed to the awful treatment of psychiatric patients during his training as a psychiatrist in Glasgow in the 1950s—when electroshock therapy, lobotomies, and induced comas were common treatments—Laing developed his own theories, chief among them that schizophrenia was caused by family units where weak personalities were over-whelmed by stronger ones. The weak retreated into seeming madness in order to protect the core of their personality.

Laing did not believe that madness was incomprehensible; the motivation for retreating into insanity was simply not understood. Laing's solution was to allow patients to act out their psychotic episodes (in a controlled and sympathetic environment) in the hope of understanding their meaning. He was against the use of chemical and electroshock treat-ments, saying that these were used to make patients more docile for the benefit of hospital staff, and they disrupted the healing process.

Review: In 1964, Laing founded the Philadelphia Associa-tion, which, over the next few years, financed a number of hostels for psychiatric patients, providing them with a more humane treatment and encouraging the patients to do as they pleased. Consequently, rumors began to spread among local residents—especially around the community at Kingsley Hall in London's East End where patients and staff lived side-by-side—about what was happening inside, and the center was closed in 1970.

Laing was accused of being anti-family (his studies in this area were published in *Sanity, Madness, and the Family* and *The Politics of the Family*) and anti-psychiatry, although he never denied that there was value in psychiatry, just that the hands-on (chemical/electrical) approach did more harm than good. His own hands-off treatment was more akin to a spiritual journey, which found favor with some during the 1960s. However, there was no consensus in medical circles that his treatment had any validity. The Philadelphia Association continues to offer support through community houses.

FURTHER READING: *The Self and Others: Further Studies in Sanity and Madness; Wisdom, Madness, and Folly: The Making of a Psychiatrist*
SEE ALSO: *Two Accounts of a Journey Through Madness* (Mary Barnes and Joseph Berke); *The Wing of Madness: The Life and Work of R. D. Laing* (Daniel Burston); *R. D. Laing: A Personal View* (Bob Mullen)

★ **Writer:** Aldous Huxley
★ **Publisher:** *The Doors Of Perception,*
★ Chatto & Windus, 1954
Heaven And Hell, Chatto & Windus, 1956

ISBN US: 978-0061729072
ISBN UK: 978-0099458203

8+

THE DOORS OF PERCEPTION AND HEAVEN AND HELL

Synopsis: Two essays based on Huxley's experiments with mescaline. Sick of Europe, Huxley, a vociferous pacifist, moved to California in 1937. It was here he first experimented with mescaline in the late 1940s. In *The Doors of Perception* he recounts the results of these experiments, summarizes the drug's effects, explains the history and science behind psychedelics, and introduces his idea—explored further in *Heaven and Hell*—that religious visionaries and mystics might benefit from the transcendental journey to "the antipodes of the mind," that psychoactive drugs offer.

Review: A rich kaleidoscope of literary, religious, and philosophical references color *The Doors of Perception.* This intellectual richness is in equal part inspiring and daunting for the lay reader (Plato, Eckhart, Buddha, and the Dalai-Lama all feature). Incidentally, Huxley would not necessarily recommend the lay reader taking psychedelics: the author considered that hallucinogens should only be used by those of great intellect, whose minds would have something to offer, if bent.

This did not stop heroes of the 1960s counterculture holding up Huxley up as their guru (The Doors were named after this book, for instance). And even if Huxley comes across as pretentious at times, there are some truly interesting ideas about legal and illegal drugs and their prohibition, which are startlingly relevant in the twenty-first century. When talking about alcohol and cigarettes, for instance, Huxley suggests that the public should try LSD or mescaline instead, that is, "to exchange their old bad habits for new and less harmful ones."

Forty years after his death, Huxley's value as a spokesperson for chemical pleasures is unabated—no more less so is his status as counterculture icon.

FURTHER READING: *The Island* (a novel in which Huxley presents a society whose mind has been opened to psychedelics)
SEE ALSO: *The Politics of Ecstasy* (Timothy Leary); *The Road of Excess* (Brian Barritt)

★ **Writer:** Michael Baigent,
★ Richard Leigh, and Henry Lincoln
Publisher: Jonathan Cape, 1982

ISBN US: 978-0385340014
ISBN UK: 978-0099682417

15+

THE HOLY BLOOD AND THE HOLY GRAIL
(HOLY BLOOD, HOLY GRAIL)

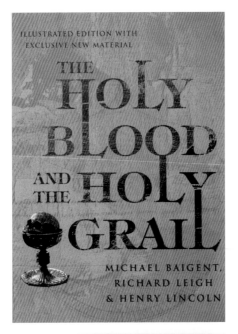

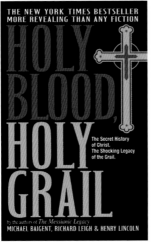

Synopsis: From the initial premise that Jesus of Nazareth married Mary Magdalene, the authors join various dots to discover that descendents of Jesus became the Merovingian dynasty, rulers of most of Gaul, and their bloodline is still maintained by the Priory of Sion (*Prieure de Sion*, actually the creation of hoaxer Pierre Plantard). The Knights Templar, the book says, was set up by the Priory as guardians and protectors of the descendents and, although officially suppressed in the early 1300s, still exists. The Templars also secretly hold the Holy Grail. The Roman Catholic Church has covered up these facts for centuries, knowing that the existence of a family line destroys the principal on which Catholic religion is founded: that Jesus died on the cross.

Review: Although some of the book's claims have been debunked and others are heavily questioned, *Holy Blood, Holy Grail* hit the headlines when its various theories became the central premise of Dan Brown's 2003 novel *The Da Vinci Code*.

The research sprang initially from a TV documentary (*The Lost Treasures of Jerusalem*) by Lincoln, which investigated the story of an obscure nineteenth-century French priest, Berenger Sauniere, who had spent vast sums refurbishing the local church and building the Tour Magdala in the remote Pyrenean foothills near Rennes-le-Chateau. Lincoln believed that Sauniere must have stumbled upon some remarkable facts. After meeting Lincoln in the UK, Leigh, an American librarian and author, brought in Baigent—a former photojournalist with whom Leigh had a mutual interest in the Knights Templar—and expanded upon the story.

In 2006, Leigh and Baigent unsuccessfully sued Random House, who published Brown's novel, the judge deciding that a fictional work based on the pair's historical research did not infringe copyright. The case raised the profile of the book considerably, sales leaping from a few thousand a year to seven thousand a week. The book remains a favorite of historical and religious conspiracy theorists.

FURTHER READING: *The Messianic Legacy*;
The Jesus Papers (Baigent)
SEE ALSO: *The Templar Revelation* (Lynn Picknett and Clive Prince); *The Jesus Dynasty* (James D. Tabor)

Writer: Richard Bach
Publisher: Macmillan, 1970
ISBN US: 978-0743278904
ISBN UK: 978-0006490340

12+ JONATHAN LIVINGSTON SEAGULL

THE GLORIOUS #1 BESTSELLER

onathan
Livingston
eagull
story

RICHARD
BACH
PHOTOGRAPHS
Y RUSSELL
UNSON

Plot: A novella-length story, heavily illustrated with black and white photographs by Russell Munson, *Jonathan Livingston Seagull* is the story of the eponymous bird who finds the everyday struggle for food among the flock increasingly frustrating, preferring to spend his time pushing his flying abilities to their limits. Threatened with expulsion, he tries his best to conform but cannot.

Jonathan meets two starlit seagulls who offer to take him to a community of other outcasts where he learns from Chiang, the Elder Gull, that "Heaven is not a place, and it is not a time. Heaven is being perfect." Jonathan becomes the teacher of a young gull called Fletcher and inspires other gulls to follow his example in flying to a higher spiritual plane.

Review: Richard Bach began flying at the age of seventeen and dropped out of college to pursue his dream of being a pilot, joining the U.S. Air Force in 1956. After twenty months, he resigned after being transferred to a desk. Dozens of jobs followed, none held for very long, including charter pilot, flying instructor, aviation mechanic, and barnstormer, interspaced with more mundane jobs. In the early 1960s he was editor of *Flying* magazine, during which time he wrote his first (non-fiction) book, *Stranger to the Ground*. Two further books about flying followed before he completed *Jonathan Livingston Seagull*, which he had started writing at the age of twenty-three.

Rejected by eighteen publishers, *Jonathan Livingston Seagull* finally appeared in September 1970. With little promotion—the handful of reviews that appeared noted the photographs but made little comment on the text—it began to sell slowly, sales building by word of mouth: by 1972 a million copies; by 1992 the figure was thirty million. Many read Buddhist or Christian philosophies in the text (at its height during thirty-eight weeks at the top of the *New York Times* bestseller list, the book's harshest critics were the Christian press). Bach has said that the book's sole message is that if you have a dream, you should pursue it.

FURTHER READING: *Illusions: Adventures of a Reluctant Messiah; There's No Such Place as Far Away*
SEE ALSO: *The Little Engine That Could* (Watty Piper); *The Little Prince* (Antoine de Saint-Exupery)

299　500 ESSENTIAL CULT BOOKS

INNER SPIRITS Top 10 Classics

★ **Writer:** Marshall McLuhan and Quentin Fiore   **ISBN US:** 978-1584230700
★ **Publisher:** Random House, 1967   **ISBN UK:** 978-0141035826
★

12+

THE MEDIUM IS THE MASSAGE

technology—radio, television, computers—were creating a less alienating learning process because they form a mosaic of information that reaches us simultaneously through several senses.

Review: In *The Medium Is the Massage*, McLuhan (with Fiore and designer Jerome Agel) condensed some of his main ideas on advertising, communication technology, and media theory into a more easily assimilated volume, creating examples using images, collages of photographs, and typography—"a collide-oscope of interfaced situations"—to illustrate how various effects can be achieved. Instead of presenting content neutrally, "all media work us over completely. They are so pervasive in their personal, political, aesthetic, psychological, moral, ethical, and social consequences that they leave no part of us untouched, unaffected, unaltered."

Critics argued that McLuhan made logical leaps in his arguments that invalidated much of his work, described by Arthur M. Schlesinger as "a chaotic combination of bland assertion, astute guesswork, fake analogy, dazzling insight, hopeless nonsense, shockmanship, showmanship, wise-cracks and oracular mystification, all mingling [with] deeply serious argument."

McLuhan became a popular figure (seminars, television, a cameo in Woody Allen's *Annie Hall*). His works have inspired much debate and critical analysis (for example, *McLuhan: Pro and Con* edited by Raymond Rosenthal and *Sense and Nonsense of McLuhan* by Sidney Walter Finkelstein). To some he is a prophet whose theories of communication are especially applicable to the internet age.

Synopsis: Having already coined the phrase "the medium is the message" in his 1964 study *Understanding Media: The Extensions of Man*, McLuhan turned his attention to the "massage"—how different graphic and typographical effects produce different reactions to what we see and watch. Media, says McLuhan, are so pervasive that they leave no part of us untouched or unaffected with their political, aesthetic, moral, or ethical consequences. *The Medium Is the Massage* expanded on McLuhan's earlier contention (in *The Gutenberg Galaxy*) that, with Gutenberg's creation of movable type, the transmission of knowledge was fundamentally changed: the printed page supplanted the old oral traditions and the linear arrangement of symbols which we call knowledge itself creates a way of thinking—linear and causal. It also led to specialization and learning in isolation. This he turned on its head in *Understanding Media*, where he claimed that modern developments in communication

FURTHER READING: *Understanding Media* (McLuhan); *Media, Messages and Language* (McLuhan, Eric McLuhan, and Kathy Hutchon) **SEE ALSO:** *Amusing Ourselves to Death* (Neil Postman); *Design Elements: A Graphic Style Manual* (Timothy Samara)

★
★
★

Writer: Carlos Castaneda
Publisher: University of California Press, 1968

ISBN US: 978-0520217577
ISBN UK: 978-0140192384

15+

THE TEACHINGS OF DON JUAN
A YAQUI WAY OF KNOWLEDGE

Synopsis: In the summer of 1960, Castaneda, a student of anthropology, was studying medicinal plants when he met Yaqui Indian Don Juan Matus at a Greyhound bus depot in Nogales, Arizona. He studied under the Yaqui shaman for five years and had many spiritual adventures. The book recounts his experiences (many of them chemical) exploring "states of nonordinary reality," how he learned to fly, how he turned into a crow, and how he ultimately achieved a state of higher consciousness. Throughout this and subsequent books, Castaneda examines and analyzes the truth of Don Juan's teachings.

Review: Described by *Time* magazine as the "Godfather of the New Age," Castaneda's work found an audience in the 1960s and 1970s, and even when doubt was thrown on his work, the ten books he wrote continued to sell—eventually eight million copies in seventeen languages.

Vivid as the writing is, Castaneda's work is generally considered a mixture of various shamanistic practices, misquotes from numerous sources, and fiction. Fiction surrounded Castaneda's life from birth to death: he claimed to have been born in Brazil in 1935, the son of a university professor, but was actually born in Peru in 1923, the son of a goldsmith; his death certificate described him as a school teacher employed by the Beverly Hills School District, but they had no record of him; he claimed to have never married, surprising news to Mrs. Castaneda and her son.

Richard de Mille, one of Castaneda's debunkers, notes that, while the books themselves are not authentic, they do contain much that is valid. Joyce Carol Oates, writing in the *New York Times Book Review*, saw them as works of art on "the Hesse-like theme of a young man's initiation into 'another way' of reality. They are beautifully constructed. The dialogue is faultless. The character of Don Juan is unforgettable. There is a novelistic momentum."

FURTHER READING: *A Separate Reality; Journey to Ixtlan; Tales of Power*
SEE ALSO: *Castaneda's Journey: The Power and the Allegory* and *The Don Juan Papers* (Richard de Mille)

★
★ **Writer:** W. Y. Evans-Wentz   **ISBN US:** 978-0195133127
★ **Publisher:** Oxford University Press, 1927   **ISBN UK:** 978-1848372375

15+ THE TIBETAN BOOK OF THE DEAD

The text illuminates and focuses the dead through each stage on his journey to liberation and reincarnation and was read over the body by a lama.

Tibetan lore describes how the text was one of the treasures hidden by Padmasambhava for future spiritual leaders to find; it was discovered on Mount Gampodar in Southern Tibet by Karma Lingpa in the fourteenth century.

Review: Walter Yeeling Evans-Wentz was an American scholar and anthropologist who studied at Oxford under Andrew Lang, author on folklore and myth. Evans-Wentz's studies of fairytales, which led to deeper enquiries into paganism and comparative religion, sent him traveling to Ceylon and India to study the mysticism and religious practices of Far Eastern religions, which, he believed, were once closely connected with religions of the West.

Evans-Wentz lived as a Buddhist monk in the Himalayan Mountains and spent three years studying with the Kazi Dawa-Samdup at Gangtok until the lama's death in 1922. Evans-Wentz subsequently published translations of four Tibetan texts (three translated primarily by Samdup), including *The Tibetan Book of the Dead*.

Carl Jung, later to offer his own psychological study of the book, noted that it "caused a considerable stir in English-speaking countries at the time of its first appearance in 1927. It belongs to that class of writings which are not only of interest to specialists in Mahayana Buddhism, but which also, because of their deep humanity and their still deeper insight into the secrets of the human psyche, make an especial appeal to the layman who is seeking to broaden his knowledge of life."

Synopsis: *The Tibetan Book of the Dead*, or the *Bardo Thodol*—sometimes translated as "Liberation through hearing during the intermediate state," or, more simply, "Liberation through hearing"—is a guide book for the dead and dying, akin to the *Egyptian Book of the Dead*. It offers instruction for the dead during the period of his Bardo existence, the forty-nine days between death and rebirth.

The text is divided into three main parts: the *chikhai bardo* describes what happens at the moment of death; the *chonyid bardo* is the dream-state immediately following death during which the dead person experiences karmic visions; and the *sidpa bardo* concerns the onset of the instinct for rebirth.

FURTHER READING: *The Tibetan Book of the Great Liberation; Yoga and Secret Doctrines: or, Seven Books of Wisdom of the Great Path; Tibet's Great Yogi, Milarepa*
SEE ALSO: *Magic and Mystery in Tibet* (Alexandra David-Neel); *Death and Dying: The Tibetan Experience* (Glenn H. Mullin)

Writer: Robert Pirsig
Publisher: William Morrow, 1974

ISBN US: 978-0061673733
ISBN UK: 978-0099322610

15

ZEN AND THE ART OF MOTORCYCLE MAINTENANCE

AN INQUIRY INTO VALUES

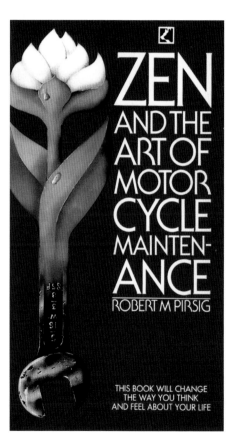

THIS BOOK WILL CHANGE
THE WAY YOU THINK
AND FEEL ABOUT YOUR LIFE

After a breakdown in 1960, Pirsig was treated at various mental institutions for schizophrenia. With no job and now divorced from his wife, he pieced his life back together, found work writing technical manuals, and began writing a book based in part on a trip he had taken with his son, Chris, from Minnesota to San Francisco via the Dakotas.

During the seventeen-day journey, the narrator is both close to his son and, initially, his traveling companions, John and Sylvia—but the very method of transport cuts him off from conversation. While traveling, the narrator tries to discover the meaning of Quality in life. Throughout he is pursued by the ghost of his past, whom he names Phaedrus. He fears that Phaedrus—in essence Pirsig's unbalanced self—will take Chris, with whom he is alienated.

Review: Reputedly rejected by 121 publishers before being picked up by Morrow, Pirsig's novel/autobiography became a huge hit on publication. The road trip and motorcycle maintenance of the title are a delivery system for philosophical exploration of Zen and Tao, a search for wholeness and quality and an inward journey to understand past experiences.

The book is a series of what Pirsig calls Chautauquas, discussions or dissertations on technical values and human values; the book began as a series of brief essays that expanded into the nucleus of a novel, and these Chautauquas became embedded in a narrative.

Pirsig believed that everyday activities—such as the ongoing maintenance of a motorcycle—could be a time for philosophical journeying as much as the traditional idea of sitting atop a mountain in isolation. At no point do you doubt that Pirsig is writing from experience and a sincere desire to understand and integrate his experiences and become a more complete person.

Plot: Something of a child prodigy (thanks to an IQ of 170, he jumped several grades at school), Robert Pirsig was an atypical student. He was studying chemistry at college aged fifteen but quickly lost interest. After serving in the army in Korea, he returned to college to study philosophy, earning his B.A. in 1950. In India he learned about Eastern philosophy before returning to the U.S. to study at the University of Chicago under Richard McKeon, the experience of which he used in his novel.

FURTHER READING: *Lila: An Inquiry into Morals*
SEE ALSO: *The Tao of the Ride* (Garri Garripoli);
Zen and Now: On the Trail of Robert Pirsig and the Art of Motorcycle Maintenance (Mark Richardson)

ESSENTIAL
CULT BOOKS

500

303

INNER SPIRITS
Top 10 Classics

★
★ **Writer:** James Redfield
Publisher: Satori Publishing, 1993

ISBN US: 978-0446671002
ISBN UK: 978-0553409024

15+ THE CELESTINE PROPHECY

Plot: The unnamed protagonist leaves his job after learning about the Insights, a series of nine spiritual ideas contained in an ancient Peruvian manuscript. Flying to Peru, he meets a historian on a similar quest, who tells him that powerful figures in both government and church want the Insight to remain a secret. As the narrator encounters various spiritually enlightened people and learns a new Insight, he also discovers that the ancient Mayans transcended into spiritual energy.

Review: After being rejected by several publishers, Redfield self-published his novel and it became a surprise hit in New Age circles. It became a bestseller when picked up by Warner Books a year later, although it is not so much a novel as a delivery system for some of Redfield's spiritual beliefs.

FURTHER READING: *The Tenth Insight: Holding the Vision;*
The Secret of Shambhala: In Search of the Eleventh Insight
SEE ALSO: *Way of the Peaceful Warrior* (Dan Millman);
The Power of Now (Eckhart Tolle)

★
★
★ **Writer:** Dante Alighieri
Publisher: Italy, c. 1300

ISBN US: 978-0679433132
ISBN UK: 978-0199535644

15+ DIVINA COMMEDIA
(DIVINE COMEDY)

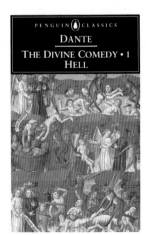

Plot: There are two quests in this thirteenth century allegory of Christianity. Firstly, Dante must seek out his lost love in the depths of hell. Secondly, he is searching for godliness and what this means to him. Partly accompanied by the poet Virgil, Dante journeys to the nine circles of hell, to purgatory, and lastly to heaven, where he is guided through its nine celestial spheres.

Review: Your first mission, if you wish to read Dante's poetry, is to find a good translation; he wrote in a colloquial Italian style, not in scholarly Latin, and your choice of translation should reflect this. This work done, you must set aside a wealth of long summer days or winter nights—weighing in at three volumes, this is not fodder for intellectual lightweights. For conscientious types only.

FURTHER READING: *Conviio*
SEE ALSO: *Paradise Lost* (John Milton); *The Odyssey* (Homer)

★
★
★
★

16

Writer: J. E. Lovelock
Publisher: Oxford University Press, 1979

ISBN US: 978-0192862181
ISBN UK: 978-0192862181

GAIA A NEW LOOK AT LIFE ON EARTH

Synopsis: James Lovelock conceived his Gaia Theory while working for NASA in the 1960s on devices used by Mars landers in the study of the atmosphere. Applying his thoughts to our own atmosphere, Lovelock considered the idea that the ecology of Earth (its biosphere, atmosphere, oceans, and soil) can be considered a single living system.

Review: Lovelock has become a powerful voice in the question of environmental science and global warming. Over the years his philosophy has become more pessimistic, believing that climate change is now inevitable as mankind has fatally polluted the atmosphere. Although many argue with the nuts and bolts of his theory here and in subsequent books, few disagree with his conclusions that drastic and immediate action is needed.

FURTHER READING: *The Ages of Gaia; Healing Gaia;*
The Revenge of Gaia; The Vanishing Face of Gaia
SEE ALSO: *Lovelock and Gaia: Signs of Life* (Jon Turney);
James Lovelock: In Search of Gaia (John Gribbin)

500 ESSENTIAL CULT BOOKS

INNER SPIRITS Best of the Rest

★
★

Writer: Neil Strauss
Publisher: Harper Collins, 2005

ISBN US: 978-0060554736
ISBN UK: 978-1847672377

8+

THE GAME

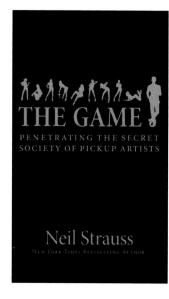

Synopsis: A journalist who is also an AFC (Average Frustrated Chump) joins a secret society where he learns how to pick up HBs (Hot Babes) and practice the society's method to FMAC (Find, Meet, Attract, Close) women. *The Game* explains this "mystery method" to the reader in a narrative rather than how-to style.

Review: Strauss starts out by asserting that modern males feel inadequate because there are "no bears to kill." His solution? Ugly males need a few lessons in the art of seduction. His method? Reducing the beautiful human act of love to a series of increasingly annoying acronyms, and suggesting the way into a woman's underwear is via a bagful of cheap tricks (including, even, actual magic tricks). Top marks for jaw-dropping sexism. Bottom marks for just about everything else . . . and yet, bars are full of Strauss-trained chumps trying his techniques.

FURTHER READING: *Rules of the Game:* taking the principles
of the above and making it into a how-to book
SEE ALSO: *Iron John: A Book about Men* (Joseph John Campbell)

★
★
★

Writer: Elaine Pagels
Publisher: Random House, 1979

ISBN US: 978-0394502786
ISBN UK: 978-0753821145

15+

THE GNOSTIC GOSPELS

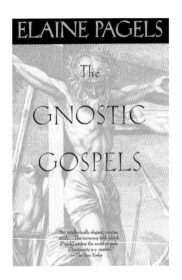

Synopsis: The Gnostic gospels refer to writings dating from around the second century AD, discovered in 1945 near the town of Nag Hammadi, Egypt. Elaine Pagels was one of the international team of scholars responsible for studying and translating them. As well as popularizing and provoking interest in the texts, her book also studies the Gnostics, an early branch at odds with other groups with more orthodox views of Christianity.

Review: Pagels argues in her book that the Gnostics were opposed to the church hierarchy already developing in orthodox Christianity, democratizing religion, and accepting women in greater roles. Although she states that she does not "advocate any side," many critics see her as being clearly on the side of the Gnostics.

FURTHER READING: *The Gnostic Jesus and Early Christian Politics;*
Beyond Belief: The Secret Gospel of Thomas
SEE ALSO: *The Nag Hammadi Library* (James M. Robinson);
Lost Scriptures (Bart D. Ehrman)

★
★
★

Writer: Joseph Campbell
Publisher: Pantheon Books, 1949

ISBN US: 978-1577315933
ISBN UK: 978-0586085714

12+

THE HERO WITH A THOUSAND FACES

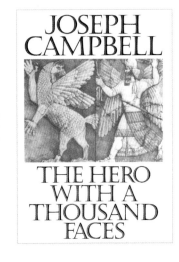

Synopsis: The central premise of *The Hero with a Thousand Faces* is that all myths, folklores, and religious tales can be boiled down to one archetypal story, the monomyth: "A hero ventures forth from the world of common day into a region of supernatural wonder: fabulous forces are there encountered and a decisive victory is won: the hero comes back from this mysterious adventure with the power to bestow boons on his fellow man." Various additional steps may complicate the journey.

Review: Although criticized on publication for being presented in an almost mystical (certainly Jungian) tone, Campbell's book found a wide audience when it was discovered that George Lucas had used the monomyth as the structure for *Star Wars*.

FURTHER READING: *The Golden Bough* (James Frazer);
The Myth of the Birth of the Hero (Otto Rank)
SEE ALSO: *The Writer's Journey: Mythic Structure*
for Writers (Christopher Vogler); *Babbitt* (Sinclair Lewis)

★
★
★
★

Writer: W. Somerset Maugham
Publisher: Doubleday, 1944

ISBN US: 978-1400034208
ISBN UK: 978-0099284864

THE RAZOR'S EDGE

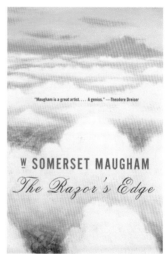

Plot: Larry Darrell, wounded during the Great War, returns home but is unable to settle back into life with his fiancée Isabel. Instead, he moves to Europe, first to Paris and the bohemian life, then to Poland and Germany where he is encouraged to find a more spiritual answer to his unhappiness and roving. This Larry does in India. Meanwhile, the lives of his friends and lovers entwine and unravel.

Review: Maugham implied that this was a true story by appearing as narrator and commentator. The title is derived from the Katha-Upanishad ("The sharp edge of a razor

is difficult to pass over"), and Larry's path to salvation is just as hard. Critically, it is considered a major modernist novel and, alongside *Of Human Bondage*, one of Maugham's most successful.

FURTHER READING: *Of Human Bondage;*
The Moon and Sixpence
SEE ALSO: *Siddhartha* (Hermann Hesse);
The Remains of the Day (Kazuo Ishiguro)

★ **Writer:** B. F. Skinner   **ISBN US:** 978-0872207783
★ **Publisher:** Macmillan, 1948 (revised 1969)   **ISBN UK:** 978-0872207783
★

WALDEN TWO

12+

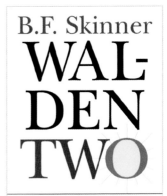

Plot: T. E. Frazier has set up a thousand-person model community founded on the principals of behavioral modification, which allows the inhabitants to do as they please as long as it pleases the community as a whole. Two soldiers and their girlfriends enlist the help of Professor Burris and his colleague to find Frazier. They travel to Frazier's contemporary (1940s) American Utopia where they discuss at length the principals and practicalities of the community. The curmudgeonly Burris is eventually persuaded to join.

Review: Named after Henry D. Thoreau's *Walden* (1854), in which the author lives a simple and spiritual life isolated in a woodland cabin, *Walden Two* was controversial in its rejection of government and family in favor of community, its inhabitants reeducated via positive and negative reinforcement of a kind studied by Skinner, a behavioral psychologist.

Including "Walden Two Revisited," a preface by B. F. Skinner on the relevance of his novel 28 years after publication.

FURTHER READING: *Beyond Freedom and Dignity*
SEE ALSO: *Understanding Behaviorism: Behavior, Culture and Evolution* (William M. Baum)

★ **Writer:** Vince Lombardi, Jr.   **ISBN US:** 978-0071420365
★ **Publisher:** McGraw-Hill, 2001   **ISBN UK:** 978-0071420365

WHAT IT TAKES TO BE #1
VINCE LOMBARDI ON LEADERSHIP

12+

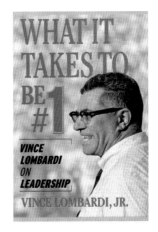

Synopsis: Vince Lombardi achieved legendary status as coach of the Green Bay Packers, who won five NFL titles and two Super Bowl championships under his guidance. His relentless drive for victory became his trademark. Compiled by his son, *What It Takes to Be #1* draws from Lombardi's writings.

Review: At the core of the book is the notion that great leaders are made, not born. Lombardi, Jr. argues that self-knowledge is the first step, and character and integrity are the two pillars of effective leadership. After that it's hard work . . . as his father once said, "The only place success comes before work is in the dictionary."

FURTHER READING: *When Pride Still Mattered*
(David Maraniss)
SEE ALSO: *The Now Habit* (Neil Fiore)

Writer: William Alcott

Publisher: Lilly, Wait, Colman & Holden, 1833

ISBN US: 978-0554091914

ISBN UK: 978-1434692412

THE YOUNG MAN'S GUIDE TO EXCELLENCE

Synopsis: Alcott has much to say on subjects as diverse as personal health, attending the theater, and masturbation. "To lie snoring in the morning assimilates us to the most beastly of animals"; "There is for the most part a union of the three—horrible as the alliance may be—I mean gambling, intemperance, and debauchery," etc.

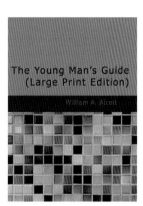

The Young Man's Guide
(Large Print Edition)

William A. Alcott

Review: American educator Alcott was a leading reformer of teaching methods, instituting changes for the comfort and stimulation of his pupils and broadening the curriculum. He also trained as a physician and promoted his ideas in numerous books. It is easy to mock his earnest and zealous prose, but there is much common sense contained in his manuals for healthy living.

FURTHER READING: *The Young Woman's Guide to Excellence; Familiar Letters to Young Men on Various Subjects*
SEE ALSO: *Boy Scouts Handbook; Essential Manners for Men*

Writer: Paul Reps and Nyogen Senzaki

Publisher: Tuttle, 1957

ISBN US: 978-0804831864

ISBN UK: 978-0140288322

ZEN FLESH, ZEN BONES

Synopsis: A collection of Zen and Pre-Zen writings, transcribed by Reps and Senzaki, in four sections: "101 Zen Stories," recounting experiences of Chinese and Japanese Zen teachers over a period of more than five centuries; "The Gateless Gate," a collection of problems (*koan*) used by Zen teachers to guide their students and first recorded in 1228; "Bulls," a twelfth-century text about the stages of awareness leading to enlightenment; and "Centering," a translation of ancient Sanskrit manuscripts that may form the roots of Zen.

ZEN FLESH, ZEN BONES:

A COLLECTION OF ZEN AND PRE-ZEN WRITINGS

COMPILED BY PAUL REPS

Review: A student of Buddhism in the 1920s, Reps was highly influential in introducing Zen philosophy to the West. *Zen Flesh, Zen Bones* is often considered his definitive volume, made up from translations he had published between 1934 and 1940, with the addition of a final piece dating from 1955.

FURTHER READING: *Zen Telegrams: Eighty-One Picture Poems; Be: New Uses for the Human Instrument*
SEE ALSO: *Paul Reps, Letters to a Friend; Living in Balance* (Joel and Michelle Levey)

POST OFFICE

A Novel By Charles Bukowski

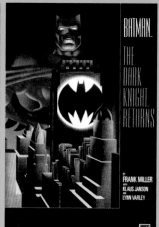

BATMAN

THE DARK KNIGHT RETURNS

BY FRANK MILLER
WITH KLAUS JANSON AND LYNN VARLEY

INTRODUCTION BY ALAN MOORE

Hatchet
GARY PAULSEN

PERFORMANCE BY PETER COYOTE

AN UNABRIDGED PRODUCTION

JIMMY

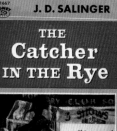

J. D. SALINGER

THE Catcher IN THE Rye

This unusual book may shock you, will make you laugh, and may break your heart— but you will never forget it

A SIGNET BOOK Complete and Unabridged

GHOST WORLD

DANIEL CLOWES

VERNON GOD LITTLE

DBC PiERRE

Julian Maclaren
Of Love and Hung

Penguin Classics

HUYSMANS
AGAINST NATURE

HERMANN HESSE
Steppenwolf

PENGUIN CLASSICS

KEN KESEY

ONE FLEW O
THE CUCKOO'S

A MAGNIFICENT FILM
BY MILOS FORMAN, STARRING
JACK NICHOLSON
FROM FANTASY FILM/UNITED ARTIST

WINNER OF THE 1994 BOOKER PRIZE

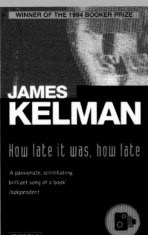

JAMES KELMAN

How late it was, how late

'A passionate, scintillating, brilliant song of a book'
Independent

MINERVA

THE SMARTEST
KID ON EARTH

WALLAC
STEV
THE PALM AT THE

EDITED BY

GEEK
LOVE

A NOVEL

KATHERINE DUNN

"Like most great novels, this one keeps the reader marvelling at the daring of the author." —THE PHILADELPHIA INQUIRER

The Stranger
ALBERT CAMUS

Faber Firsts

The
Bell
Jar

SYLVIA PLATH

JOHN KENNEDY TOOLE

A
CONFEDERACY
OF DUNCES

'Every reviewer has loved it.
For once, everyone is right'
Rolling Stone

CHAPTER 9

OUTCASTS AND LONERS

FREAKS, GEEKS, MISFITS, AND MAVERICKS

We're no statisticians, but we imagine the demographic of cult-book buyers is made up largely of outsiders (we include ourselves among this number). You know, the kind of person who had their nose stuck in a book in high school while others were outside playing sports (or getting laid). Maybe someone like you? Lucky for us, the cult-book canon has forever been a welcoming home to authors who have put such feelings of alienation into print—cult fiction being a place that embraces the outsider with open arms, offering a kind of literary consolation to those square pegs in the round hole of school, society, or life.

Of course by their very nature you might not identify with all our outcasts and loners, but among them we're sure you may feel some twinge of recognition of what it feels like to be on the outside looking in—a feeling that is perhaps stronger than ever as our culture slides ever deeper into homogeneity.

TOP 10

OUTCASTS AND LONERS

★
★
★
★
★

Writer: John Fante
Publisher: Stackpole Sons, 1939

ISBN US: 978-0876854433
ISBN UK: 978-1841953304

15+

ASK THE DUST

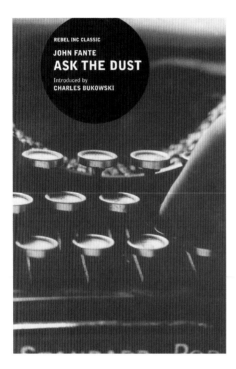

Plot: Bunker Hill, L.A., the 1930s. Arturo Bandini lives in a seedy hotel, attempting to eke out an existence as a short-story writer and subsisting on oranges and drink. His twisted love affair with a waitress—his "Mexican princess" Camilla Lopez—is at the center of the story, but it is literary success and himself that Bandini cares about most.

Along the way Camilla descends into madness (a progression not helped by Bandini's cruel behavior), and Bandini dodges landlords and bills, spewing vitriol about his thwarted efforts to be a good writer, lover, and, above all, human being. The book ends with Bandini's literary career looking up, but with a telling visual metaphor that has us questioning whether this angry young man will let himself live up to his potential.

Review: If John Fante's writing were a weather report, the outlook would be bleak. But don't let that put you off. The second in his Bandini quartet of novels is a humdinger of a piece of fiction: poetic, funny, and melancholy.

Fante was unjustly overlooked for most of his lifetime, partly because the marketing budget for *Ask the Dust* was blown by his publisher on a legal battle with none other than Adolf Hitler (they had published a pirated copy of *Mein Kampf*). He eventually received the recognition he deserved when his work was praised by Charles Bukowski in the 1970s, and his writing bears comparison with his perhaps best known fan: both authors offer some of the starkest, angriest, and most convincing writing about America during their respective epochs. "Fante," said Bukowski, "was my God." Fante's position as a literary deity has, rightly, been secure ever since.

FURTHER READING: The rest of the *Bandini Quartet*
SEE ALSO: *Women* (Charles Bukowski);
Hunger (Knut Hamsen)

★
★
★
★

Writer: Written and illustrated by Frank Miller
Publisher: DC Comics, 1986

ISBN US: 978-1563893421
ISBN UK: 978-1852867980

12+ # BATMAN THE DARK KNIGHT RETURNS

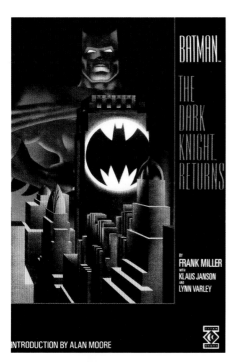

INTRODUCTION BY ALAN MOORE

Plot: Batman, ten years retired, is assaulted by a gang called "The Mutants" who are causing untold chaos on the streets of Gotham City, where a heat wave has caused "civil violence." Enraged, he dons his old cape and teams up with a thirteen-year-old girl, Robin, to defeat many an old enemy, as well as a friend. All the gang are here—Robin and Alfred the Butler, as well as the dastardly villains (Batman always had the best villains) Two-Face and The Joker—but the roles have been deliciously subverted in Miller's 1986 revisionist version of the Batman legend.

Miller accompanied this new-style Batman with dark and grimy drawings and a touch of noir, which gave the caped crusader an altogether grittier feel.

Review: Could Frank Miller's reincarnation of the Batman legend be the ultimate fictional outcast? Hear us out, the evidence is on our side: he's an old man playing the young man's game of superheroics, a bachelor despite the potential his wealth and status offer, and his closest confidantes are a thirteen-year-old girl and his butler, Alfred. The ultimate paradox (and evidence) of his superlative position as the ultimate outcast is that he is a crimefighter but one who is loathed, indeed, hounded by the Establishment.

The press, fans, and Batman neophytes loved the new, darker version of the Batman legend and *The Dark Knight Returns* was an instant hit. The accolades must have been a pleasant surprise since, for most of the general public, Batman would previously have been associated with the camp sixties TV series and a fistful of Pows!, Zaps!, and brightly colored clothing.

In rewriting the formula, Miller helped push graphic novels headlong into the mainstream (Alan Moore's *Watchmen* found success around the same time)—a place they have more or less enjoyed since.

BATMAN: THE DARK KNIGHT RETURNS
FRANK MILLER
with KLAUS JANSON and LYNN VARLEY

FURTHER READING: *Daredevil; Sin City; The Dark Night Strikes Again*
SEE ALSO: *Watchmen* and *Batman: The Killing Joke* (Alan Moore)

★
★
★
★

Writer: Sylvia Plath
Publisher: William Heinemann Ltd, 1963

ISBN US: 978-0061148514
ISBN UK: 9 780571 245642

12+

THE BELL JAR

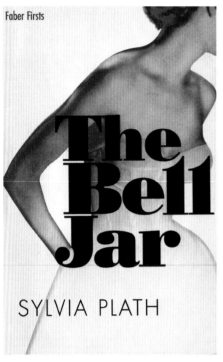

Faber Firsts

The Bell Jar

SYLVIA PLATH

Sylvia Plath

THE BELL JAR

EVERYMAN'S LIBRARY

Plot: An account of the young Esther Greenwood's mental breakdown and subsequent treatment by electric shock therapy, and in a mental institution.

Her illness originates, in the main, from the impossible conundrum of female sexual and professional fulfillment in the rigidly male-centric world of 1950s America. Greenwood's potential, like Plath's and like so many others, must cede to the mores of the times; slowly, painfully, this idea inches into Greenwood's mind with increasing horror. She becomes isolated, depressed, an outcast, as society places expectations on her that she cannot live with.

Review: A wealth of imagery in this, Plath's only novel, attest to her better-known career as a poet. In one extended simile, for instance, Greenwood thinks of her potential as a fig tree: "From the tip of every branch, like a fat purple fig, a wonderful future beckoned and winked." In the tree's fruits she sees the chance to be a poet, a "brilliant professor"; to travel; to take lovers; to marry with kids. Her conclusion is that, "choosing one meant losing all the rest." This is her inner struggle.

Gloom and dark imagery aside, there is also humor and perceptiveness. From the description of the awkward taking of Greenwood's virginity, to the cattiness of female friendships, Plath evokes a time in many women's lives they'd possibly care to forget.

Undoubtedly, though, The Bell Jar is the most famous literary account of living under the black cloud of depression—and it is arguably the best. "To the person in the bell jar . . ." Greenwood/Plath, says, "the world itself is the bad dream." A description that is all the more poignant considering Plath's suicide weeks after the novel's first publication.

FURTHER READING: *Johnny Panic and the Bible of Dreams* (short stories); *Ariel* (poems)
SEE ALSO: *The Catcher in the Rye* (J. D. Salinger); *Girl, Interrupted* (Susanna Kaysen); *A Room of One's Own* (Virginia Woolf)

Writer: J. D. Salinger
Publisher: Little, Brown & Co, 1951

ISBN US: 978-0316769174
ISBN UK: 978-0140237504

THE CATCHER IN THE RYE

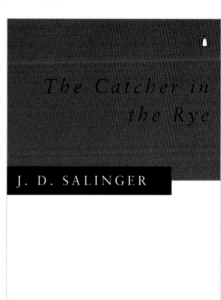

Plot: Phoneys, the rich and famous, those with affectations—don't even mention them to Holden Caufield, Salinger's legendary teenaged narrator. Holden, we learn as the book begins, is "flunking out" of his boarding school, Pencey Prep, for underachievement. What follows is a weekend of random encounters and moments of at once hilarious and unsettling introspection as Holden roams New York before facing the music with his parents at the start of his Christmas vacation.

Review: First person narration allows us intimate access to Salinger's immensely likeable and wickedly funny—yet ultimately depressive—narrator. Add to this a simple colloquial style, and you have a book that strikes a poignant chord with teenagers to this day.

Young adults will also identify with Holden's anti-establishment and anti-grown-ups stance, though his alienation is compounded by the fact he is not that fond of his peers either. He pushes those he likes away, while constantly feeling "on the other side of life." Yet, his mistrust of adults also shows a keen understanding of teenage emotion. Adults, he contends, are all phoneys who are in denial about their phoniness. It might just be this take on teenage rebellion that gives the book its enduring appeal.

That Salinger has lived as a recluse since 1953, that many U.S. states have banned *The Catcher in the Rye* from their libraries and schools for decades, and that John Lennon's murderer is said to have carried a copy of the book in his back pocket only add to the cult status of this classic novel.

FURTHER READING: *Franny and Zooey;*
For Esme with Love and Squalor
SEE ALSO: Many have tried but nobody could really be said to have captured the spirit of Salinger's Caufield

★
★
★
★

Writer: John Kennedy Toole
Publisher: Louisiana State University Press, 1980

ISBN US: 978-0807126073
ISBN UK: 978-0140282689

15+

A CONFEDERACY OF DUNCES

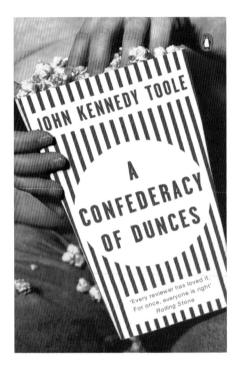

'Every reviewer has loved it.
For once, everyone is right'
Rolling Stone

A
Confederacy
of DUNCES

The Pulitzer
Prize-winning novel
featuring Ignatius Reilly
and his marvelous,
madcap adventures in
New Orleans

JOHN KENNEDY TOOLE

Plot: Lumbering. Medievalist. Opinionated. Devoted to the causes of "theology and geometry," but firmly against "offences against taste and decency," Ignatius J. Reilly lives with his momma in 1960s New Orleans. When, pressed for cash, she forces him to find work, he takes up a variety of low-paid jobs and becomes the catalyst for ludicrous adventures involving a pornography ring, a stripper with a parrot, political homosexuals, an unsuccessful undercover cop, a hot dog stand, an unsuccessful pants factory, a wily black janitor, and a mysterious copy of Anicius Manlius Severinus Boethius' *Consolations of Philosophy*.

Review: Even before it appeared in print, this was a cult book. Convinced of the work's merit, yet unable to find a publisher (Simon and Schuster, unbelievably, rejected this roaring comedy of ideas because "it isn't really about anything"), Toole committed suicide in 1969. His mother discovered a carbon copy of his manuscript and persuaded an initially reluctant Walker Percy (teacher at Loyola University

New Orleans and himself a noted author) to read it. Convinced of its strength, he was eventually able to see the book into print, and it rapidly found an audience, winning the Pulitzer Prize for fiction.

What of the book itself? The many characters are brilliantly varied, each with their own utterly distinctive voice, and the New Orleans setting provides the perfect backdrop to Reilly's adventures. Despite the anarchic action, the plot is well orchestrated. Yet it is the lumbering, paradoxical figure of Ignatius himself who dominates the work—one of the great creations of modern fiction, creating chaos wherever he goes.

FURTHER READING: This is Kennedy Toole's only adult work
SEE ALSO: Mind-bogglingly individual, it defies comparison

Writer: Mikhail Lermontov
Publisher: Russia, 1840

ISBN US: 978-1604244618
ISBN UK: 978-0140447958

★
★
★
★

15+

GEROY NASHEGO VREMENI
(A HERO OF OUR TIME)

A HERO OF OUR TIME
MIKHAIL LERMONTOV
TRANSLATED BY MARTIN PARKER AND NEIL CORNWELL
ONE WORLD CLASSICS

PENGUIN ● CLASSICS
MIKHAIL LERMONTOV
A Hero of Our Time

Plot: A series of five interwoven episodes center around a nineteenth-century Russian aristocrat, Pechorin, and his attempts to relieve the boredom of his stultifying existence with a series of schemes. These include the wooing and destruction of a Princess, the killing of an acquaintance in a duel, and the abduction of a noblewoman. The novel is an unflattering portrait of its protagonist and of the Russian society in which its author grew up, and was harshly criticized on publication in 1840. In particular, Lermontov's detractors insisted that the vile bully Pechorin must be autobiographical. Lermontov scoffed at this suggestion, noting the book is not a self-portrait but "a portrait of the vices of our whole generation in their ultimate development."

Review: For the literary misfit to have artistic merit, we must be repelled by their misanthropic misdeeds, but equally they must tell us something about ourselves and about the human condition. Lemontov's Pehcorin is just such an antihero, teaching us about the dualism of human nature.

A psychological casebook of sorts, then, which paved the way for the great Russian novels of Dostoyevsky and Tolstoy.

Seeing Pechorin through the eyes of different protagonists (and his own diaries) allows us to build a multi-faceted and comprehensive picture of a man frustrated by a mediocre world that won't recognize his brilliance, but who can find no useful channel for that brilliance other than ruining the lives of others. He's nothing if not self-aware, however. "If I cause unhappiness in others, I'm no less unhappy myself." The episodic structure leaves us in the dark as to whether this self-awareness will lead to a change of character, and this deliciously damning portrait of Lermontov's "superfluous man" is all the more riveting for that.

FURTHER READING: Lermontov was killed in a duel at the age of twenty-six and this was his only novel
SEE ALSO: *Anatol* (Arthur Schnitzler); *Dangerous Liasons* (Choderlos de Laclos)

★
★
★
★

Writer: James Kelman
Publisher: Martin, Secker and Warburg, 1994
ISBN US: 978-0393327991
ISBN UK: 978-0749398835

18+

HOW LATE IT WAS, HOW LATE

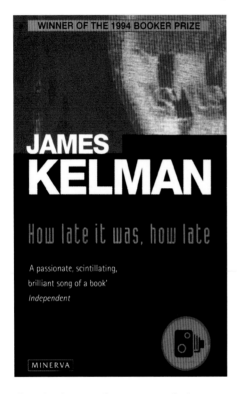

Plot: Kelman's 1994 Booker Prize winner tells of Sammy, a Glaswegian drunk, ex-convict, and all-round hopeless case. When he comes round after a binge of drinking and fighting, he's faced with two nightmare dilemmas: his girlfriend Helen has gone missing, and he cannot see. Sammy must try to make his way to the Sight Loss Department at the Central Medical—but will they believe he is blind? In his blackly comic attempts to convince them, he is caught up in the dual struggles of being physically incapacitated and overcoming a Kafkaesque mountain of bureaucracy.

Review: Kelman has always fiercely defended the profuse swearing in his work (one of the judges of the 1994 Booker called it "a disgrace"). In *How Late It Was, How Late* he pushes our tolerance of obscenities to the limit. Kelman would argue this generous flourishing of the wand of profanity is necessary, saying that it shows how a certain section of the British population, speak, act, and live—his London-centric critics are elitist and racist, he says.

As someone who has spent a lot of time in Glasgow, Scotland, on a Saturday night, I'd agree. In fact I'd go so far as giving Kelman that overused label of "genius" for his capturing of the spirit, the rhythm, and the sound of those lost souls who use "sweary words" and violence to deal with the reality of their harsh existence. A pleasant or easy read this isn't, but it's uplifting all the same.

FURTHER READING: *Busconductor Hines*; *Kieron Smith, Boy* (the latter if you like the sound of Kelman-light without the profanity) **SEE ALSO:** *Buddha Da* (Anne Donovan); *Poor Things* (Alisdair Gray)

Writer: Blaise Cendrars
Publisher: Bernard Grasset, 1926

ISBN US: 978-1590170632
ISBN UK: 978-0140186369

★
★
★
★

5+

MORAVAGINE

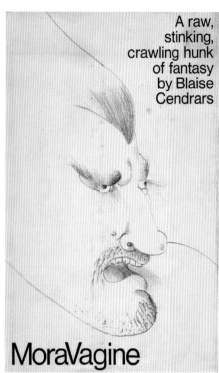

A raw, stinking, crawling hunk of fantasy by Blaise Cendrars

Plot: A doctor releases one of his patients from a lunatic asylum and together they go on a global rampage carrying out various scams, from organizing a coup in Russia, to prospecting for gold, to writing a novel. On the strange duos' return to Europe, World War I is breaking out, when "the whole world was doing a Moravagine." Narrated by the doctor and with a cameo appearance by Cendrars himself, the writing is pleasingly descriptive, with a metafictional touch.

Review: A cacophony of madcap adventures, bizarre schemes, and violent crimes combine to create a picaresque novel of unrivaled weirdness. To take two examples: the narrator first spots Moravagine masturbating into a goldfish bowl, and later we're told of a sexual encounter with a stovepipe and a lead ingot. That's before we've even mentioned the disemboweling of a girlfriend.

Moravagine is not without a philosophical message, however. "There is no truth," our narrator tells us. "There's only action, action obeying a million different impulses, ephemeral action, action subjected to every possible imaginable contingency and contradiction. Life." In other words, the madness of *Moravagine* is synonymous with the moral entropy and chaos of the world in the 1900s.

Nevertheless, the unflinching depiction of rape, and the murder of little girls, may leave some feeling the author did not go far enough in calling his own creation "an idiot and a monster." And yet we could argue that *Moravagine*'s unabashed psychotic leanings are partly what gives this poem to insanity its charm. A divisive book then, but worth a look.

FURTHER READING: *Sutter's Gold*
SEE ALSO: *Journey to the End of the Night* (Céline)

★
★ **Writer:** Charles Bukowski **ISBN US:** 978-0876850862
★ **Publisher:** Black Sparrow Press, 1970 **ISBN UK:** 978-0753518168
★

18+ POST OFFICE

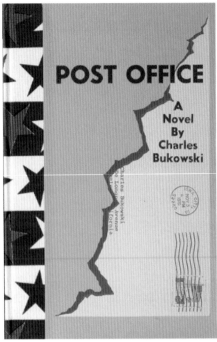

Plot: Tedious and degrading work hauling mail bags, rough one-night stands, moments of wild drunkenness, winning or losing at the racetrack . . . repeat ad infinitum. This is the long and short of the life of Bukowski's Henry Chinaski, his fictional alter ego, and the main protagonist of this account of a misanthropic postal worker.

"All these mail men do is drop their letters and get laid. This is the job for me, oh yes yes yes," Chianski enthuses at the novel's start. But Chianski/Bukowski was not made to endure the hierarchies, routines, and emotional burdens of clerical work, and at the end of the story he wakes up from another drinking spree having made a life-changing decision.

Review: Cynical, ugly, grubby, and explicit—descriptions of Bukowski's work that could come from either fan or detractor. His first novel is shocking, the language bold, and makes for a depressing picture of the life of a menial worker.

Post Office was born of an offer from John Martin, the publisher of Black Sparrow Press, who promised Bukowski $100 a month to write for the rest of his life. It paid off—the book was an instant hit and *Time* was soon calling Bukowski "the laureate of American low-life," a crown which hasn't been surrendered to another writer to this day. Others have not been so impressed by his at times degrading views of women, and he has often been labeled misogynist.

As for this reviewer's view of the book, let's call it cynical, ugly, grubby, and explicit . . .

FURTHER READING: *Ham on Rye; Women*
SEE ALSO: *Ask the Dust* (John Fante);
Hunger (Knut Hamsun)

★
★
★
★

Writer: Hermann Hesse
Publisher: S. Fischer Verlag, 1927
ISBN US: 978-0312278670
ISBN UK: 978-0140282580

15+

STEPPENWOLF

Plot: *Steppenwolf* is the record of a man (Harry Haller) who thinks himself to be half-human and half-wolf in an unnamed interwar German town. As the novel begins the suicidal Haller is wallowing in a mire of depression. On the one hand he loathes the bourgeoisie with which he is associated, with its repression of sensuality and pleasure. On the other, he aspires to live on a more spiritual level; this dichotomy between the cold Apollonian intellect and fiery Dionysian lust for life that makes us human is at the center of the novel, and indeed much of Hesse's other work.

Back to the plot, and things are looking up for Harry when he finds a theater with unusual signage, "MAGIC THEATER—ENTRANCE NOT FOR EVERYBODY." Once inside he discovers a booklet that perfectly describes his mixed up feelings at being a "wolf of the steppe." He also becomes acquainted there with a young woman, Hermine, who takes him to paroxysms of hedonism he'd hitherto only dreamed of. Eventually, though, he will have to pay for these pleasures, Hermine says, in that he will have to kill her.

Review: If you are looking for an easy read with an obvious message, you are best off looking elsewhere. (Hesse was forced to add a note to his book in 1961 to say it had been "violently misunderstood.") If, however, you are looking for an interesting examination of intellectual hypocrisy and a study of the artistic temperament, then do give it a try. Do please note, though, that the gloom and doom might be too much for some, even if there is a small ray of hope at the end.

FURTHER READING: *Siddartha*;
The Glass Bead Game
SEE ALSO: *Metamorphosis* (Franz Kafka);
The Outsider (Albert Camus)

★
★
★
★

Writer: Joris-Karl Huysmans
Publisher: Charpentier, 1884

ISBN US: 978-0140447637
ISBN UK: 978-1414230689

15+ # AGAINST NATURE

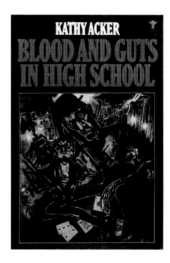

Plot: In *Against Nature*, Huysmans vomits forth his revulsion for bourgeois society in fin-de-siècle Paris. In an unstructured narrative he tells of Jean des Esseintes, an aristocratic Parisian who escapes to the countryside to live a solitary life as an aesthete, conducting strange intellectual experiments to remove himself from "nature."

Review: A plethora of moral indignation greeted Huysman's misanthropic novel, which was later described by an English poet as a "breviary of decadence." By contrast, many writers commended it, and Huysmans still has a host of admirers among the literary fraternity. You might fear pretentiousness but, actually, this bizarre gem of a novel is seductively accessible.

FURTHER READING: *The Damned*
SEE ALSO: *The Picture of Dorian Gray* (Oscar Wilde)

★
★
★

Writer: Kathy Acker
Publisher: Grove Press, 1984

ISBN US: 978-0802131935
ISBN UK: 978-0802131935

15+ # BLOOD AND GUTS IN HIGH SCHOOL

Plot: Janey Smith has an incestuous relationship with her father, escapes to New York, joins a gang, is sold into prostitution, and eventually makes her way to Tangiers, where she buddies up with the writer Jean Genet. Just a few of the plotlines in this ultra-modern take on the rites-of-passage novel.

Review: It's as if Kathy Acker has taken a literary tin of paint, flung it at the wall, and waited to see what turns out, considering the bewildering array of techniques used here, including: dialog laid out like a film script, dream maps, drawings, and a Persian phrasebook. Whether you go in for experimentation or not, you'll have to agree, nobody does it quite like Kathy Acker did.

FURTHER READING: *Great Expectations;*
Politics; Empire of the Senseless
SEE ALSO: *Barf Manifesto* (Dodie Bellamy):
Your Body Figured (Douglas A Martin)

★
★
★
★

Writer: Fyodor Dostoyevsky
Publisher: Russkii Vestnik, 1866

ISBN US: 978-0679734505
ISBN UK: 978-0140621808

12+

CRIME AND PUNISHMENT

Plot: An ex-student, Raskolnikov, commits a double murder in the poetically evoked slums of St. Petersburg. "I wanted to make myself a Napolean and that is why I killed her," he says of killing his landlady. This grand assertion and his self-justification for the crime are eventually worn down, both by Raskolnikov's conscience and by the psychological methods of the detective, Petrovich.

Review: A weighty tome of classic Russian storytelling, this is a powerful read. The persistent reader will find in its pages a fascinating study of what happens when moral laws are transgressed, and how one man's alienation from society compels him to commit the most gratuitous of crimes.

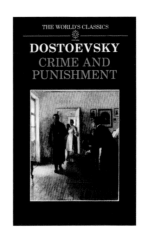

THE WORLD'S CLASSICS

DOSTOEVSKY
CRIME AND PUNISHMENT

FURTHER READING: *The Idiot; Notes from the Underground*
SEE ALSO: *The Secret History* (Donna Tartt); *A Hero of Our Time* (Mikhail Lermontov)

★
★
★

Writer: Katherine Dunn
Publisher: Random House, 1989

ISBN US: 978-0375713347
ISBN UK: 978-0349100869

15+

GEEK LOVE

Plot: Olympia (Oly) Binewski, an albino, hunchbacked dwarf, is one of four children deliberately deformed (by pills and radioactivity during pregnancy) by her parents in order to create a freak show for their failing traveling carnival. Years later, Oly, now living in a boarding house in Portland and spying on and protecting her daughter (who knows nothing of her parents), recounts her youth and the rise of her brother, Arty, to cult leadership.

Review: The "geek love" of the title refers to the love of a mother for her daughter and the familial love of the geek family. By intertwining the two stories (past and present), the characters have to be constantly reevaluated, as does the notion of normalcy in the society that surrounds them, especially among those who visit geek shows and Arty's followers.

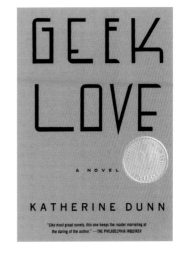

GEEK LOVE

A NOVEL

KATHERINE DUNN

"Like most great novels, this one keeps the reader marveling at the daring of the author." —THE PHILADELPHIA INQUIRER

FURTHER READING: *Truck; One Ring Circus: Dispatches from the World of Boxing*
SEE ALSO: *Freakery: Cultural Spectacles of the Extraordinary Body* (Rosemary Thomson); *Sideshow U.S.A.: Freaks and the American Cultural Imagination* (Rachel Adams)

★
★
★
★
★

Writer: Daniel Clowes
Publisher: Fantagraphic Books, 1997

ISBN US: 978-1560974277
ISBN UK: 978-0224060882

15+

GHOST WORLD

Plot: In the backdrop of the "ghost world" of small town America, two girls are coming of age. Bespectacled Enid, "a restless outcast," and Rebecca, "her uneasy counterpart," are considering their futures in the long, uncertain summer after high-school graduation.

Review: While Clowes tones down the lavish surrealism of his earlier graphic novel *Like a Velvet Glove Cast in Iron* and avoids the wonky caricature of others of his *Eightball* comics, *Ghost World* does share something of their strangeness. With simple atmospheric techniques, such as using a blue tint over the black and white line drawings, he evokes the "ghostliness" alluded to in the title. "Post-adolescence" has rarely been portrayed with such exactitude and unerring bleakness.

FURTHER READING: *David Boring; Like a Velvet Glove Cast in Iron*
SEE ALSO: *Black Hole* (Charles Burns); *Buddy Does Seattle* (Peter Bagge)

★
★
★
★
★

Writer: Patrick Hamilton
Publisher: Constable, 1941

ISBN US: 978-1933372068
ISBN UK: 978-0141185897

12+

HANGOVER SQUARE

Plot: Set in the gin-soaked, gas-lit pub land of interwar London, *Hangover Square* tells the story of the schizophrenic George Harvey Bone. Unbalanced by drink and infatuated with the prostitute Netta Longdon, Bone suffers from "dead" moments when he experiences murderous intentions that he will later forget. "This Netta business had been going on too long," he thinks. "When was he going to kill her?"

Review: Hamilton creates unforgettable characters in the vulnerable drifter Bone and the coquettish and cruel Netta. He is equally adept at ratcheting up an inexorable sense of foreboding as the object of Bone's affections treats him with increasing disdain. Bleak chic at its best.

FURTHER READING: *Slaves of Solitude; The Gorse Trilogy*
SEE ALSO: *They Drive by Night* (James Curtis);
Under the Net (Iris Murdoch)

★
★
★
★

Writer: Gary Paulsen
Publisher: Bradbury Press, 1987
ISBN US: 978-1416936473
ISBN UK: 978-0330439725

12+

HATCHET

Plot: Thirteen-year-old Brian Robeson, on his way to be reunited with his estranged father, watches in horror as the pilot flying him over the Canadian wilderness dies of a heart attack. After haphazardly crashing the plane, which sinks into a lake, Brian has to survive on his wits, a hatchet being the only modern tool to hand.

Review: Although Brian has led a sheltered, urban upbringing, he manages to make fire, build himself a shelter, find food, and survive, although author Paulsen never gives his scared and fatigued young hero an easy time. Already distressed by memories of his parents' divorce and with his life threatened constantly, Brian learns by trial and error, coping with disasters with determination, perseverance, and growing maturity.

FURTHER READING: *The River; Brian's Winter; Brian's Return;* and *Brian's Hunt*
SEE ALSO: *Swiss Family Robinson* (David Wyss); *Island of the Blue Dolphins* (Scott O'Dell)

★
★
★
★

Writer: Carson McCullers
Publisher: Houghton Mifflin, 1950

ISBN US: 978-0618526413
ISBN UK: 978-0141185224

15+

THE HEART IS A LONELY HUNTER

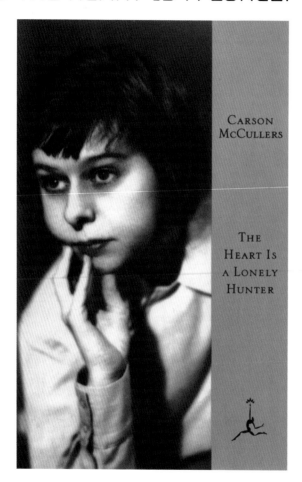

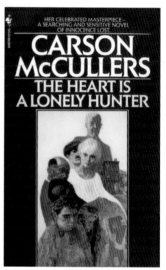

Plot: Character is paramount in this story which centers on the deaf-mute John Singer and the people who come to him with their sadnesses. Using her protagonists to complete a desolate picture of life in the South, McCullers takes us on a journey to the more wretched side of the human condition.

Review: A prescient advocacy of civil rights from a precocious literary sensation. (McCullers wrote the book when she was twenty-three). From the poetic title to the melancholia that hangs in the air throughout and until each character's unfortunate resolution, McCullers presents life's woes with a humbling veracity. Moreover, she famously depicts a shared humanity between black and white that was unusual when book was published in 1940.

FURTHER READING: *The Ballad of the Sad Café*
SEE ALSO: *To Kill a Mockingbird* (Harper Lee);
The Color Purple (Alice Walker)

★
★
★
★

15+

Writer: Saul Bellow
Publisher: Viking Press, 1964

ISBN US: 978-0140189438
ISBN UK: 978-0141184876

HERZOG

Plot: Moses Herzog is falling apart at the seams. He is no good as a father or husband; he is no good at his job; his wife has taken a lover . . . and that lover is his best friend. What is a man to do? Revenge is foremost in his mind, but there is also the small matter of composing letters he will not send: to colleagues, to friends, to enemies, and to famous folk—both dead and alive.

Review: With *Herzog* Bellow established himself as one of the greatest exponents of writing about that inner angst that makes us human, and it brought him to the bestsellers list for the first time. Pleasingly labyrinthine interior monologue and vitriolic dialog between the cuckold and his wife compensate for the lack of plot. "If I am out of my mind, it's alright with me," Herzog recounts. It's alright with us too.

FURTHER READING: *Humboldt's Gift*
SEE ALSO: *A Severed Head* (Iris Murdoch);
Who's Afraid of Virginia Woolf? (Edward Albee)

★
★
★

15+

Writer: Scott Bradfield
Publisher: Knopf, 1989

ISBN US: 978-0312140892
ISBN UK: 978-0330334129

THE HISTORY OF LUMINOUS MOTION

Plot: At the age of eight, Phillip Davis is traveling on the seemingly endless California highways, the trip punctuated by nights in motels and his mother's lovers. The journey seems to be at an end when mom settles down with a hardware-store owner. Phillip kills him, sending the pair back on the road. They finally settle, mom in an alcoholic stupor, leaving Phillip to explore the world of drugs, burglary, and the occult with his new friends.

Review: Narrated in the first person, Phillip's philosophical outpourings are unlike any you would expect from the mind of the average eight-year-old. Unless he is in motion, Phillip is lost. Even when his father reappears, Phillip sees it as deadening rather than offering stability. Bradfield's debut novel split critics, summed up by Michiko Kakutani's comment that the book was "by turns dazzling, irritating, and exhausting."

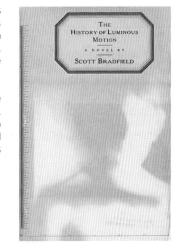

FURTHER READING: *Good Girl Wants It Bad; Hot Animal Love*
SEE ALSO: *We Have Always Lived in the Castle* (Shirley Jackson)

★ **Writer:** Chris Ware
★ **Publisher:** Fantagraphics, 2003
★

ISBN US: 978-0224063975
ISBN UK: 978-0224062107

15+

JIMMY CORRIGAN
THE SMARTEST KID ON EARTH

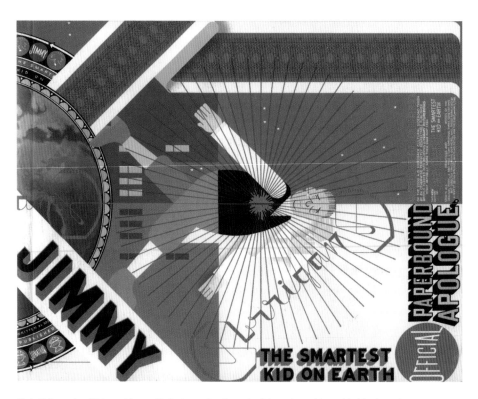

Plot: At the center of this graphic novel is Corrigan, a lonely office worker, and his dysfunctional family. The book pieces together his relationships with his absentee father and domineering mother, and—in a series of flashbacks—the equally miserable story of his bullying grandfather's youth in the Chicago of the 1890s.

Review: Highly commended by mainstream critics, less so perhaps by comic book aficionados. The mainstream success is all the more remarkable considering the book's main strength lies in its visual storytelling; the author is not afraid to leave some pages free of words and let his illustrations speak for themselves, and there is ingenious and highly original use of panel layout. The muted colors of the palette of the art emphasize Jimmy's alienation, while the fact the book is partly autobiographical lends a poignant tone to an already moving story. Utterly original, if perhaps too bleak in its outlook to be entertaining.

FURTHER READING: *Acme Novelty Library: No. 19; Quimby the Mouse*
SEE ALSO: *David Boring* (Daniel Clowes)

★
★
★

Writer: Italo Svevo
Publisher: Putnam, 1930 (originally in Italian, 1923)

ISBN US: 978-0375727764
ISBN UK: 978-0140187748

15+ # LA COSCIENZA DI ZENO

(CONFESSIONS OF ZENO)

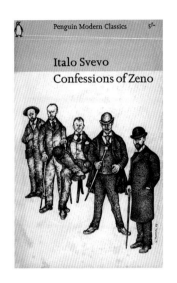

Penguin Modern Classics   5/-

Italo Svevo
Confessions of Zeno

Plot: Zeno Cosini visits a psychiatrist to understand his addiction to cigarettes and, at the suggestion of his analyst, he keeps a diary through which he reveals various aspects of his life: how he began smoking, the death of his father, meeting his wife, his affair with an aspiring singer, and his work as a businessman. Through free association and exploring his subconscious, he examines his addictions, neuroses, and obsessions.

Review: Experimental in form and heavily influenced by the author's reading of Freud, Svevo's novel was initially (self-) published to utter silence from critics. Championed by James Joyce, it eventually found an audience, and is now seen as the first Italian novel of psychology.

FURTHER READING: *Further Confessions of Zeno*
SEE ALSO: *If on a Winter's Night a Traveler* (Italo Calvino);
The Smoking Diaries (Simon Gray)

★
★
★
★

Writer: Jean Cocteau
Publisher: Grasset, 1929

ISBN US: 978-0811200219
ISBN UK: 978-2253010258

15+ # LES ENFANTS TERRIBLES

Plot: A brother (Paul) and sister (Elisabeth) cut off the outside world to share their childhood only with a "Game" whose rules they must obey. Their fantasy world becomes a nightmare scenario when Elisabeth invites another girl (Agatha) to share their isolation. Sibling jealousy ensues . . . as does melodrama and inevitable tragedy.

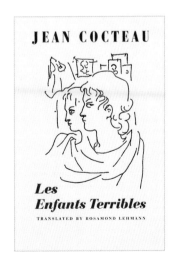

JEAN COCTEAU

Les
Enfants Terribles
TRANSLATED BY ROSAMOND LEHMANN

Review: Intriguing phantasmagoria from Jean Cocteau, whose multi-disciplinary talent (he wrote poetry, prose, films, and drama) is given play here. "A wolfish phosphorescence," rises from one of the sibling's hearts. Another character's physical features become, "separate stars of one great constellation." Pretentious? Maybe. The best poetic prose of a generation? Definitely.

FURTHER READING: *Opium*
SEE ALSO: *Our Lady of the Flowers* (Jean Genet);
The Counterfeiters (André Gide);
The Cement Garden (Ian McEwan)

ESSENTIAL
CULT BOOKS

500

331

OUTCASTS AND LONERS
Best of the Rest

★
★
★
★

Writer: Albert Camus
Publisher: Gallimard, 1942

ISBN US: 978-2070360024
ISBN UK: 978-0141182506

12+

L'ETRANGER (THE STRANGER)

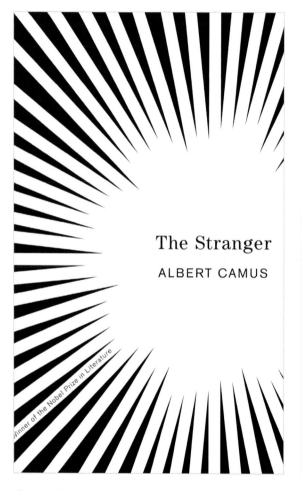

The Stranger

ALBERT CAMUS

Winner of the Nobel Prize in Literature

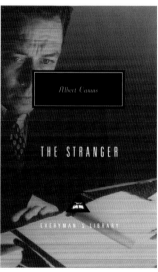

Plot: The ultimate existential novel follows Meursault, a bachelor, living in Algiers. It opens with the death of his mother and continues with an act of violence that sees him on trial for murder. That Meursault responds to all these events without emotion is the crux of the book.

Review: In not crying at his mother's funeral, Meursault is presented—as one character notes—as, "A man whose heart is so empty it threatens to engulf society." Camus evokes a powerful message here: that those who do not "play the game," those who don't conform, must live outside society, or else. What fascinates is that this message remains frighteningly pertinent to this day.

FURTHER READING: *The Plague*
SEE ALSO: *Metamorphosis* (Franz Kafka); *Nausea* (Jean-Paul Sartre)

★
★
★
Writer: Samuel Beckett
Publisher: Routledge Kegan Paul, 1938

ISBN US: 978-0802150370
ISBN UK: 978-0571244584

 12+

MURPHY

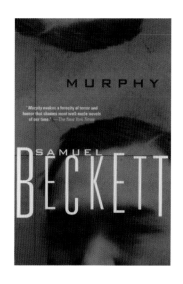

Plot: Through a chance meeting with Mr. Ticklepenny, Murphy obtains a job as a nurse at the Magdalen Mental Mercyseat, despite a lifetime avoiding work. His attempts at a meaningful, loving relationship with Celia become secondary to his futile fascination with one of the patients, Mr. Endon. Depression, a game of chess, and death follow.

Review: Beckett's second novel (although the first to see print) was rejected by forty-one publishers before being accepted. Unlike his later work, which strips away context, leaving only bare words to convey meaning (and meaninglessness), *Murphy* was written at a time when Beckett was still emerging from the shadow of James Joyce. *Murphy* owes more to Schopenhauer, Descartes, and especially Arnold Geulincx, whose "Where you are worth nothing, there you should want nothing" was central to the novel.

FURTHER READING: *Watt; Malone Dies; The Unnamable*
SEE ALSO: *The Grove Companion to Samuel Beckett* (ed. C. J. Ackerley and S. E. Gontarski)

★
★
★
Writer: Julian Maclaren-Ross
Publisher: Allan Wingate Publishers, 1947

ISBN US: 978-0141187112
ISBN UK: 978-0141187112

 12+

OF LOVE AND HUNGER

Plot: A vacuum-cleaner salesman plays an unsuccessful game of hide and seek, avoiding his debtors and a busybody landlady, while forever on the look-out for a decent new job or girl.

Review: Maclaren-Ross' desperate and gloomy *Of Love and Hunger* has a colloquial style and clipped prose whose simplicity nonetheless perfectly evokes its dingy seaside town setting. In the background, war looms with ominous inevitability—in fact everything in this novel set in the Depression could be said to loom: the arrival of the bailiffs, the ending of a seedy love affair, and the hero's call-up to the war effort all cast a portentous shadow from start to finish. What a pity that the Bohemian lifestyle consumed Maclaren-Ross before he could realize his full potential as a novelist.

FURTHER READING: *Bitten by the Tarantula and Other Writing*
SEE ALSO: *Fear and Loathing in Fitzrovia* (Paul Willets)

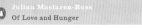
Julian Maclaren-Ross
Of Love and Hunger

Writer: Ken Kesey
Publisher: Viking Press, 1962

ISBN US: 978-0140283341
ISBN UK: 978-0330235648

ISBN US: 978-0140283341
ISBN UK: 978-0330235648

15+

ONE FLEW OVER THE CUCKOO'S NEST

Plot: *One Flew Over the Cuckoo's Nest* is narrated by Chief Bromden, a paranoid man on a psychiatric ward, whom the authorities believe to be a deaf-mute. When a new patient arrives a whirlwind of rebellion and disorder ensues, disrupting the authority of the formidable Nurse Ratchet.

Review: Every once in a while a book comes along that spurns the values of its epoch: this is just such a book. Its portrayal of minorities and women, in particular, fly in the face of the equal rights movements of the 1960s. Yet Kesey does have something meaningfully liberal to say about the abominable treatment of mental patients, and, in any case, this is above all a satisfyingly good story with an unexpectedly tragic ending.

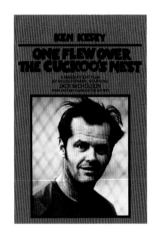

FURTHER READING: *Sometimes a Great Notion*
SEE ALSO: *The Electric Kool-Aid Acid Test* (Tom Wolfe)

Writer: Wallace Stevens
Publisher: Knopf, 1971

ISBN US: 978-0679724452
ISBN UK: 978-0679724452

ISBN US: 978-0679724452
ISBN UK: 978-0679724452

12+

THE PALM AT THE END OF THE MIND
SELECTED POEMS AND A PLAY BY WALLACE STEVENS

Synopsis: A collection of many of Stevens' best works, arranged chronologically, with some text corrected and restored. Poems include "The Idea of Order at Key West," "The Emperor of Ice-Cream," "The Man with the Blue Guitar," and some 230 others, plus the play "Bowl, Cat and Broomstick."

Review: Edited by his daughter, Holly Stevens, *The Palm at the End of the Mind* is a fine introduction to the work of Wallace Stevens, one of America's most respected poets. He often used his work to explore the essence of poetry and his choice of themes and vocabulary have on occasion made him appear, as one critic described, a "willfully difficult poet." Most agree, however, that while his work demands much, it repays re-reading.

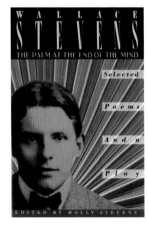

FURTHER READING: *Collected Poetry and Prose*
(ed. Frank Kermode and Joan Richardson)
SEE ALSO: *A Reader's Guide to Wallace Stevens*
(Eleanor Cook)

★
★
★

Writer: DBC Pierre
Publisher: Faber and Faber, 2003

ISBN US: 978-1841954608
ISBN UK: 0-571-21516-5

18+

VERNON GOD LITTLE

Plot: *Vernon God Little* is set during the aftermath of a high-school massacre in the "barbeque sauce capital of Texas." Accused of playing a role in the murders, Vernon Gregory Little escapes the media vultures circling the town and attempts to flee to Mexico.

Review: Junk food, the acquisition of white goods, TV—everything, in fact, that modern America holds dear—is satirized here through the distinctive voice of the adolescent Vernon, a Texan vernacular that bounces off the page and is done, like a juicy barbequed spare-rib, to perfection. *Vernon God Little* recently topped a list of books that people have left unread. More fool them. Persist, and you'll enjoy a darkly comedic take on where the Big Brother generation could land us.

FURTHER READING: *Ludmila's Broken English: A Novel*
SEE ALSO: *The Lost Honor of Katharina Blum* (Heinrich Böll);
We Need to Talk About Kevin (Lionel Shriver)

★
★
★

Writer: Jeffrey Eugenides
Publisher: Farrar, Straus and Giroux, 1993

ISBN US: 978-0446670258
ISBN UK: 978-0747560593

15+

THE VIRGIN SUICIDES

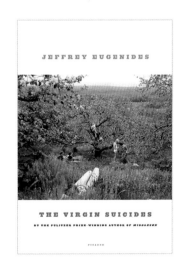

Plot: Over the course of a year, the five Lisbon sisters, all noted beauties, commit suicide in their "comfortable suburban home" outside Detroit.

Review: Moral panic about mass teenage suicides is a staple of the media and, as such, Eugenides has been accused of peddling sensationalism. This misses the point that the accomplished novelist evokes adolescent longing and angst to a T. When, after her first suicide attempt, a doctor tells Celia she has much to live for, she replies. "Obviously doctor, you've never been a thirteen year old girl." While on this level it works, as an allegory for something bigger, it doesn't quite hit the spot. Original nonetheless, particularly for the first person plural narration.

FURTHER READING: *Middlesex*
SEE ALSO: *The Three Sisters* (May Sinclair);
A Thousand Acres (Jane Smiley);
King Lear (William Shakespeare)

★
★
★

Writer: Louis-Ferdinand Céline
Publisher: Denöel & Steele, 1932

ISBN US: 978-0811216548
ISBN UK: 978-0714541396

15+

VOYAGE AU BOUT DE LA NUIT
(JOURNEY TO THE END OF THE NIGHT)

Plot: A vaguely autobiographical novel sees Céline's fictional antihero Bardamu become an army volunteer in World War I, traveling to Africa and America, and—by the end of novel— qualifying as a doctor in the 1930s.

Review: *Journey to the End of the Night* is a sulfurous book, containing some of the most pessimistic views on the human condition ever written. Nevertheless, the misanthropic Bardamu's expatiating on the misery of social degradation was praised at the time of publication, and Céline is now celebrated as one of the foremost modernist French novelists. This, despite his alleged collaboration with the Nazis and his open anti-Semitism. Stomach this, and you might enjoy his darkly humorous novel and its free use of 1930s Parisian argot.

FURTHER READING: *Death on the Installment Plan*
SEE ALSO: *Hunger* (Knut Hamsun);
Ask the Dust (John Fante)

★
★
★
★

Writer: Nelson Algren
Publisher: Farrar, Straus and Cudahy, 1956

ISBN US: 978-0374525323
ISBN UK: 978-1841956800

5+

A WALK ON THE WILD SIDE

Plot: "The book asks why lost people," Nelson Algren said, "sometimes develop into greater human beings than those who have never suffered their whole lives." Algren animates this notion through the tale of Dove Linkhorn, who leaves Great Depression-era Texas to look for work in New Orleans. Here he encounters the wild side of life in the company of hookers, bootleggers, amputees, and other dispossessed human beings.

Review: A meticulously observed tale of those at life's sharp end, where Algren himself was at times. The story's raw realism will appeal to those who like their novels well grounded, while the language has an idiosyncratic poetry that will satisfy those with literary pretensions: a twofold crowd-pleaser, then.

FURTHER READING: *The Man with the Golden Arm; The Neon Wilderness*
SEE ALSO: *Last Exit to Brooklyn* (Hubert Selby, Jr.) *Conversations with Nelson Algren* (Donohue)

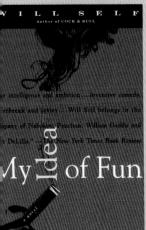
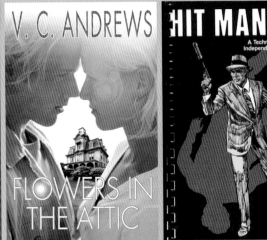

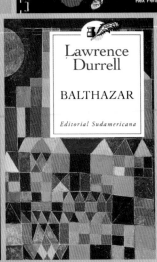

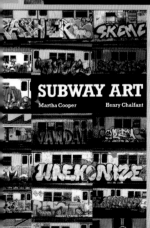

GENRE-DEFYING ONE-OFFS
AND VERY ODDBALL STUFF

We finish the book with the jewels in the crown from our vault of cult book treasures: the One of a Kind titles. Cynics might suggest there's a "try hard" feel to some of our recommended authors' attempts at innovation, and admittedly literary experimentation can sometimes go off with more of a pfft than a bang, but you need only delve into our One of a Kind selection, to see that occasionally, by some alchemy of great writing and mad ideas, such literary experi- ments can be nothing short of explosive. Sure, we've already reviewed a wealth of diverse and original books in previous chapters, but we've saved the most outré for last: forget non-linear plots (so con- ventional!), what follows is everything from subversive self-help guides to outlandish meta-fic- tion, from eighteenth-century poetry to how to write a number one hit. In short, anything goes.

★
★
★
★

Writer: Michael Chabon
Publisher: Random House U.S., 2000

ISBN US: 978-0312282998
ISBN UK: 978-1841154930

12+

THE AMAZING ADVENTURES OF KAVALIER AND CLAY

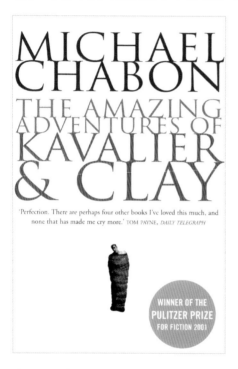

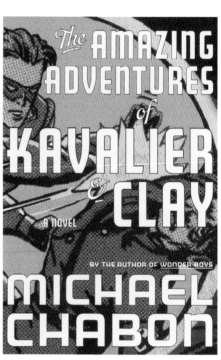

Plot: New York, 1939. Two teenage Jewish cousins, Sam Klayman and Josef Kavalier, embark on a career in the new industry of comic books. Together, they devise a new, Houdini-esque superhero, The Escapist, who will eventually bring them fame and fortune. The early years of their friendship, though, are overshadowed by events thousands of miles away—for Kavalier is a Czech Jew, whose family are left behind in occupied Europe, and The Escapist is the only means the young men have of fighting back at the Nazi regime.

Review: For a time in summer 2001 it seemed as if just about everyone was reading Chabon's masterpiece. Winning the Pulitzer Prize for fiction that April, its huge readership not only encompassed the literary fiction crowd but also swathes of comic book fans, fascinated by the new light Chabon threw on the origins of their favorite tales; it is their passionate response that has made this a real cult classic.

Notable for its fresh take on the life of mid-century Jewish New York—surely one of the most extensively fictionalized milieux in literature—*The Amazing Adventures* is a novel full of tension. The creative heroes face constant commercial pressures, the all-powerful Escapist highlights their impotence in the face of Nazi oppression, and there's also a sensitively drawn love triangle, with both the men becoming involved with the artistic Rosa. It's the push and pull of these conflicts, recounted in Chabon's precise, well-timed, and detailed prose, that make this novel so gripping.

FURTHER READING: *Wonderboys; Summerland*
SEE ALSO: *Michael Chabon Presents . . . The Amazing Adventures of the Escapist* (a collection of comics starring the novel's comic book hero)

Writer: Raymond Queneau
Publisher: Editions Gallimard, 1947

ISBN US: 978-0811207898
ISBN UK: 978-0714542386

★
★
★
★
★

EXERCICES DE STYLE (EXERCISES IN STYLE)

Synopsis: Ninety-nine times over, using a variety of tech-niques, styles, and tenses, Queneau retells the same basic story, which can be summarized in standard prose thus: a twenty-something man with a long neck gets on a bus during rush hour. The bus is crowded, and our "hero" gets annoyed, jostles a fellow passenger, and flings himself onto a vacant seat. Later, the narrator encounters the young man again in front of the Gare Saint-Lazare. This time the fellow is getting sartorial advice from a friend, who tells him, "You ought to get an extra button put on your overcoat." And, in terms of plot for each of the ninety-nine versions of the story, as the French say: "C'est tout."

Review: Okay, so this is not exactly the kind of book you'd give a difficult relative for Christmas—although it might be fun to watch their faces when they open the parcel—but it is a top-notch stocking-filler for those with a love of language and literary mavericks. Queneau uses the retellings to challenge our perceptions of how a story should be told and the result is a highly pleasing hodgepodge. Some of the ninety-nine tales are extremely funny ("Pig Latin" and "Ono-matopoeia," for instance), some quite dull but instructive nevertheless ("Past" and "Present Tense," and "Reported Speech," for instance), and yet others erudite ("Aphaeresis" and "Apocope," teaching us unusual linguistic terms). Don't worry if this all seems inaccessible, you'll giggle when you see how it's done.

An indispensable tool for all would-be writers (whether of fact, fiction, or fantasy), a must-read for all linguistic students, and a key text for cult book devotees, *Exercises in Style* is endlessly fascinating. Oh, and hats off to the translator of the English edition, Barbara Wright, for her splendid exercises in translation.

FURTHER READING: *Zazie in the Metro*
SEE ALSO: *253* (Geoff Ryman);
99 Ways to Tell a Story:
Exercises in Style (Matt Maden)

★
★   **Writer:** Virginia Andrews   **ISBN US:** 978-0671729417
★   **Publisher:** Simon & Schuster, 1979   **ISBN UK:** 978-0006159292

15+ # FLOWERS IN THE ATTIC

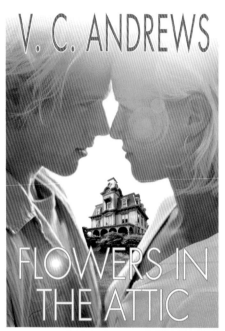

Plot: Families don't come much more dysfunctional than the Dollangangers, the stars of this, Virginia Andrews' debut novel. First we have mom, a woman who (following the death of her husband) locks her kids in her parents' attic (for reasons of financial gain), poisons them with baked goods, and generally goes all out for winning "world's worst mom" award. Next up is grandma, an accessory to the children in the attic atrocity, who takes pleasure in calling her grandkids "the devil's spawn." Meanwhile Cathy (our narrator) and Chris, the two eldest kids of four locked in the attic, conduct an incestuous relationship.

And after that, as the old joke goes, plot-wise, it's all downhill from there...

Review: A copy of this book passed around our high school until it made it back, dog-eared and disintegrating, to its owner. To this day huge numbers of adolescent girls can be found thrilling to its (mostly implied) naughty delights under the bedclothes with a torch.

Why, though? Books really don't come much sillier or more melodramatic than this—the number of exclamation marks alone would gain the author a fail on most creative writing courses. As for the writing itself, well, here is an example from grandpa Dollanganger: "Look at you, standing there in your iron-grey dress, feeling pious and self-righteous while you starve small children!" Eek!

But the book retains a huge cult following, and the Andrews franchise has seen over eighty-five million copies sold worldwide. The clue to this enduring mainstream and cult success can probably be explained by the author, who said she wrote about, "unspeakable things my mother didn't want me to write about." And then you remember. A fourteen year old girl, lit torch under the quilt, an innate wish to rebel, and it all becomes crystal clear.

FURTHER READING: The remaining titles in the Dollanganger series
SEE ALSO: *Just Take My Heart* (Mary Higgins Clark)

★
★
★
★

Writer: David Foster Wallace
Publisher: Little, Brown & Co, 1996

ISBN US: 978-0316066525
ISBN UK: 978-0349121086

15+

INFINITE JEST

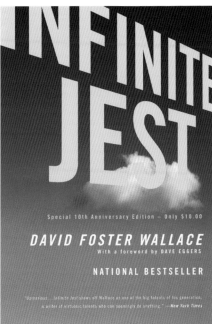

Plot: Fellow author Rick Moody writes that the late Foster Wallace's second, and last, novel is "so grand in its portrait of degraded, mass-merchandised, drug-afflicted contemporary America, that it's almost impossible to summarise." But let's have a try.

It is America of the near future. The United States is a member of the "Organization of North American Nations" federated with Canada and Mexico; a place where big corporations rule the roost, and culture has reached a new nadir. Set against this nightmarish vision is a tennis academy that hothouses promising young sports stars, including pot-smoking Hal Incandenza; meanwhile in a rehab half-way house, one Don Gately, a former criminal and addict, counsels drug addicts. Linking the two plot lines, and several others, is a movie, "Infinite Jest," a kind of cultural snuff movie, which holds all those who view it in its thrall.

Review: A post-modern labyrinth that will have you earning your cult fiction stripes, if you make it through all 1079 pages.

And it's not like we have here 1079 pages of breathtaking description, complex plotting, or the usual deep character-isations of the longer novel. On the contrary, the book has a laboratory's worth of forensic detail: there is page upon page on the minutae of professional tennis games, medical information about drugs, and even, at one point, ten pages about taking down a bed (diagrams included).

This won't be to everyone's taste, for sure, but thoughtful types will love *Infinite Jest*'s Shakespearean inventiveness, mind-bending complexity, and snowflake-like intricacies. Page-turner lovers—well, not so much.

FURTHER READING: *A Supposedly Fun Thing I'll Never Do Again; Oblivion* (short stories)
SEE ALSO: *A Heartbreaking Work of Staggering Genius* (Dave Eggers)

★
★
★
★
★

Writer: Charles Baudelaire
Publisher: Poulet, Mallasis et de Broise, 1857

ISBN US: 978-2266083263
ISBN UK: 978-2070409044

15+

LES FLEURS DU MAL

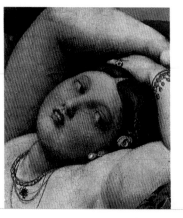

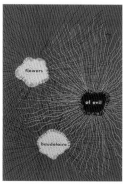

Synopsis: *Les Fleurs du Mal* is a series of 101 lyric poems that explore the temptations of good and evil and the dual nature of mankind. Highly personal in subject matter, they also present the poet's isolation and melancholy as he battles with the aforementioned conflicts.

Split into five sections, a central theme dominates the poems, namely the two opposing influences on the human condition, "the spleen" and "the ideal." By "spleen" Baudelaire means all the ills of the world: disease, depression, and, crucially, ennui, or boredom; while the "ideal" are the sensual ways in which we can overcome the spleen through alcohol, opium, and lust.

Lesbians, sex, and violence all feature highly throughout, while vampires and other creatures of the night serve to remind us of our own mortality—death being the ultimate victory of the spleen.

Review: On publication *Les Fleurs du Mal* were greeted with outrage; *Le Figaro* called them "immoral" and six of the poems were banned. A collection of hymns to beauty, lust, and the devil, it's not hard to see why. "A Celle Qui est trop Gai," one of the six banned poems, was particularly maligned. In it the poet describes creeping "softly" toward an unsuspecting woman: "To whip your joyous flesh/And bruise your pardoned breast. . . ."

But Baudelaire's intention was not to shock. Rather, he wished to point out that in an industrial society morality is not always the realistic outcome, and he mocks the hypocrisy of his readers. He does this with a magical poetic flourish that touches on all the senses, leaving the reader trembling in a dark recognition of what potentially lies within their souls.

FURTHER READING: *Le Spleen de Paris*
SEE ALSO: *Afternoon of a Faun*
(Stéphane Mallarmé);
Poèmes Saturniens (Paul Verlaine)

★
★
★
★

Writer: Laurence Sterne
Publisher: J. Dodsley, 1767

ISBN US: 978-0141439778
ISBN UK: 978-1853262913

15+

THE LIFE AND OPINIONS OF TRISTRAM SHANDY, GENTLEMAN

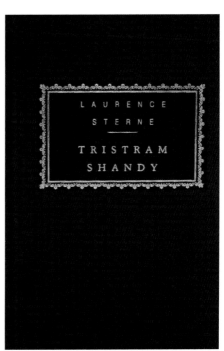

Plot: A fictional autobiography in which Tristram attempts to tell the story of his life from his very conception. This moment is dealt with in the first chapter (it's something of an accident: his mother distracts his father at the crucial moment, asking him if he had remembered to wind the clock, and Tristram is the result) but despite valiant efforts, and hundreds of pages, the narrator never gets into his stride. Instead of an ordered life the book offers us anecdote after anecdote—many of them about Tristram's beloved uncle Toby, an old soldier whose interminable military reminiscences give way, under Mrs. Wadman's influence, to more romantic leanings.

Review: "Digressions, incontestably, are the sunshine;—they are the life, the soul of reading," declares Tristram in the twenty-second chapter of the book. "Take them out of this book for instance, you might as well take the book along

with them." He's absolutely right. Hundreds of pages of "auto-biography" only take Tristram into infancy. Instead of a coherent plot, what Sterne gives us is a glorious mess of anecdotes, comic episodes, philosophical asides, and digressions. At one point, Shandy demonstrates his indirect narrative technique by drawing meandering lines across the page; at another, one page is printed entirely black. Unsurprisingly it has been called the first "anti-novel" in English. And yet it comes together as a rich mixture of family life, linguistic playfulness, sexual politics, and literary experiment. An influential classic.

FURTHER READING: *A Sentimental Journey*
SEE ALSO: *At-Swim-Two-Birds* (Flann O'Brien); *Pale Fire* (Vladimir Nabokov); *Nausea* (Jean-Paul Sartre), all considered fine examples of the anti-novel

★
★
★
★

Writer: Tim Burton
Publisher: Rob Weisbach Books, 1997

ISBN US: 978-0060526498
ISBN UK: 978-0571224449

15+

THE MELANCHOLY DEATH OF OYSTER BOY

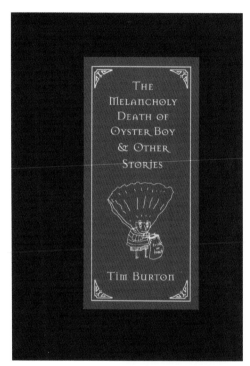

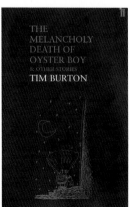

Synopsis: A collection of poems from the perennially original filmmaker, Tim Burton, with a cast of tragic, yet sweet, characters: "Stick Boy and Match Girl," who fall in love with obvious dire consequences; "The Boy With Nails in His Eyes," whose attempts to decorate a Christmas tree are futile; and poor "Oyster Boy" of the title, who comes to a macabre and sticky end.

"Mummy Boy" is a good example of Burton's style: "They took a baseball bat and whacked open his head/ Mummy Boy fell to the ground; he finally was dead."

It's probably not unfair to suggest that Burton's rhyming couplets won't be winning a poetry prize anytime soon. The illustrations, on the other hand, are a delight; that MOMA recently exhibited over 700 of his drawings, paintings, and storyboards is testament to his enormous skill in this field.

Review: Tim Burton, is, of course, much better known for his movies than his books, but both share a gothic quality, an underlying malevolence, and a captivating brilliance. But, where *The Nightmare Before Christmas*, *The Corpse Bride*, and *Edward Scissorhands* can be enjoyed by youngish children, these poems go further into the shadows. Maybe too far, in fact? Murder, sexual deviancy, and drug abuse feature highly in the collection. Not exactly all-ages stuff.

Nevertheless, positivity, in a creative sense, abounds here: you sense that the book has been lovingly created from cover, to endpaper, to spine; from the odd yet endearing illustrations that accompany the poems, even as far as the chosen font (Scripps College Oldstyle), which we are told is a "simple design lacking freakish qualities." Those same freakish qualities which otherwise distinguish this subversive and entertaining little book.

FURTHER READING: *The Nightmare Before Christmas*
SEE ALSO: *The Gashlycrumb Tinnies*; *The Doubtful Guest* (Edward Gorey)

★
★
★
★
★

Writer: Weegee
Publisher: Essential Books, 1945

ISBN US: 978-0306812040
ISBN UK: 978-0306812040

12+

NAKED CITY

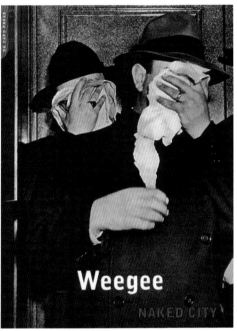

"Through his sense of timing, Weegee turns the commonplaces of a great city into extraordinary psychological documents."—Nancy Newhall, Acting Curator of Photography, Museum of Modern Art

ESSENTIAL
CULT BOOKS

500

349

ONE OF A KIND
Top10 Classics

Synopsis: A photographic response to one of the most dynamic, exiting, and dangerous cities in the world: New York. The time is the early 1940s and the photos are the work of Wegee (né Arthur Fellig), who presents his view of "The Naked City" from Harlem to Coney Island, in an album depicting everyone from high class ladies at the opera to lowlifes in the gutter.

Transgender prostitutes, bums, victims of gun crime and domestic violence, and sleeping and lost children are among his subjects, a cast of characters who recall the work of Raymond Chandler, John Fante, and Hubert Selby, Jr. This is noir at its most in-your-face, and its most realistic.

The collection includes perhaps his best-known photo, "The Critic," depicting two high-class women in their handbags and gladrags outside the opera house, being eye-balled by a critical-looking female bum.

Review: We are, one reviewer has said, "all eye witnesses and voyeurs" when we look at Weegee's work. This statement is also, perhaps, the perfect description of the tabloid photo journalism of which Weegee is the progenitor as well as the master. Even if we could blame him for the plague of celebrity snappers, and photos, we have to suffer nowadays, his work remains a feast for the eyes. Captions illuminate some of the background to the pictures, but cleverly, so that we still pause for thought: what did the young mother think when she lost her child on Coney Island?; Did the 3am beach lovers stay together? And how did Weegee come by such a strange nick name?

Actually, we can answer that last one: apparently the photographer was so given to being in the right place at the right time, camera in hand, that his colleagues nicknamed him after ouija boards, popular at the time.

FURTHER READING: *Weegee's People*
SEE ALSO: *The Americans* (Robert Frank);
Weegee's World (Miles Barth)

★
★ **Writer:** Valerie Solanas
★ **Publisher:** Self-published, 1968

ISBN US: 978-1873176443
ISBN UK: 978-1859845530

18+ # THE SCUM MANIFESTO

Synopsis: More radical feminist pamphlet, or tract, than complete book, the central argument of this diatribe against men is that all males have a latent desire to be female. This "pussy envy," Solanas opines, has led to men's creation of all the things she considers to be the ills of the world: money, government, war, prejudice, The Arts, marriage, and religion. Men have then dominated these hierarchical structures to create the patriarchy, perpetuating their domination by convincing women that they want to stay at home "with babies chomping away on their tits."

Not one to shirk the issues, however, Solanas offers a solution: women should join The Society for Cutting Up Men, kill all men, "fuck up the system," and selectively destroy property. Babies—exclusively females—would then be born in test tubes.

Review: Vitriolic would be a good place to start to describe this at times hard-to-follow rant. Insane might be our next adjective of choice. Indeed Solanas did end up in a mental institution after she stalked and shot Andy Warhol in the late 1960s.

And yet to pass this off as the work of a lunatic lesbian would be misleading at best, grossly unfair at worst. Amid the vomiting up of misandrist bile, there are some valid points (particularly entertaining is a section on the passive aggressive nature of "hippies"), and it's actually quite a lively read; you can't help admiring Solanas' sheer audacity, however screwy the train of thought. In any case, the author would later claim she wrote the tract as a satirical piece to invoke debate. In that context, this is nothing short of a blazing success.

FURTHER READING: *Up Your Ass*
(this play is the remainder of Solanas' literary legacy, premiered posthumously in 2000 in San Francisco)
SEE ALSO: *I Shot Andy Warhol* (Mary Harron; script from the movie about Valerie Solanas); *Popism: The Warhol Sixties* (Andy Warhol)

★
★
★
★

Writer: Joseph Moncure March/Art Spiegelman
Publisher: First Published in this edition by
Pantheon Books, 1994

ISBN US: 978-0375706431
ISBN UK: 978-0679424505

15+

THE WILD PARTY

Plot: "Queenie was a blonde and her age stood still/And she danced twice a day in vaudeville. . . ." Meet Queenie, the anti-heroine of *The Wild Party*, a melodrama in spiky, memorable verse. A jaded Broadway dancer, she and her vicious lover Burrs resolve to throw a party to relieve the boredom and the stifling heat of a New York summer. We're then introduced to a cast of characters ranging from the merely seedy to the downright terrifying; lascivious, drunk, their sins unseen in the candlelight, they party harder than you'd imagine was possible in times of prohibition. And with the arrival of that most dangerous of creatures, an honest, honorable man, matters take a turn for the dangerous.

Review: *The Wild Party* was successful on its initial publication in 1928 before fading into comparative obscurity over the following decades. Then, in 1994 (almost twenty years after March's death), a new edition was published with gloriously dark illustrations by Art Spiegelman. While these are great in their own right, the verse remains the star—instantly memorable, sexy, punchy, full of life, swinging like ragtime jazz, and as lustful and tragic as the deepest blues. The mood swings from exhilarated to chilling as Queenie's party continues on its inexorable downwards course, and by the end the reader is gripped. Don't worry if you've not read a poem since your schooldays—you'll love this, for sure.

FURTHER READING: *The Set Up*
SEE ALSO: This is truly one of a kind

★
★ **Writer:** Lawrence Durrell   **ISBN US:** 978-0571086092
Publisher: Faber & Faber, 1962   **ISBN UK:** 978-0571225569

15+

THE ALEXANDRIA QUARTET

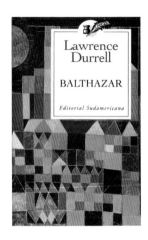

Plot: A tetralogy of works, "Justine," "Balthazar," "Mountolive," and "Clea," revolving around the life and loves of an expatriate writer, L. G. Darley, in Egypt after World War II. Through a plethora of characters and the exotic backdrop of Alexandria, Darley learns "the politics of love, the intrigue of desire, good and evil, virtue and caprice, love and murder."

Review: Although best known for its fecund eroticism, *The Alexandria Quartet* is also celebrated for its modern, experimental style. We'd love to say this adds up to an exotic literary extravaganza, but, honestly, the melodrama and dated sexual politics might prove this quartet's double whammy of disappointment for the modern reader.

FURTHER READING: *The Avignon Quintet*
SEE ALSO: *The Book of Secrets* (M. G. Vassanji);
Six Nights on the Acropolis (George Seferis)

★
★ **Writer:** Robert Frank   **ISBN US:** 978-3865215840
★ **Publisher:** Robert Delpire, 1958   **ISBN UK:** 978-3865215840
★
★

12+

THE AMERICANS

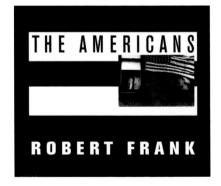

Synopsis: Funded by the Guggenheim Museum, Robert Frank traveled with his family across America from 1954–1957, taking over 20,000 photos of a wide cross-section of American society, of which eighty-three were included in *The Americans*—perhaps the most famous photography album of all time.

Review: Conventional images of America—cars, jukeboxes, cowboys, star-spangled banners—are mixed with other, less flattering portraits, a mix the public in the late fifties was not quite ready for, some going so far as to call Frank "Un-American." Soon, though, his innovative new style won over his detractors and Frank's place in photography history was secured. A fiftieth-anniversary edition of *The Americans* was published in 2007, its layout no less compromised by intrusive captions than the original 1959 U.S. edition.

FURTHER READING: *The Lines of My Hand*
SEE ALSO: *Naked City* (Weegee); *The Decisive Moment*
(Henri Cartier-Bresson); *New York* (William Klein)

★
★
★

Writer: William Powell
Publisher: Lyle Stuart, 1971

ISBN US: 978-0848811303
ISBN UK: 978-0974458908

8+ # THE ANARCHIST COOKBOOK

Synopsis: *The Anarchist Cookbook* contains assorted recipes for bombs and explosive-making, as well as other hints and tips for the direct action protestor, including how to make a ball-bearing catapult to lob at police during demonstrations.

Review: William Powell now wants to see his 1971 cult smash pulped, rescinding on the central idea within *The Anarchist Cookbook* that "violence is an acceptable means to bring about political change." You might disagree and want to give the recipes a shot, but be warned: some of them are said to be disastrously ill-conceived. Of course, the proof of the pudding is in the eating but, needless to say, we don't suggest you try this theory out at home.

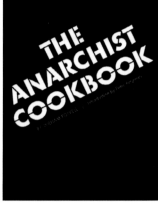

FURTHER READING: *The First Casualty* (a novel)
SEE ALSO: *Recipes for Disaster: An Anarchist Cookbook;*
Rebel, Rebel: The Protestor's Handbook (Bibi van der Zee)

★
★
★

Writer: Nick Cave
Publisher: Black Spring Press, 1989

ISBN US: 978-1880985724
ISBN UK: 978-0141044873

8+ # AND THE ASS SAW THE ANGEL

Plot: "Slopped into the world with all the glory of an uninvited guest." The birth of Euchrid Eucrow, a Southern hillbilly, sets the tone for the rest of Cave's Gothic horror tale of an outcast who slips slowly into insanity after suffering the religious hypocrisy of his townsfolk.

Review: It's the inventive language of Euchrid that makes Australian singer-songwriter Cave's novel stand out; a language Cave has called, "a kind of a hyper-poetic thought-speak, not meant to be spoken—a mongrel language that was part-Biblical, part-Deep South dialect, part-gutter slang." Indeed, a more memorable idiolect since the Namsat of Burgess' *A Clockwork Orange* is hard to imagine—Cave's gifts as a lyricist are more than evident here.

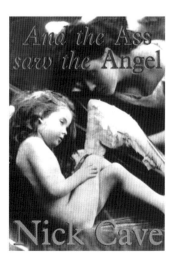

FURTHER READING: *The Death of Bunny Monro*
SEE ALSO: *House of the Seven Gables* (Hawthorne);
Wieland (Brockden Brown)

★
★
★

Writer: Richard Nicholls
Publisher: Running Press, 1977

ISBN US: 978-0894717413
ISBN UK: 978-0894717413

15+ # BEGINNING HYDROPONICS

Synopsis: A comprehensive guide to the process of growing plants in sand, gravel, or liquid, with added nutrients, but without soil. The book begins with an entertaining history of hydroponics (the process has been used since the time of the Aztecs) before moving on to the how-to sections.

Review: That hydroponics can be used to cultivate cannabis plants accounts for this seemingly innocuous book's cult status—the beauty of the soil-free method being that you don't have to get your hands dirty. (Horticulturally speaking, that is; the law may beg to differ.) Whatever you choose to grow, though, Nicholls' 1977 book is a great starting point, detailing in simple language the methods, necessary equipment, and problems of growing plants without soil.

FURTHER READING: This is Nicholls only work on the subject
SEE ALSO: *How-To Hydroponics* (Keith F. Roberto);
Marijuana Horticulture: The Indoor/Outdoor Medical Grower's Bible (Jorge Cervantes)

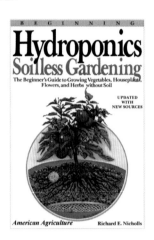

★
★
★

Writer: Leonard Cohen
Publisher: McLelland and Stuart, 2006

ISBN US: 978-0061125614
ISBN UK: 978-0141027562

15+ # BOOK OF LONGING

Synopsis: A collection of poetry, some prose, and song lyrics from Canadian singer-songwriter Leonard Cohen, in which he ponders growing old, sex and desire, spirituality, music, and the waning spirit of the 1960s. Accompanying the texts are the author's scratchily inked illustrations, which perfectly evoke the above mentioned themes.

Review: "I am one of the fakes, and this is my story," Cohen states in the poem "Thousands," playing down his status as a respected poet. Shame that, because he was a poet before he wrote songs, and the ones here are actually very pleasing. Okay, not every poem is memorable, but quatrains like "The Book of Longing," "Nightingale," or "Split" will do it for those who love a pleasing rhyme, a carefree beat, and a simple message. A browse-worthy collection, and not just to be appreciated by Cohen fans.

FURTHER READING: *Book of Mercy; Stranger Music*
SEE ALSO: *Tarantula: Poems* (Bob Dylan);
Auguries of Innocence (Patti Smith)

★
★
★
★
★

Writer: Voltaire
Publisher: G. and P. Cramer, 1759
ISBN US: 978-0486266893
ISBN UK: 978-0140623031

12+

CANDIDE

With an Appreciation by André Maurois

ESSENTIAL CULT BOOKS

500

355

ONE OF A KIND
Best of the Rest

Plot: Exiled for kissing the Baron's daughter, Candide and his tutor, Pangloss, are caught up in a series of unfortunate events: Candide's quest to be reunited with his love sees him press-ganged into the army, ship-wrecked, and nearly feasted on by cannibals. All the while Pangloss instructs Candide in his philosophy of optimism, eventually renounced by the latter as, "a mania for insisting all is going well when things are going badly."

Review: Voltaire's *Candide* caused a scandal on its publication across Europe in 1759. But those who criticized his godlessness had him all wrong. Although this philosophical diatribe sends up Government and the Church, the bad boy of the Enlightenment was a Deist whose leading principle, "Think for yourself," could sum up this, *the* cult novel of the eighteenth century.

FURTHER READING: *Lettres Philosophiques* are worth reading for his satirical view of the English nation, but mainly he is better known in France as a playwright
SEE ALSO: *Encyclopédie* (Denis Diderot); *Gulliver's Travels* (Jonathan Swift)

★ **Writer:** Jeff Chang
★ **Publisher:** St Martin's Press, 2005
★

ISBN US: 978-0312425791
ISBN UK: 978-0091912215

15+ # CAN'T STOP, WON'T STOP
A HISTORY OF THE HIP HOP GENERATION

Synopsis: *Can't Stop Won't Stop* is the accessible and entertaining story of the rise of a movement that started on the streets of the Bronx and grew to define a generation, taking in music, dance, art, and politics, across its thirty-year history. Chock full of original interviews with hip-hop's progenitors, Chang's comprehensive, in-the-know account tells you everything you need to know about America's biggest musical export since rock 'n' roll.

Review: Weighing in at a voluminous five-hundred pages, you might think that this is for hip-hop fiends only. Not so. As Chang has said, the story of hip-hop is "a window on the last three decades of the twentieth century." Besides, as DJ Kool Herc writes in his introduction, "Even if you didn't grow up in the Bronx in the '70s, hip hop is there for you." That includes you.

FURTHER READING: *Total Chaos: The Art and Aesthetics of Hip-Hop*
SEE ALSO: *Subway Art* (Chalfant and Cooper)

★ **Writer:** Lawrence Ferlinghetti
★ **Publisher:** New Directions, 1958
★
★

ISBN US: 978-0811200417
ISBN UK: 978-0811200417

18+ # A CONEY ISLAND OF THE MIND

Synopsis: Poetry from City Lights bookshop owner Ferlinghetti, which name-drops creative luminaries such as Goya, Chagall, and Dante, while at the same time having a jazzy, free-spirited style that is by no means pretentious. Ferlinghetti borrowed his title from Henry Miller's *Into the Night Life*, because, he states, his poems are, "a kind of coney island of the mind, a kind of circus of the soul." Their emotional and thematic diversity attest to that.

Review: Ferlinghetti's most famous collection of poems forms an honest, if unflattering, portrait of the changing political mood of America in 1958. In the insipid, establishment-friendly world of the 2000s, his "conscientious non-objectors" seem no less out of place—while the problems he alludes to (the nuclear arms race, political indifference, religious dogma) rage on. Readable and relevant.

FURTHER READING: *Pictures of the Gone World*
SEE ALSO: *Howl* (Allen Ginsberg)

★
★
★

Writer: Anthony Powell
Publisher: Heinemann, 1951–1975

ISBN US: 978-0226677149
ISBN UK: 978-0099436683

15+

A DANCE TO THE MUSIC OF TIME

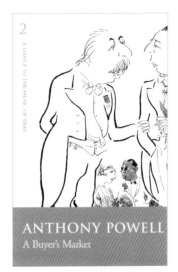

Plot: An ambitious series of twelve novels, which began in 1951 with *A Question of Upbringing* and concluded in 1975 with *Hearing Secret Harmonies*. The books follows the life of Nicholas Jenkins, who watches his peers grow up from their days at upper-class boarding school, Eton, to the "winter" of old age.

Review: As the series title suggests, the passage of time and its effects on human relations is a prime concern of the author. Jenkins notes that human beings are driven "at different speeds by the same Furies." Powell wanted to write the English response to Proust's *A La Recherche Du Temps Perdu*, and he succeeded in this comic rendition of that wit peculiar to the English upper classes.

**FURTHER READING: If you've not had enough of Powell after the dozen titles in the series, try *Afternoon Men* or *From a View to Death*
SEE ALSO:** *A La Recherche du Temps Perdu* (Marcel Proust); *The Magic Mountain* (Thomas Mann)

★
★
★
★

Writer: Franz Kafka
Publisher: Kurt Wolff, 1915

ISBN US: 978-0805210552
ISBN UK: 978-0486290300

15+

DIE VERWANDLUNG (METAMORPHOSIS)

FRANZ KAFKA

THE METAMORPHOSIS

ADAPTED BY **PETER KUPER**

Franz Kafka
Metamorphosis and Other Stories

Plot: The premise of this novella is presented in its famous first line: "When Gregor Samsa awoke one morning from troubled dreams he found himself transformed in his bed into a monstrous insect." What follows is the reaction of Samsa's employer, his sister, and his parents to the "unpleasantness," as well as the coolly detached reaction of Samsa himself.

Review: There has been no finer depiction of alienation and the absurdity of existence since Kafka published *Metamorphosis*, written in a single frenzied night of wordsmithship.

Whatever Kafka's message, and many have tried to find one, reading it is akin to drinking three consecutive double espressos: paranoia-inducing, unsettling—the stuff, in fact, of nightmares. Best not read at bedtime.

FURTHER READING: *The Trial; The Castle*
SEE ALSO: *Nausea* (Jean-Paul Sartre);
Institute Benjamenta (Robert Walser)

★
★
★
★

Writer: Jonathan Safran Foer
Publisher: Houghton Mifflin Company, 2002
ISBN US: 978-0060529703
ISBN UK: 978-0141008257

15+

EVERYTHING IS ILLUMINATED

Plot: Aided by a local guide (Alex Perchov), who has a poor command of English, a young American Jew (named after our author) travels to Ukraine to seek out the woman who fifty years previous had saved his grandfather from the Nazis.

Review: The meta-fictional approach of Safran Foer's debut novel is probably what won him plaudits from the literary establishment. To the likes of you or I, though, this approach might come across as literary grandstanding. Fret not—we're brought straight back down to Earth by the comic effect of Perchov's slips of the tongue and a flatulent dog. In short, if cheeky meta-fiction and a hilarious take on the English language appeals, enjoy the illumination. If not, better skip your bedtime reading and go straight to lights out.

FURTHER READING: *Extremely Loud and Incredibly Close*
SEE ALSO: *The Chosen* (Chaim Potok); *Herzog* (Saul Bellow)

★
★ **Writer:** Rex Feral
Publisher: Paladin Press, 1983

ISBN US: 978-0873642767
ISBN UK: 978-0873642767

18+ # HIT MAN
A TECHNICAL MANUAL FOR INDEPENDENT CONTRACTORS

Synopsis: Spoof instruction manual for wannabe hit men, including all you need to know about equipment, surveillance, and fitness, as well as dealing with the triple dangers that threaten the hit man: ego, women, and partners.

Review: Some books are born cult, some books achieve cult status, some have cult status thrust upon them—this one is all three, its cult status being both inevitable, down to its popularity, and the fact it was pulped when a judge ruled it had contributed to a triple murder in 1993. Since then the book has been unavailable, although the internet has both aided and abetted its continued existence—if you really want to, you can find the text online.

FURTHER READING: This was an anonymous effort so we're left in to the dark as to the author's other work
SEE ALSO: *The Anarchist Cookbook* (William Powell)

★
★
★
★ **Writer:** Allen Ginsberg
Publisher: City Lights Books, 1956

ISBN US: 978-0872860179
ISBN UK: 978-0141190167

18+ # HOWL

Synopsis: *Howl* is a three-part poem that rocked America to its sneakers and saw its author and publisher on trial for obscenity in 1957. It is an ode to the "best minds of my generation destroyed by madness," the "angel-headed hipsters" of Ginsberg's acquaintance—those, that is, living on the fringe of society—and a battle cry against those in authority who oppress them.

Review: Uncompromising in its language, style, and content (Ginsberg did not heed the advice of others to tone the language down), this is a howl of discontent to the straight-laced and authoritarian postwar era. Love it or loathe it, Ginsberg's, and this poem's, influence on American poetry and culture—as well as its cult aura—should not be underestimated.

THE POCKET POETS SERIES

HOWL
AND OTHER POEMS

ALLEN GINSBERG

Introduction by
William Carlos Williams

NUMBER FOUR

FURTHER READING: *Kaddish*
SEE ALSO: *Pictures of the Gone World* (Lawrence Ferlinghetti); the work of Bob Dylan, a friend of Ginsberg's

★
★ **Writer:** Nicholas Middleton
★ **Publisher:** Sinclair Stevenson, 1992

ISBN US: 978-1857990126
ISBN UK: 978-1857990126

15+ LAST DISCO IN OUTER MONGOLIA

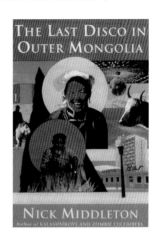

Synopsis: In 1982 Nick Middleton decided to visit Outer Mongolia. Five years later he finally got his visa and managed the trip. However, with no map or guidebook to hand, his journey was not without incident. In 1990, as the country shifted toward democracy, Middleton visited Outer Mongolia again: both trips, and the intervening changes to the country, are described in this book.

Review: If Outer Mongolia conjures up thoughts of Genghis Khan, just read Middleton's deft and entertaining travelogue and you'll soon be conjuring up images of much, much more: the concrete city of Ulan Bator, the Gobi desert, and meals of tadpoles and yak's curd being some of the more lasting impressions Middleton creates.

FURTHER READING: *Kalashnikovs and Zombie Cucumbers: Travels in Mozambique; Surviving Extremes: Ice, Jungle, Sand, and Swamp*
SEE ALSO: *Video Night in Kathmandu: And Other Reports from the Not-So-Far-East* (Pico Iyer); *Catfish and Mandala: A Two-Wheeled Voyage Through the Landscape and Memory of Vietnam* (Pham)

★
★ **Writer:** Le Comte de Lautréamont
★ **Publisher:** Albert Lacroix, 1868–69
★

ISBN US: 978-1878972125
ISBN UK: 978-1878972125

15+ LES CHANTS DE MALDOROR
(THE SONGS OF MALDOROR)

Plot: An inhumane universe of murderous intentions, unholy deeds, fallen angels, child-molesters, and hermaphrodites see Maldoror, the titular anti-hero, plunging into the abyss of evil. Told as a series of six "cantos," this episodic book of ultra-violent yet strangely compelling images sees Lautré-amont not only presenting the dangerous possibilities extended by the human psyche, but twisting the literary conventions of the nineteenth century.

Review: The heavy influence of Lautréamont's Maldoror cannot be exaggerated, from the time of its publication (on the twentieth-century Surrealists, for instance) to the present day (films, records, and bands have all recently been made about or named after the book). A shocking orgy of poetic, deranged, and startling moments it may be (not least the murder of a child)—but isn't that everything you want from a cult book?

FURTHER READING: None—Lautréamont died young
SEE ALSO: *Une Semaine De Bonté: A Surrealistic Novel in Collage* (Max Ernst); *The Book of Disquiet* (Fernando Pessoa)

★
★   **Writer:** Alan Sillitoe   **ISBN US:** 978-0007792146
★   **Publisher:** W. H. Allen & Co, Ltd, 1959   **ISBN UK:** 978-0007792146

15+

THE LONELINESS OF
THE LONG DISTANCE RUNNER

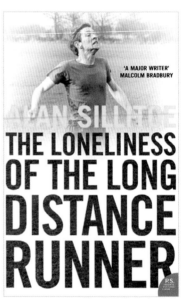

Synopsis: A collection of short stories set in England's Midlands in the postwar period, characterized by cigarettes, fish and chips, soccer matches, and a lack of "lolly" (money). The stand-out story gives the collection its title, in which a seventeen-year-old lad in a young offender's institute first realizes there's a "them and us" scenario in life.

Review: If you think English working class life in the fifties sounds grim, rest assured humor is in plentiful supply here. And, even if the sense of place and time is drawn to a T, don't think the stories will alienate you either. On the contrary: though slight in scope and stature, Sillitoe relates themes of self-realization, youthful anger, and emotional turmoil, which all human beings should relate to, no matter where they're from.

FURTHER READING: *Saturday Night and Sunday Morning*
SEE ALSO: *The Life of a Long Distance Writer: A Biography of Alan Sillitoe* (Richard Bradford); *Look Back in Anger* (John Osborne)

★
★

Writer: The Timelords
Publisher: KLF Publications, 1988

ISBN US: 978-0863596162
ISBN UK: 978-0863596162

12+

THE MANUAL
HOW TO HAVE A NUMBER ONE THE EASY WAY

Synopsis: Advice and tips from British musicians and pop-culture icons Bill Drummond and Jimmy Cauty (better known as the KLF) on how to have a number one single—even if you are lacking in finances and musical talent.

Review: On the one hand the notion that pop music success can be reduced to a formula opens up a Pandora's Box of worries about the state of our pop culture; on the other hand, what's stopping you getting a copy and trying your luck at the music biz game—after all, in their guise as the Timelords, Drummond and Cauty had a number one with *Doctorin' the Tardis*, and there really is some decent step-by-step advice in here, witty banter aside. Good luck!

FURTHER READING: A one hit, ahem, wonder
SEE ALSO: *How to Write a Hit Song* (Molly Ann Leikin)

THE
MANUAL
(HOW TO HAVE A NUMBER ONE THE EASY WAY)

JIMMY CAUTY   BILL DRUMMOND

★
★
★

Writer: Will Self
Publisher: Bloomsbury, 1994

ISBN US: 978-0679750932
ISBN UK: 978-0747582335

15+

MY IDEA OF FUN

Plot: Hallucinogenic, bizarre, and never boring, Self shocks (deliberately) here, while at the same time making a judgment on contemporary society. The story, if we can call it that, is of Ian Wharton, a lonely boy growing up in a caravan park with his overly libidinous mother. Finally, through the strange Mr. Broadhurst (aka the Fat Controller), he learns the secret of the dark arts.

Review: Traditionally novelistic qualities—plot and character, for instance—don't come easy to Self, who admits, "I have largely written about ideas." But this is not storytelling in the classic sense. Verbose and difficult, Self neophytes might be better off starting off with the short stories, or the highly entertaining *Book of Dave*. But this is the book that made Self's name.

FURTHER READING: *The Quantity Theory of Insanity; The Book of Dave*
SEE ALSO: *Adventures in Capitalism* (Toby Litt); *Money* (Martin Amis)

W I L L   S E L F
Author of COCK & BULL

"For intelligence and ambition...inventive comedy, heartbreak and levity...Will Self belongs in the company of Nabokov, Pynchon, William Gaddis and Don DeLillo."—The New York Times Book Review

My Idea of Fun

ESSENTIAL
CULT BOOKS

500

363

ONE OF A KIND
Best of the Rest

★
★
★

Writer: Susan Sontag
Publisher: Farrar Straus, 1977

ISBN US: 978-0312420093
ISBN UK: 978-0141035789

15+

ON PHOTOGRAPHY

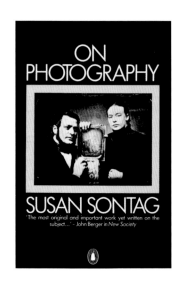

'The most original and important work yet written on the subject...' – John Berger in New Society

Synopsis: Photography has changed our lives in both positive and negative ways: it can offer us views of a world of marvels that is out of reach for most, yet it can just as easily show us the horrors of the world. Photographs can usurp reality and have created a voyeuristic culture.

Review: *On Photography* is not just about photographs but the way we process information, how information is processed for us, and that the knowledge we gain of the world is mostly second hand. Even when we ourselves are taking photographs, for most it is a way of documenting and cataloging experience in a way we understand. Robert Hughes cheekily summed up the book in a *Time* review by saying that "not many photographers are worth a thousand of her words."

FURTHER READING: *The Volcano Lover; Regarding the Pain of Others*
SEE ALSO: *About Looking* (John Berger); *Camera Lucida: Reflections on Photography* (Roland Barthes); *Classic Essays on Photography* (ed. Alan Trachtenberg)

★
★
★

Writer: Stephen King
Publisher: Scribner, 2000

ISBN US: 978-0743455961
ISBN UK: 978-0340820469

12+

ON WRITING
A MEMOIR OF THE CRAFT

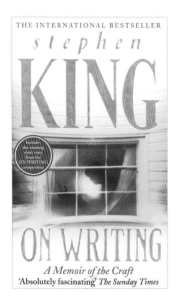

THE INTERNATIONAL BESTSELLER

stephen

KING

ON WRITING
A Memoir of the Craft
'Absolutely fascinating' *The Sunday Times*

Synopsis: Part memoir, part textbook for aspiring authors, King describes firstly his resume: his childhood inspirations, the early years of writing, and his meteoric rise to fame and addiction. The second part of the book, "on writing," offers hints and tips on how to write. Lastly he tells of an incident with a van in 1999 . . .

Review: As someone who has frowned on the notion of creative writing courses, it may seem strange that King has penned a book on this very subject. But this is not how to write by numbers, or indeed, letters. Rather, with a rare display of authorial honesty and generosity, King reveals so much about his life and the writing process that aspiring writers will weep in grateful appreciation.

FURTHER READING: Just about any of the novels, and *Secret Windows: Essays and Fiction on the Craft of Writing,* a companion piece to *On Writing*
SEE ALSO: *The Elements of Style* (William Strunk, Jr. and E. B. White)

★
★
★
★
★

Writer: James Hogg
Publisher: Longan, 1824

ISBN US: 978-1590170250
ISBN UK: 978-1853261886

15+

THE PRIVATE MEMOIRS AND CONFESSIONS OF A JUSTIFIED SINNER

VINTAGE **HOGG**

The Private Memoirs and Confessions of a Justified Sinner

THE PRIVATE
MEMOIRS AND
CONFESSIONS OF A
JUSTIFIED SINNER

JAMES HOGG

INTRODUCTION BY
MARGOT LIVESEY

Plot: Recounting the misadventures of an outcast, this is a cautionary tale of religious fanaticism set on the dark, dingy, and dangerous streets of seventeenth-century Edinburgh. Robert Wringhim, convinced by a shady, perhaps diabolic, character that he is born of God's elect and can do no wrong, is led into a series of crimes, including murder.

Review: Lovers of the psychological tale will lap up Wringhim's inner struggles, while those who like a challenging style will be satisfied by the interlocking narratives and dialogs offered by Hogg. From lowly stock, Hogg was a shepherd before writing ballads as a poet, but it's for his prose he's best known, and justifiably so: *Private Memoirs and Confessions of a Justified Sinner* is devilishly good.

FURTHER READING: *The Three Perils of Man*
SEE ALSO: *Moravagine* (Blaise Cendrars); *Maldoror* (Comte de Lautréamont)

★
★
★
★

Writer: Robert Tressell
Publisher: G. Richards, 1914

ISBN US: 978-0199537471
ISBN UK: 978-0199537471

12+

THE RAGGED TROUSERED PHILANTHROPISTS

Plot: This classic socialist novel centers on a group of painters and builders in late Edwardian England, slogging their guts out for a pittance and thinking nothing of it. Until, that is, Frank Owen joins their fold, and tries to convince his colleagues of the Marxist notion that "Money is the real cause of poverty."

Review: *The Ragged Trousered Philanthropists* has seen a revival of interest in recent years. And justly so, for, despite being written a century ago, the pointed social and political commentary that lies within its pages should resonate with those who have ever scrabbled around for work or fallen victim to the unjustness of capitalist society. It's a long read, but it's funny one too.

FURTHER READING: Published posthumously, due to the efforts of Tressell's daughter
SEE ALSO: For the American view on things: *Common Sense and The Rights of Man* (Thomas Paine); *The Jungle* (Upton Sinclair)

★
★
★

Writer: Bryan Lee O'Malley
Publisher: Oni Press, 2004

ISBN US: 978-1932664089
ISBN UK: 978-1932664089

12+

SCOTT PILGRIM'S PRECIOUS LITTLE LIFE

Plot: "Scott Pilgrim is dating a high-schooler!" we learn as this fun-packed graphic novel commences. Further biographical details include: our hero is twenty-three, plays in a cool band called Six Bomb Omb, and lives with his gay pal in Toronto. All in all, Scott Pilgrim has the same life, pretty much, as any twenty-something comic book geek—until, that is, rollerblading Ramona Flowers invades his dreams and his waking hours. To win her heart Pilgrim must defeat her seven "evil ex-boyfriends."

Review: Cute Manga-style artwork mixes with cute schoolboy humor and the two work perfectly together to create one of the most memorable graphic novel characters of recent years. No wonder there's a further four volumes out there, a fifth in the works, and a movie planned.

FURTHER READING: Four further volumes of Scott Pilgrim books
SEE ALSO: *Fruits Basket* (Natsuki Takaya)

★
★
★
★
★

Writer: Ring Lardner
Publisher: *Chicago Tribune*, 1916–19

ISBN US: 978-0141180182
ISBN UK: 978-0141180182

12+

SELECTED STORIES

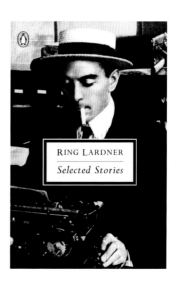

Synopsis: A tableau vivant of American manners in short story form, including: "You Know Me Al," six tales of semi-literate baseball player Jack Keefe; "Some Like Them Cold," which sees a brief romance played out in letters following a chance meeting; and "Alibi Ike," a portrayal of an outfield baseball player who has an excuse for everything.

Review: Lardner was a hugely successful sports journalist who began writing short stories to earn an extra buck. Thank goodness he did: the stories are excellent, depicting the vagaries and disappointments of human relationships with a pin-point precision rarely captured since. Lardner was among the first to write English dialog as actually spoken by real Americans, influencing a plethora of writers from Salinger to Hemingway. If you only ever pick up one short story collection, make it this one.

FURTHER READING: *How to Write Short Stories*
SEE ALSO: *For Esme With Love and Squalor* (J. D. Salinger)

★
★
★

Writer: Edgar Lee Masters
Publisher: The Macmillan Company, 1919

ISBN US: 978-1580493390
ISBN UK: 978-0486272757

12+

SPOON RIVER ANTHOLOGY

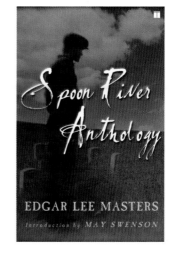

Synopsis: Masters creates a *comédie humaine* in the fictional small town of Spoon River in the American Midwest, through the self-penned epitaphs of 244 of its residents. From Hortense Robbins, who only in death realizes how self-aggrandizing she was in life, to Amanda Barker, who declares her supposedly loving husband a murderer, to uppity Judge Sommers, these tales from the crypt present the whole gamut of human existence.

Review: This is a lively—if not living—portrait of small town life, with all its petty jealousies, lofty ambitions, and dark secrets. Even if the collection enjoyed huge success and has literary merit, the poems are probably best enjoyed nowadays in the smallest room of the house, having that flick through-able quality that makes for perfect bathroom reading.

FURTHER READING: Masters did not come close to the success he'd enjoyed with his first book
SEE ALSO: *Under Milk Wood* (Dylan Thomas);
Lake Wobegon Days (Garrison Keiller)

ESSENTIAL
CULT BOOKS

500

367

ONE OF A KIND
Best of the Rest

★
★
★

Writer: Robert McKee
Publisher: Harper Collins, 1997

ISBN US: 978-0060391683
ISBN UK: 978-0413715609

STORY

SUBSTANCE, STRUCTURE, STYLE, AND
THE PRINCIPLES OF SCREENWRITING

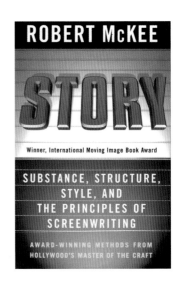

Synopsis: Robert McKee's cult guide is based on his Story Seminars, which for over fifteen years have taught screenwriters and novelists the crucial nature of "story design" when writing a screenplay or novel.

Review: McKee uses a mix of creative argument—emphasizing the importance of the art of the story, and fear: only a handful of the 35,000 scripts logged every year with the Writers Guild of America become movies—to convince the aspiring screenwriter on the need for, and efficaciousness of, his method. McKee's credentials are festooned with a list of movies written, directed, or produced by his former students.

FURTHER READING: *Adaptation: The Shooting Script*
SEE ALSO: *Adventures in the Screen Trade* (William Goldman)

★
★
★

Writer: Cooper and Chalfant
Publisher: Thames & Hudson, 1984

ISBN US: 978-0805006780
ISBN UK: 978-0500514542

SUBWAY ART

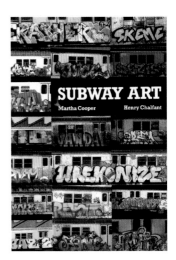

Synopsis: In the early 1980s huge swathes of New York City were desperately poor; from this urban deprivation sprang hip-hop, encompassing not only music but new styles of dancing and graffiti art. The city's determined graffiti artists used subway trains as their canvases, covering entire carriages with amazing, innovative new letterforms and graphics.

Review: Cooper took photos of the trains as art objects in themselves, while Chalfant shot them on the elevated lines, using the housing projects where the artists lived as a backdrop. The combination of the two styles with the stories of the painters themselves forms a compelling record of the period. Subway trains are safer, and cleaner, now—but infinitely less visually exciting.

FURTHER READING: *R.I.P.: New York Spraycan Memorials*
SEE ALSO: *Wall and Piece* (Banksy); *Graffiti Planet* (Alan Ket)

★
★
★
★
★

Writer: Flann O'Brien
Publisher: MacGibbon & Kee, 1967

ISBN US: 978-1564782144
ISBN UK: 978-0007247172

5+

THE THIRD POLICEMAN

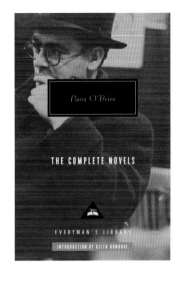

Plot: In places this is a conventional story that sends up regional bureaucracy through the eyes of a murderer; in others it is a surreal allegory about heaven and hell. A key element of the book is a man's unrequited love affair with his bicycle, which, believe it or not, is not the oddest.

Review: Word for word, the most satirical, and possibly funniest, novel to have come out of Ireland. Almost as intriguing as the novel itself is the story of its gestation. When *The Third Policeman* was turned down by O'Brien's publisher for being too "fantastic," he invented a series of imaginative excuses to friends of how he had come to lose the manuscript. Thankfully, his comic and surreal *tour de force* was eventually posthumously published.

FURTHER READING: *At-Swim-Two-Birds*; *The Hard Life*
SEE ALSO: *Ulysses* (James Joyce); *Murphy* (Samuel Beckett)

★
★
★
★

Writer: Dylan Thomas
Publisher: Dent, 1954

ISBN US: 978-0811202091
ISBN UK: 978-0140188882

12+

UNDER MILK WOOD

Plot: A "play for voices" from Welsh poet Dylan Thomas, depicting one day in the lives of the inhabitants of the fictional Welsh village of Llareggub. Originally penned for radio, the play can now be enjoyed in either audio or print form.

Review: The sixty or so characters in Thomas' poetic masterpiece make a lilting and lyrical noise as they sing out their stories as the day unfolds. Through the medium of pastoral, Thomas celebrates the idyll of the seaside country town and the voices of his characters, even if the villagers are not idealized themselves, being, as Reverend Eli Jenkins says, "neither wholly bad or good." The play was an instant hit and has never been out of print since its first publication shortly after Thomas' premature death—blame "the drink" for that, but raise a glass to Thomas for *Under Milk Wood*.

FURTHER READING: *The Collected Poems*
SEE ALSO: *Spoon River Anthology* (Edgar Lee Masters)

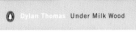

ESSENTIAL
CULT BOOKS

500

369

ONE OF A KIND
Best of the Rest

★
★
★
★

Writer: Haruki Murakami
Publisher: Kodansha, 1997

ISBN US: 978-0375725807
ISBN UK: 978-0099461098

12+

UNDERGROUND
THE TOKYO GAS ATTACK AND THE JAPANESE PSYCHE

Synopsis: In a journalistic style, Murakami presents the story behind the Tokyo Gas attack by the Aum Shinrikyo cult on March 20, 1995. In the first part he interviews victims, while in the second he focuses on the perpetrators.

Review: Murakami takes the true crime genre to a new, expansive level, presenting the attack in the context of the modern Japanese psyche. Intriguing questions raised include just why so many educated people and professionals joined the Aum Shinrikyo cult, or why the authorities reacted so ineffectively to the attack. The detached style of Murakami's fiction is put to clever use, being the perfect analytical approach to a subject that, in lesser hands, could so easily have come across as angry, defensive, or mawkish.

FURTHER READING: The novels, of course, but further non-fiction works such as *What I Talk About When I Talk About Running*
SEE ALSO: *In Cold Blood* (Truman Capote); *Zodiac* (Robert Graysmith)

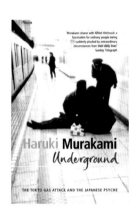

★
★
★
★

Writer: Arthur Rimbaud
Publisher: Self-published, 1873

ISBN US: 978-0811201858
ISBN UK: 978-0195017601

15+

UNE SAISON EN ENFER
(A SEASON IN HELL)

Synopsis: A series of symbolic prose poems in which Rimbaud sums up his experiences of writing poetry and love in his life, to date.

Review: After being shot by his lover, Paul Verlaine, Rimbaud shut himself away on his mother's farm and, consumed by both professional and personal inner conflict, he penned *A Season in Hell*. It's a work of dualism: his love life with Verlaine is both described ecstatically and reviled, and he rejoices in poetry only to spew out harsh criticisms of his previous poems, his "magical sophisms through the hallucination of words." Quitting while he was ahead, Rimbaud gave up poetry to travel the globe at the age of nineteen. His legacy, the first masterful example of prose poetry, remains.

FURTHER READING: *The Last Poems; Illuminations*
SEE ALSO: *Les Fleurs du Mal* (Charles Baudelaire); *Les Chants de Maldoror* (Le Comte de Lautréamont)

★
★
★
★

Writer: John Berger
Publisher: BBC/Penguin Books, 1972

ISBN US: 978-0140135152
ISBN UK: 978-0141035796

15+

WAYS OF SEEING

Synopsis: "Seeing comes before words. The child looks and recognizes before it can speak." So Berger's challenge to our visual perception of the world begins, telling us how "seeing . . . establishes our place in the surrounding words." His way of looking at classical and modern art revolutionized art criticism, and *Ways of Seeing* is now a seminal work for all students of art and cultural history.

Review: Out of the seven essays (three of them without text) included in the book, of particular interest to the modern reader is the section on publicity, the "density of visual images" Berger describes being ever more prevalent as the twenty-first century progresses. In fact, in the age of the internet and its plethora of pop-up ads, the book is probably more relevant than ever.

FURTHER READING: *From A to X*
SEE ALSO: *The Work of Art in the Age of Mechanical Reproduction* (Walter Benjamin); *How the Mind Works* (Steven Pinker)

★
★
★
★

Writer: Walter Benjamin
Publisher: In Illuminations, Harcourt Brace & World, 1968
(originally in German as *Das Kunstwerk im Zeitalter seiner technischen Reproduzierbarkeit*, 1936)

ISBN US: 978-0674024458
ISBN UK: 978-0141036199

15+

THE WORK OF ART IN THE AGE OF MECHANICAL REPRODUCTION

Plot: Benjamin explores how art, photography, and film have changed human perception, especially now (the 1930s) that they could be reproduced and distributed to the masses. The uniqueness of experiencing the authentic, be it art, a landscape, or an actor on stage, means the reproduction loses something of its aura.

Review: Benjamin is particularly critical of film over painting: viewing a painting allows the spectator a chance to bring something of himself to it; with film, no sooner has the eye grasped a scene than it has changed. Film lives up to the old lament that the masses seek distraction where art demands concentration.

FURTHER READING: *Berlin Childhood Around 1900*
SEE ALSO: *On Photography* (Susan Sontag); *Camera Lucida: Reflections on Photography* (Roland Barthes)

JACK LONDON

*The Call of the Wild,
White Fang, and Other Stories*

THE #1 NEW YORK TIMES
& WALL STREET JOURNAL
MOST SOUGHT-AFTER
OUT-OF-PRINT BOOK RETURNS!

THE CULT CLASSIC NOVEL
ONCE A
RUNNER
JOHN L. PARKER JR

PICADO

htaking...
completely
at *Book World*

F A
HA

DIN

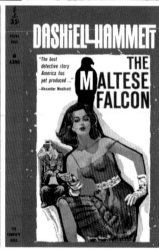

35

PIXNA
BOOK

M
A200

DASHIELL HAMMETT

"The best
detective story
America has
yet produced..."
—Alexander Woollcott

THE
MALTESE
FALCON

SNOW CRASH
NEAL STEPHENSON

A NEBULA AWA
THE
FORE
WA
JOE HALL

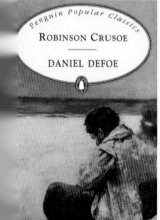

Penguin Popular Classics

ROBINSON CRUSOE
—
DANIEL DEFOE

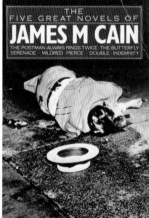

THE
FIVE GREAT NOVELS OF
JAMES M CAIN
THE POSTMAN ALWAYS RINGS TWICE · THE BUTTERFLY
SERENADE · MILDRED PIERCE · DOUBLE INDEMNITY

RAYMOND CAR

This blind man, an old friend of my wife's, he was on his w
night. His wife had died...

cathed

WILLIAM S.
BURROUGHS

AN

Penguin Popular Classics

SPIRITS OF THE DEAD:
TALES AND POEMS

EDGAR ALLAN POE

LIFE
A
USER'S
MANUAL
Georges
Perec

Translated by David Bellos

THE INTERNATIONAL BEST-SELLER

ORTHERN LIGHTS

Now a major movie starring Nicole Kidman and Daniel Craig

FILMED AS

THE
GOLDEN
COMPASS

VINTAGE **MARX AND ENGELS**

THE
COMMUNIST
MANIFESTO

REFERENCE
INDEXES AND CREDITS

INDEX BY TITLE

INDEX BY AUTHOR

ESSENTIAL
500 CULT BOOKS

REFERENCE
Index by Author

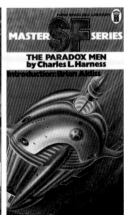

PICTURE CREDITS

All book covers are copyright © their respective publishers and are included here for review purposes. Every effort has been made to credit the publishers whose covers have been reproduced in this book. We apologize for any omissions, which will be corrected in future editions, but hereby must disclaim any liability.

KEY:

T   Top   R   Right
B   Bottom   C   Center
L   Left

281B Atomised: Vintage
282T Locas: Fantagraphics
282B Moscow Stations: Faber
283T My Secret Garden: Pocket
283B My Troubles with Women:
      Last Gasp
284T Our Band Could Be Your Life:
      Little, Brown & Company
284B The Politics of Ecstasy: Ronin
285T Portnoy's Complaint: Vintage
285B The Rum Diary: Bloomsbury
286T The Secret Diary of Laura Palmer:
      Penguin
286B Sex, Art, and American Culture:
      Vintage
287T The Sexual Life of Catherine M.:
      Serpent's Tail
287B Tropic of Cancer: Grove Press
288L Truisms: Messageries du Livre
288R Pig Tales: Faber
289T Wonderland Avenue: Abacus
289B Young Adam: William Heinemann

CHAPTER 8

294L&R The Complete I Ching:
        Inner Traditions
295L   Dianetics: The American Saint Hill
       Organization
295R   Astounding Science Fiction: Dell
296T&B The Divided Self: Pelican
297T   The Doors of Perception and
       Heaven and Hell: Penguin
297B   The Doors of Perception: Vintage
298T   The Holy Blood and the Holy Grail:
       Century
298B   Holy Blood, Holy Grail: Delacorte
299:   Jonathan Livingstone Seagull: Avon
300   The Medium is the Massage:
       Penguin
301T   The Teachings of Don Juan:
       Ballantine
301B   The Teachings of Don Juan: Penguin
302   The Tibetan Book of the Dead:
       Bantam
303   Zen and the Art of Motorcycle
       Maintenance: Corgi
304T   The Celestine Prophecy: Gramedia
304B   The Divine Comedy: Penguin
305T   The Ages of Gaia: Bantam/Dell
305B   The Game: It Books
306T   The Gnostic Gospels: Vintage
306B   The Hero with a Thousand Faces:
       Pantheon
307L&R: The Razor's Edge: Vintage
308T   Walden Two: Hackett
308B   What it Takes to be #1: McGraw-Hill
309T   The Young Man's Guide: BiblioLife
309B   Zen Flesh, Zen Bones: Doubleday

CHAPTER 9

314L&R Ask the Dust: Canongate
315T   Batman: The Dark Knight Returns:
       Titan/DC Comics
315B   Batman: The Dark Knight Returns:
       DC Comics
316T   The Bell Jar: Faber
316B   The Bell Jar: Everyman's Library/Knopf
317L   The Catcher in the Rye: Signet
317R   The Catcher in the Rye: Penguin
318L   A Confederacy of Dunces: Penguin
318R   A Confederacy of Dunces: Wings
319L   A Hero of Our Time: Oneworld Classics

319R   A Hero of Our Time: Penguin
320L   How Late it Was, How Late: Minerva
320R   How Late it Was, How Late: Delta
321L   Moravagine:
       New York Review of Books
321R   Moravagine: Doubleday
322T&B Post Office: Ecco
323L&R Steppenwolf: Penguin
324T   Against Nature: Penguin
324B   Blood and Guts in High School:
       Grove Press
325T   Crime and Punishment:
       Oxford University Press
325B   Geek Love: Vintage
326T   Ghost World: Fantagraphics
326B   Hangover Square: Penguin
327L&R Hatchet: Listening Library
328L   The Heart is a Lonely Hunter:
       Modern Library
328B   The Heart is a Lonely Hunter:
       Bantam
329T   Herzog: Penguin
329B   The History of Luminous Motion:
       Knopf
330   Jimmy Corrigan: The Smartest Kid
       on Earth: Jonathan Cape
331T   Confessions of Zeno: Penguin
331B   Les Enfants Terribles: Harvill Press
332L   The Stranger: Vintage/Knopf
332R   The Stranger: Everyman's Library
       Knopf
333T   Murphy: Grove Press
333B   Of Love and Hunger: Penguin
334T   One Flew Over the Cuckoo's Nest:
       Picador
334B   The Palm at the End of the Mind:
       Vintage
335T   Vernon God Little: Faber
335B   The Virgin Suicides: Picador
336L   Journey to the End of the Night:
       W. W. Norton & Co.
336R   Journey to the End of the Night:
       Oneworld Classics
337L   A Walk on the Wild Side: Ace
337R   A Walk on the Wild Side:
       Farrar, Straus and Giroux

CHAPTER 10

342L   The Amazing Adventures of Kavalier
       & Clay: Fourth Estate
342R   The Amazing Adventures of Kavalier
       & Clay: Random House
343L   Exercices de Style: Gallimard Jeunesse
343R   Exercises in Style: Oneworld Classics
344L   Flowers in the Attic: Pocket
344R   Flowers in the Attic: Simon & Schuster
345L&R Infinite Jest: Little, Brown & Co.
346T   Les Flueurs du Mal: J'ai Lu
346BL The Flowers of Evil: BOA
346BR The Flowers of Evil: New Directions
347L   The Life and Opinions of Tristram
       Shandy, Gentleman: Modern Library
347R   The Life and Opinions of Tristram
       Shandy, Gentleman:
       Everyman's Library/Knopf
348T   The Melancholy Death of Oyster Boy:
       HarperCollins
348B   The Melancholy Death of Oyster Boy:
       Faber
349T   Naked City: Da Capo
349B   Naked City: Essential Books
350T   SCUM Manifesto: W. W. Norton & Co.

350B   SCUM Manifesto: AK Press
351   The Wild Party: Pantheon
352T   Balthazar: Sudamericana
352B   The Americans: Scalo
353T   The Anarchist Cookbook: Ozark
353B   And the Ass Saw the Angel:
       Black Spring Press
354T   Beginning Hydroponics:
       Running Press
354B   The Book of Longing: Ecco
355L   Candide: Everyman's Library/Knopf
355R   Candide: Bantam
356T   Can't Stop Won't Stop: Picador
356B   A Coney Island of the Mind:
       New Directions
357L   A Question of Upbringing: Arrow
357R   A Buyer's Market: Arrow
358L   The Metamorphosis:
       Three Rivers Press
358B   Metamorphosis: Penguin
359L   Everything is Illuminated:
       Houghton Mifflin
359R   Everything is Illuminated:
       HarperPerennial
360T   Hit Man: Paladin Press
360B   Howl: City Lights
361T   The Last Disco in Outer Mongolia:
       Phoenix
361B   Les Chants de Maldoror:
       Le Livre de Poche
362L   The Loneliness of the Long Distance
       Runner: Pan
362R   The Loneliness of the Long Distance
       Runner: HarperPerennial
363T   The Manual: Ellipsis
363B   My Idea of Fun: Vintage
364T   On Photography: Penguin
364B   On Writing: New English Library
365L   The Private Memoirs and Confessions
       of a Justified Sinner: Vintage
365R   The Private Memoirs and Confessions
       of a Justified Sinner:
       New York Review of Books
366T   The Ragged Trousered Philanthropists:
       Granada/Panther
366B   Scott Pilgrim's Precious Little Life:
       Oni Press
367T   Selected Stories: Penguin
367B   Spoon River Anthology: Touchstone
368T   Story: It Books
368B   Subway Art: Holt
369T   The Complete Novels:
       Everyman's Library/Knopf
369B   Under Milk Wood: Penguin
370T   Underground: Vintage
370B   A Season in Hell & Illuminations: BOA
371T   Ways of Seeing: Pelican
371B   The Work of Art in the Age of
       Mechanical Reproduction: Penguin

378   The Crimson Rivers: Harvill Panther
379   Hunger: Canongate
       The Paradox Men:
       New English Library

R 011 MC
2010
1080591

ACKNOWLEDGMENTS

Gina McKinnon would like to thank Nick Jones and Roly Allen at Ilex Press for their ideas and support putting together this book. From Ilex, Ellie Wilson's and Julie Weir's input is also much appreciated. Our list of 500 titles was selected by Nick, Roly, and myself, and I am thankful to Rehana Ahmed, Sam Hayden, Jonathan and Alison Spooner, Jo Blackmore, and Alex Reeve, who offered different perspectives on the final selection. We are also grateful to those same people for the loan of books, and to Paul and Debbie James for the same reason. Finally, many thanks to Steve Holland for writing many of the entries in the Incredible Worlds, Inner Spirits, and Rebellious Voices chapters of this book.